Praise for *Fire on the Levee*

"In the chaotic days after Hurricane Katrina, the charred body of a man last seen in the custody of police officers is discovered, and it falls to a young federal prosecutor to determine what happened and why. The grievous case of Henry Glover exposed the entrenched secrecy and tribalism that underlies so much police violence in America. In *Fire on the Levee*, that prosecutor, Jared Fishman, with Joseph Hooper, has told the riveting tale with care and expertise."

—**David Simon, creator of *The Wire, Treme* and *We Own This City***

"*Fire on the Levee* is a gripping true crime thriller about one of the most shocking police killings in recent history, and the obstacles to holding the police accountable. Jared Fishman moves beyond illuminating what is broken in the American justice system and insightfully points the way to how we can begin to fix it."

—**Shane Bauer, author of *American Prison: A Reporter's Undercover Journey into the Business of Punishment* and *A Sliver of Light: Three Americans Imprisoned in Iran***

"This is an important story that reflects the injustice and chaos of post-Katrina New Orleans. Jared Fishman and Joseph Hooper tell it brilliantly. Sadly, this story tells us as much about New Orleans, whose Black population remains, for the most part, disrespected and vulnerable. This is a real page turner. The story of post-Katrina New Orleans is incomplete without this revealing tale."

—**Roberta Brandes Gratz, author of *We're Still Here Ya Bastards: How the People of New Orleans Rebuilt Their City***

"A true crime whodunit set against the backdrop of Hurricane Katrina where all the prime suspects are police. The effort to solve this senseless murder and its grisly cover-up is a miracle of dogged investigation, told in a way that keeps the reader turning the page. Mandatory reading for anyone who cares about better policing in the U.S."

—**Gary Rivlin, author of *Katrina: After the Flood***

"A vital and eye-opening account of the quest to excavate the truth and find justice for one of Katrina's horrors. *Fire on the Levee* is both an important chapter in the history of police abuses and a blueprint of the hurdles to holding the blue line accountable."

—**Ronnie Greene, author of *Shots on the Bridge: Police Violence and Cover-Up in the Wake of Katrina***

FIRE

ON THE

LEVEE

JARED FISHMAN with JOSEPH HOOPER

FIRE ON THE LEVEE

The Murder of Henry Glover
and the Search for Justice
after Hurricane Katrina

HANOVER
SQUARE
PRESS

HANOVER
SQUARE
PRESS™

Recycling programs
for this product may
not exist in your area.

ISBN-13: 978-1-335-42926-1

Fire on the Levee

Hanover Square Press
22 Adelaide St. West, 41st Floor
Toronto, Ontario M5H 4E3, Canada
HanoverSqPress.com
BookClubbish.com

Printed in U.S.A.

In memory of Henry Glover, Asel Asleh, Raymond Robair, Walter Scott, Tamir Rice, Zachary Hammond, Claudia Patricia Gómez González and far too many others whose lives were needlessly cut short.

To A. and J., may you leave the world a little better than you found it.
To Fiona, with love.

—Jared Fishman

To David, who would have been proud of this book.
And to Kate, always.

—Joseph Hooper

TABLE OF CONTENTS

SELECTED INDIVIDUALS 11

AUTHOR'S NOTE 17

PROLOGUE... 19

CHAPTER 1: A THIN BROWN FOLDER 27

CHAPTER 2: DROP ME OFF IN NEW ORLEANS 35

CHAPTER 3: PEELING THE ONION 55

CHAPTER 4: A BAD SHOOT..................................... 67

CHAPTER 5: "OR WHATEVER" 83

CHAPTER 6: US AND THEM..................................... 98

CHAPTER 7: A THOUSAND WORDS 121

CHAPTER 8: UNUSUAL SUSPECTS........................141

CHAPTER 9: TOURIST ATTRACTION 150

CHAPTER 10: WRONG PLACE, WRONG TIME......... 163

CHAPTER 11: CHARGED 179

CHAPTER 12: ON THE THRESHOLD...................... 199

CHAPTER 13: SPEAK THE TRUTH 214

CHAPTER 14: TELLING STORIES................... 225

CHAPTER 15: CASE-IN-CHIEF........................ 239

CHAPTER 16: SPEAKING UP 264

CHAPTER 17: NOT A FRIENDLY PLACE.................283

CHAPTER 18: A SOCIETY FOR THE LIVING............. 297

CHAPTER 19: HANDLE THE TRUTH 319

CHAPTER 20: THE LAST WORD.................... 333

CHAPTER 21: SENDING A MESSAGE 350

CHAPTER 22: IN BETWEEN.......................... 363

CHAPTER 23: GROUNDHOG DAY 381

CHAPTER 24: BREAKDOWN................................... 403

CHAPTER 25: CHASING JUSTICE..................... 409

EPILOGUE 420

ACKNOWLEDGMENTS 439

ENDNOTES.. 443

SELECTED INDIVIDUALS

The Federal Team

Bobbi Bernstein, deputy chief in Jared Fishman's Department of Justice office, who led the prosecution team in the Danziger Bridge case.

Jared Fishman, attorney in the Criminal Section of the Civil Rights Division of the Department of Justice, who led the prosecution team during the Glover investigation and trials.

Ashley Johnson, rookie FBI agent, who led the Bureau's investigation of the death of Henry Glover.

Tracey Knight, Assistant US Attorney in New Orleans, who investigated and prosecuted the Glover case.

Mike Magner, Assistant US Attorney in New Orleans, who prosecuted the first Glover trial.

Glover Family and Friends

Bernard Calloway, best friends with Henry Glover, with him when he was shot. Also, common-law husband of Patrice Glover, Henry's sister.

Edna Glover, Henry's mother.

Patrice Glover, Henry's older sister.

Rebecca Glover, Henry's aunt and civil rights advocate.

Edward King, older brother of Henry Glover, and one of the three men who tried to rescue Henry after he was shot.

Kawan McIntyre, Henry's first cousin, who reported him missing, with Edna Glover and on her own.

William Tanner, the Good Samaritan who picked up a wounded Henry in the street and tried to find emergency medical care.

New Orleans Police Department (NOPD)—Fourth District

Keyalah Bell, a rookie officer in 2005.

Alec Brown, a rookie officer in 2005 who partnered briefly with David Warren.

Linda Howard, a veteran officer, stationed at the DeGaulle mall on the day of the shooting.

Robert Italiano, a lieutenant (and Fourth District's second-in-command) who oversaw the District Investigative Unit. He responded to the incident at Habans School.

David Kirsch, the captain of the Fourth District at the time of Katrina. He responded to the incident at Habans School.

Travis McCabe, a sergeant who wrote a report on David Warren's weapon discharge.

Joseph Meisch, a lieutenant, expected to head up the Fourth District Investigative Unit after Italiano retired.

Purnella "Nina" Simmons, a police sergeant who responded to the shooting scene and afterwards drove to Habans School, accompanied by Officer Keyalah Bell.

David Warren, a rookie officer from the Seventh District who was temporarily reassigned to the Fourth District in the aftermath of Hurricane Katrina. He was partnered with Linda Howard on the day of the shooting.

New Orleans Police Department, Special Operations Division (SOD)

Joshua Burns, an officer stationed at Habans School after Hurricane Katrina.

Greg McRae, an officer responsible for maintaining the automotive fleet and armory at Habans School.

Jeff Sandoz, a sergeant at Habans School.

Dwayne Scheuermann, a lieutenant and SOD's second-in-command.

Jeff Winn, NOPD captain who commanded SOD.

Other NOPD

Gerard Dugue, Detective Sergeant with NOPD's Cold Case Homicide Unit, who led NOPD investigations into the deaths of Henry Glover and Raymond Robair, and the shootings on the Danziger Bridge.

Attorneys/Judge

Lance Africk, the federal judge hearing the Glover case.

Frank DeSalvo, attorney for one of the two NOPD unions, the Police Association of New Orleans (PANO), who represented Greg McRae and Melvin Williams.

Jeff Kearney, who represented Dwayne Scheuermann.

Steve Lemoine, who represented Robert Italiano.

Julian Murray and Rick Simmons, attorneys for David Warren.

Mike Small and Allyn Stroud, who represented Travis McCabe.

Mary Howell, a noted New Orleans civil rights attorney.

Acronyms

ATF—Federal Bureau of Alcohol Tobacco and Firearms

AUSA—Assistant United States Attorney, locally based federal prosecutors

CBP—Customs and Border Protection

DIU—District Investigative Unit

DMORT—Disaster Mortuary Operational Response Team

DOJ—Department of Justice

FEMA—Federal Emergency Management Agency, the federal agency responsible for disaster response

ICE—Immigration and Customs Enforcement

NOPD—New Orleans Police Department

PIB—Public Integrity Bureau, NOPD's Internal Affairs

SOD—Special Operations Division, NOPD's Special Weapons and Tactical (SWAT) team (also sometimes called Tac)

AUTHOR'S NOTE

The individuals in this book are real people I met during the course of this case. I use the real names of those who testified in court proceedings or whose names appear in the public record. I wanted the reader to hear from key participants in their own words, to the extent that space allowed. The quotes that appear, with limited exceptions, are taken verbatim from court records or from other publicly available sources, such as media accounts, or from interviews my co-author and I conducted for this book. In every case, we have noted the sources for these quotes in the Endnotes.

At the time of the Henry Glover investigation, interviews were not recorded, per FBI policy. The quotes that appear in Chapters 1 through 10, covering that investigation, come from other sources, mostly court transcripts. They are, however, fair representations of what was said at that time.

In writing this book, I rely on information that exists in the unusually extensive public record. Additionally, I have had conversations with many of the participants in these events, in an effort to be as complete and as accurate as possible. I have tried to provide readers with enough information to make their own assessments of what is credible and true.

I have no doubt that some people will take issue with how they are represented, or of my account of some of the events described. I acknowledge that I come to this story with my own biases. Though I believe I have a unique perspective to offer, it's just that, a perspective. As well, in a book that covers a thirteen-year period, much had to be left unsaid. My hope is that *Fire on the Levee* sparks a continuing conversation about how to win justice for Henry Glover.

The views and opinions expressed herein are mine, the author, alone. They do not represent the views of the US Department of Justice.

Jared Fishman

PROLOGUE

The images broadcast across my television were unlike anything I had ever expected to see in America: mothers struggling to hold their children above the water; dead bodies floating in the muck or covered under blankets by the side of the highway; families holding up signs pleading for rescue.

On August 29, 2005, Hurricane Katrina slammed into New Orleans, causing protective levees to breach and submerging 80 percent of the city underwater. Though most of the city's residents had heeded evacuation orders and left before the storm hit, those who stayed—the poor, the sick, the stubborn—found themselves living in a city drowning in toxic lake water, fouled with sewage, petrochemicals, and death.

Four days after the storm, when President George W. Bush made his belated visit to the region, New Orleans was in desperate shape. That Friday afternoon, he and the city's mayor, Ray Nagin, and the state's governor, Kathleen Blanco, toured the city by helicopter. They surveyed some of the scenes that would come to define the tragedy of Katrina: the mostly African American Lower Ninth Ward, adjacent to the breached levee of the Industrial Canal, still covered in water; the Louisiana Superdome, a squalid refuge of last resort that had warehoused an estimated 30,000 people without adequate food, sanitation, or medical assistance.

After the tour, standing on the airport tarmac, an uncertain and overmatched President told the city, "I want you to know that I'm not going to forget what I've seen."

But on that Friday, it was an event that almost no one had taken notice of, in the often-overlooked Algiers section of New Orleans, that in time would assume its own resonant, macabre significance. For fourteen years, I would be consumed with trying to redress what had happened there. The effort would shape who I became as a lawyer and fundamentally change how I understood the American justice system.

Algiers sits on the West Bank of the Mississippi, and owing to its higher elevation, did not flood after the storm. Though the hurricane's high winds and torrential rains felled trees, damaged roofs, and shattered plenty of windows, Algiers was spared the devastation of much of the rest of the city.

In the first few days after Katrina, the Algiers residents who stayed likely figured they had successfully ridden out the storm. The neighborhood had taken a beating but seemingly not worse, or not much worse, than what other storms had delivered in the past.

The reality, however, was that Algiers was too cut off from the rest of the city to understand just how isolated it really was. There was no power or television, telephone lines were down, and cell phone service was spotty at best. News and rumors, often indistinguishable, filtered in by word of mouth. Few in Algiers could fathom that on the other side of the river, most of New Orleans was underwater, and unlike after past storms, essential city services would not be coming back anytime soon.

As the days dragged on, the unsettling thing about Algiers was the desolation. The few remaining people seemed lost in their own neighborhoods. One resident, an officer with the New Orleans Police Department (NOPD) Fourth District, which patrols Algiers, later compared what she saw to a horror movie. "Everybody was...just walking around like zombies. The street looked like a ghost town."

In the first days after the hurricane hit, law enforcement had been widely regarded as heroic by many in New Orleans. The local police traveled city streets that had been transformed into murky canals in their small boats, plucking residents out of their attics. The national coast guard hovered over houses in their helicopters, lowering metal-framed cages down to citizens stranded on their rooftops, withering under a brutally hot sun.

But as the days passed, and incompetence and political infighting bogged down the government relief effort, the mood on the city streets turned ugly. Looting became rampant. Many residents took basic supplies from abandoned stores simply to survive, while others went on a shopping spree that included consumer electronics, luxury cars, and guns.

By September 2, most of the people left in Algiers fell into one of two camps: the poorest of the mostly African American population, and the police. Relations between these two groups were becoming increasingly tense. If you were low-income and Black and still in the city, you were likely viewed by the police, both White and Black officers, with deep suspicion.

City officials, most notably the mayor and the police chief, often exaggerated the unrest, passing on rumors, later debunked, about murder and rape in the Superdome, and New Orleans being under martial law. Governor Blanco sounded the apocalyptic tone on September 1, announcing the dispatch of the National Guard to New Orleans to restore order. "These troops know how to shoot and kill," she proclaimed, "and they are more than willing to do so if necessary and I expect they will." New Orleans began to feel like a city under military occupation.

★ ★ ★

On the morning of September 2, General Charles DeGaulle Boulevard, a busy six-lane thoroughfare that serves as Algiers's main commercial artery, was strangely quiet. The streets were an obstacle course of downed trees. The DeGaulle mall, normally a hub of working-class commerce with its dollar stores, beauty parlors, and Chuck E. Cheese restaurant, sat virtually empty, an easy target for looters.

A police substation on the mall's second floor was deserted, its computers and file cabinets exposed to the elements when the office's plate glass windows shattered.

One part of Algiers humming with activity was the Paul B. Habans Elementary School, a quarter mile from the mall. After its headquarters had flooded on the other side of the river, the police department's Special Operations Division (SOD) commandeered the school, turning it into a paramilitary outpost. Fifty or so SOD officers grabbed meals there and, when they weren't in the field, hunkered down for what little sleep they could catch in the sweaty, mostly un-air-conditioned fetor.

A mile and a quarter north of Habans, the Patterson Road levee, a ridge of raised earth, protects the higher-priced homes from the Mississippi. Algiers's Fourth District police station, home to the area's regular patrol units, is located two blocks from the levee.

Midmorning that day, a plume of black smoke slowly rose from behind the levee. As the morning dragged on, the smoke grew denser and darker, reaching a height of fifty feet and filling the air with the stench of burning rubber, metal, and gasoline. At the foot of the levee, obscured by the scrubby, storm-battered underbrush, sat the source of that smoke, a white Chevy Malibu, devoured by flames.

Random fires were not unusual after Katrina. But this fire was different. Entombed inside the Chevy, visible to anyone who happened to approach it after the flames subsided, were the incinerated remains of a body.

All that remained was a skull, some ribs, and a leg bone. The flesh was reduced to ashes and char. Seven days after the fire, those remains would be recorded by an out-of-state retired corrections officer who came upon the scene and shot an impromptu video. Later, he told an interviewer, "The magnitude of the way [the body] was destroyed…was telling a story—'I don't want no one ever to find out what I did.'"

PART I

INVESTIGATION

CHAPTER 1

A THIN BROWN FOLDER

January 2009

In January 2009, a thin brown folder appeared on my desk at the
US Department of Justice, in Washington, DC. The folder con-
tained only two items. One was an autopsy report that briefly de-
tailed what was left of the incinerated remains of a man named
Henry Glover. The other was a recently published article from *The
Nation*, which raised questions about Glover's death.

At the time, I was a relatively junior attorney in the criminal
section of the Civil Rights Division of the Department of Justice
(DOJ), the office responsible for enforcing federal civil rights law.
Our mandate included prosecuting hate crimes, human trafficking, and "color of law" cases.

Color of law cases made up the bulk of my docket. These cases
involve crimes committed by people empowered to act as enforcers

of the law—police and corrections officers, federal agents, judges, and prosecutors—who abuse the rights of people in their charge. This covers a variety of misconduct, including excessive force, sexual assault, theft, and fabricating evidence. (The old-fashioned-sounding term first shows up in this country in late nineteenth-century American civil rights legislation, but its origins can be traced back to thirteenth-century England.)

Stuck to the front of the thin brown file was a handwritten yellow Post-it note from one of the deputy chiefs of the section, Bobbi Bernstein: "I don't know if there is anything to this, but at least this should be interesting."

First, I read *The Nation* story that had caught the deputy chief's attention. Its author, *ProPublica* investigative reporter A.C. Thompson, had spent months in New Orleans meticulously collecting documents and first-person accounts which, three and a half years after Katrina, were painting a disturbing picture of police behavior in the wake of the storm.

Thompson had pored over autopsy records of people who had died under unusual circumstances in the days after Katrina. The strangest such report cursorily described the burned remains of a thirty-one-year-old Black man named Henry Glover. The Orleans Parish Coroner's Office had originally left the "cause of death" blank, as if the coroner couldn't be bothered to worry about how Glover died. A few months later, his death was upgraded to the hardly more specific "unclassified." It is difficult to imagine physical evidence more suggestive of foul play than an incinerated body, but the coroner never referred this highly suspicious death to NOPD's homicide division for further investigation.

According to an article by *The Nation*, on September 2, 2005, Glover, a resident of Algiers, had seemingly disappeared. He had last been seen in police custody, but his family had no certain idea of what had befallen him until seven and a half months later, when a DNA sample that they had submitted matched his remains, which had been sitting in the city morgue.

Thompson pieced together Glover's last day by tracking down

two of the three people who had tried to come to his aid. Edward King, Henry's brother, had been at home when Henry's best friend, Bernard Calloway, rushed in, yelling that Henry had been shot. The two men ran towards the nearby DeGaulle shopping mall and found Henry crumpled on the street, bleeding. Calloway told King that he and Henry had been at the mall when somebody on the mall's second-floor breezeway fired off the single shot that pierced Henry's torso. According to the article, no one knew who fired the shot.

Minutes later, King flagged down William Tanner, a stranger driving in the area. Tanner shepherded the men—Calloway, King, and the gravely injured Henry—into his Chevy Malibu and took off for the nearest place he thought he could find emergency medical help, an elementary school that had been commandeered by members of NOPD's Special Operations Division.

At Habans Elementary School, Tanner and King said a group of officers yanked the three would-be rescuers out of the car and beat them. Henry continued to bleed in the back seat of the Chevy. While the men were detained in front of the school, one of the officers drove off, with Henry still in the back seat, by now most likely dead. That, Tanner and King said, was the last time they saw Henry Glover.

One person who could have given Thompson a first-person account of what happened at the mall was nowhere to be found. Bernard Calloway had fled New Orleans and had dropped out of sight.

According to *The Nation* story, NOPD responded to Thompson's queries with a two-sentence email that said the Orleans Parish Coroner's Office had conducted an independent investigation and "found no evidence to rule the death of Mr. Glover a homicide," nor did they have any information "to support or corroborate" Tanner's and King's claims.

Thompson found an off-the-record police source who showed him photos of Tanner's burned-out car by the levee with Henry's remains in the back seat. The source said the photos had been taken by officers from the Fourth District whose station was across the street. The remains sat in the torched car for two weeks before a federal disaster relief agency finally brought them to the city morgue.

The anonymous officer quoted in the article suggested that NOPD moved the body out of the SOD barracks to prevent it from rotting in the late summer heat. ("Have you ever smelled a dead body?" the cop asked. "They smell horrible.") Thompson had uncovered no evidence of a more sinister motive. But clearly what he'd heard persuaded him that an SOD officer driving a dead body to an out-of-the-way spot and then having had nothing to do with its subsequent incineration was, at the very least, worth a closer look. "If the NOPD ever bothers to learn who set fire to Glover," he wrote, "the department's first step should be questioning its own personnel: a trail of clues leads right back to the police force."

All of this certainly *seemed* suspicious. Thompson's article painted an entirely different picture of the post-Katrina chaos than I was used to reading about. His article had police officers running amok, beating up citizens seeking help. And though it didn't make a direct claim, the article suggested police involvement in Glover's burning, which in turn suggested that the police might have killed him as well.

But there were endless other possible scenarios. The cops could have shot Glover. But it could also have been a trigger-happy shop owner protecting his property, or an enemy settling old scores. Given what we then knew of the timeline, the burning could have occurred up to two weeks after Henry was killed, so the killer, whoever that was, could have located the body and burned it after the police moved the car. Or the burning and shooting could have been unrelated.

Just like the Post-it note said, however it played out, this case promised to be "interesting."

I had been at DOJ Civil Rights for slightly over two years, with just enough seniority to have recently been upgraded to an office with a window, albeit one facing an alley lined with dumpsters.

As a thirty-three-year-old attorney in an office of some fifty lawyers, I'd mostly handled lower-level cases of law enforcement abuse. Most of my early days at DOJ were spent investigating corrections officers for abusing inmates, generally in the out-of-the-way places where American prisons tend to be located, like Tiptonville, Tennessee; Winton, North Carolina; and Del Rio, Texas. I had started asking the four deputy chiefs in the office if they had any challenging prospective cases that I might be right for. "Interesting" sounded great, but more than that, I was looking for a case that might shine a light on some of the bigger issues confronting the criminal justice system.

When I was in law school, I never considered becoming a prosecutor. For that matter, I didn't think I would even be "a real lawyer." I had spent my pre-law-school days working in international conflict zones, and I hoped to use my law degree to help rebuild legal systems in postwar countries. I was fascinated by the question of what it would take for a society to recover after such destruction. I thought at least part of the answer lay with reestablishing "the rule of law" and developing new legal frameworks to create stability. My first job out of law school, as a program officer at the US State Department, gave me the chance to find out. I was shipped off to the Balkans to work with local police and prosecutors as they reconstructed their legal system.

In the winter of 2004, I was driving through the frozen Kosovo countryside to interview a regional police commander with a senior colleague, Markus Funk, who had spent much of his career in Chicago prosecuting high-ranking mobsters and abusive priests. We talked about my career ambitions, and I told him that I wanted to work on justice reform. He told me that if I wanted to be effective, I needed to work inside the system first. Markus told me I should be a prosecutor.

I could not imagine myself working a job whose endgame was sending people to prison. If I were to work inside the system, I said, I would rather be a defense attorney. I cared too much about civil rights.

In that case, he shot back, then I *really* should be a prosecutor.

In the US criminal justice system, prosecutors are the most powerful actors. More than anyone else, they have the power to affect case outcomes, from who is arrested to who is incarcerated and for how long. They have an inordinate amount of power when it comes to determining whether the legal process is fair—or not.

The suggestion that prosecutors were key to creating a more just system was a fairly novel idea at that time. I was persuaded enough to take advantage of a fellowship program that allowed me to do a yearlong "rotation" as a prosecutor in the Washington, DC, US Attorney's Office. My caseload mostly consisted of misdemeanor domestic violence and sex crime cases.

Much to my surprise, I loved the job. I loved the energy of the courtroom, the drama of criminal trials, and the window it gave me, an upper-middle-class Jewish kid from suburban Atlanta, into the lives of people whose backgrounds were very different from mine.

But my experience also gave me a front row seat to the enormous racial and socioeconomic inequity that mars our criminal legal system. It was impossible not to recognize that almost every defendant in our courtrooms was Black or Hispanic, usually from lower-income communities. I handled hundreds of cases at a time, with limited ability to assess what really had happened in any given case. I depended on police officers to be completely truthful, even though I instinctively knew they sometimes weren't. Every day, I watched the lives of large numbers of people of color—victims and defendants alike—change for the worse, often for no discernable public good. It was hard to call what we were doing "justice."

If I were to continue as a prosecutor, I decided, I wanted to use the power of the position to enforce our civil rights laws on behalf of the nation's most vulnerable individuals and communities. The most potent way to do that, I figured, was to go after abusive law enforcement officers. The Civil Rights Division of the Justice Department allowed me to do just that.

In January 2009, when the Henry Glover folder landed on my desk, I had only tried two cases in front of a jury, and neither involved a homicide or the police. That did not deter me. If my suspicions about the new case were proved right and NOPD was implicated in both the shooting and the burning of Henry Glover, then his death could reverberate well beyond New Orleans.

And if my suspicions were wrong? Well, at least I would spend lots of time in New Orleans, certainly a better draw than Tiptonville.

I began by reading the autopsy report, a cold, mechanical exercise that sometimes offers the necessary clues to begin to figure out what happened. But this autopsy report was the skimpiest one I have ever seen, cataloging in two short paragraphs what was left of the body of Henry Glover. The only charred bone fragments that could be positively identified were nine ribs, the humerus or upper arm bone, and the hyoid, a small bone that anchors the tongue inside the mouth. Contrary to standard autopsy protocol, there were no photos.

An autopsy report typically walks the reader through the body starting with the head. Here, the skull, which A.C. Thompson saw in the photos from his cop source, was missing, presumably removed from the scene sometime after the fire and before the body collection two weeks later.

The report documented the existence of metal fragments, but they were so small and deformed by the heat of the fire—estimated by one visiting forensic pathologist who examined the remains as between 1,500 and 2,000 degrees—they couldn't be identified as coming from a bullet. But as the pathologist told Thompson, "When I heard he was found in a burned car, I thought that was a classic homicide scenario: you kill someone and burn the body to get rid of the evidence."

The autopsy provided no physical proof of how Glover actually died.

My first phone call was to Special Agent Ashley Johnson in New Orleans. Typically, DOJ Civil Rights prosecutors partner with FBI agents, similar to how police team up with their local district attorney's office to investigate a crime. In the wake of *The Nation* article, my office and the New Orleans FBI opened a preliminary investigation into Glover's death.

No one in my office had ever heard of Ashley Johnson, which wasn't surprising since she had only recently graduated from the FBI Academy at Quantico, Virginia, and was still a "probationary" agent. She had even less law enforcement experience than I had, which gave me a sense of the FBI's modest assessment of the case's merits.

FBI agents can often be territorial. They usually don't want the lawyers mucking around with their cases until their criminal investigations are almost complete, or only if they need us for something, like grand jury subpoenas. Ashley wasn't like that.

A week earlier, William Tanner, the Good Samaritan who picked up Henry by the side of the road, walked into the FBI building looking for reimbursement for his burned car. Ashley had taken his complaint and set up a follow-up meeting. "I'm interviewing Tanner next week," she told me on the phone. "Why don't you come on down?"

CHAPTER 2

DROP ME OFF IN
NEW ORLEANS

February 2009

I had visited New Orleans twice before, both typical booze-fueled college pilgrimages to Mardi Gras over a decade earlier. The city I found in February 2009 was very different. Driving in from the airport to the FBI building, I experienced a New Orleans still staggering from the devastation of Katrina. Even though three and a half years had passed since the storm, in neighborhoods like Lakeview and the Seventh Ward, some homes still bore the spray-painted marks indicating how many dead bodies had been found inside. I drove past roofless, gutted buildings, still waiting for demolition. Parts of the city reminded me of the conflict zones where I had spent early parts of my career.

The FBI building sits in Gentilly, a neighborhood on the south-ern edge of Lake Pontchartrain that endured substantial flooding and wind damage. It looked impervious: five stories of steel, brick, and sparkling glass. I walked through the high-ceilinged lobby atrium, where I met Special Agent Johnson.

Agent Johnson didn't look like most of the button-down, law-and-order-minded (primarily White male) FBI agents I had interacted with over the years. She was a petite, soft-spoken young woman from a middle-class African American family in Mobile, Alabama. She, like me, had taken an unconventional path to law enforcement—in her case, starting out as a social worker and probation officer.

That morning, Ashley, crisply turned out in black slacks and a blazer, came down from her fifth-floor cubicle to greet me inside the marble-floored atrium. "Attorney Fishman?" she asked with surprising formality. "You can call me Jared," I said with a smile.

We did not have much time to trade small talk or even compare notes on the case. William Tanner was already waiting for us in the interview room.

Normally, in police misconduct investigations, before interviewing witnesses, the first thing I do is pull all the police records. Cops produce an inordinate amount of paperwork: incident reports, call logs, radio traffic, and shift rosters. Ashley had been trying to collect documents, but so far had found nothing. She had been hearing—as we would continue to hear in the coming weeks—that routine police documentation did not exist for the weeks and months after the storm. This, it would turn out, was only partially true.

And so, without much else to go on, we started by meeting with William Tanner. We were joined by a more senior agent who often worked civil rights cases in New Orleans.

The FBI interview room would look familiar to anyone who watches TV police procedurals—no windows, a one-way wall mirror, a low-budget table with a few nondescript plastic chairs around it, plus a metal bar attached to a wall in case a witness needed to be secured.

Tanner was a tall, lean, forty-one-year-old Black man who made a living doing various odd jobs, including working at a junkyard and as a maintenance man at an apartment complex. He wore crisply pressed blue jeans, and a patchwork quilt shirt with logos of Negro League baseball teams. His clear brown eyes were almost mesmeric in their intensity. A visible scar ran diagonally across his smooth, mostly bald head. "That's from the surgery they did," he told us at the outset. "That's where I went flatline four to five minutes on the operating table." Tanner tilted his head sideways and gave me an awkward, crooked smile. I wondered how seriously to take this guy.

Tanner was a natural-born storyteller. He spoke with an unusual cadence and sentence structure, misusing words, or inventing them outright. But his story immediately drew me in.

Tanner described himself as a "weather junkie" who stuck around New Orleans because he wanted to know what a hurricane felt like. "I stayed and videotaped the situation before and after effects of the hurricane," he said. "It's just me. I'm a very adventure-type person." As the hurricane made landfall, Tanner pretended to be a news weatherman, standing in the rain with an umbrella and a camera.

But four days after the storm hit the city, Tanner had had his fill of Katrina adventure. He found himself driving his 2001 Chevy Malibu fruitlessly looking for a gas station that hadn't been emptied of gas or commandeered by law enforcement. He had planned to drive to Texas to join his wife, coincidentally named Catrina, who had decamped before the storm.

While driving through the ghostly streets of Algiers, dodging fallen tree limbs, Tanner heard a single gunshot. He heard someone shouting, "Henry got shot!" Tanner instinctively drove *towards* the danger.

Within a minute, a frantic Edward King flagged him down, desperate for assistance. The two men drove a few blocks to the corner of Texas and Seine, at the edge of the DeGaulle strip mall, where they found a distraught Bernard Calloway hovering over the body of his best friend, Henry Glover, bleeding in the street.

Tanner had never met any of these men before. "I didn't know them from Sam Elliott," he said, which I found easy to believe since he consistently mangled their names during our interview. But he committed to helping them.

Tanner checked Glover's pulse. Henry was still alive. The three men lifted a barely conscious Glover into the back seat. They sped off, but not in the direction of West Jefferson Hospital, the closest hospital, at least fifteen minutes away, in neighboring Jefferson Parish. West Jeff, as it was known, fell under the jurisdiction of a sheriff notorious for racially profiling people driving what he called "rinky-dink" cars. "If there are some young Blacks driving a car late at night in a predominantly White area, they will be stopped," Sheriff Harry Lee declared in a 1986 press conference. "If you live in a predominantly White area and two Blacks are in a car behind you, there's a pretty good chance they're up to no good."

Tanner made a quick decision: "I couldn't go to West Jeff because Harry Lee had that sealed off. You have four brothers in the car, one shot. We would have never made it past the mall. So I figured that Habans School would be the best way to go."

Habans Elementary School was just blocks away, and Tanner hoped to find emergency medical facilities there. Just a few days earlier, again in Good Samaritan mode, he'd jump-started the car of two stranded police officers near the school. He saw a truck stuffed with what he thought might be medical supplies next to Habans. "I assumed they were going to do the job of taking care of the people."

When Tanner pulled into the school driveway, a group of officers armed with assault rifles and shotguns immediately surrounded his car. "I had a bunch of police officers in tactical uniforms putting laser sights and guns to my glass [window] and [they] told me get out of the car—not so very nicely."

Tanner told us that he, King, and Calloway were pulled out of the car, shoved to the ground, and handcuffed. The officers called them "niggers" and accused the men of being looters. One of the men had a large tattoo on his arm, he recalled. Nobody in uniform paid any attention to Henry Glover, dead or dying in the back seat. King finally lost it, yelling out wild threats about retribution. "He said he was going to shoot the person who shot his brother," Tanner said, which enraged the cops.

"They start waling on me. They hit me, kicked me in the ribs twice, hit me with [an] M-16 rifle on the side of my face."

Though Tanner told us that no one gave Glover medical care, he did see one officer taking photos. "They ain't much touched him. That was the cruelest thing a person can do to a man, let him bleed to death in a car like that."

Throughout the beating, Tanner kept an eye on his car. One of the officers who beat him rummaged through the trunk and extracted routine items: jumper cables, a Stanley toolbox and a gas can. Then, Tanner said, the officer searching his car disappeared into the school building and returned with a couple of road flares sticking out of a pocket of his cargo pants. Not long afterwards, the officer drove away with Tanner's car with Glover still in the back seat, followed by another cop in a pickup truck. At that moment, Tanner thought, "I'm not going to see that car no more."

After the car disappeared, officers brought the three remaining men to the back of the school, out of sight, and handcuffed them to a metal picnic table. Then Tanner's luck, if you could call it that, changed. The White female police officer whose car he jump-started a few days earlier recognized him. After she conferred with the officers guarding the detained men, they released Tanner. King and Calloway remained cuffed.

Tanner asked about his car. An officer told him, "The car is in police custody. It's under investigation."

King and Calloway told Tanner where he could find their families. Tanner walked a mile and a half to the Skyview apartments, a low-income complex near the DeGaulle mall, to tell their families what had happened. Then, stripped of his car, he waited for two days, stranded, until his wife retrieved him in a borrowed car and brought him to Texas.

Tanner handed us a photo of his car, which was completely burned out, rusted, and covered with spray-painted markings. He said he had taken the photo the week before.

"Wait, the car is still there?" I asked, not quite believing that his car hadn't been moved in three and half years.

"Yeah. It's still there."

After Tanner left the building, we tried to make sense of what we'd heard. He was undoubtedly eccentric and spoke with a certainty that at times felt exaggerated. More disconcertingly, he could sound more concerned about reimbursement for his car than Henry Glover. And yet he had done something that few of us likely would. He stopped to help a man who had been left for dead, risking his life for a stranger in the midst of civic chaos.

The more senior agent was deeply unimpressed. Not only did he find Tanner strange, he found it difficult to believe that cops would beat a group of men seeking help, even during Katrina. And even if they had, years of hard experience had taught him that the DOJ often "opened" civil rights cases that ate up a lot of Bureau investigative resources and then rarely brought charges.

I had no idea whether we would ever be able to bring charges. The only possible federal crime for which we currently had any admissible evidence was an excessive force claim for the beating at Habans, and we were a long way away from having a prosecutable case. For one thing, we didn't have a clue who the suspects were. On top of that, I had never heard of anyone successfully prosecuting such a case on victim testimony alone. Most likely, we needed police officers to corroborate Tanner's account. For the time being, we didn't know the name of a single law enforcement witness at the school that day.

Ashley and I quickly got the message from her bosses that the FBI would not commit resources to the case unless we could quickly uncover some promising evidence that NOPD might be responsible for the shooting or incineration.

The only thing we knew that *might* implicate NOPD in the shooting was the location of an abandoned police substation on the second floor of the strip mall where Glover was shot. Our only lead on the burning was Tanner's assertion that a police officer drove off with Henry's body.

Burned-out car belonging to William Tanner, "the Good Samaritan," by the Patterson Road levee.

Though I found much of what Tanner had to say credible, one detail hung me up: the officer with the road flares in his pocket. By the time we met Tanner, he knew his torched car was sitting by the Patterson Road levee. The detail about the road flares—an unlikely thing to notice while being beaten—seemed like it could have been his attempt to link the cops with the burning, payback for the theft of his car and the beating he'd received at their hands. I found it hard to believe that an officer would carry road flares on a bright sunny day, and I found it unlikely that anyone would choose to set a car on fire with something as unwieldy as a road flare. If Tanner invented this, it undermined his credibility about everything else.

Tanner had never received compensation for the car. When he and his wife returned to New Orleans in October 2005, two months after the storm, he went to the Fourth District police station in Algiers, where an Immigration and Customs Enforcement (ICE) officer, temporarily assigned to New Orleans, located the car by the levee. Tanner then took his story to a local nonprofit, Safe Streets/Strong Communities, and even to the Department of Homeland Security, hoping for restitution, but with no luck. His own insurance company turned him down. "I called my insurance people and told them the NOPD stole my car. The company replied that when the police take your car, it isn't stealing, and that there was nothing that they can do."

And so, Tanner kept paying down the loan on the Chevy. Every month, he wrote out a check to pay for a car that was burned out and rusting next to the Mississippi River. Finally, by 2009, he'd paid off the note in full and felt emboldened to push his story to the media. "When I tried to go to the news media the first time with this situation, they said I was a raving lunatic trying to blame something on NOPD," he said later. But A.C. Thompson, the author of *The Nation* article, saw Tanner doing a TV interview and tracked him down. "And once that happened, the wheels started slowly turning," he said. "I pursued it the best way that I can. And I promised my father I would take care of this."

If anything, the FBI's indifference to Tanner and the whole

Glover case brought Ashley and me together as a team. At the time, the Bureau had a nationwide policy prohibiting recording most witness interviews and required its agents to conduct interviews with a law enforcement partner to verify what was said. (In lieu of recordings, the FBI relied on agents to file written summaries, so-called 302s, to document the interviews.) The junior agents who worked with Ashley seemed more focused on their own cases, and the senior agents wouldn't touch ours. Some of them were outright hostile. And so I became her partner during the first months of the investigation.

As we were discovering, Ashley and I were temperamentally very different. I'm an extrovert, gregarious, and, whenever possible, informal. She is more reserved, polite—all business. But we clicked, which doesn't happen as often as you might think. Misalignment between prosecutors and agents is a big reason why so many police misconduct cases never get pursued by the feds. Sometimes the prosecutor just doesn't like the odds of winning in court, or the agent, for whatever reason, doesn't feel motivated to do the necessary investigative legwork. These days, a lot of cases show up on DOJ's radar thanks to video footage shot by the police or by bystanders, and any ensuing media coverage. But in 2009, it was the DOJ-FBI partnership that made or broke cases, and from the outset, Ashley and I were both totally caught up in the "whodunit"—what really had happened to Henry that day?

Most excessive force cases turn on the question of the officer's "intent"—was there any legal justification for the use of force?—but here we were starting with a mystery. Two mysteries, actually: Who pulled the trigger? Who burned the car? We figured it was our job to find out whether A.C. Thompson's insinuations and Tanner's story really were as outlandish as the senior FBI agents seemed to think.

Ashley had grown up in a family that venerated Dr. King and the civil rights leaders of his generation, and she joined the FBI with hopes of working cases that would advance the cause. Instead, the Bureau assigned her to health-care fraud. This was the type of case she always imagined working on.

★ ★ ★

Ashley and I spent the next few days in her FBI-issued golden Chevy Impala, driving around the still-battered streets of New Orleans trying to find anyone who could tell us something about what had happened to Henry Glover. We had no idea where to find Edward King or Bernard Calloway, so we began with Henry's mother, Edna Glover.

Ms. Glover lived in the Fischer Community in Algiers, in the area informally known as the Fischer Projects, where Henry had grown up. For decades, it had been synonymous with urban crime in New Orleans, and a focal point for violent clashes between residents and police. The Projects' old high-rise and low-rise buildings had been demolished in the early 2000s, replaced by low-density and much more attractive pastel-painted town houses. It was the kind of upgrade that you saw in some of the city's housing projects, improving the quality of life for some lower-income New Orleanians, yet drastically reducing the housing options for the rest.

Ms. Edna (as I came to call her) was sitting with friends on the porch of her taupe-colored town house when we arrived. A woman in her late fifties, she seemed older than her years. She invited us inside.

The house was filled with the aromas of freshly fried chicken. Ashley describes the smell as "family." The walls of Edna's living room were covered with photos of her five kids that captured years of happy memories. My sense was this home was filled with love.

Two photos jumped out. One was of Reginald, Edna's eldest son, proudly marching down a city street in his handmade white-feathered Mardi Gras Indian suit. (Black New Orleanians have marched in the streets on Mardi Gras dressed or "masked" in these ornate, intricately handmade outfits since the 1800s, an homage to Native American peoples who aided those escaping slavery.)

In the center of the wall was another photo of a young man, dressed in a white tuxedo, set against a backdrop of an ethereal blue sky with white puffy clouds. Printed at the bottom of the photo: *Henry Glover—10-02-73 - 09-02-05.*

The moment I saw it, Henry Glover transformed in my mind

from the bones and ash of the autopsy report into a son, a brother, and a father.

Edna had a gentle demeanor and spoke in a soft voice. As she talked about her son, she began to cry. She didn't have any firsthand information about his death. After the storm hit, she evacuated to Texas. Henry's oldest brother, Reginald, had commandeered an unattended school bus and drove some family members, including his mother, out of the city. Edna knew only what she'd gleaned from her daughter Patrice and her son Edward—mostly that Henry was shot behind the mall and was last seen at Habans School.

Edna spoke about the agony of not knowing what had happened to Henry. The family spent their first few days in exile in Dallas making phone call after phone call trying to find out something, anything. They called missing persons hotlines, the coroner's office, the police department, and any other possible leads they could think of, all without success.

After several months in Texas, Edna came back to New Orleans and went to the Fourth District police station. Since Henry was last seen in police custody, she figured the officers there might have some information. But the first visit ended in abject failure—the cops said they didn't know what she was talking about and dismissed her. After weeks of getting no answers, she returned to the station and spoke with a Black police officer who filed a missing persons report. The officer told Edna that she should hear back from him in the next week or so.

At that time, Edna had no idea that the car in which her son's body was burned was sitting only about a minute's walk from the police station.

"When did you first hear back from NOPD?" I asked.

"I never heard back."

I was incredulous. In three and half years, no one from NOPD contacted her? Even after Glover's body was autopsied in October 2005 and conclusively identified by DNA in April 2006, no one from the police department ever called her?

"Do you know how we can find Edward King?" Ashley asked about Edna's other son.

"He's in Gretna Jail," Edna responded.

"Gretna Jail? Why is he in jail?"

"Unpaid tickets, I think."

Edna gave us a soft handshake and a weary smile. She seemed defeated. Ashley and I told Ms. Glover that we couldn't make any promises, but that we would do our best to figure out what had happened to Henry. I wasn't feeling particularly optimistic.

We knew from *The Nation* article and Tanner's account that Henry's sister Patrice had briefly been by Henry's side as he lay dying on the corner of Texas and Seine, not far from the mall. But even more importantly, she'd grown up with Henry and, we hoped, could give us some sense of her brother who was, for us, the absence at the center of our investigation.

Ashley and I pulled into Patrice's apartment complex, a two-level, boxy brick building in the heart of Algiers. Patrice didn't know why two federal investigators would drop in on her unannounced, but she graciously invited us in. She was surprised and pleased that finally, almost four years after her brother had been killed, somebody in a position of authority was taking an interest in the case. Her youngest child, two-year-old Bernard, or Little B, ran around the apartment in his diaper, delighted with the unexpected company.

Patrice's mood was subdued. Clearly, she keenly felt the loss of Henry, and the uncertainty around his death. Nobody had ever told her what had happened to Henry, so Ashley and I proceeded cautiously. As much as we wanted new information, it was more important to us to gain Patrice's trust and build a rapport.

Patrice had come of age with Henry in the Fischer Projects. When Ashley and I had met her, she had moved into a blue-collar apartment building, not far from where she had grown up. She thought of her life as a success story. While her four siblings mostly worked in constantly changing off-the-books jobs, not uncommon in this part of Algiers, she had earned a steady paycheck in the decade leading up to Katrina, as a customer services rep for Harrah's hotel and casino.

"I was excited I had a job," Patrice recalled, "and that means

Edna Glover holding a photo of her son, Henry Glover.

CHANDRA McCORMICK

you're doing better than the average person in a poor area in New Orleans. And I had the father of my kids, my boyfriend [Bernard Calloway], in my life too. I was like, 'We can work together to do the best with what we have.' Stay out of trouble, take care of your family, and good things happen to you, that's where I was in my life." Her father had died when she was two years old, and her mother, Edna, was hampered by ill health. Patrice had been "the one that kept the family together."

She had a special affection for Henry, her baby brother, two years her junior. Patrice described Henry as a sweet, easygoing man who, after a couple of run-ins with the police in his teens and early twenties, had pretty much straightened his life out. He was a hard worker who held down two part-time jobs, moving furniture at a furniture store and doing maintenance at a local cemetery. He excelled at fixing anything electronic. People from the neighborhood brought him broken televisions, stereos, and video game machines, and Henry fixed them for whatever money they could pay.

"They'll call Henry and say, 'Henry, such and such is broken, can you come fix it?' And he'll go fix it and make it work." Within the family, Henry played a similar role. "'Say brother, I need you to come to my house and fix something.' That's the kind of brother he was, always there for me. He was a little on the quiet side, but he was fun. He had a good sense of humor and he fed off other people's energy too."

Remembering Henry made Patrice tear up, but she plowed on, giving us the context for the events of September 2. Before Katrina hit, Harrah's put her and her family up in a room at the Hilton Hotel downtown to weather the storm.

Soon after the ferocious winds and rain had died down, she and Bernard and their two kids returned to their modest apartment in the Skyview apartment complex, near the DeGaulle mall. They figured they had made it through the worst part of the storm. "Storms have passed," she said, "and in a day or two or three, you know, the lights usually come back on." She figured that it wouldn't be long before they were "living our regular lives." Word hadn't yet filtered back to them that the levees had collapsed, and that floodwaters were quickly submerging much of the city.

Four days after the storm, she said, the full weight of that miscalculation had sunk in. The family planned to squeeze into her compact four-door Kia with as many members of their extended family as could fit and head to somewhere in Texas. But she discovered that someone had siphoned most of the gas out of her car, a routine type of petty theft after the storm.

Henry left his nearby apartment that morning to find an alternative mode of transportation. Later in the morning, he arrived at Patrice's apartment with a Firestone truck he had taken from an abandoned auto parts store. He and Bernard drove off to collect Henry's things in preparation for the family exodus. Patrice gave Henry a hug and said, "Brother, be careful out there."

Roughly thirty minutes later, Bernard rushed back to the apartment, screaming that Henry had been shot. She sprinted to the spot where Henry lay bleeding on the street, some fifty yards from the mall parking lot.

Patrice asked Henry to blink his eyes if he could hear her. He did, so she knew he was still conscious. Within minutes, her brother and her boyfriend were swept up by a stranger in a white sedan to drive Henry to the hospital, she assumed, leaving Patrice alone in the street. Slowly, a group of onlookers began to gather.

Patrice told us that cops in separate cars drove up to the scene to deal with the crowd of people. One of the officers was a Black woman in NOPD uniform whom she recognized from the neighborhood; she'd seen her handing out bottles of water in the first days after the storm.

Another cop, a White male, arrived in an unmarked car, wearing a tactical uniform and brandishing a long gun. Patrice said she confronted him: "One of your officers shot my brother." He responded, "Get the F back before I shoot you." We asked Patrice why she thought a cop had shot Henry. She admitted she didn't know for sure, but both she and Bernard were well aware of the police substation on the second floor of the nearby mall. "It only could have been the cops that done it because them are the only ones that was out."

Several hours later, the stranger with the white car, William Tanner, burst in to report what had happened at the school. She then took off for Habans, a ten-minute walk, where she encountered a Black officer who told her, "We let the motherfuckers go." By the time she returned to the apartment, Bernard and Edward were there waiting for her, their faces bruised and swollen.

"I just want to find out what happened to my baby brother and I couldn't get any answers," Patrice told us. "I just want some kind of justice."

It was a big request, as she must have known. Patrice had formed her first impressions of the New Orleans police as an eight-year-old girl, living through one of the most notorious episodes of NOPD criminal behavior.

The modern era of police abuse in New Orleans began with a vengeance in 1980. After a White patrolman was killed, a group of his fellow police officers, on a mission to find out who did it, went on a rampage in the projects, killing four Black civilians, including the girlfriend of a suspect who was shot naked in a bathtub.

"I remember the cops coming in, knocking on all our doors, just waking us up, had us terrified, guns drawn," Patrice recalled in a later conversation. "I remember asking: 'Momma, what's going on?' [She said,] 'Just stay inside. Get under the cover, get under the bed, the police are out there.' I think my momma probably had Henry in her arms. Trying to shield and protect him. [The police] voices loud you know: 'Get inside! Get the fuck inside!' With their loud angry voice like that, it was a lot."

The so-called Algiers 7 case was grotesque on a grand scale. Cops conducted interrogations of young Black men that, as New Orleans's leading newspaper, *The Times-Picayune*, reported, "border[ed] on torture." Police marched men through the projects like prisoners of war, hands in the air, guns to their heads. Witnesses, including one police officer, said they witnessed mock executions. The department did its best to cover up the killings, and the officers who were present mostly kept their mouths shut. In the end, no one was charged in connection with the four deaths. Of the seven officers charged for abusing civilians during the search, only three were convicted.

A federal appeals court summarized some of the allegations. Several of the victims were hit with fists or books, and two individuals "were also 'bagged,' a process whereby the officer placed a bag over the victim's head and temporarily sealed off the bottom to cut off the air supply."

The case generated public outcry and modest efforts to reform the NOPD. But over the ensuing years, both public interest and police reform waned. Then, a decade after Algiers 7, the city was roiled by the killing of Adolph Archie, a Black man with a record of arrests for low-level crimes. Archie stole a gun and fled through the middle of downtown, chased by a small army of cops. In the ensuing melee, he shot and killed an officer. A young officer apprehended and cuffed him after the officer realized Archie had run out of bullets and posed no lethal threat. The officer was subsequently ostracized by his police peers for not following an unwritten NOPD dictum—anyone who kills a New Orleans cop should be killed before an arrest can be made.

Archie never lived to see a trial. As police radio began to fill up with death threats from other officers, the cops driving the wounded Archie to the hospital changed course. They brought him to the station of the officer who had been killed, where Archie's head and torso were bashed in. No officer was ever indicted in the case.

Frank Minyard, the coroner who initially determined that Archie's smashed head was caused by a "slip and fall," was the same coroner who examined Henry's ashes and bones and determined that the cause of death was "unclassified," rather than a suspected homicide.

We needed to find Edward King, and both Edna and Patrice had told us they thought we could find him in Gretna Jail.

Only a fifteen-minute drive from Patrice Glover's house, Gretna sits just over the New Orleans city line in Jefferson Parish. The Jefferson Parish Correctional Center, like most county jails I've seen, is a dingy assemblage of concrete blocks and razor wire and reeks of industrial cleaners.

Different jails are bad in different ways. But I hate going to any of them. Even though as a prosecutor, I knew I could leave whenever I wanted, I found even the temporary experience suffocating. The inmates, mostly men from communities of color, are locked in cells, many confined for nonviolent offenses. Usually they emerge from incarceration emotionally damaged, barred by virtue of their convictions from most legal employment, with drastically reduced opportunities in life.

Edward King entered the small interview room wearing a bright orange jumpsuit, and he wobbled slightly, the penguin walk of a prisoner in leg shackles. Edward looked confused, and nervous. Clearly, he didn't get many visitors in dark suits. We explained that we were federal agents looking into his brother's death, and that seemed to put him at ease.

He told us that he was in jail for unpaid municipal fines. The city issued a warrant, and he was arrested, not long after he was quoted in *The Nation* article.

It seemed unfathomable to me that a person could be jailed for owing the government money. But every year, thousands more people just like him are jailed across America for nonpayment of fines and fees connected to minor traffic and municipal code violations and misdemeanors.

Across the US, many municipal governments fund their criminal legal system and other government services on the backs of the poorest in their communities, using fines and fees associated with law enforcement. Nonpayment regularly results in escalating penalties, including additional fees, license suspension, loss of voting rights, and far too often, imprisonment. This cycle of punishment and poverty can lead people to lose their jobs, their homes, and even custody of their children. Gretna, where King was being held, had the distinction of being the "arrest capital" of America, jailing more people per capita than anywhere else in the US, mostly on low-level charges. Few things drive home the realities of our country's racial and economic caste system more vividly than interviewing a man in leg shackles and an orange jumpsuit who has been jailed for being too poor to pay his municipal debts.

Edward laid out for us his family tree. He was the second of five children, Henry the youngest. (The two eldest children, Edward and Reginald, were born before their parents married; they bear Edna's maiden name, King.) When the storm hit, Edward was living in Algiers, in the Skyview apartments with his wife. His sister Patrice and Bernard Calloway and their children lived in an apartment in the same complex. Just down the block, in the Jackson's Landing apartments, was Henry, with his girlfriend and their daughter.

The families had stocked up on food and had a decent supply of water, so when the storm hit, they decided to stay put in Algiers. Edward said that Henry especially didn't want to abandon his home. But by the evening of September 1, as supplies dwindled, even Henry agreed that it was time to leave.

On the morning of September 2, Edward was at home when Bernard came running into the apartment, screaming that the police shot Henry. Edward didn't have time to ask him how he knew it was the police.

Edward, Bernard, and Patrice ran down the street to the corner of Texas and Seine, fifty yards beyond the strip mall, finding Henry lying facedown, his white T-shirt soaked with blood, his breathing shallow. After loading Henry into the back seat of Tanner's car, Edward cradled Henry in his arms as the three men sped through the streets looking for help.

Edward's account of what happened at the school was similar to Tanner's, only more emotional. "Last time I saw my brother [was] when they took me out of the car and put them handcuffs on," he said mournfully. "That's the last time I saw him." The beating by the cops, he said, lasted, off and on, for two hours, so intense that at times he lost consciousness.

He recalled one officer in particular, the cop who followed the Chevy in a pickup truck. He called the officer "Schumacher." "He beat me good. I grew up in a neighborhood project, I mean fighting three, four times a day. But I never got beat how this man beat me with my hands behind my back, kicking me in the face, spitting in my face, whenever he felt like it."

Edward couldn't get over that after all this time, we were talking to him about his brother. "I can't believe you're here," he said with a look both gratified and disoriented.

Even for Ashley, who had spent plenty of time working with marginalized communities, meeting Edward was a revelation. She told me afterwards, "At that moment, a lightbulb kind of went on in my head, that there was a segment of our population that just felt like nobody gave a damn about them. They were beaten, they were in jail when they shouldn't be, and it was just the norm."

It was obvious to both of us that whatever baggage Edward had been carrying before September 2 must have gotten heavier. "Every time I pass that school, I get flashbacks," he said later. "Sometimes, I dream about it. I was thinking after a while, it would go away. It's not going away... And I'm trying to deal with this every day. It's hard, man. I feel like something just is gone, [something] that I had in my heart is gone."

Edward told us that he and Bernard collected their families and packed up all their belongings, and got out of New Orleans immediately. The Glover extended family, ten people in all, made the thirty-minute walk to the Algiers Ferry station where buses waited to take them out of the city.

I asked, in retrospect a little naively, why he hadn't tried harder to find out what had happened to his brother when he got back to New Orleans. Edward looked somewhat puzzled by my question: "When it's the police who do this to you, who do you call?"

CHAPTER 3

PEELING THE ONION

March and April 2009

In the early weeks of the investigation, while we were still awaiting documents from NOPD, A.C. Thompson posted a follow-up online to his article in *The Nation*. The new post identified the officer whose car William Tanner had jump-started and who had helped get him released from Habans on September 2. Thompson showed Tanner a copy of the 2005 NOPD yearbook, the cop version of a high school yearbook. Tanner pointed to a middle-aged White woman who worked with SOD.

I didn't like the idea that we were in a race against a reporter to find witnesses, but I was happy for our first real law enforcement lead.

Ashley and I spent much of the early days of the investigation driving around the New Orleans area in her Chevy Impala. It served as our mobile office and war room.

One morning at the end of March 2009, Ashley picked me up at my hotel in the French Quarter, my New Orleans home away from home. The officer lived an hour-plus drive away, much of it on the Causeway, the longest continuous bridge in the world, running twenty-three miles across the middle of Lake Pontchartrain. Driving across it feels something like crossing the ocean on a tightrope.

Ashley and I had decided to show up at her home unannounced, hoping that by catching her by surprise, we might get a more honest account of events before she could coordinate her story with anyone else. The downside of this strategy is that we often came up empty. A half hour off the Causeway, we found ourselves in deep rural Louisiana, on back roads in densely forested country that took us to the officer's wooden cabin. We knocked on the door, but she wasn't home. As Ashley and I waited in her unmarked car, we felt more and more conspicuous, a mixed-race couple with no obvious business being there, as local pickup trucks passed by, scattering dirt on our vehicle. The officer never showed up.

We woke up early the next morning and started over again. Ashley walked by a rusty old refrigerator on the porch and knocked on the front door of the cabin. A groggy woman emerged in her patterned flannel pajamas and slippers, surrounded by a pack of dogs and cats. She pointedly did not invite us inside, so Ashley and I interviewed her in the woods in front of her home, alongside her loudly barking dogs.

Ashley was not in her element. She was afraid of dogs in general, and this pack did nothing to make her feel at ease, growling and displaying their fangs. Each time a dog moved closer to her, I could see her hand inch closer to the gun on her hip.

The officer was chatty enough, but didn't offer much information about what had happened to Henry Glover. She explained away her haziness on the details with a line we would hear, delivered with varying degrees of convincingness, throughout the investigation: *You've got to understand, it was Katrina.*

As the officer retreated inside her cabin with the dogs, Ashley eased up, and we hopped back in the Impala for the long drive back to the city.

★ ★ ★

Ashley and I located the SOD timesheets and matched them to pictures in the NOPD yearbook, looking for potential witnesses who could help us understand what happened at Habans that day. But truth can be an elusive commodity, especially in a police investigation. I typically start by interviewing people on the periphery of the case, then work my way closer to the subjects of the investigation, a technique known in my office as "peeling the onion."

We wanted to start by interviewing cops who had the least chance of being mixed up in the crimes against Henry, trying to accumulate as many "truth nuggets" as possible from which we could build a case against our actual suspects, whomever they turned out to be. We needed to find evidence of police involvement in the shooting or the burning quickly, or New Orleans FBI would likely shut us down. Plus, the statute of limitations for most of the federal crimes we were investigating is five years, so we didn't have a lot of time.

After looking at some fifty yearbook photos of officers who had likely been at Habans that day, we developed a small list of priority interviews. They were all Black officers who had either left NOPD or transferred out of SOD since the storm.

We hoped that finding officers who no longer worked in SOD would lessen a sense of group allegiance that might interfere with telling the truth. We also knew from our interviews with Tanner and King that the officers who beat them and who seemed to be in charge were all White. While some Black officers were present during the beating, and some joined in the verbal attacks, and one even slapped Edward, all of the main assailants were White.

We made an unannounced visit to the home of a former SOD officer who now worked for the Louisiana State Police. He lived in a middle-class neighborhood with a well-trimmed lawn and two cars in the front driveway. Like many of the other SOD officers we would meet, he told us he did not know anything about a gunshot victim showing up at the school, or three civilians being beaten and detained there. Likewise, he denied even hearing about the shooting behind the mall, or about the man burned behind the levee.

All this we found hard to believe given that *The Times-Picayune* had recently run articles rehashing the allegations in Thompson's piece. Picking up on our skepticism, he countered, *You have to understand what it was like after Katrina.*

In normal times, SOD headquarters sits on the East Bank of the Mississippi. On August 30, as floodwaters poured into the building, the first order of business, he told us, was keeping the equipment dry. The officers moved their fleet of cars, trucks, boats, and a small armory's worth of military-grade weaponry, as much as they could manage, into Habans Elementary School in Algiers.

SOD's fifty-plus officers quickly made the school their home. They set up cots and fold-out beds in the empty classrooms and converted the school cafeteria into an officer's mess hall. When fuel was available, generators provided intermittent refrigeration for food, including meat that was either donated by fleeing citizens or commandeered from abandoned stores by the cops themselves. A barbecue grill was set up in the back of the school. Word got around, and Habans became an attraction, not only for SOD, but for officers from state and federal agencies working in the area who dropped by on break. Some simply moved in.

During the day, SOD responded to calls throughout New Orleans, primarily in the flooded East Bank. Officers split into two twelve-hour shifts, though in reality, many worked around the clock. In the early days, they primarily performed search and rescue duties—often going door to door, or more accurately, roof to roof. SOD had a few boats, and some officers used their own fishing boats to navigate the floodwaters. Sometimes, they found dead bodies rotting in attics, or floating in the stagnant waters. They plucked survivors off rooftops and ferried them to dry land. Without sufficient water and food, many of the elderly were dead before morning.

At night, hollow-eyed men padded around Habans in fatigues and undershirts, looking grimier and smelling gamier as the days wore on. Officers grabbed whatever sleep they could in the brutal late summer heat and humidity. Some slept in their cars so they could run the AC. It was difficult to get more than two to three hours of sleep at night.

With city power out, the darkness was all-enveloping and oppressive. Time itself was fluid. "…[W]e didn't know what day it was," another officer told us. "…[Y]ou know daylight was there, you knew nighttime came… And weeks went by."

As we ended our interview, I took one last shot. "Do you think SOD could have had anything to do with the burning car?"

He shook his head. "Sounds like bullshit to me." And then he gave us the shutdown question that we would get a lot over the course of the investigation: "Were you here for Katrina?"

"No," we answered.

"Then you couldn't possibly understand."

The implication was clear: *Who are you to come down here now and try to judge us?* If all our interviews went like this, I doubted we would ever figure out what happened to Henry Glover.

With the *Times-Pic* running front-page articles about possible police involvement in the burning of Henry Glover, our investigation was no longer a secret. The upside was that we knew cops would start talking. The allegations were hard *not* to talk about. Over time, we knew that talk around the department could yield valuable leads. But how, as outsiders, to tap into the chatter we knew was happening?

We needed a source inside the department, ideally, someone who had access to both SOD and the Fourth District, and who had lived through Katrina and NOPD's response. Most importantly, our source needed to be trustworthy, not so easy in a department as notoriously corrupt as NOPD.

Ashley's colleague introduced her to an officer who had helped the FBI during several investigations. She gave him a call, and then stopped by his office. During her first visit, she expressed her reservations about Tanner, and questioned how seriously she should take the allegations. The source paused and gave her a look "like a parent would give a child who's been goofing off at school," according to Ashley. A look that conveyed, "You need to take this seriously."

It seemed this officer was the only one in NOPD who shared that sentiment. It was unclear what motivated him. He had risen through the ranks during some of the most notorious scandals in the department's checkered history. Maybe he had gotten his hands dirty years before and was looking for atonement. Maybe he was just sick of watching his colleagues get away with the abuse.

Ashley had an instinct that her source needed to be protected, an instinct that would grow sharper as we received clearer signals from people in NOPD and New Orleans FBI that they would prefer the Glover case go away. Ashley wouldn't even tell me who her source was. From that point on, we simply referred to him as "The Source."

The Source had given Ashley some names of officers he said we should talk to. "Who are these people?" I asked. Ashley told me she didn't know.

"What do you mean you don't know?"

"He didn't tell me anything about them."

"All right then. Let's go find them."

Even with a list of names, it was not easy to find our witnesses.

We showed up at one address and found a house still completely unlivable, with blown-out windows and trees strewn across the front lawn. A FEMA (Federal Emergency Management Agency) trailer sat in the front driveway, apparently hooked up for some basic utilities, though it did not appear that anyone really lived there.

We eventually tracked down Purnella "Nina" Simmons, who, at the time of Katrina, worked in NOPD's Fourth District. Sergeant Simmons, a twenty-five-year veteran, was assigned to the backwater "compliance" section at police headquarters. With her singsongy voice and deferential manner, she had the demeanor of a preschool teacher.

Simmons seemed surprised that two feds had shown up un-announced at her office at NOPD headquarters. She wondered whether she had to speak with us. We told her the interview was voluntary but that we hoped she could clear up a few things for us about what had taken place after Katrina. She reluctantly started talking.

Simmons had been patrolling a storm-damaged and largely deserted Algiers in her squad car with a rookie partner named Key-alah Bell when she received a cell phone call from her friend Linda Howard, another veteran female Black officer. Howard sounded frantic: "Get over here now!"

Howard had been stationed at the Azalea Plaza mall, known to most as the DeGaulle mall. She was assigned to protect the District Investigative Unit (DIU) police substation on the mall's second floor, its plate-glass window shattered by the hurricane's piercing winds, its computers and files vulnerable to the elements and to theft.

Simmons and Bell sped to the mall to find Howard pacing by the stairway that led up to the police substation. "He just shot someone, he just shot someone," she cried.

"Who?" Simmons inquired.

Howard pointed at David Warren, a forty-year-old rookie officer from another district loaned to the Fourth when floodwaters prevented him from reaching his regular post.

Simmons described Warren as "almost nonchalant." He told Simmons that two men had approached the building, and he yelled to them to get away. "And [they] disregarded what he was saying and he fired a shot." Warren told her that he didn't think his shot had hit anybody.

Simmons didn't ask too many questions of Warren or Howard. She kicked in a distress call to alert other officers and then she and Bell got back in their car and drove to the rear of the strip mall, where Howard indicated the man had fallen.

As Simmons and Bell looked around for clues, a crowd gathered at the intersection behind the mall.

"As the crowd came up…they were telling us that somebody

had been shot. The police had shot somebody. And we were asking where they were at, where the person was at."

A woman stepped forward in the crowd. "She walked up to me and said...my brother has been shot by the police... And I told her I don't know, I was there to find out the same thing."

Some people in the crowd told Simmons that the man had been driven to a hospital. Several police officers—Simmons thought they were SOD—arrived at the scene. The scene was growing increasingly tense, and the officers began dispersing the crowd.

Ashley and I exchanged a look. This corroborated Patrice Glover's account of how she tried to get answers from a Black female officer she had recognized from the neighborhood, before being run off by a group of gun-toting cops.

Around the same time, another call came out over the police radio from Habans School about a shooting victim, and Simmons thought it might be related to the shooting at the mall. Without making any effort to secure the shooting scene—calling a supervisor or crime scene unit to find and preserve the physical evidence of a police-involved shooting—Simmons and Bell drove to Habans School, a quarter mile north of the strip mall.

At Habans, they found a crowd of police officers, mostly people Simmons did not know who worked in SOD. Three men sat on the ground in handcuffs, surrounded by armed officers. Off to the side, a white four-door sedan was parked diagonally. One of the handcuffed men was sporadically yelling, "Somebody's shot in the car." Simmons said she never looked inside.

Among the collection of officers at Habans, Simmons saw Captain David Kirsch, the senior leader of the Fourth District, and Lieutenant Robert Italiano, the district's number two.

Simmons told her supervisors about the possible connection between the mall shooting and the car at the school; the timing, proximity, and circumstances all pointed to such a connection. She thought Italiano would be particularly interested in this since he led the DIU, whose office David Warren and Linda Howard had been guarding.

Kirsch told Simmons that the two incidents were not related. "It's a different situation," he declared. Simmons tried to explain what Howard and the sister had told her at the mall, but Italiano interrupted her. "They are separate incidents. They are not the same."

Sergeant Simmons didn't push the issue, responding meekly, "Yes, sir." The scene was crowded with police officers, who seemed to have the situation under control.

She asked Italiano if she should write a report about the shooting at the mall, and he told her no.

Along with Bell, Simmons went back to the mall to check on her friend Linda Howard, but didn't do any further investigation. She didn't look for shell casings or any other evidence of the shooting. She didn't secure the scene. She didn't seize Warren's weapon—a personally owned assault rifle—or relieve him from duty. Since Italiano told her she didn't need to file a report, she didn't document anything about the shooting.

Ashley and I pressed Simmons about not doing more.

"I spoke with the captain. I knew they would take care of it. I told them about the shooting, and that was my job, so that DIU could do the investigation." She sounded matter-of-fact: "We were doing the best that we could for the times that we were in."

Months later, Italiano told her to write a report. Ashley and I had been looking for any reports on the shooting but so far had come up empty. Simmons told us she didn't have a copy, and hadn't seen it since she had written it.

We needed to find this report.

Robert Italiano, the former Fourth District lieutenant, also lived nearby, so we went there next. It was dusk by the time we pulled up to his house, in a comfortable, mostly White neighborhood in Algiers. Again, it was a "cold call," and the retired lieutenant wasn't in.

We headed over to Keyalah Bell's house, a modest but cozy bungalow in a less affluent neighborhood a ten-minute drive away. As we pulled into the driveway, Ashley received a call from the second-in-command of the New Orleans FBI field office, the Assistant Special Agent in Charge, the ASAC in Bureau lingo. He was Ashley's boss's boss.

I could hear the yelling on the other end of the line. I could only make out a few words, but it was clear to me that the ASAC wasn't happy about our unannounced visit to Lieutenant Italiano's house.

Ashley hung up the phone and seemed a little shaken, but brushed it off like a pro. She put on her game face and rang Bell's doorbell. Bell, who had partnered with Simmons the day of the shooting, seemed nervous to see us, but nonetheless invited us inside. She looked about thirty, and she was in the middle of cooking dinner for her two children.

Bell's young daughter pranced across the floor in a pink tutu as Ashley and I took seats on the living room sofa. Our presence felt intrusive. It was a ridiculous time to interview a witness about a homicide, but Bell was willing to talk, and we were not about to lose the opportunity.

Bell seemed thoughtful and forthcoming, if somewhat measured. Her account echoed what we'd heard from Simmons. She described arriving at the mall and finding Howard acting "very hysterical." Howard just said, "Talk to him," as she gestured at Warren.

Bell spoke to Warren who said he had fired his weapon. She said, "He had this really...calm demeanor, like nonchalant... He just said, 'They were looting.'"

Bell and Simmons drove around to the parking area behind the mall, where Warren had said he had seen the "looters." Bell said that the gate that separated the parking lot from a stairway leading to the mall's second level, where Warren had fired his weapon, was locked with chains. She told us that the only way to access the area where the officers had been was through the front of the mall.

Behind the mall, near the intersection of Texas and Seine, Bell noticed a pool of blood and either a bloody white towel or T-shirt. But quickly their attention was diverted by a group of angry neighborhood residents who'd heard about the shooting and were walking towards them. "They were pretty hysterical also, just yelling." A car full of officers with assault rifles arrived and took control of the scene, so she and Bell got back in their patrol car.

"…[A]t that point we just looked at each other and we knew we had to get out of there."

Then they heard a call over the police radio requesting officers to handle an aggravated shooting at Habans, so they drove over to the school. At Habans, Bell said, armed SOD officers were milling around, some in uniform, some in plain clothes.

A group of officers surrounded some handcuffed men in front of a squad car. The men looked dazed. "They were just sitting on the ground. One of them looked at me and I looked back at him and he just put his head down in disbelief—just put his head down and shook his head."

When Simmons went over to brief Captain Kirsch and Lieutenant Italiano, Bell stayed behind near their patrol vehicle. She observed a Fourth District detective walk over, look at the car, and comment that they had "a good 30" on their hands, police talk for a homicide. She noticed one person taking photographs. Bell told us she never looked inside the car.

When Simmons returned from her conversation with Italiano and Kirsch, the two women went back on patrol, and headed back out to the mall, where Bell told us she encountered Henry's sister at the corner of Texas and Seine.

"She just asked, 'I know my brother was shot. I just want to know where he is.'"

"I told her I did not know. Because, you know, at the time, I didn't know who the person in the car was." She *wanted* to tell the sister, "He's at Habans," but she wasn't 100 percent sure, given how dismissive the ranking officers had been. She was sure, as a rookie, it wasn't her place to share this information.

Though she didn't say it directly, Bell gave us the impression that, Katrina notwithstanding, the way this shooting was handled was not normal. We also had the distinct sense that she had more information. We knew we would need to talk to her again, probably not at dinnertime, with children clamoring for her attention.

That night, as Ashley was getting ready for bed, she received a call from Bell on her cell phone. "I remembered something," the officer said.

She confessed that she had, in fact, seen a bloodied body inside the white car at Habans, untended to and apparently lifeless, splayed out on the back seat. After this revelation, she burst into tears.

CHAPTER 4

A BAD SHOOT

April 2009

As Ashley drove me back to my hotel in the French Quarter, we tried to make sense of the ASAC's irate phone call. At one level, we understood. In a hierarchy-driven law enforcement culture, we could see how the idea of a rookie agent showing up unannounced at a senior police officer's house might be problematic. The FBI relied on NOPD to execute warrants and conduct joint investigations, the basis of a close working relationship that only got closer in the difficult months after Katrina, when the FBI and NOPD operated out of the same headquarters, at The Royal Sonesta Hotel.

But, we agreed, the ASAC's reaction was over-the-top. Unannounced visits to officers are a standard tactic in police misconduct cases, particularly where there is a suspicion of obstruction by the department. Ashley had gone over her list of potential interviewees with her immediate supervisor, who hadn't flagged any problems.

Furthermore, Italiano had only been a lieutenant—a higher-ranking officer, sure, but still many layers away from the top of the chain of command. Even more unusual, he wasn't even currently employed by NOPD. He had retired two years earlier.

For whatever reason, the ASAC didn't seem to want us interviewing Italiano without being there himself, and he set up a meeting for the next day, first thing in the morning, in his office.

We didn't know what to make of this. Italiano was someone we certainly wanted to talk to, but based on what we had heard from Simmons and Bell, he seemed to be further "inside the onion" than we were ready to deal with. Warren shot Henry Glover from the police substation that Italiano had commanded. He had been present at the Habans School while Henry's unburned body lay in the white Chevy. We wanted more time to process all this, but that wasn't an option.

Doing a first interview with such a potentially important witness in a meeting hosted by the FBI Field Office's second-in-command, who was not directly involved in our investigation, struck me as a real old boys club way to do business. But, I thought, maybe that's just the way they do things in New Orleans.

Ashley greeted me in the FBI lobby, and we went up to her cubicle to regroup for a minute. She had just learned from her supervisor that Captain Kirsch, who had overseen the Fourth District during Katrina and had been Italiano's then-boss, would also join the meeting. I felt blindsided.

It's rare to interview two witnesses in the same room at the same time, particularly early in an investigation, and especially when there is an allegation of a cover-up. You don't want to give them the chance to synch up their versions of events while they're talking to you. By interviewing them separately, you may uncover discrepancies, which, in turn, may create leverage to push a witness to cooperate.

I didn't see a way out of this compromising mess, particularly considering the ASAC's chewing out of Ashley just the day before. I thought about calling DOJ deputy chief, Bobbi Bernstein, back in DC, who assigned me the case, for some quick advice. Bobbi is an iconic figure in civil rights legal circles, known for her dogged investigations, brutal cross-examinations, and compelling court-room arguments. She was in the early stages of investigating the most high-profile instance of post-Katrina NOPD criminality, an incident where a truckload of cops opened fire on unarmed civil-ians crossing the Danziger Bridge. We regularly compared notes. But it wasn't yet 8:00 a.m. I decided not to bother her.

Ashley and I decided we would be respectfully curious, and we wouldn't push too hard. If we were lucky, maybe we'd get another crack at Italiano and Kirsch, separately.

The ASAC's office was neatly decorated with professional regalia—FBI awards, ceremonial police challenge coins, and a photo of the Twin Towers. When Ashley and I walked in, Kirsch hadn't arrived yet. The ASAC and Italiano sat together on the of-fice couch making small talk. The ASAC called him "Bobby."

Bobby, for his part, looked less comfortable. Italiano was in his early sixties, with silver hair, an angular face, and a goatee. He pro-jected a hardness that comes from thirty-seven years of policing.

I introduced myself, and he reluctantly shook my hand. His glare conveyed, "Who the fuck do you think you are?" I have to admit, it was intimidating.

The ASAC took charge of the interview, inviting Bobby to tell us about the mall shooting. In Italiano's retelling, he and Kirsch were patrolling the streets of Algiers together that day. They heard a call over the police radio. An officer—he wasn't sure who—reported that a shooting had occurred near the Fourth District DIU at the mall. The officer communicated that the man who had been shot had left the scene in a truck.

Then, moments later, another call came in over the radio, saying a car arrived at Habans School with a dead body in the back seat. Italiano said he and Kirsch assumed the calls were describing the same incident, a shooting and its aftermath. They drove to Habans, geographically within their jurisdiction, but at that moment under the control of the department's tactical unit, SOD.

At this point, Italiano's recollection grew remarkably vague, even granting the three and a half years' passage of time. He told us he saw the three Black men who arrived in the car and heard them say there was a fourth man who had been shot, inside the car. He wasn't sure whether he actually saw the car at the school or the body inside it.

He saw Nina Simmons at Habans, who informed him about the David Warren shooting at DIU, and she suggested that the two scenes might be connected.

Italiano told us that at Habans, he had begun to think that was not the case. The call from DIU had mentioned a truck, whereas the body at Habans was in a car. We couldn't check him on this, because no police radio logs existed. But even if this were true, it seemed that this one word—which could have been an honest miscommunication since Henry and Calloway had arrived at the mall in a truck—was pretty flimsy grounds for such a definitive conclusion. But we let it go.

Italiano had no recollection of talking to Linda Howard, either on the day of the shooting or afterwards. He had briefly spoken to Warren about the shooting, though the timing of this conversation was unclear. Warren told him that the man whom he shot at was rushing at him and may have been armed. The officer thought his shot had missed.

Kirsch showed up midway through Italiano's account. He didn't say much. He spent much of the meeting hunched over his Black-berry, which could have been the genuine business of a district commander or a convenient distraction.

Ashley and I focused our attention on the question at the heart of the case. Was there a connection between the shooting and the burning of Glover's body? Italiano acknowledged knowing about the burned car with the body inside, but said he had no information that it had anything to do with the firearm discharge by David Warren.

We asked about the investigation that followed, and Italiano told us there hadn't been one. He said that he never went to the mall the day of the shooting. We asked about the report Simmons said she authored on the shooting, and he denied that such a report existed. We asked about the missing persons report that Edna Glover had made, and he said that the district was not writing missing persons reports after the storm.

He explained in a condescending tone that these were not "normal times." To Ashley's mind, "It was like he was saying, 'How stupid are you? There was a hurricane going on.'" As if we needed the reminder.

We would have loved to push Italiano harder on all of this, especially his conversations with Simmons and Warren, and the suspicious lack of a documentary paper trail. But Ashley and I were still stuck in deferential mode. We were young and green, and under the watchful eye of an FBI higher-up. A thirty-seven-year police veteran was adamant that we were totally on the wrong track.

As far as we could tell, no one had ever seriously looked into the death of Henry Glover. But now, in the wake of *The Nation* article and Ashley's and my preliminary efforts, NOPD had opened its own investigation. Detective Sergeant Gerard Dugue, a veteran investigator with the NOPD's Cold Case Homicide Unit, the office responsible for investigating all police-involved killings, had been assigned the case and requested a meeting.

At that time, DOJ rarely started a full-scale investigation into a police misconduct allegation until after the local inquiry had ended. But given that NOPD had done nothing for the past three and half years, we found ourselves in the unusual position of conducting a parallel investigation.

I did not expect much from the meeting with Dugue, given our experience to date with official NOPD channels. But even if he didn't assist our investigation, at least we could coordinate our efforts. We knew he had already interviewed some witnesses, and we wanted to make sure that his involvement wouldn't complicate our own attempts to identify and interview others.

Ashley and I met Dugue in the FBI lobby. A genial, older, Black gentleman, in his dark suit and tie and carrying a manila folder, he looked like the seasoned investigator he was. He greeted us with a warm smile and a firm handshake and, as evidence of his professional affability, offered to share what he had learned from his investigation that began in January, but only now in April was picking up speed.

Our meeting was brief and to the point. We never even sat down. Without ceremony, he handed us the manila folder.

Inside there were copies of four color photographs taken by an officer with Customs and Border Protection (CBP) who had been stationed in Algiers after Katrina. A few days earlier, we had received the same photos from a CBP agent via email, but this was the first time we were seeing them blown up on letter-size paper.

The first two photos depicted Tanner's car, fully engulfed by bright orange flames, and spewing black-and-white smoke. The car sat surrounded by trees, one of which had partially caught fire. In the foreground of both photos sat a downward-sloping concrete slab, part of the Patterson Road levee. The photographs were taken during the day, though the exact time was not obvious.

The second two photographs, taken after the fire had subsided, showed the inside of the car. Only the metal shell and some wire remained. Strewn throughout the back seat were bits of charred human flesh, fractured bone, and ash. Only two body parts were easily recognizable: the skull and the spinal column.

As significant as the photos themselves was the date stamp at the bottom of the photos—*SEPT 2 2005*—evidence that the burning had occurred on the same day as the shooting. That radically shrank the number of people with the opportunity to incinerate the car and the body inside. It didn't prove the police had burned the car but made it much more likely.

Underneath the photographs was a stack of papers. These were totally new to us. Dugue hadn't located a report on the shooting itself, but he had found the missing persons report written in November 2005, after Edna Glover's visit to the Fourth District police station. The guts of the report, a one-and-a-half-page handwritten narrative, offered up a remarkably detailed picture of Henry's last day, from the shooting at the mall to the beatdown of the three men at Habans to Henry being driven out of the school by an officer driving Tanner's car.

The existence of the report refuted Italiano's claim that the department wasn't producing missing persons reports after Katrina and confirmed that people inside NOPD knew about the connection between the police shooting at the mall and the body that arrived at Habans, at least as early as November 2005.

It was particularly striking to see the name of the detective assigned to follow up on the report: Robert Italiano.

Dugue agreed to remain in touch during our respective investigations. He said he would give us first crack at interviewing Warren.

As Ashley and I walked away from the meeting, I wondered whether my skepticism of Dugue had been warranted. Maybe he could be another inside source, an official one at that.

Back in DC, I found the case hard not to talk about. I tested out theories and asked for investigative advice from my colleagues. I couldn't have been in a better spot. The Civil Rights Division of the Department of Justice was home to some of the best civil rights lawyers in the country.

The Division was created as a part of the Civil Rights Act of 1957, the nation's first civil rights law since Reconstruction. In the 1960s, it had played a pivotal role in dismantling segregation and securing voting rights for African Americans in the South.

The Criminal Section, where I worked, led some of the nation's most significant criminal civil rights prosecutions. Our attorneys prosecuted nineteen men for murdering three civil rights workers in 1964 and led investigations into racially motivated crimes like the bombing of the Sixteenth Street Baptist Church in Birmingham and the assassination of Medgar Evers, a civil rights activist and the NAACP's first field secretary in Mississippi.

In 2009, the criminal section was an amazingly collegial place. Although most of the attorneys were on the road at any given time, whoever happened to be around would gather in the conference room for lunch and share war stories. Serious stories, about defeating Klansmen and neo-Nazis, dismantling forced labor rings, and bringing down whole shifts of sadistic corrections officers. As much as we celebrated victories, we mourned the righteous cases we lost, which, given that we were civil rights lawyers, were not uncommon. (The office never stood a chance of convicting an abusive Mississippi sheriff's deputy who was also Elvis's cousin.)

My friend and mentor, senior DOJ attorney Barry Kowalski, told many of the biggest and best stories. A bald, diminutive man who often rode his bike to work, Barry made an impression, sauntering around the office in his spandex shorts.

Barry's work touched on many key moments in American civil rights history. He investigated the assassination of Martin Luther King to determine whether James Earl Ray acted alone. (The investigation concluded he did.) Once, in order to gain a tactical advantage with the jury, he managed to convince the notoriously racist governor of Alabama, George Wallace, to make him an honorary colonel in the Alabama National Guard.

Barry was best known for leading the federal prosecution of the Los Angeles cops responsible for the brutal 1991 beating of Rodney King, the most famous police misconduct case my office ever handled. When state prosecutors failed to convict the officers, despite damning video evidence, LA went up in flames—sixty-three lives lost and a billion dollars of property destroyed in some of the city's most impoverished neighborhoods. It was a worst-case demonstration of what can happen when cops aren't held accountable for their actions. Barry secured the federal convictions, helping to ensure the city wouldn't burn again.

Barry, who died in 2019, taught me how to use a grand jury to build a case; how to pick a jury; how to prepare a victim to testify; and how to effectively present a police abuse case to a jury that might not be inclined to convict. (Barry was a proponent of finding a pithy phrase that concisely summarizes your theme. In the Rodney King case, he famously declared in his closing argument, "Let's call it like it was. They were bullies with badges.")

The brutal travel schedule at DOJ Civil Rights chewed up most attorneys within three years. If I were going to stick around, I wanted cases that had the kind of impact that Barry's had. It seemed like the Glover case could be that starting point.

Though Ashley and I felt confident that a police officer had shot Henry Glover, we had yet to locate anyone who had witnessed the shooting. Our efforts to track down both Bernard Calloway and Linda Howard had led nowhere. We also kept hearing from Glover family members and neighbors about a "boy on a bike" who had seen the shooting, but no one could provide us his name.

We needed to find a witness.

When Ashley and I had interviewed Patrice Glover two months earlier, she told us that she and Bernard Calloway had split up during the family's exile in Dallas. After some months in Texas, she told him that she had to return to New Orleans to find out what had happened to her brother. "I knew his mind wasn't going to be right, so I was like, 'Take care of yourself, you get help, get yourself together.' It messed him up."

She and Calloway were now completely estranged. We eventually tracked down his phone number, but he would only call back Ashley on her office number after working hours. It was a frustrating yet tantalizing one-way form of communication that went on for weeks.

Even after Ashley finally reached Calloway and explained that we were investigating Henry's death, he remained reluctant to speak with us. "His attitude at first was, 'I'm past that, I'm trying to move on with my life,'" Ashley says. "And it was like we were trying to resurrect something that he had buried." Calloway didn't want to meet with us in New Orleans. He had internalized the last thing he had heard from police officers before fleeing the city: come back and we'll kill you.

Ashley and I flew to Tulsa where he was temporarily living. It was a hand-to-mouth existence, working construction when he could find work, and sleeping on a co-worker's couch. Calloway was stocky and imposing, and stared at me as if he were sizing me up.

My assumptions about Calloway at the start of the conversation could be reduced to one ugly word: *thug*. This had something to do with his size and chilly demeanor. But it was no doubt influenced by the darkness of his skin and the association of Blackness and criminality served up daily by the news media and popular culture: the Black Man as criminal.

It did not take me long to realize just how wrong I had been. Bernard was a gentle, soft-spoken man who had been deeply traumatized by Katrina and what followed. "No food, no water, no communication with the outside world," he told us. But however much Katrina had damaged him, the murder of his best friend had done worse.

Bernard woke up groggy on the morning of September 2, having slept fitfully under the window, where he could better hear if anyone tried to break into the apartment. Four days after the storm—before the National Guard arrived to restore a modicum of civic order—the city felt lawless, he said. Many low-income residents, Bernard included, took food from abandoned stores for survival, but others were predators. "I woke up after a horrible night of hearing...people getting their doors kicked in and getting robbed and stuff."

Bernard told us that he improvised a family breakfast, cooking some meat that hadn't yet spoiled on a small charcoal grill, when Henry showed up. Henry was Bernard's common-law brother-in-law, but over the fifteen some years they'd known each other, they had become more like brothers. Henry drove a pickup truck he had taken from a Firestone auto parts store to evacuate the family.

Driving back to Henry's apartment a few blocks away to collect his things, they passed the sister of Henry's girlfriend and her friend, two women who were a part of the impending family exodus. The women asked Henry to drive to the mall to pick up some items they had stolen from Tuesday Morning, a down-market home goods store. The women failed to mention to Henry that they left the stolen goods in the mall parking lot after being run off by a police officer with a rifle.

Doing the favor was typical of Henry, Bernard said, generous and easygoing to a fault. When they pulled into the back parking lot of the mall, they didn't notice anyone. The two men exited the truck, and Bernard began to lift a heavy piece of luggage into the truck. Henry smoked a cigarette.

Bernard heard the crack of a single gunshot and a booming voice yell, "Leave now!" from above, virtually simultaneously. Bernard told us he never saw the man who fired, but he figured it had to be police. He knew there was a police substation on the second floor and, and he added, "Normal 'hood people don't talk like that."

Henry and Bernard took off running towards their apartments. Bernard looked over at Henry, who stumbled, clutched his chest, and collapsed in the middle of the street. Bernard ran over to his best friend, who was struggling to breathe, and placed a towel under his head.

"I'm dying," Henry said. "Tell my mama I love her." Bernard ran back to the apartments to get Henry's siblings, Patrice and Edward King, and they returned to Henry.

Tanner, the Good Samaritan, showed up minutes later, and the three men loaded Henry into the car and drove off to find help.

The scene Bernard described at Habans School dovetailed with what Tanner and Edward had told us. "When we got there, they drew all them automatic weapons on us and threw us on the ground, handcuffed us real rough... I got hit in the back of the head." The police heaped verbal abuse upon them, and called the men "niggers." One officer yelled at them that they were looters who were "pieces of shit trying to steal from good people." Another threatened to "cut their tendons and throw them in the river." At some point, Bernard said, Edward "went off," yelling, "Whoever killed my brother, I'm going to kill him." The officers "grabbed him on his neck and started choking him.

"Then I said, 'You ain't got to do him like that.' That's when they started beating on me... [W]e was back on the ground at this time. I remember getting punched and stuff... I could see Mr. Tanner and [Edward] getting beat too."

As vividly as Bernard summoned these images for Ashley and me, he could not identify any of the SOD officers at Habans from official NOPD photos that we showed him. Perhaps too much time had elapsed, and the well-scrubbed faces in the photos did not closely resemble the haggard, unshaven faces that confronted them at the school.

But Bernard came up with an officer's name, or at least an approximation of one: Schumacher. Bernard had seen the letters *S*, *C*, *H*, *M*, and *A* on the uniform of the SOD officer who seemed to be in charge. He recognized the name Schumacher from the lyrics of a Scarface rap song. Schumacher, Bernard said, had been the one who beat Edward. Edward had given us the same name when we interviewed him two months earlier, though when we checked with NOPD, they didn't have any officers with that name.

Eventually the beating stopped, and the men were moved to the back of the school. Schumacher told the men he was "going to investigate." When he returned a while later, "he said, 'Man, your brother and your brother-in-law had been shot for looting.' And he said that we can get the body from the coroner's. And he instructed them guys to give us a bottle of water." Tanner was released first, and then Bernard and Edward. They were told to leave New Orleans, or they would be killed.

Bernard and Edward ran back to their apartments, gathered the rest of the family, in all seven adults and six kids, and loaded their belongings onto a hotel luggage cart. They made their way through the empty Algiers streets, through the dense and draining heat, until they arrived at the ferry station, where they boarded the bus that would take them to Dallas. Dead bodies littered the streets. Bernard blindfolded his kids with pieces of clothing. He didn't want them to see his city like this.

As Ashley and I were leaving, Bernard mentioned something in passing. One of the officers at Habans had called Henry Glover a "piece of shit" and "nothing but a thief." That particularly bothered him. "I knew that he didn't really know [Henry] because if he knew him, he wouldn't say none of that."

We needed to find Linda Howard, the only other identified eyewitness to the shooting, to hear her account of what happened.

After multiple unannounced visits to her house, all we had managed was a brief chat with her mother. The day after we returned from Tulsa, we finally found Howard at home, but she was curt, telling us simply to call her lawyer. That, we figured, was trouble. Often, when officer witnesses take cover behind a lawyer or a police union rep, it signals they are unlikely to talk.

The next day, Howard's lawyer told us that, contrary to our expectations, she would meet with us. We arrived at the attorney's office, a run-down 1950s-era office building in center city. The elevator was broken, so Ashley and I took the stairs. Inside the office, Howard, a forty-seven-year-old Black woman, offered a reluctant handshake. She seemed anxious.

It didn't take long for the words to pour out of her.

Despite having been spared the worst of the flooding, the Algiers she described was straight out of a horror movie. "Everybody looked like a shadow," she said, trembling. "You really couldn't put faces with people because everything was…chaos…. The streets really looked like a ghost town."

I had assumed we would struggle to get information about the shooting itself. Interviewing cops in misconduct cases is usually an exercise in patience and perseverance. As Howard began to talk about the day of the shooting, we knew we needn't have worried about the reluctance.

On the morning of September 2, her sergeant assigned her to work with David Warren, a man she had never met before, at the DIU substation on the DeGaulle mall second floor. Warren normally worked in the Seventh District on the other side of the river, but the flooding cut him off from his post, so he was temporarily reassigned to the Fourth District, where he lived.

Howard didn't like the idea of working with a stranger in these uncertain times. She especially didn't like the idea of working with this particular stranger, a forty-year-old rookie who seemed fixated on guns.

En route to the mall substation, Warren took a detour to his house, located in an upscale neighborhood nearby. He grabbed some weapons from his personal arsenal, including shotguns and a sniper rifle. He asked her if she wanted a rifle for herself. She declined, telling him that she was fine with her department-issued Glock.

Warren and Howard arrived at the strip mall and positioned themselves on a second-floor breezeway, adjacent to the damaged police substation. It was hot and the air was still. "We was talking. It was quiet. They didn't have anybody around."

From their position on the breezeway, both officers heard a loud, screeching sound—the grinding of car gears. Howard first noticed the two men pulling into the mall's rear parking lot in the Firestone truck.

As Howard spoke, she clutched the table in front of her for support. She closed her eyes, reliving the experience. "Back there, two guys back there," she said in a raised voice, as if acting out the scene. Howard and Warren ran towards the rear of the building to get a better look.

The two men jumped out of the truck and moved towards a shopping cart filled with stolen items left near the back curb of the parking lot.

Warren yelled out a terse warning to the men, like, "Police!" The men looked up and then started running. Warren leveled his personally-owned sniper rifle.

The loud bang startled her. She kept her eyes on the two men running. One of the men fell to the ground.

She yelled at Warren in disbelief: "Why did you do that?" Howard told Warren that she needed to "call the rank"—the standard protocol.

Warren, replied, ridiculously casually, it seemed to her, "Why?"

"Because you just shot someone!" she yelled again.

Warren said he missed, even though the wounded man lay in the street below, after collapsing about fifty yards away from them. Howard told Warren to come and see for himself. "But he wouldn't come."

She wanted nothing to do with Warren: "Get away from me!" When Warren fired, the men were over sixty feet away from them, a level below, and running away. She said the men appeared to be unarmed. Even if they had wanted to, the men in the parking lot could not have reached the officers, blocked by a locked gate that separated the mall from the lot. Howard said she never thought even to reach for her service revolver.

We asked if she had any reason, in that moment before Warren pulled the trigger, to fear for her safety.

"No. Because we were up high behind locked gates, bottom and top. They were running away. There was no reason for me to feel threatened."

Was there any justification for the shooting? we asked.

Howard was unequivocal: "No."

She said that nothing much happened the rest of the day. Howard remained at the mall with the officer who had gunned down another man for no apparent reason. No one ever came by to relieve Warren of his gun, examine the scene, or search for evidence.

"I just wanted to get away from there," Howard told us. "I didn't know what was going on...in Officer Warren's head.... I just didn't want to stay there anymore.

"He had just shot someone, and I was the only witness."

Howard described a completely unjustified police shooting with little need for any probing questions on our part. During the twelve subsequent years that I investigated police misconduct, I never met another police officer who was so forthcoming with incriminating evidence against a fellow police officer. Even cops disturbed by the misconduct they've witnessed usually minimize bad cops' behavior, shade the truth, or neglect to mention key details. Some outright lie.

The evening after the shooting, Howard returned to the Fourth District police station at the end of her shift, where she ran into the second-in-command, Lieutenant Robert Italiano, in the hallway.

"He asked me if it was a 'good shooting.'" In other words, was the shooting legally justified and within department policy? Howard said she grimaced and shook her head sideways to indicate "no."

"He didn't say nothing... I think he might have said, 'Okay.'" Then Italiano walked away. No one asked her anything else about the shooting in the years that followed, so she shut down those memories as best she could and got on with the job.

That is, until she was questioned by Detective Gerard Dugue.

As we were leaving our meeting with Howard, her lawyer mentioned, almost in passing, that Detective Dugue had interviewed her. In our meeting with him, he never mentioned talking with her.

Howard's attorney handed us a transcript of the interview that Detective Dugue conducted as a part of NOPD's internal investigation. Dugue had interviewed her two days *before* we had met with him.

CHAPTER 5

"OR WHATEVER"

May 2009

The transcript of Howard's interview with Dugue was flimsy—just seven pages long, including the two pages of pro forma introduction. The entire recorded interview had lasted less than twelve minutes, a far cry from the two-plus hours that Ashley and I had spent with her.

Howard had given us a clear, vivid, and highly emotional account of an execution without much probing from Ashley or me. In contrast, with Dugue, Howard seemed reluctant to talk much about the shooting at all, and Dugue did little to push her.

Reading Howard's statement, it was difficult to make out what, exactly, she had witnessed. It is possible to read her words and conclude that she had not seen the shooting. More likely, I thought, she had worded it so that it was impossible to tell.

She had told Dugue, "I went through the breezeway that was on the side of the office and I saw a couple of guys down there. You know, they were just talking... So I alerted him [Warren] and told him that they had some guys down there. We re-switched places. He went to the back, I came to the front or whatever. And then a while later I heard a gunshot. It startled me. I went back to...where he was at, and he came back to the front or whatever."

Only hours earlier, Howard had described how Glover clutched his chest after being hit by Warren's bullet, then crumpled to the ground. She was absolutely certain that Warren had hit his target. She saw the wounded man being loaded into a white car that sped away. But in her statement to Dugue only days before, everything was open to interpretation.

"And I saw a guy lying down. I don't know if the guy was ducking because of the shot, the fire or whatever... So I went back to the area where I saw the guy lying down at and he was gone... And that's all I can remember."

Judging from the transcript, Dugue seemed content to leave the interview a brief, muddled mess. In fact, it seemed plain to us that he interviewed Linda Howard in such a way as to *not* find out what happened. He failed to ask her any of the most obvious follow-up questions: *Did you see Warren fire his weapon? What were the men doing at the point the shot was fired? Did the men have anything in their hands? Did you think you and Warren were in danger? What happened to the man after Warren shot him? Did the man appear wounded?*

I was baffled how Howard could have given such different versions of events only twelve days apart. I knew Ashley and I had to straighten these inconsistencies quickly.

We met with Howard again the next day at the US Attorney's Office, inside the federal courthouse. She seemed more at ease, but I was anxious, uncertain which version of the shooting we would hear. I was relieved when she assured us that the account she had given Ashley and me the day before had been true.

Howard explained that when she got a call from Dugue asking to meet, she had been on medical leave for three days after an allergic reaction. She asked to delay the meeting because she was taking medication three times a day, a prescription dose of Benadryl that left her feeling drowsy.

Dugue pressured her to give a statement. "He said, 'Just do the best you can but I need to get this done.' ...I was tired. I was, you know, sleepy...but...I had to do what I had to do. I had to make the statement."

Howard told us that she had done her best not to think about the shooting in the intervening years. When it had become obvious to her that NOPD wasn't interested in doing any real investigation, she tamped down the painful memories from that day.

"The way everything was...in order to make it from day to day..." She trailed off, searching for the words. "I just tried to blot it out like it didn't happen. Even though it did happen, I just tried to blot it out so I can make it."

A few days after the recorded interview, Dugue called her back and suggested meeting at the mall, at the scene of the shooting. Howard went back to the strip mall for the first time in three and a half years. Howard said the experience of returning to the mall "was like somebody had pressed play," causing memories to flood back with a vengeance.

At the mall, Howard told Dugue the whole story of the shooting: where she and Warren had been positioned, how Warren shot one of the men while he was running away, and how that man had crumpled to the ground.

Ashley asked if Dugue recorded their second conversation.

"No." She shrugged. Dugue, she said, had not bothered to bring his recorder.

It was hard to know what to make of Howard's explanation. Clearly, she had not been at her best on the day Dugue first interviewed her. We verified that she had been on medical leave during the interview, and confirmed she was on medication. But on the recording, she didn't sound particularly disoriented. Her responses to more general questions about Katrina were evocative and clear.

How was it that she became so vague and ambiguous only when she was talking about the shooting?

I could certainly appreciate that Linda Howard would have liked more than anything to forget about the shooting. Earlier in my career, I had spent enough time with survivors of wartime trauma, in Bosnia, Rwanda, and Kosovo, to understand the defense mechanism of compartmentalizing and blocking out painful memories.

But I also knew that recovering a memory is not like watching a movie. While visiting a place, hearing a sound, or smelling a scent can trigger recall, people rarely completely forget about the central traumatic event—in this case, the shooting.

I could only imagine how little incentive Howard had to dredge up those painful memories for Dugue. The absence of follow-up questions must have signaled his lack of interest in uncovering the truth, much like the Fourth District rank before him. She would have risked being labeled a rat or getting fired and losing her pension a few years away from retirement, quite likely, for nothing.

Regardless of what kept her from telling the whole story to the detective, we believed Linda Howard was telling the truth now. Her account was consistent with Bernard's description of a shot coming out of nowhere, and her emotional outpouring when discussing the shooting was in line with how Bell and Simmons described her at the mall: in a state of shock after watching a senseless killing. Furthermore, it seemed highly unlikely that she would just make up a story about a fellow officer executing a civilian, putting her own career, maybe her own life, in jeopardy.

I also knew that a defense attorney would have a field day in court with the Dugue interview. I figured we would deal with that if that day ever came.

Months into the investigation, we still had not located any written documentation of the shooting, which was highly unusual. Ashley and I suspected that some sort of report about the shooting existed, but having gone three months without finding it, we felt increasingly pessimistic that it would ever surface.

Simmons had told us she had written a report months after the shooting at Italiano's direction, but that she hadn't seen it since then. Italiano, on the other hand, had vehemently denied that any such report existed.

Officer Keyalah Bell had told us she had seen a copy of the report in 2006 and had been disturbed by what she had read. As best she remembered, it whitewashed the shooting. She was determined to find the report.

Weeks after our chaotic dinnertime interview, Ashley received a call from Bell. Unbeknownst to us, she had enlisted the help of an IT friend within the department who uncovered a copy of the shooting report for her, which she passed on to us.

As I read the report, which was signed by Sergeant Simmons and Lieutenant Italiano, I could see why Bell had been troubled. Everything about this document screamed cover-up, beginning with how it was classified. The report was classified as a "Signal 21," a catch-all designation for incidents of lesser importance, like a misplaced police radio or a neighborhood noise complaint. Signal 21s typically do not receive any follow-up by a detective.

The report consisted of two parts. The first was a shorthand summary of the incident in Simmons's own handwriting. The second was a fuller accounting, a one-and-a-half-page typed narrative, that told the story this way: two Black men in a Firestone truck pulled into the mall's rear parking lot and ran towards the back entrance of the mall. Warren yelled out a warning, "Police—get out." The men looked right at him and continued moving towards the building. "Officer Warren saw an object in the passenger's right hand which he perceived was a weapon. Fearing for his safety and noting the subject[']s unwillingness to comply, Officer Warren fired a single shot from his rifle in the direction of the passenger." The two men ran away.

The report states that Warren believed his shot had missed, and supports the claim by saying "several officers arrived" who "began an exhaustive search of the area for the subject[']s whereabouts, with negative results."

Based on what we heard from Simmons and Bell, their brief efforts to find a shooting victim could hardly be described as "exhaustive." Although they found a bloody shirt or towel, which certainly suggested that someone might have been hit, it was not mentioned in the report.

Another group of cops, likely SOD, had showed up near the spot where Henry had collapsed, but they were busy yelling at and dispersing the neighborhood crowd, rather than investigating a police shooting. The crowd of neighbors gets mentioned only in passing, noting "a group of civilians standing a block away in the 3400 block of Seine Street advised a man had been shot and was taken to a hospital by an unknown person."

Besides noting that she heard noises and saw the men by the back of the building, Linda Howard barely figures into the report. "Officer Howard was in a different position on the balcony and was unable to observed [sic] all that Officer David Warren observed prior to him discharging his firearm."

If Howard was basically written out of Simmons's report, a different officer, nowhere near the mall that day, was written in. Three days before Henry Glover was killed, a Black officer, Fourth District Officer Kevin Thomas, had been shot in the head while patrolling the streets of Algiers. He and his partner encountered four Black men near a gas station convenience store. The details of what happened next were, and still are, somewhat murky, but a .45 bullet struck Thomas's head, nearly killing him. The man identified by Thomas's partner as the shooter later was acquitted by a jury. A different man was subsequently tried for the attempted murder of Thomas. The case hinged on the testimony of Robert Italiano, who testified that Thomas's partner had identified the *wrong* shooter. Somehow, this second suspect was convicted at trial.

Thomas survived, barely. Within NOPD, his close call instantly became confirmation of officers' worst fears about what could happen to them on the street after the storm. Although Warren's weapon discharge had no connection to the Thomas shooting, the report went out of its way to link the two events: "It should be noted that at this time the entire City of New Orleans was plagued by looters at almost every section of the city. It is also a fact that Police Officer Kevin Thomas had been severely wounded by being shot to the head by a looter. These brazen criminal acts had all police officers on high alert."

Incident reports are typically bare-bones recitations of the facts: the who, what, where, when. This read to me more like an excerpt from a defense attorney's closing argument to a jury, attempting to justify what might in normal times be unjustified, which seemed particularly odd, given Warren's stated belief that his shot had missed.

The report concludes by mentioning that, in the aftermath of the storm, neither DIU nor Cold Case Homicide were available to conduct investigations. Nonetheless, the report stated that after an "initial investigation," conducted by Simmons, Italiano, and Kirsch, "it was determined that the use of force by Officer Warren was justified and was within the guidelines of the Departmental Policy [on]... Use of Force."

When Bell handed us the report, she was incredulous. This report went out of its way to absolve Warren of any blame, describing an officer afraid for his life and defending himself in the line of duty.

"What was the fear?" Bell asked. "They had a locked gate. There was no other entrance to the building other than going all the way across [to the front of the mall] or finding some bolt cutters to cut the chain-linked locked gate [at the rear entrance]." When she had spoken to Warren after the shooting, he acted as if nothing had happened, and he never mentioned fearing for his life or seeing any weapons, telling her only that they were "looters."

Bell then gave us a new piece of information about a strange meeting between Simmons and the two ranking commanders for the Fourth District.

One evening a few days after the shooting, while Simmons and Bell were on patrol together, Simmons received a call from Italiano and Kirsch, asking her to stop by the mall. The two female officers arrived in the late afternoon and waited for what felt like a very long time until the sun finally went down. Electrical power had not yet been restored in New Orleans, and the entire city was pitch-dark. For the first time in her lifetime, Bell could see stars at night in Algiers.

The rookie officer grew increasingly anxious that the two women were alone in the dark. As they prepared to leave, a squad car pulled up behind them, its glaring headlamps the only illumination in the vicinity. Simmons walked over to her bosses' car to confer with them. Bell was left by herself for the next fifteen minutes as her fears escalated.

"…[B]y the time they arrived it was pitch black dark and no one knew I was there with her… [I]t's like what are you going to see there? What possibly do you want to see?… [W]hether it's a female or a male, you're there by yourself in an area where a possible shooting occurred. And…she was by herself that they knew of."

Bell thought it might be a setup. "I was afraid for Sergeant Simmons," she said.

Fifteen minutes later, Simmons returned unharmed. As far as Bell knew, that was the only "investigation."

When Bell handed us the report, it was obvious that she had been deeply affected by the Glover shooting. She told us yet another story of why she had the feeling that the department was trying to cover up the shooting. In the late fall of 2005, when Edna Glover returned from Dallas and went to the Fourth District station looking for answers about her missing son, Bell had been on duty. Based on the details Edna provided, she figured Henry had to be the man Warren had shot. Bell found Italiano in the back of the station and asked him how to handle this, noting the similarities to the dead man who arrived at Habans. He was dismissive. He told her to tell Ms. Glover to "check the morgue."

"At that point I was upset," Bell told us, "because I had to bring information to tell a lady, 'Oh, by the way, check the morgue,' with the knowledge I had that something wasn't right…" Back in 2005, as a Black female rookie officer, she felt she hadn't been able to push back harder. And she was certain that if she had, no one would have listened. In handing us the report almost four years later, she hoped she could finally make it right.

Finding the report was certainly a break, but now we confronted a new challenge: the report contradicted much of what Simmons had told us about the shooting. At least on paper, Simmons seemed like she was part of a NOPD cover-up. This posed a serious dilemma since she would testify before the grand jury in two days.

The US Constitution requires that anyone charged with a federal felony offense must be indicted by a grand jury, an investigative panel consisting of between sixteen and twenty-three citizens. A grand jury's primary function is to determine if there is "probable cause" that a crime has been committed. Theoretically, this serves as protection against overzealous prosecution. In reality, probable cause is a remarkably low bar, anything more than a 50 percent certainty. Most scholars believe that the grand jury no longer provides any real check. In legal circles, people joke that a grand jury would "indict a ham sandwich." In my experience, this is mostly true. The only times I have ever seen a grand jury reject (or "no bill") charges have been in the context of police misconduct investigations. Police officers, apparently, are harder to indict than ham sandwiches.

Often, prosecutors appear before a grand jury only when they are ready to indict, sometimes presenting only a single witness to summarize the evidence supporting probable cause. However, the grand jury can also be used as a forum to get at the truth, by requiring witnesses to answer questions under oath with their answers recorded verbatim. The grand jury also allows prosecutors to see how regular civilians evaluate the credibility of witnesses and the overall merits of the case. In a case where we were still trying to figure out what happened, this would be very useful.

The grand jury can have an intimidating aura. Its proceedings are closed to the public, both to protect the identity of people who have not yet been charged with a crime and to encourage truthfulness from witnesses. Lying can subject witnesses to perjury charges. I hoped the power of the grand jury would compel Nina Simmons to truthfully explain the contradictions in the report.

My plan was to take Simmons through the account of the shooting aftermath she'd given Ashley and me, "locking in" her testimony. This would make it harder for her to back away from her testimony later if we ever had a trial. Then I planned to ambush her with the Signal 21 report. I needed her to explain who was responsible for the cover up. I hoped the surprise would push her to tell us the truth about how this false report came to be written. I assumed she had been directed to write the report by a superior, and, based on his signature on the document, the evidence pointed towards Italiano.

It wasn't a terrible plan, as the alternative carried its own risks. Talking over the problematic report with Simmons before the grand jury appearance would give her more time to back off from what she had originally told us.

I drastically overestimated the power of the grand jury to compel the truth.

Simmons was sworn into the grand jury, an assortment of twenty-some civilians from the New Orleans area, who sat in a nondescript conference room in the courthouse. As I worked my way through questions about the shooting, everything seemed to go to plan. Simmons provided testimony consistent with our first interview, incriminating Warren in a bad police shooting. Simmons confirmed that Linda Howard believed that Warren had hit the man he shot at, that this man was unarmed, and that he had fallen in the street.

Then I pulled out the Signal 21. I hammered Simmons with the report, line by line, noting the contradictions between her testimony and the report's narrative. I asked her to explain to the grand jury why these facts were left out of the report. She stammered and had no explanation. I asked about the part of the report that asserted Warren saw an "object" and feared for his life, since she had told us that he never said anything like this immediately after the shooting. Again, she had no explanation for the discrepancy.

However, when I asked her if Italiano had ordered her to justify the shooting in the report, she denied it. "No one was there when I wrote the report. I sat down and wrote the report."

The harder I pushed, the wobblier and wobblier she became, but

I couldn't break her. She took full ownership of this report, and she would not implicate anyone else. About twenty-five different times, she claimed to have written the report by herself.

Strangely, she didn't try to claim that the report accurately documented the shooting, though she couldn't explain why she would intentionally write a misleading report.

I took one last shot, invoking the awesome power of the grand jury that at this moment didn't feel so awesome. I reminded Sergeant Simmons that she was under oath before a federal grand jury. That often seemed to work on television.

It didn't. She put her head down and shook her head. "I wrote this report."

Normally, a confession about writing up a false report of a shooting would be a gold mine in the prosecution of a police officer.

Lying before a grand jury, a federal felony, is punishable by up to five years in prison. But the perjury statute has a "recantation" provision that protects witnesses from prosecution if they correct their previous false testimony. It was obvious that Simmons was lying, and she seemed shaken by the experience.

As we left the grand jury room, I turned to Tracey Knight, the local prosecutor from the New Orleans US Attorney's Office, who assisted us that day. "She'll be back," I told Tracey. I didn't know how long it would take, but I was certain Simmons would retain a lawyer and return.

A few days later, I got a call from the lawyer. The sergeant wanted to "clarify" her earlier testimony.

Ashley and I met Simmons at the attorney's office, a renovated warehouse with lots of wood and natural light. A chastened Simmons spoke in a soft voice, head slightly bowed. She admitted she had lied.

Simmons seemed genuinely remorseful. She told us that three months after the shooting, Italiano unexpectedly ordered her to write the report. He didn't tell her what to put in the report. Simmons spoke with both Warren and Howard and wrote up a brief narrative section.

However, she said, the one-and-a-half-page narrative in the official report was not what she had written in December 2005. She had authored the report's handwritten sections, but not the longer typed section. It seemed that someone had switched out the narrative section. This someone, she didn't know who, had replaced her truthful version—which offered no opinion on the lawfulness of the shooting—with the sanitized version with which I had ambushed her.

Days before her grand jury testimony, she told us, Detective Dugue had called her in for a meeting, and provided her with a copy of the typewritten narrative that she swore she had never seen before. He assured her that we hadn't seen it either but strongly implied that she should conform her upcoming testimony to the contents of the sanitized report.

When I asked her why she had taken ownership of the report under oath, she betrayed some of the panic that had gripped her in front of the grand jury. "It showed my name on that report...I couldn't see my way out of it... I could not prove the other part was not mine..."

As for the moment when I had produced the report in front of the grand jury, she said, "Words cannot express the anger I felt, the humiliation, the embarrassment, feeling like I was targeted now."

She also said her sense of loyalty to the NOPD held her back from telling the truth. She didn't want her testimony to implicate the fellow officer, whoever it was, who had manipulated the report. Remarkably, Nina Simmons had only a vague sense that whoever wrote the narrative had thrown her under the bus.

It's hardly an unknown practice for police departments to write up internal reports that shade the truth so as not to incriminate the officers involved. I've since read hundreds of them. But in my experience, this switch-out—if true—was different than anything I had seen before.

For the next two months, Ashley and I tried to find Simmons's missing narrative. We issued more subpoenas and search warrants. We discovered that the computer used by Simmons in 2005 had been subsequently destroyed, and in those days, reports were not being uploaded to external servers. A flash drive she said might have contained the report had gone missing from her desk.

Ashley and I marched ahead with the investigation, following up with pretty much anyone who had worked in the Fourth District during the storm, including Travis McCabe, a sergeant at the time of Katrina, subsequently promoted to lieutenant. He told Ashley and me to meet him at Whole Foods, where he worked a security detail, a typical moonlighting gig for an officer in this underpaid department.

As Ashley and I walked into the Whole Foods, we saw McCabe eating lunch with the head of the Fourth District, Captain David Kirsch. As they saw us coming, Kirsch hastily tossed his half-eaten lunch in the garbage and hurriedly exited the store with his head down.

We had been talking to McCabe for about fifteen minutes, mostly asking what he knew about the burned-out car, when we moved on to the Warren shooting. He offered up a surprising amount of detail. It seemed, at moments, as if McCabe were quoting verbatim the narrative that Simmons had said was false. This was puzzling because there was little reason why he should have seen it.

Initially, McCabe said he had read the Signal 21 report. Ashley and I showed him the copy we had received from Bell. He then told us, "I wrote the report with Nina Simmons."

Ashley and I exchanged perplexed looks. Simmons had never mentioned McCabe's name. "You wrote the report?" Ashley asked.

"Sergeant Purnella Simmons…came to me. She was very stressed… She asked for help and I said, 'Of course, I'll help you.'"

As I'd done with Simmons in the grand jury, we went through the one-and-a-half-page narrative, line by line. McCabe vacillated between claiming 100 percent authorship and portraying himself as a glorified stenographer, merely typing what Simmons dictated. McCabe claimed that he had also interviewed both Howard and Warren to prepare the report.

★ ★ ★

We tried to make sense of McCabe's revelations. We followed up with Simmons, and she denied ever talking to McCabe about the report. She said he seemed like a strange guy, and she always kept her distance. And we checked with Howard, who said she had never spoken with McCabe about the shooting. She too found McCabe off-putting.

We located old reports written by both Simmons and McCabe. The language of the report certainly sounded more like McCabe's writing than Simmons's.

Two weeks later, McCabe testified before the grand jury. He continued to assert he wrote the Signal 21 with Simmons. He was dismissive of Simmons and her ability to write a report. "She just wasn't capable of putting together a police report. And I sat down with her and basically helped her type the report."

Notwithstanding his involvement in writing the report, he blamed Simmons for its content. "It's solely her responsibility," he said.

McCabe did, however, take credit for the language describing the Kevin Thomas shooting and "the brazen criminal acts [that] had all police officers on high alert." "They're my words," he acknowledged, "but that was the situation we were in."

McCabe had no explanation as to why he would insert his perspective into someone else's shooting, other than to say, "I would have to say all of us were in that same state of mind."

Three months later, we approached McCabe at the Whole Foods again, this time with a "target letter," stating he was under investigation for perjury. Ashley told him that she didn't believe that he had interviewed Linda Howard or that he had written the report with Simmons. We wanted to know where he got the report from.

McCabe said, "Who do you think I got it from?"

Ashley responded, a little coyly, "I don't know. You tell me."

"Do you think I got it from David Kirsch or Robert Italiano?" McCabe replied.

"I don't know. Did you get it from both of them?"

McCabe's first response was, "No. I got it from Italiano." Then he quickly changed course: "I don't know. Maybe I got it from Italiano." And then he clammed up altogether.

Ultimately, we felt we could make a pretty good case against McCabe for writing a false report and for perjury, based on his words alone, but he seemed like a bit player in the cover-up. Over the following months, Ashley and I hoped and even expected he would come clean and give us the names of the higher-ups who directed the cover-up of the shooting, but he didn't.

CHAPTER 6

US AND THEM

May through July 2009

In late May, I found myself bleary-eyed in Ashley's car, parked under old-growth oak trees. We sat outside of David Warren's house in Algiers on a bucolic suburban street, a departure from the more neglected neighborhoods where Ashley and I spent much of our time. It was 6:00 a.m., and I was mindlessly sipping bad hotel coffee to stay focused. Neither one of us had gotten enough sleep. Ashley had been up since 4:00 a.m., executing a search warrant in another case. I couldn't sleep in anticipation of my first opportunity to come face-to-face with the man who killed Henry Glover.

Our hope was that we would catch Warren leaving for work—he had recently left NOPD to work for an electrical utility company— or at least, we could catch him at home after the kids had left for school. We figured that approaching him alone, by surprise, might improve our chances that he would speak to us.

We hunkered down for a stakeout. I was excited, even though Ashley's supervisor Kelly had warned me that stakeouts generally involve a lot of sitting around waiting for something interesting to happen that rarely does. This early in the morning, the only thing going on was the chirping of a mockingbird.

By this point in the investigation, Ashley and I had spent a lot of time in the car talking through the case. The thing we discussed most was the mystifying link between the shooting of Glover and the incineration of his body.

We had run into one roadblock after another trying to unravel the burning. Three months into the investigation, we didn't know much more than what *The Nation* had reported in December 2008. Our one significant advance, thanks to the date stamp on the photos taken by the Customs and Border Protection officer, was establishing that the burning occurred on the same day as the shooting.

Our only real suspect was the unnamed SOD officer who drove away in Tanner's Chevy. And we had no evidence suggesting that whoever did that also torched it, save for Tanner's claim about road flares, about which Ashley and I remained skeptical.

It made sense that SOD would want to move the body *somewhere*. Five days after Katrina, as the death toll mounted around the city, the city morgue was overwhelmed. A thousand-plus bodies remained littered across the city. The city simply lacked resources to collect the dead. It was not uncommon to drive down the street and see bodies left where they fell, covered by sheets, cardboard, or corrugated metal. In one morbid photo taken by a visiting federal agent, a Black man lay stretched out by the side of the road, wrapped up in a brown paisley rug, his stockinged feet poking outward. The only acknowledgment of his humanity was a homemade cardboard sign that read, *This man died here.*

Understandable, then, why SOD officers didn't want a dead body in a car decomposing in ninety-plus-degree temperatures in front of the building they called home. But it was hard to fathom why they would burn the body, destroying the physical evidence of a fatal shooting that would fall to NOPD to investigate, particularly if they had no knowledge that the man had been shot by another cop. Even if they were aware of that, why would SOD cross the line into flagrant criminality to protect an officer they didn't know?

Ashley and I, stuck in the car, played out classic "means, motive, and opportunity" scenarios. Sitting in front of Warren's house, it struck me for the first time how close he lived to the levee where Glover's body was burned—just over a mile away.

It was conceivable that somebody at the Fourth District had told Warren that the body of the man he had shot that morning had been moved from Habans to the levee. He could have found the car before darkness fell and destroyed the evidence of his crime. The time window was tight, but possible. Of all the people in the case, Warren certainly had the most motive to burn Glover's body. As far as "means," burning a car didn't seem too hard to pull off, especially for a guy who, we would later learn, had a couple of engineering degrees.

It was all speculation, of course, but with little evidence and lots of time, we had seemingly endless possibilities to sort through. But by the second hour of the stakeout, we were ready to talk about something else.

Though Ashley and I got along well and enjoyed each other's company, we rarely spoke about our personal lives. This morning, I shared some about my home life in DC, the joys and challenges of raising a ten-month-old daughter with my wife, Fiona, while spending nearly half my workweek on the road. It felt like I was living two disjointed and disconnected lives: one as an investigator trying to solve a horrific crime, and another as a husband and hands-on father who, when I was home, pureed baby food, changed diapers, and sang songs at bedtime. I hadn't yet heard the expression "work-life balance," but I certainly didn't have it.

Up to that point, I knew very little about Ashley's life. I knew she lived in Madisonville, a sleepy town on the edge of Lake Pontchartrain, a forty-minute commute from downtown New Orleans. It was quiet, with cheaper rents and good seafood. "It's where most of the FBI agents live," she told me, "but I'm probably one of two

Black people there, so when I go out somewhere, I stand out." If she had much of a social or a dating life, she never mentioned it, and given the barrage of emails I received at all hours of the night, it didn't seem likely.

This morning, we had time, maybe too much time, to think about the paths that had brought us both here. We were an odd couple, by Louisiana law enforcement standards anyway, a Black female agent and a Jewish government lawyer. But we had our similarities: we were about the same age, early thirties; we both grew up in the South, she in Mobile, Alabama, me in the Atlanta suburbs. And neither of us had expected to wind up in law enforcement.

Ashley was raised in an integrated neighborhood in Mobile. Her parents grew up lower-income, and through hard work and education, made their way into the middle class. Her father was a social worker, and in his spare time, he played a prominent role in the community as a city councilman and a church pastor. Ashley's mother taught at a local elementary school.

Church was central to Ashley's upbringing. Her family went to church every Sunday, where her father would preach. Her parents made sure that she stayed on the straight and narrow. Her dad emphasized the need for hard work and good grades. Her mom imparted the need to conduct oneself in a way that was always above reproach.

"She is very proper," Ashley said. "To go to the grocery store that was four minutes away, she's going to put on full makeup and wear a suit. How you ate, how you sat, how you spoke, she's very into that. I was the only child in my school that would show up every day wearing an Easter dress."

I tried to imagine a younger Ashley heading to school every day dressed for church. "You dressed that way for school?"

"Yeah. In elementary school, the kids would make fun of me, so I used to sneak shorts and a T-shirt into my book bag and change in the school bathroom." The Ashley I knew was always impeccably dressed in smart-looking pantsuits. "As I've gotten older," she said, "I think I am my mother."

Ashley had always figured she would be a schoolteacher like her mother. She loved spending her days as a kid pretending to be a teacher, giving lessons in front of a huge chalkboard to an imaginary classroom full of stuffed animals. Later, a stint as a student teacher with real, and less compliant, students made her rethink her options.

She switched her focus to social work, following in her father's footsteps. She got her BA and a master's degree from her hometown university, the University of South Alabama in Mobile, and then another master's from the University of Alabama in Tuscaloosa. In graduate school, she took a class on criminal justice, and was intrigued by a guest speaker from the FBI who talked about careers at the Bureau.

Ashley had never before considered a job in law enforcement. As a child, she didn't have much exposure to the police. To the extent the police entered her thinking, it had to do with occasional showdowns between her dad and the police chief at city council meetings, usually over police budgets.

But when a classmate decided to take the FBI entrance exam, Ashley went along with her on a whim. She never heard back from the Bureau and after a while stopped thinking about it. She worked as a probation officer, and later as a social worker in a local hospital, much of it in the psych ward.

Three years later, Ashley got a call from an FBI recruiter, asking if she was still interested. She was. Her ambition to become a social worker inside the school system had been stymied by the lack of job openings so she decided to enter the FBI Academy at Quantico.

Though she had wound up in the criminal justice system by accident, it seemed to suit her. She appreciated clear lines—something was right, or it wasn't—the kind of certitude that she had always found in the church. "Growing up, the church was the core," she said. "Everything centered around that. When I moved away from Mobile, I didn't go to church every Sunday, but I've never strayed from the tenets and the teaching."

★ ★ ★

I could relate to the importance of family and religion in Ashley's life. Though neither of my parents grew up particularly religious, being Jewish was central to their identity. For the first fifteen years of my life, my parents sent me exclusively to Jewish schools. They wanted me to learn the rules and traditions of Judaism, and to bring the teachings back to the family. My teachers thought I would become a rabbi or a lawyer.

My understanding of the world was shaped by the contrasting perspectives of my parents. My dad's worldview was heavily influenced by his parents, who fled Austria in the late 1930s, before the Nazis exterminated much of their community. My grandparents were refugees who had lost everything. And yet my father managed to build a successful accounting practice that lifted him into the upper-middle class. For him, America meant opportunity.

But the Holocaust was always in the background. My dad would regularly remind me that, at any moment, even in America, we too could lose everything we had. He was a big supporter of Israel, donating substantially to Zionist causes. In his mind, Israel was a backup plan in case things ever took a severely bad turn in the United States.

I couldn't imagine that happening in my country. I had grown up in a world sheltered from that kind of hate, and then one morning in sixth grade, I arrived at my Jewish elementary school to find it vandalized with anti-Semitic graffiti, swastikas and *Heil Hitler* applied in red spray paint. (Two decades later, I investigated a similar hate crime.) "Never again" was the mantra instilled in me as a kid. I'm sure it laid the foundation for my subsequent interest in the genocides in Bosnia and Rwanda.

My mother had a more optimistic worldview. She was a product of the 1960s, protesting the Vietnam war, marching for civil rights, burning her bra, and helping lower-income women of color find employment. Eventually she became a stay-at-home suburban mom, focusing her attention on me and my little sister, and volunteering extensively with Jewish organizations. My mother encouraged me to do community service, to do my part to make the world a better place, however ill-defined that notion was.

The Jewish concept that most shaped my worldview was the medieval Jewish ideal of *Tikun Olom*, an exhortation to "repair the world." I accepted the fact that the world was broken, and that I had an obligation to try to fix it.

The reality was, my world was very small, the homogenous bubble of prosperous suburban Jews I spent my days with, from school to after-school sports to summer camp. I didn't know any Black people, apart from Martha, the woman who cleaned our home.

My eyes began to open to a bigger, messier reality when I moved on to an integrated public high school. The student body was roughly equal parts White and Black students—many of whom bused in from the other side of the city—and a sizable minority of "others," mostly new immigrants from Latin America and South Asia. I interacted with classmates whose lives didn't resemble anything I had been familiar with. One of my Black classmates, Brandon Williams, a well-loved sports star voted "best smile," was killed by a stray bullet when a fight broke out after a basketball game in his neighborhood. The police never solved the crime.

And yet I still saw the world mostly through a Jewish lens. I had adopted my father's position on Israel and his strong sense that the Arabs were a major threat to my people's ability to maintain our homeland.

My world began to expand in college at the University of Pennsylvania, when my Middle Eastern Studies advisor told me I should gain exposure to Arab and Islamic history and culture, considering that Arab peoples lived in the region too.

That exploration would eventually provide me with my first exposure to state-sanctioned police violence, setting off a chain of events that in some ways led me to sitting in the car with Ashley.

Ashley and I had other witness interviews lined up for later that morning, so we couldn't spend the whole day camped out in front of Warren's house. After about two hours, we called it.

We walked up to the sturdy brick home with its meticulously

manicured lawn. Ashley rang the doorbell, and Warren stepped out. Medium height, pale blotchy complexion, and a soft, doughy physique, he looked like an unthreatening suburban dad from a *Happy Days*–style sitcom, an image at odds with someone who shot a man in the back with a sniper rifle. Inside the house, we could see, as we peeked around him, his wife homeschooling his five children. That explained why no one had left the house.

Warren told us he was not interested in speaking to us and handed us his lawyer's business card. He was soft-spoken and polite. He told us to have a nice day.

Winning an excessive force case before a jury generally comes down to proving two things: that an officer used force that was "objectively unreasonable" and excessive under the circumstances, and that the officer acted "willfully," a legal standard often described as the highest level of intent in the criminal code.

On its face, the shooting appeared inherently unreasonable. Warren was on the second floor of a building, locked behind metal gates, shooting down at a person who was, by our estimate, over sixty feet away. The law is clear: when a suspect poses no immediate threat to an officer, that officer is not justified in using deadly force to make an arrest.

Proving "willfulness" is generally a lot harder. The law requires proof that the officer acted voluntarily and with "bad purpose to either disobey or disregard the law." Jurors are typically leery of second-guessing decisions made by officers in the line of duty, particularly when it comes to lethal force.

Many jurors find it hard to conceive that police officers would ever act with such intent, particularly in the days before the internet was awash in excessive force videos. Broadly speaking, jurors, especially White jurors unfamiliar with how minority communities are policed, don't want to believe that the people to whom society has given a license to kill would intentionally use force for a "bad purpose."

As hard as this "willful" standard is to meet generally, it's usually harder in the case of shootings. Hands-on force generally takes longer and often continues well after the victim has stopped putting up any resistance. Sometimes, the officer will call the victim names or use racial slurs or boast about how the victim is getting what he deserves, all which makes it easier to demonstrate "bad purpose."

Shootings by their very nature almost always happen quickly. The typical jury instruction, drawing from Supreme Court precedent, tells jurors to take this into account, advising that "police officers are often forced to make split-second judgments in circumstances that are tense, uncertain, and rapidly evolving about the amount of force that is necessary."

Even by Howard's and Bernard's accounts, the whole of the interaction between Warren and Glover took less than ten seconds. One barked command—something like "Leave now!"—and a single shot. And certainly, the aftermath of Katrina could be characterized as "tense, uncertain, and rapidly evolving" circumstances.

We needed evidence that would shed light on what was going on in Warren's head at the moment he pulled the trigger. Without that, I knew that a jury might be inclined to accept whatever defense Warren presented, which certainly would include a claim that he "feared for his life," the defense in practically every police shooting I've ever investigated. The assumption of most jurors is that when an officer says he "feared for his life," that fear is genuine.

To convict Warren, we would need to explain why he would kill a man who posed no threat. But Warren was refusing to talk, and even the Fourth District officers who spoke to us didn't know much about him.

David Warren had the most unconventional résumé for a cop that I had ever seen. He grew up in Wisconsin, and as a young man had prepared himself to take over his family's small business that manufactured school furniture, things like cafeteria tables and choir risers. He had earned two undergraduate engineering degrees and then went on to get an MBA, all from the University of Wisconsin-Milwaukee.

Friends in his social circle introduced him via email to a young woman in Louisiana. Warren eventually visited her there, and they formed a bond. They married and raised their large young family back in Wisconsin.

After his father died, Warren inherited part ownership of the family business. He later sold his share of the company and moved to New Orleans to be closer to his wife's family. He felt like he had enough financial independence to pursue other dreams. Then, in 2003, this forty-year-old father of five young children did something that I found incomprehensible. He entered the police academy, becoming what I imagined was one of the oldest rookie officers in NOPD history. Most of the other recruits were almost half his age.

The main thing that people knew about Warren was his interest, bordering on obsession, with guns. A number of officers told us that, in the days after Katrina, Warren carried a small arsenal around with him, offering up and passing around his personal rifles and shotguns to NOPD officers and National Guardsmen alike. His gun of choice for personal protection was a .223-caliber SIG SG 550 sniper rifle, designed for precision shooting at long distances, that Warren bought for $7,500. It was the gun that would end Henry's life.

Before he ever became a police officer, Warren invested thousands of dollars and weeks of his time taking "use of force" classes at the Lethal Force Institute, a training program once described by the *Boston Phoenix* weekly as "the…seminar to take when you absolutely, positively need to kill someone tomorrow." Warren fired grenade launchers and Tommy guns, and attended lectures on the limitations on legal force. He also studied at the Orleans Regional Security Institute, where he passed the NRA's National Instructor Program with perfect marks. He taught a class on the nomenclature of handguns.

His mentor at the Orleans Regional Security Institute suggested that Warren enter law enforcement as a way to put his gun expertise to practical use. This mentor told him that New Orleans needed well-educated officers.

One thing was certain, Warren was a hell of a shot. He regularly participated in distance shooting competitions, firing at targets hundreds of *yards* away. When he graduated from the police academy, he received NOPD's Precision Shooter Award in recognition of his near-perfect scores.

Warren certainly didn't strike us as someone who was likely to take a shot with a scoped sharpshooter's rifle from sixty feet away and miss. Or believe he had missed.

Though Warren's fixation on guns was unsettling, it didn't explain why this engineer-businessman-turned-cop would shoot someone for no good reason. We got a lead from an unlikely source, William Tanner, our Good Samaritan, a man whom Warren had never met.

Tanner had been desperate to locate his car in the weeks after the SOD officer drove off with it. While he had no luck with NOPD, eventually, he connected with a federal agent with Immigration and Customs Enforcement (ICE) who came to his house to take his complaint.

After a few days of digging around, the ICE agent found the charred car by the Patterson levee, just across the street from the Customs and Border Protection headquarters. He reported his find to supervisors in the Fourth District.

We had no expectation that the ICE agent would lead us back to David Warren. But as the agent told us about the burned-out car, and, more generally, the horrors that had been visited upon New Orleans in the days after the storm, another memory surfaced. Because the NOPD had been so undermanned—249 officers walked off the job—federal agents partnered up for a period with officers from the Fourth District to patrol Algiers.

The ICE agent mentioned almost in passing that he had paired up for a few days with a young officer who had seemed bothered by the burned car and body by the levee and maybe knew something about it, possibly even about the shooting that had preceded it. The agent was unclear about the particulars, and he couldn't remember the officer's name. But he knew the officer was White, recently graduated from the academy, and lived in Algiers. That was enough for Ashley and me to start searching.

Ashley pulled records of the last three cadet classes at NOPD and cross-referenced them against Fourth District officers who worked during the storm. We came up with a list of three officers who fit the bill.

After striking out with our first two candidates, Ashley and I arrived at the third officer's house fairly optimistic that the process of elimination would deliver us to the right man.

We rang the doorbell, and a large Black man in sweatpants stumbled to the door, looking irritated to have been woken up. Ashley, exasperated by our search, asked him with a straight face, "By any chance, were you White in 2005?"

As it turned out, a fourth officer, Alec Brown, fit our criteria but somehow fell through the cracks, perhaps because he had moved to the other side of the country. Ashley finally tracked down Brown's phone number in Salt Lake City. When she identified herself on the phone, he said, "You're good. You found me."

Brown knew about our investigation and was still in touch with a few officers on the force. He was hesitant to talk, so Ashley flew out to Salt Lake to meet him in person, hoping her presence would reassure him.

He came to the door in a T-shirt with cutoff sleeves, showing off his sinewy arms and a Confederate flag tattoo. "My first thought was, 'uh-oh,'" Ashley told me after the visit.

And yet Brown was respectful and forthcoming. He graduated from the police academy a month or so before Katrina but, almost immediately, began seeing things he didn't like. He told us about one officer who drove around with small baggies of drugs in his trunk to plant on people. The officer's philosophy was, the people he policed were always "guilty of something, even if we didn't catch them this time." By 2008, Brown was sufficiently fed up that he quit the department and moved out to Utah, where he found work in a movie theater.

Ashley overcame Brown's initial reluctance, and he agreed to fly to New Orleans a few days later, where I met him for the first time.

Brown told us that he had been on vacation in Panama City, Florida, just before Katrina made landfall. When the storm hit, all lines of communication went dead, so he got in his Jeep and drove back to New Orleans. The trip was a multiday ordeal—the highways only ran one way, out of the city—and when he finally arrived, he was astonished at the destruction.

Two days after his return, near the end of the shift, he told us he drove his car up to the top of the levee, just wasting a little time before clocking out for the day.

There he found a "burned-up vehicle, four-door" and, in the back seat, a charred human skeleton. There was still "flesh on the chest cavity, a little bit on the legs…and a little bit of flesh on the small, like, the little minor bones, like the arm bones and leg bones, stuff like that." He got a close enough look to see what he thought might be a gunshot hole in the skull.

Brown reported the disturbing find to his commanding officer, Sergeant Travis McCabe, as soon as he got back to the station. The same Travis McCabe, we knew, who had told Ashley and me that he'd "helped" Purnella Simons write the report of the shooting.

Brown said he was surprised when McCabe evinced no curiosity about an incinerated car and body sitting less than a quarter mile from the station. "He said that they knew about it and don't worry about it." And then the sergeant made an offhand statement that struck Brown as particularly strange.

"Police need to stick together," McCabe told him. Brown understood that McCabe was telling him to forget about what he had seen, but the message, however coded, seemed to have the opposite effect.

Brown couldn't imagine why anyone would light a car on fire that close to a police station, where cops would likely see, or smell, whatever was going on. Whenever he got the chance, he'd casually bring up the subject of the car and the body to officers he was friendly with, hoping to glean some useful piece of information. One time, McCabe overheard and upbraided him: "I told you we already know about it. Just leave it alone."

As callous as many of his fellow officers sounded before the storm, Brown said, afterwards, he could feel a hardening in their attitudes towards the civilians left behind. No one embodied that shift better than David Warren.

Brown had been back in New Orleans for less than a week when he was partnered with Warren, patrolling the streets of the Fourth District. Just as Linda Howard had said, Brown immediately got a bad feeling. Warren took him to his house and offered him a choice of rifles. Brown, like Howard, declined: "You have a [NOPD-issued] .40-caliber Glock... If you can't stop something with that, you need to [call] backup." In addition to his gun collection at home, Warren traveled with two or three rifles in the trunk of his car, all with scopes, "lasers, flashlights attached, different things like that."

Brown said that Warren never went anywhere without his personal assault rifle. "He would jump out of the [patrol] vehicle, no matter whether it was a little routine stop, somebody walking down the street... He always had that rifle out and ready."

Brown described for us one incident when they were driving in the Fischer Projects and heard gunfire. Warren was all set to drive straight into the projects, guns blazing. Brown managed to talk Warren down. Brown backed the car up by a tree, which provided cover, and then called in SOD, better equipped and trained for these kinds of situations.

Warren's would-be Rambo act was undoubtedly extreme, even by NOPD standards. But Brown's depiction of Warren's feelings about post-Katrina looting gave us, we felt, a better sense of the mentality that had taken root in the minds of a lot of officers during those first sleep-deprived and stressed-out weeks after the storm (the worst of which Brown had missed). He described the mindset as "Us versus Them."

One day, as Brown and Warren drove around Algiers, their conversation turned to the widespread looting that had broken out across the city, an exchange that Brown recalled for us verbatim. Brown made a distinction between the people who were taking advantage of confusion to steal things like televisions or cars versus the greater number of people who were taking items they needed for their own survival, like food, water, and batteries.

Warren disagreed, telling him that the looters "'were all animals and they deserved to be shot, and they were doing nothing but destroying the city.'"

Brown pushed back. "'Well, that's not right. So, you can't tell me that somebody that is stealing food is the same as somebody that's taking a TV. It's completely different.'"

"'No, that's the same exact thing. All they are doing is tearing up the city and stealing.'"

"'Well, you can't tell me that if it was your kid, you're not going to go off and try to get food and everything to provide for your kid, because I know I sure will… We have hamburgers at the station… from Walmart. You're eating that, so are you just as bad? Because you're the one eating, basically, looted food… It's for your survival, so you can eat. It's the same as everybody else.'"

"'Well, that's different,'" Warren told him.

One day, Brown and Warren were driving on Patterson Road and passed the Chevy Malibu by the levee. Brown asked Warren what he knew about the body in the burned-out car. "'Did you see that body in it?'" Brown asked. "'I wonder what kind of happened?'"

There was an awkward silence. "He kind of put his head down," Brown recalled. Then, in a quiet voice, Warren said, "'I don't know. Maybe he was just a looter.'"

When officers told me, "If you weren't here for Katrina, you can't understand," I took their point. I certainly was not in New Orleans for Katrina. When the storm hit, I was a thousand miles away watching the unfolding events on cable news. At that time, I still worked at the US State Department, weeks away from making the transition to prosecutor.

And yet I could relate to the feelings I heard many officers express. When I lived in Jerusalem, the Israeli-Palestinian peace process fell apart, and daily violence became my reality. Suddenly and unexpectedly, I was living in a society that seemed to be on the verge of collapse. I watched firsthand how conflict and uncertainty quickly divided the world into "us and them." And I saw how, when that happens, it's easy for violence against "them" to begin to feel righteous and justified. It was just this mindset that killed my young Palestinian-Israeli friend.

My journey to Jerusalem started in Morocco. In the summer of 1997, at the prompting of my college advisor, I studied at an Arabic language institute in Morocco, which seemed like the least threatening of the Arab countries for a Jewish kid to study in. My Arabic language skills were rudimentary, but I didn't let that stop me. Even though I was still suspicious of the locals and what they might do to me if they found out I was Jewish, I visited the most remote places, usually alone. One morning, at my budget guidebook's suggestion, I climbed through a sprawling network of dark caverns, led by my guide, a ten-year-old boy with a plastic flashlight.

Hours later, after we emerged into the light, I wandered through the countryside by myself, taking in the arid, rocky landscape punctuated by lush almond and olive groves. A shepherd tended to a flock of goats; a Muslim man halted his work in the fields for his afternoon prayer in the shade of a palm tree.

After a few hours, running low on food and water, I hitchhiked in the back of a dusty pickup truck to a nearby village. I asked the first man I saw if he could take me to a local restaurant.

He offered an amused smile and told me to follow him. He brought me to a palm tree and told me to wait. There was no one else around, and I sat in complete silence. *Should I be worried?* I wondered.

Moments later, like a scene from the Bible, the man reappeared with hot pita bread and olive oil and a teapot of sweet mint tea. *"Ahlan wa sahlan,"* he said. "You are with your people, so be at ease."

I needed a place to sleep for the night, so my host brought me to a group of four Arab men camping on the edge of town. *"Ahlan wa sahlan,"* they welcomed me.

One man in the group spoke enough English so that between us we could carry on a rough conversation using two broken languages and a range of wild hand motions. As the evening sky turned dark, we settled down around a campfire. I tried to push away an anxious feeling. In all likelihood, my hosts had never thought about my religion. But if they discovered I was Jewish, could things get uncomfortable or even dangerous?

As we ate dinner together, the group's leader asked me if I had any music with me. This being the late '90s, I traveled with a beat-up Sony Walkman and four cassettes, which included mixtapes and Pink Floyd's *The Dark Side of the Moon* album.

"We love Pink!" he yelled with genuine excitement.

The man placed the tape in his small boom box. Midway through the album, I relaxed as the saxophone played the introductory melody on the seventh track, "Us and Them." When the vocals kicked in, I felt like the lyrics had been written specifically for the moment. In the song, the speaker realizes the people on the other side of an unnamed war are, like him, just "ordinary men."

Sitting by the campfire, it struck me how narrow my worldview had been. I saw the Arab peoples exclusively through the lens of the Jewish-Arab conflict, a perspective defined primarily by fear. And yet these men had shown hospitality to a stranger for no other reason than kindness. At that moment, I felt at ease.

A year after my epiphany in Morocco, I found myself in rural Maine, surrounded by teenagers from conflict zones. While most of my college friends took summer internships in finance, technology, and consulting, I signed up to be a counselor at Seeds of Peace, an American-based nonprofit summer camp that fostered dialogue between teenagers from countries at war.

The Seeds of Peace camp had many similarities to classic American summer camps. We lived in bunks, swam in the lake, and played epic games of capture the flag. But most of our campers came from Israel and the Arab world, the Balkans, and Cyprus. We shared cabins and ate meals together. For two hours each day, these teenagers engaged in conversations, facilitated by the staff, about issues that went to the heart of their respective conflicts: history, identity, religion, and power.

On any given day, the camp produced moments like the one I

had experienced in Morocco. At night, I would often stay up late with my bunkmates, thirteen- and fourteen-year-old boys from Gaza, Tel Aviv, Hebron, and Jerusalem, talking through ways to someday end the conflict that had defined their lives. I found myself believing it might just be possible for people of different backgrounds to work together for a common good.

When I graduated college, I moved to Jerusalem to help launch the Seeds of Peace Center for Coexistence, where I designed and led year-round programming for returning campers. The Israeli-Palestinian peace process was ongoing, and we traveled freely across borders in delegations of mixed nationalities. I took a group of Israelis to visit their friends in a refugee camp; brought Palestinians to run workshops in Israeli schools; and celebrated Jewish, Muslim, and Christian holidays while eating copious amounts of home-cooked food.

The political moment felt promising. People spoke with real enthusiasm about the possibility of "coexistence," and a two-state solution of two nations living side by side seemed almost inevitable. But I knew the situation was fragile. Our work bringing mixed groups of people to talk, work, and play together was regularly criticized as "naive" and even "dangerous."

"They," I was told (by Israelis and Palestinians alike), "don't really believe in peace." My photograph once showed up in an article in a Hamas-affiliated newspaper that accused the program of corrupting Palestinian teenagers.

That year, tensions grew over the slow pace of progress in the peace negotiations. A 2000 summer summit failed to finalize an agreement, increasing a sense of hopelessness, and ratcheting up tensions. On the one-year anniversary of my arrival in the region, the peace shattered, ushering in a period known as the Second (or *Al-Aqsa*) Intifada.

On September 28, 2000, the leader of Israel's right-wing opposition party, Ariel Sharon, accompanied by 1,500 armed police, entered a part of Jerusalem known to Muslims as the *Haram al-Sharif*, and to Jews as the Temple Mount, a move intended to demonstrate Israel's sovereignty over this sacred space, and to provoke a violent response from Palestinians.

As Sharon left the Temple Mount that day, Palestinians and Israeli police clashed; the Palestinians threw rocks, and the Israeli police fired rubber-coated metal bullets. Scores of Palestinian civilians were injured in the exchange, as well as a smaller number of police officers.

I went to Jerusalem's Old City that day. I went because, like William Tanner during Katrina, I could sense the moment would be historic, and I felt compelled to see how it played out with my own eyes.

After Sharon left, my friend Sami brought me to the *Haram al-Sharif.* Wounded civilians lay sprawled out on the ground of the holy complex. An old Palestinian woman wailed at no one in particular, *"Wayn a-salam?"* "Where is the peace?" she cried out, tears running down her face.

Sami was a Palestinian who had lived in the Old City his whole life, and who served as a mentor to me. I asked him when this violence would end. "Three days," he said reassuringly.

"I hope so," I said, though not at all convinced. "If not, it won't end for three years." Both of us drastically underestimated how quickly things would escalate and how much destruction would follow.

Demonstrations spread across Israel, the West Bank, and Gaza, and the Israeli army and police increasingly resorted to firing live ammunition, often in violation of their own protocols. Palestinians increasingly turned to attacks on police and soldiers using rocks, bottles, and firebombs. Amnesty International estimated that at least 80 percent of the Palestinians killed during the first month of the Intifada were noncombatants, who were either bystanders or had participated in nonviolent demonstrations.

Asel Asleh, a seventeen-year-old Palestinian citizen of Israel, was one of those killed.

I knew Asel from his time as a camper at Seeds of Peace. Asel was one of the program's stars, a gregarious teen with a disarming smile that made you love him instantly. He over-delivered on the organization's call to "make one friend" from "the other side," befriending scores of people across nationalities and religions.

Asel identified as a Palestinian, but he was also a citizen of Israel, two identities that, in many of his peers, seemed to be at war with each other. Asel used his complicated identity as a bridge to bring people together. He wasn't afraid to call out injustice or demand that he and his people be treated fairly. But he was keen to imagine a mythical place where, as he said, he could hit the "reset button" and start over. He would comfortably quote both the hip-hop lyrics by Tupac Shakur about the need to start making changes, and the fourteenth-century Sufi poet Rumi ("Out beyond the ideas of wrongdoing and rightdoing, there is a field. I'll meet you there"). "We should never forget," Asel once wrote, "but we should forgive."

On October 2, Arab youth gathered near Asel's village of Arrabe to protest the killing of demonstrators in a neighboring village the day before. Some of the young people at the protest threw stones; police responded by firing tear gas into the crowd. Asel stood off to the side, watching the confrontation, seemingly out of harm's way. "He was like an observer, or a journalist," one eyewitness later testified. As he so often did, Asel wore his green Seeds of Peace T-shirt.

Suddenly, two groups of officers charged towards the crowd, which dispersed in panic. Multiple officers chased Asel into an olive grove. Several times, he slipped and fell while being chased by the police. One officer caught up to Asel, hit him in the back of his head with the butt of a gun, and then shot him in the back of the neck at close range. A police checkpoint prevented his ambulance from reaching the hospital in time. He died en route.

In the months that followed, the Israeli government formed the Or Commission to determine what had happened to Asel and the twelve other Palestinians killed inside Israel during the first days of the Intifada.

I assumed that the police would try to justify killing Asel by claiming they had acted in self-defense and falsely accusing him of taking part in the violence. Instead, the officers and police officials who testified during the hearings had no answer for why Asel was targeted and pursued, or why he was killed, calling it a "mystery."

In the end, the police officer who most likely fired the fatal shots was never forced to explain the shooting or justify his actions. The Or Commission concluded, "The police reaction was excessive given the circumstances, since there was no real danger that required a lethal response." And yet none of the officers involved in Asel's death (or the twelve others) were ever prosecuted for their actions.

As the months passed, the violence reached unprecedented levels. A roadside bomb exploded on a road I walked every day to get to my office. Palestinian suicide bombers detonated increasingly lethal attacks across Israel, including a pizza shop and market that I frequented. Machine gun fire and explosions from Israeli helicopter gunships disturbed the otherwise quiet Jerusalem nights. Saddam Hussein, Iraq's dictator, announced he was mobilizing thousands of troops to "liberate" Jerusalem. When three Israeli soldiers were kidnapped on the border of Lebanon, it seemed like full-scale regional war could break out at any moment.

During the early days of the Second Intifada, a large convoy of US Marines in black armored SUVs pulled into the parking lot of the Seeds of Peace Center. They had come to evacuate our neighbors who worked for the American Consulate in Jerusalem.

Eight marines in full battle dress rushed our neighbors into the vehicles, and in a few moments, they were gone. As I stood out on the balcony of the center with my colleagues, many of whom were also American citizens, I wondered why we weren't being evacuated as well. For the first time in my relatively privileged life, I felt like *I* had been left behind.

Over the following months, I watched the two societies retreat to their generations-old posture of mistrust and mutual dehumanization. The casualties piled up, and the participants in my program, who lived in almost every city in Israel, Gaza, and the West Bank, continuously added names to the list of friends killed in the conflict.

My own work at the center contracted. The peace movement,

once seemingly full of possibility, disappeared practically overnight. It became impossible to bring our teenagers across borders or hold meetings with groups of mixed nationalities. Kids turned their backs on friends from the other side. Most dishearteningly, some of those who knew Asel began to doubt that he had been gunned down without justification, no matter what the Or Commission concluded. "I love my country and I believe the soldiers are just trying to protect me," one of my young friends said. "I don't think they shot him for no reason."

Those who held on to their old idealism were affected in other ways. One Israeli boy I regularly brought to see his Palestinian friends elected to spend his mandatory army service in Gaza. He felt the army needed people like him who could see the Palestinians as people, not just the enemy. The war broke him. Within months, he received a psychological discharge. It was impossible for him to recognize the humanity of the people he policed and continue to serve as a soldier.

For the Palestinian citizens of Israel in the program, the mounting death toll was proof that Israel would never really accept them. I, as an American, had the option of leaving, and seven months into the fighting, I returned to the States to enter law school. I dreamed that one day I'd use that law school education to come back to the Middle East to help build a democratic Palestinian state alongside Israel. (I'm still waiting.)

Not long after I left, the Israelis built a thirty-foot concrete wall that physically and irreparably divided the two societies. The next four years saw waves of suicide bombings, targeted assassinations, and a reoccupation of Palestinian cities that had been self-governing during the peace process.

There was no mistaking it: we had returned to a time of Us versus Them. All told, at least three thousand Palestinians and one thousand Israelis were killed during the Second Intifada. It has only gotten worse since then.

Four months after I returned to the US, hijacked planes crashed into the World Trade Center and the Pentagon. Then I watched how quickly my own country could retreat into a world of Us and Them.

★ ★ ★

When I first flipped through the Glover file back in January 2009, Asel popped into my mind. Asel's and Henry's deaths felt similar. Coincidentally, Asel had been killed on Henry's birthday. When I got back from one of my first trips to New Orleans, I framed an old picture of Asel and hung it in my office at the Justice Department as a reminder. No one had ever been held accountable for Asel's death. I hoped to do better for Henry's family.

CHAPTER 7

A THOUSAND WORDS

Summer 2009

By early summer, Ashley tracked down the Customs and Border Protection (CBP) officer Daniel Stanley who had taken the photo of Tanner's car on fire. We hoped he had information about the person or people who had ignited the car.

Stanley was among the many out-of-town law enforcement officers who poured into New Orleans to help contain the lawlessness that had spread throughout the city in the week after Katrina. Stanley and five other agents, who typically spent their days guarding America's border, were sent to the city to secure the CBP's armory, located opposite the levee and next to the Fourth District station.

While sitting on the front porch of the CBP compound, the agents noticed a thick black plume of smoke rising from behind the complex. They couldn't tell exactly where the smoke was coming from, or what had caused it. They heard a "whooshing sound," and were assaulted by the smell of burning rubber, metal, and gasoline. Concerned that a large-scale fire could rapidly spread to surrounding buildings and family homes, Stanley and the other agents walked in the direction of the smoke.

The levee ran parallel to the river, a high man-made ridge of earth, overgrown with wild grass, and topped with a flat gravel landing that cars could drive on. By the time the agents reached the top, the heat had grown oppressive. Looking down at the bottom of the levee, the agents could see a small four-door sedan engulfed in yellow-and-orange flames. The black smoke grew denser and darker, reaching over fifty feet into the sky.

The CBP agents tried to approach the car to see what was inside, but the scalding heat prevented them from getting any closer. Stanley grabbed his camera and snapped a few pictures, then headed back to the base. When the agents returned to their compound, they struck up a conversation with two New Orleans police officers.

The talk naturally turned to the burning car just a few hundred feet away on the other side of the levee. The only thing that any of the agents recalled was the dismissiveness of the officers, one of whom commented curtly, "There is nothing we can do… Just another casualty of the storm."

When the fire died down later that evening, some of the agents returned to take a look at the car. They found the remains of a human body scattered across the back seat, including a skull. It looked to Stanley like the man might have been shot in the head.

Stanley snapped a few more pictures and went back to the compound. He'd seen a lot of dead bodies over the past few days, but this was the first one that had been incinerated.

He and another agent walked over to NOPD's Fourth District police station on Richland Road, a few hundred yards away. He reported the body and the car to a senior-ranking Fourth District officer. Another day, he made a point of informing one or two Fourth District officers about the body when he stopped by for a meal. Unfortunately, none of the CBP agents could give us useful physical descriptions of any of the cops they talked to.

Weeks later, the FBI lab recovered the "metadata" from those photos that pinpointed the car in flames at 10:49 a.m. With the much narrower time window, Ashley and I were convinced that the SOD officer who drove off with Tanner's car most likely had something to do with the fire. Unfortunately, we didn't know who that was.

Throughout the summer, Ashley and I doubled down on our efforts to interview SOD officers. Someone—likely, many someones—at Habans School that day knew exactly who drove off with Glover's body. At least fifty officers had been based at the school. We would try to interview every single one. We were nothing if not persistent.

We interviewed officers throughout May and June, but it didn't feel like we were making any substantive progress. Most interviewees claimed not to know anything about the morning the gunshot victim showed up at the compound. To the extent that anyone acknowledged witnessing what had happened, almost to a man—and they were all men—they said they had only been at the scene for minutes.

One afternoon, Ashley got a tip that got our attention.

"Schumacher is Dwayne Scheuermann."

Both Bernard Calloway and Edward King told us that an officer named "Schumacher" had been in charge at Habans. It was their best-guess reconstruction of the letters they saw stitched on the uniform shirt of the SOD officer who had beaten King.

The rumor going around was that Lieutenant Dwayne Scheuermann and Officer Greg McRae set the car on fire.

We came to appreciate that Scheuermann was either a hero or a villain depending on which side of the "thin blue line" you found yourself on. He was revered within much of the department as a "cop's cop," ever willing to put himself on the line in the high-risk encounters that were SOD's specialty. His record of arrests was so prolific, he had even received national recognition from then–President Bill Clinton for "outstanding productivity throughout his career."

But that productivity came with a price, in the form of more than fifty complaints in his file. One such civilian complaint sheds light on the scope of on-the-job abuse Scheuermann was accused of by members of the community. During one drug bust in 2002, he allegedly conducted an improper body cavity search of a suspect. (According to New Orleans civil rights attorney Mary Howell, there was a period during the 1990s and again in the early 2000s when complaints regularly surfaced about some NOPD officers using anal cavity searches, sometimes in public places, as a way to humiliate and terrorize young Black men.) Then, straddling the handcuffed man, the lieutenant purportedly punched and pepper-sprayed him. At some point during the bust, Scheuermann pointed his shotgun at some people near the arrest scene. Neither the body cavity search nor the wielding of the shotgun was mentioned in the report he filed.

In another extraordinary incident from 2003, Scheuermann allegedly ordered two women officers under his command to search the buttocks and vaginas of three females, ages 51, 23, and 1. The officers, according to the *Times-Pic* account, were searching, unavailingly, for "a shotgun, a rifle, two body armor vests, two license plates, a flashlight and a holster."

Scheuermann's methods occasionally raised eyebrows within the NOPD. After the drug bust incident, he was suspended by the department, but successfully appealed the decision to the city's Civil Service Commission. The strip search of the females resulted in the city paying out $45,000 in damages to settle a civil rights lawsuit brought by the family, but Scheuermann suffered no serious professional repercussions.

The frequency with which he fired his service weapon also received some scrutiny. He had discharged his weapon in the line of duty at least fifteen times, whereas most cops never fire their guns in their entire careers. A year before Katrina, an NOPD deputy chief was so concerned over his use of firearms—three gun discharges in one three-month period—he ordered him not to lead operations.

But for the most part, Scheuermann's police career was Teflon-coated. Notwithstanding the numerous complaints, he continued holding leadership positions throughout the department, including the vice-presidency of one of the two NOPD unions, the Police Association of New Orleans (PANO). At the time of Katrina, this trim fortysomething family man was an NOPD lieutenant and second-in-command of SOD.

In some ways, Katrina brought out the best in him, at least during those calamitous first few days. In a PBS *Frontline* report that aired four years after the storm, the viewer gets a montage of dramatic still photos that capture Scheuermann piloting his fishing boat through the flooded city, working round-the-clock to save scores of stranded citizens, pulling them out of second-story windows or cutting through roofs with axes to grab them.

A New Orleans blog that covered the local criminal justice beat captured one iconic Scheuermann moment. When a boat he was towing capsized and the passengers, including a baby strapped to a baby carrier, were tossed into the filthy water, the lieutenant reportedly dove into the muck and surfaced with the baby. The baby was brought back to life with CPR.

We knew far less about McRae, in his late forties, who had served in SOD back in the 1980s until serious injuries from a crash sustained in a car chase had removed him from street duty at the end of the decade. In the years leading up to Katrina, he'd spent most of his career working behind the desk. Four days before the storm hit, he returned to SOD to help maintain its vehicles and the weapons in the unit's armory.

Ashley and I tried to speak with both Scheuermann and McRae, but like Warren before them, they passed us on to their respective lawyers. Scheuermann was represented by Frank DeSalvo, the head lawyer for the PANO union.

DeSalvo cut a Falstaffian figure, portly and jovial. He was a mainstay of the New Orleans bar, locally famous for his ready wit and his knee-jerk defense of police officers in the quotes he offered up to *The Times-Picayune* as frequently as possible. When the feds opened an investigation into off-duty police officers who allegedly beat a group of Black streetcar drivers while using racial slurs, and then planted a gun, destroyed video evidence, and intimidated witnesses, DeSalvo commented in print, "I think that the FBI would have better things to do than investigate a barroom fight."

When the *Times-Pic* ran an article in early June outlining allegations against police officers in three separate investigations—our case, and shootings at the Danziger Bridge and at the convention center—he unsurprisingly predicted that the federal investigations would clear all of the NOPD officers involved.

With Scheuermann and McRae out of reach, Ashley and I were back to hitting the pavement, trying to find officers who could, at a minimum, confirm that Scheuermann and McRae were even at the school when Henry showed up on September 2.

In late May, Ashley and I interviewed Sergeant Sherman Joseph, who had led an SOD platoon after Katrina. Joseph still worked as an SOD sergeant and had asked Ashley and me to meet him at SOD headquarters, which had since moved back to its usual location on the East Bank of the Mississippi.

From the outside, it was an old redbrick warehouse with a green metal roof. But inside, the compound felt like an airplane hangar with high ceilings and open spaces that enclosed a series of trailers that served as offices. Scattered throughout were boats, armored cars, and riot gear.

SOD, like similar SWAT units that had sprouted up all over the country since the 1970s, was typical of the growing militarization of American policing. As the war on drugs took on the trappings of an actual war, SWAT units amassed military-grade hardware like M-16s, flash-bangs, and armored personnel carriers, often through federal programs that repurposed surplus military hardware from the wars in Iraq and Afghanistan. The weaponry was used to respond to hostage situations or to serve "no-knock" search warrants where officers bang down doors and storm houses, most often for drug offenses.

The first thing we saw upon entering was two or three military-grade Humvees. Heavily armed men in tactical gear, some carrying assault rifles, casually milled around. We got plenty of ugly looks. It wasn't the most inviting environment for an interview.

Sherman Joseph said he and his partner had been the first officers to spot the Chevy Malibu as it neared Habans that morning. They were sitting at a stop sign when they saw the car, a Black male in the passenger seat, window open, waving his arms as if signaling for help. Rather than stopping for the patrol car, the Chevy accelerated and beelined for the school.

Not sure what was going on, Joseph and his partner flipped on their police lights and siren and gave chase for about one long block, momentarily losing traction on wet leaves, which created distance between them and the Chevy. Joseph said that by the time they arrived at the school, the men were already out of the car and handcuffed.

Joseph's version, if true, could explain why so many officers reacted with such initial aggression. That morning, the cops had been mostly cleaning weapons that had gotten wet over the preceding days, preparing to leave for the day's missions. Then, suddenly, they hear the siren, see the flashing lights, and a car with three yelling Black men roars into the school with a gunshot victim bleeding in the back seat.

Joseph didn't have much information on what happened next. Like most of the SOD officers, he claimed he only hung around for a matter of minutes. "The only thing I remember is one of the guys was saying something about his brother, and I figured that person in the back seat was his brother."

I asked Joseph why he left so quickly. After all, he was a squad leader.

Lieutenant Scheuermann, he said, was handling the situation.

By June 2009, it was hard to imagine that any NOPD officer had not heard about the federal investigation into the death and burning of Henry Glover. Articles about the case regularly appeared in the *Times-Pic*, and stories ran on local TV news stations. By the middle of June, the paper had disclosed that the officer who killed Glover was David Warren. Subsequently, someone spray-painted *Henry Glover* on the NOPD headquarters building to keep the case front of mind for police leadership.

For us, this heavy local media coverage created new problems. The cops were put on notice, even more so when the police unions got into the act. New Orleans had two police unions: PANO and the Fraternal Order of Police (FOP). I had been warned by colleagues that unions could gum up an investigation, making it hard to speak to police officer witnesses.

At this point, DeSalvo appeared to represent both Scheuermann and McRae, and neither would speak to us.

For its part, FOP sent out an email to its entire membership, advising officers—regardless of whether they were a suspect or a witness in the investigation—to get a lawyer. Many cops took them up on the suggestion. It felt like every criminal defense lawyer in New Orleans was working this case.

One day in late June, Ashley got word from senior FBI leadership about the existence of a photograph that might finally answer the question of who drove off with Glover's body.

At her FBI cubicle in New Orleans, Ashley gingerly opened the paper envelope from a pharmacy photomat. The photo showed Henry sprawled out in the back of Tanner's car, before the burning. It revealed a slim Black man, facedown in the back seat, wearing a white T-shirt and denim jeans. Perfectly centered in the back of his shirt was a small, bright circle of blood. The photo suggested a single gunshot wound to the back, just as Bernard and Howard had described. There was no visual evidence that he had been shot in the head, as Alec Brown and the CBP agents who had seen Henry's skull had suggested.

What the photograph did not show was who was driving the car. But we felt fairly certain that the photographer, a Black NOPD officer, would be able to identify the driver.

We met him in a fast-food restaurant near his home. This low-ranking officer was not happy to see us. He wore a hat pulled down low over his face, and he slouched in the booth, clearly hoping that no one he knew would see him with us.

When the officer had learned about our investigation into Glover's death, he knew he was sitting on important evidence. But when he had handed over his photo to the FBI, he was hoping, as if he'd somehow forgotten everything he'd ever known about criminal investigations, that that would be the end of it. He grumbled that he wanted it to remain anonymous.

He said, on the morning he took the picture, he was standing across the street from Habans when a white sedan pulled up. Initially, he only noticed one person in the car—the driver. Then he saw the man lying motionless in the back seat, covered in blood, evidently a shooting victim. The officer snapped two quick photos. He was taking pictures of lots of the strange things he was seeing during Katrina, and this fit the bill.

"Who was driving the car?" I asked.

He said he didn't recall. Great, I thought, another witness with post-Katrina memory issues.

He told us it could have been a Black civilian. Or maybe a White police officer. He couldn't be sure. When we asked why he thought that it *could* have been a police officer, he said there were other police officers around, so it would have been unusual for officers to do nothing if they came across a civilian driving around with a dead body.

Whenever I've investigated allegations of police misconduct, I've always tried to get involved in the case as early as possible. Many FBI agents I have worked with had a knee-jerk inclination to take the word of their fellow law enforcement officers at face value. I always wanted to be in the room with the agents during those first interviews with police witnesses to push back a little, if necessary.

With Ashley and me, the roles were somewhat reversed. Without corroborating evidence, I tried to keep an open mind about whether a cop was telling the truth or not. Ashley, especially when it came to the cops, was more skeptical. Her starting point was often, "Give me a reason to trust you."

When it came to trusting her gut, Ashley leaned heavily on her pre-FBI professional experience. Her work as a probation officer exposed her to plenty of self-exculpatory storytelling. Her skepticism only grew during her time as a social worker in a psych ward. She often saw traits in our witnesses that suggested bigger psychological issues. To her, they might come across as "pathological liars," "paranoid," or "narcissists."

She and I balanced each other well. Although we never consciously strategized about our roles going into interviews—who was going to play the good cop, who the bad—pretty quickly, our styles emerged. I tended to ask most of the questions, so I imagine I came off as the aggressive one. Ashley preferred to sit back and observe, noting mannerisms, body language, and tone of voice.

The witnesses likely had no idea she was the tougher judge of character and, I suspect, more often than not, the more accurate one. But we were both convinced that our photographer-cop was lying.

As the investigation wore on into the summer, it seemed like we were losing our leverage. All the officers were lawyering up, many refused to speak with us, and those who would talk were choosing the locations of our meetings. They often wanted to be interviewed in their police stations, which generally indicated that we wouldn't learn anything useful.

We interviewed one former SOD officer, at his request, at the Second District police station, where he then worked. We sat down in a conference room and had just gotten through some of our background questions when the district commander burst into the room, red-faced and screaming at us: "How dare you come in here! Get the fuck out of my station!"

We tried to explain that the officer had chosen the station for the interview, but that did nothing to appease the commander. For its part, the *Times-Pic* later referred to the abortive meeting as a "legend," noting "a gnawing sense of anxiety within the department." They were afraid of us. Which indicated to me, they had reason to be afraid.

Subsequently, we learned that the assistant special agent in charge—the same one who had berated Ashley for our unannounced visit with Italiano—had called the commander that same night to apologize for his "agents' behavior." Once again, I felt sold out by the senior leadership of the FBI for doing my job.

Later in the summer, Ashley and I added a new member to our team, Tracey Knight, a New Orleans native and prosecutor in the local US Attorney's Office.

Tracey sat in during the first few weeks of grand jury, filling in for the Assistant US Attorney (AUSA) who usually handled civil rights cases and who happened to be on vacation. Even after the AUSA returned to work, Tracey kept coming. The case got to her. "I just remember thinking at the time, 'This story cannot be true,'" she told me later. "I just can't believe this happened in my community."

At the end of June, as Ashley and I struggled to identify who had burned Tanner's car, Tracey came up to me after a particularly intense grand jury session. "I want in," she said.

Unlike Ashley and me, relative rookies, Tracey was a fifteen-year veteran of the criminal justice system. She exuded calmness and warmth. Soft-spoken and deliberate, she seemed the opposite of the archetypal hard-charging prosecutor.

Usually, federal civil rights cases bring together a prosecutor or two from the Justice Department in Washington (often called "Main Justice") and at least one Assistant US Attorney who is based locally. In theory, it's a complementary pairing. The AUSA knows the local legal landscape: the defense lawyers, the judges, even the judges' clerks. DOJ attorneys bring subject matter expertise and knowledge of the intricacies of civil rights law. With their much smaller caseloads, DOJ attorneys have more time to go deeper into cases, which in police investigations is a virtual prerequisite.

In practice, the DOJ/US Attorney's Office collaboration can degenerate into a clash of legal egos, which isn't surprising. A civil rights case involving a police shooting is big news. It's often *the* thing that everyone in their city is talking about. Local federal prosecutors often want to lead the investigation and don't like the idea of outsiders from Washington telling them what to do. And DOJ prosecutors have been known to display an arrogance that doesn't win them many local friends. I've had more than a few cases blow up because the federal legal players, all ostensibly on the same team, couldn't get along.

The Glover case was that rare instance where the team came together the way it's supposed to. Early in the investigation, the New Orleans US Attorney's Office took a back seat, supporting us with staff, as Ashley and I issued subpoenas and booked grand jury time. But the office's greatest contribution to the cause was Tracey and her extraordinarily skillful legal assistant Laura Orth.

The first time Ashley did an interview with Tracey instead of me, I reached out to her for her assessment. "She's great," Ashley assured me. "If you were a woman, we could be the 2009 Charlie's Angels."

The Glover case was personal for Tracey, an African American New Orleanian, in ways that it couldn't be for me. She attended a local Catholic school, St. Ursuline Academy, went to college at Howard University in DC, and then returned to the city for law school at Tulane. Tracey had been a Katrina refugee. She had left the city with her two-year-old daughter a few days before the storm hit and didn't come back for a year, temporarily resettling in the suburban DC area and working at the US Attorney's Office in Maryland. When the levees broke and her hometown was drowning, she had been staying in a hotel in Houston, where her sister lived. She had been distraught watching the Katrina coverage on TV. Now, as she was learning the details of the Glover case, she was coming to realize that things were worse in her city than she could ever have imagined.

I hoped that Ashley and Tracey would have better luck with our photographer-cop without me growing visibly frustrated with his steady stream of bullshit. Over the course of a few hours during a July meeting, they got him to back off the idea that the driver of the Chevy was a civilian, but he still refused to give them a name.

He gave the clearest explanation to date of why he was seemingly incapable of attaching a cop's name to the crime. He was afraid. He said he knew better than to "go around asking a whole lot of questions," because then you get labeled a "rat." Then he said, "It is my ass that is out there. I have to look in my bushes. My life is on the line. And I live with that every single day."

When Ashley and Tracey debriefed me on the interview, I figured we'd gotten as much out of the officer as we were ever going to.

People lie for a variety of reasons. If you can figure out *why* someone is lying, sometimes you can address the source of their anxiety and get at the truth. People often lie out of simple self-preservation—they don't want to lose their jobs or, worse, face jail time. In those circumstances, we can cut them a deal, offer a reduced sentence, or even offer immunity from prosecution.

Sometimes we catch a witness in a lie that we can objectively disprove. Now we have leverage. Coming clean may be the subject's best chance to avoid charges. Oftentimes, witnesses, who may not have done anything wrong themselves, lie out of loyalty, to protect their friends and colleagues. (SOD, with its paramilitary ethos, was particularly good at closing ranks.) In those cases, sometimes it works to appeal to a sense of higher duty. Do they want to be able to look into their kids' eyes and know that they did the right thing?

But when fear of physical harm to oneself or one's loved ones is the primary motivation for lying, there isn't much I can do. This officer's fear ran deep. He was afraid that he would be assassinated by other cops. It was hard to assess if this fear was credible. But this was New Orleans. By now, I had absorbed enough NOPD history to understand that his fears were not farfetched.

In the '80s, high-profile police abuse cases typically involved White cops brutalizing Black citizens, most notoriously the Algiers 7 case that Patrice Glover remembered so well. But by the '90s, the department had added a number of abusive Black officers to the ranks. Under intense community pressure to diversify,

NOPD actively recruited minority candidates but the department's notoriously low salaries, and its then-policy that required officers to live in the city, reduced the number of people who wanted or were eligible for the job. Admissions standards were often lowered and routine background checks ignored.

The result was a toxic milieu of temptation and highly temptable cops. Throughout the decade, traditional graft hummed along as usual—for instance, cops shaking down restaurants and clubs in the French Quarter. The new wrinkle was an infusion of dirty Black cops, sometimes working in league with the drug dealers they'd grown up with. The city as a whole got more dangerous. By the mid-'90s, New Orleans had the highest per capita murder rate in the country.

As New Orleans civil rights attorney Mary Howell noted, "We had police officers doing bank robberies. We had police officers involved in arson, rape, kidnapping. We used to say that people in New Orleans were more afraid of the police than they were of the criminals, and it was hard to tell the difference."

"Want less crime?" went the familiar local joke. "Hire fewer policemen!"

The personification of the NOPD officer as law unto himself was Len Davis, aka Robocop, a ruthless neighborhood enforcer who was in the drug business with a local hit man. In October of '94, Davis and his partner assaulted a teenager in the Lower Ninth Ward. Kim Marie Groves, a local resident whose children were friends of the teenager, witnessed the assault and filed a complaint with the department's Internal Affairs office against Davis and his partner.

Davis figured the complaint might interfere with his cocaine operations. He called up his drug partner and ordered a hit on Groves, the mother of three. The conversation was overheard by FBI agents who had tapped his phone as part of a drug-running investigation, even though they initially failed to understand the significance of the coded language they heard.

That evening, Groves was murdered, execution-style, a shot to the back of the head. Davis was subsequently convicted in federal court and sentenced to be executed for his role in the murder of Kim Marie Groves. He was the first police officer in the history of the United States to be sentenced to die for a civil rights crime.

The Davis hit was chilling, but more to the point as far as our cop-photographer was concerned was the story of Antoinette Franks, a young Black female officer and a bona fide sociopath. Franks was a clueless rookie officer. She became dangerous when she became romantically involved with a small-time drug dealer not yet out of his teens. Like many New Orleans cops, she supplemented her modest salary by moonlighting as security, in her case, at a Vietnamese restaurant owned by the Vu family. Franks became incensed when her former NOPD partner Ronnie Williams, who also worked security at the restaurant, told her to stop inviting her lover and her brother to freeload off the restaurant.

Late one evening in March 1995, Franks and the boyfriend showed up at the restaurant bent on revenge. The boyfriend killed Officer Williams with a shot to the head, and both he and Franks fatally shot two younger Vu siblings—a son who was training to be a priest, a daughter to be a nun—while the older sister, Chau Vu, cowered in a walk-in cooler. Franks left the scene and returned in uniform, hoping to pass herself off as an officer responding to a distress call. When the cops who had arrived to investigate the murders asked Chau Vu to describe what had happened, she yelled at Franks: "You were there. You know everything!"

New Orleans had the baleful distinction of having two former cops, Len Davis and Antoinette Franks, sitting on death row. Our cop witnesses surely knew that recent history better than we did.

Throughout the interview with Tracey and Ashley, the photographer-cop kept looking at Ashley, as if she might somehow extricate him from this jam. If anything, it seemed to me that Ashley was tougher on the Black cops who were withholding information. Later she explained to me, "I think I had this expectation when I interviewed these guys that they would understand—'A Black man has been murdered and you're covering up for it. That could be you down the road.'"

The officer fixed her with what Ashley called "The Look," the entreaty to racial solidarity. And then he made his meaning plain: "As a Black woman, you should understand what I'm going through."

Ashley paused. "Between you and the dead guy in the car," she said, "I'm with the dead guy in the car."

As signs pointed to police involvement in both the shooting and the burning of Henry, the FBI began putting more resources into our investigation. In addition to getting support from some senior FBI agents from the New Orleans field office, we picked up a rotating cast of temporary duty agents who would drop into New Orleans for sixty to ninety days at a time and help out with whatever we needed.

From May to July, our team spent countless hours interviewing officers whom we had heard had been at Habans on September 2. Most of the officers we interviewed claimed not to know anything.

Almost as frustrating as the "deniers" were the "hinters," officers who would drop clues or photos that they couldn't explain. Enough to make us do more work, not enough to be admissible in court. These cops passed on "rumors," for instance that Scheuermann and McRae burned the car. But when we asked them where they learned this information, we'd get back something like, "Everybody's talking about it, to be honest with you."

A different officer explained why there was so much chatter. "Basically everybody's speculating that everybody's going to jail, you know, because the federal government is investigating them. You are referred to as 'those people.'"

"I think we've been called worse things," I replied. We had heard what some of the cops called us. We were "the Black girl" and "the Jew."

As a relatively new father and traveling prosecutor, my life generally consisted of two things: work and parenting. Back home in DC, after a half week or sometimes a week of being away, I did my share of parenting so my wife could get a reprieve. We were two full-time working parents, juggling a baby, Fiona's rapidly growing company tackling global income inequality, and the biggest case of my career. We didn't get out much.

So when I was in New Orleans, I made the most of life without child-rearing responsibilities. My release was music, and some of the best I heard wasn't in the bars or the clubs. On particularly nice summer nights, I'd wander the streets of New Orleans with an Old Fashioned in hand, listening to whatever was on offer, anything from a solo saxophonist playing over backing tracks to a full brass band of high school students. Every so often, I'd see some of my favorite musicians playing for tips in the French Quarter.

I had my acoustic guitar with me on one trip to New Orleans. One beautiful night, I grabbed my guitar and headed out to Jackson Square. I left my hotel in the French Quarter and walked down Chartres Street, passing through the eighteenth-century heart of a splendid Franco-Spanish colonial city that became American by virtue of the Louisiana Purchase. While the storm damage had been cleared up in this part of town, many of the storefronts remained vacant. Even in the heart of the city's tourist district, New Orleans wasn't all the way back.

I sat down on the front steps of the St. Louis Cathedral, the iconic church that towers over the northwest corner of the square, and began to play. I was a little self-conscious, but I had heard plenty of other amateur musicians in the Quarter who weren't any better than I was.

My mother told me once that whenever she saw someone playing guitar on the street, she would throw a few dollars in their case. "It could be you one day," she joked.

Deeply missing my wife and child, I played a song I'd written not long after the birth of my daughter and the death of my mother. In the middle of working a grim case that I was completely wrapped up in, I was having a private musical moment, in public, in this city I was growing to love.

And then, a woman roughly my mother's age walked by and tossed a dollar in my case.

When I told Bobbi Bernstein about my busking in Jackson

Square, she was concerned. "Is that legal?" she asked. "I think so," I said somewhat uncertainly. New Orleans seemed to be overflowing with musicians playing for money on the street, none of whom had any permits as far as I could tell.

"Be careful," she warned me. She worried that if I were recognized, I could be targeted by NOPD. The last thing she wanted was for me to get arrested for illegally playing music.

Fiona was a little less concerned. "Frankly, I don't think the NOPD could ever contemplate that a suit from DC was busking."

Regardless, from then on, I stuck to listening to other people play.

After one particularly unsuccessful week, trying to come up with admissible evidence that might persuade a jury that Scheuermann and McRae were responsible for the burning, I headed out to Frenchmen Street to unwind, and reset for the next day.

As I crossed Esplanade, the street that divides the French Quarter from the Marigny, I got a call on my cell phone. It was Ashley. She sounded tired and frustrated.

"What's our strategy?" she asked.

"What do you mean?" It seemed like a strange thing to ask, given that almost all Ashley and I ever did was talk strategy.

But she was under pressure. While some senior leaders at the FBI wanted the case to go away, others were pouring resources into the investigation, and wanted to know when we would have indictments.

"What are we going to do to break through SOD?"

I didn't have a great answer. "We will keep following every lead." I tried to reassure her, "Eventually, we will bust this thing wide open."

I was losing my patience too. I knew we had to keep at it. But man, was I ready for a breakthrough.

Ever since our first interview with Officer Keyalah Bell back in April, we had been trying to find the man with a "professional" camera that she'd seen taking photos at Habans.

After a lot of digging, we were fairly sure he was Alex Brandon, a photographer for the *Times-Pic* embedded with SOD after the storm. He had captured some of the most powerful images after Katrina.

It took months for us to get access to Brandon. At the time, DOJ required a remarkable amount of paperwork to subpoena a member of the news media, including a sign-off from the attorney general. In 2009, Brandon was working with the Associated Press, covering the Obama White House. Because he was living in DC, Ashley flew up, and we interviewed him at my office.

Brandon told us that he had been at Habans the morning Henry arrived. He'd been about to take a photo of Tanner, King, and Calloway surrounded by the SOD officers. But Officer Greg McRae, a man he'd known casually from covering NOPD, had come up to him and told him not to. "It was, for lack of a better term, an order," Brandon told us.

Later that evening, over a meal at the Habans cafeteria, Brandon asked McRae what had happened with the man in the back seat of the car. McRae ran his hand across his throat in a slicing gesture. Then, he curtly replied, "NAT," cop talk for "Necessary Action Taken."

"I got the impression that that was the end of the conversation," Brandon said.

Brandon had been at Habans with a federal agent from the Bureau of Alcohol, Tobacco, and Firearms (ATF). The agent also had his camera out. Brandon thought he might have snapped some photos.

I was on vacation when Ashley tracked down the agent. We desperately hoped he had the photos we needed. The agent had seen three handcuffed men sitting near the back bumper of a patrol car, surrounded by SOD officers. He had seen a Black man sprawled out on the back seat who looked like he was dead. He had heard from the officers that the man in the back seat had been shot for looting.

And then the ATF agent told Ashley that he had *not* taken any photos. Two days later, the ATF agent called Ashley and said that, after his interview, he found a hard drive of backup photos with hundreds of photos from the storm, a catalog of Katrina's most terrible images.

When Ashley received the hard drive, I was on vacation, staying in an off-the-grid cabin in the woods on a lake. I was checking my emails on my government Blackberry at the end of the dock, one of the few parts of the property with cell service.

I read through the first email from Ashley. It felt like she was taunting me. "You are gonna love what I have…we just bust this thing wide open."

I opened the second email and waited. The download was excruciatingly slow, as two photos revealed themselves slowly, line by line. It was hard to make out from the details on what felt like the world's smallest screen.

The first photo was of Henry lying facedown, covered in blood in the back seat of Tanner's car, similar to others we already had.

As the second picture finally loaded, I blurted out, "Holy shit."

The photo showed Tanner, King, and Calloway, sitting on the ground handcuffed, surrounded by six menacing-looking police officers, some of them carrying assault rifles, just as Henry's three allies had told us.

One of the cops, shaved head, shirtless, and carrying an assault rifle, had a large tribal-style tattoo on his arm. Tanner had described one of the men, who he believed had beaten Calloway, as having a tattoo like "The Rock," the actor Dwayne Johnson.

Tucked behind one of the officers was a sliver of a face of a man wearing sandals. Ashley identified him as Dwayne Scheuermann.

And there was Greg McRae, a scowl on his face, who looked like he was about to tell the photographer to go to hell. In his hand, just as Tanner had said, were two road flares.

CHAPTER 8

UNUSUAL SUSPECTS

August and September 2009

In a single image, the photo Ashley had sent me captured the extreme power disparity between White law enforcement and Black men in the South: three forlorn African American detainees, handcuffed on the ground, towered over by a bunch of heavily armed White men. The image was from the late summer of 2005, but save for the modern cop car and weaponry, it could just as easily have been from the depths of Jim Crow. In this moment, however, it was our best evidence that we really could solve the mystery of who burned the body of Henry Glover. We set to work confirming the identities of the officers in the picture.

Tanner was one of our first stops after getting the ATF photo. We figured if Tanner could give us a clear sense of what each officer had done at Habans, we could proceed onion-style, "from the outside in," first interviewing the SOD cops with the least criminal culpability to get leverage on the cops with the most.

We had made six redacted versions of the photo—in each photo, only one face was visible—so Tanner could only focus on one face at a time. He said he didn't get a good look at faces, since he kept his head down during most of the incident. We told him to do his best.

We showed him the sliver of the face of the person we knew to be Dwayne Scheuermann. Even more than recognizing the face, Tanner recognized the footwear: sandals. Tanner identified Scheuermann as the officer in charge, who hit Edward and who had followed his Chevy out of Habans in a truck. The last photo we showed to Tanner was McRae. We had blacked out the road flares to see if Tanner had an independent recollection of McRae's involvement.

"That's the guy with the road flares who drove off with my car," Tanner said, pointing at McRae's face in the photo. He said the officer punched him in the stomach and rib cage twice, and hit him with a rifle.

Ashley and I then showed him a copy of the fully unredacted photo, with McRae holding the road flares. Tanner looked up at me and gave me one of his off-kilter grins.

"I told you!" He laughed. "You didn't believe me, but I told you!"

There were two officers in the ATF photo that Tanner didn't have much to say about, one White, one Black, so Ashley and I figured we'd start there—"from the outside in." The White officer, Chris Abbot, didn't shed much light on what happened that morning at Habans School but his Katrina experiences were a vivid illustration of what some of the NOPD officers had endured.

Hours after Katrina had begun to pummel New Orleans with lashing rain and winds in excess of eighty miles per hour, the 17th Street levee broke. Water from Lake Pontchartrain poured into the city, engulfing Abbott's home in the low-lying lakefront neighborhood of Lakewood.

Abbott climbed to his attic to escape the rapidly rising floodwaters. His recorded 911 call was saved by the NOPD, along with other SOS calls it received: "I can't get out of my attic. The water is rising…I'm trying to get out. It's up to my neck." There was no way anyone could reach him in the hurricane-force winds. Abbott's captain coolly instructed him to use his service revolver to shoot a circle of holes in the attic roof and then punch his way out. "The water's up to my mouth," Abbott answered, trying to fight back the panic. "I really don't know that I'm going to make it."

When Abbott's radio went dead, the officers on the other end of the line figured their colleague had drowned. Forty-five minutes later, he came back on the line, out of breath: "I'm on a roof. I need someone to come and get me." Hours later, Abbott was plucked off the roof by NOPD officers in a boat. He was badly shaken, and he'd lost his Lakewood home, but within a day he was back on the job, and according to one account, working more than a month straight before taking a day off.

His near-death experience during Katrina was only the latest in his perilous NOPD career—Chris Abbott was a hard man to kill. In 1998, he was patrolling a public housing project in the uptown Central City district of New Orleans when he took a bullet to the chest, and was saved by his bullet-proof vest.

That episode paled in comparison to another incident three years later in the Treme, when Abbott stopped a man he believed was carrying a concealed weapon. Brandy Jefferson, who had "no mercy" tattooed on his forehead, opened fire. He shot Abbott twice, in the stomach and the shoulder, and then twice more, into the back of the officer's head.

Amazingly, Abbott recovered and returned to the job. The shooter was prosecuted for attempted murder. At trial, Jefferson claimed that he had a protection agreement with Abbott, paying him off so he could deal drugs in the area without attracting NOPD interest. Jefferson testified that when he wanted out of the deal and threatened to turn Abbott in to the FBI, the enraged officer attacked him, prompting the shooting.

It was a wild claim, although in New Orleans not an inconceivable one. The jury rejected it, and Jefferson got life in prison under Louisiana's habitual offender law.

(Years after I met him, Abbott was shot a third time, in the leg, while working an approved off-duty neighborhood watch detail. As of this writing, he's still with NOPD, working as an officer peer support counselor.)

We met with the Black officer from the ATF picture, at a small booth in a run-down McDonald's next to the interstate highway. He didn't waste any time getting down to business. "I didn't kill my dog!" he blurted out.

Ashley and I exchanged puzzled glances, and then Ashley said, "I'm sorry, you didn't do what?"

The officer, it turned out, was currently under investigation for "malfeasance in office" for the death of his police dog. He had brought the dog with him to work at a late-night detail for a private company, sweeping the now shuttered and abandoned Charity Hospital for vagrants. Left unattended, the dog pushed his way past a partially propped open elevator door and plummeted seventeen floors down a flooded elevator shaft to his death. The officer compounded this lapse of judgment by allegedly writing a misleading incident report about the circumstances surrounding the K-9's demise.

"We are not here about the dog," Ashley said. He looked visibly relieved.

"We are here about this." Ashley placed the photo on the table. He looked at the picture of three detained men being surrounded by six cops. "Oh," he said, suddenly nervous again. He said he vaguely remembered the day, but that he had only been at Habans School for a short time that morning.

(Four years later, the officer was found not guilty of malfeasance at trial.)

Tanner, Calloway, and King all remembered seeing Jeff Sandoz at Habans that day, the burly shaved-head SOD sergeant with large tribal tattoos standing in the center of the ATF photo. They said he used racial slurs and called them names. None of them could re-call Sandoz hitting anyone, which was somewhat surprising, since Tanner had previously told us that an officer with tattoos like The Rock had been the one who beat him.

We subpoenaed him to the grand jury to hear his testimony under oath. I was curious to see whether he would simply assert his Fifth Amendment rights, the protection against self-incrimination, or whether the threat of a perjury indictment might actually induce him to tell us the truth. He took the third path: lying.

Sandoz minimized his time on the scene. He claimed that he couldn't remember who was at Habans, and what, if anything, happened there that day. He attributed his "lack of memory" to Katrina: the destruction of his home, friends injured and killed, missing his son, and the grim living conditions.

As clear as it seemed to me that Sandoz was lying, it's hard to prove that someone remembers something when they say they can't. I hoped that, like Nina Simmons, Sandoz would walk out of the grand jury, get a lawyer, and come back to correct his testimony. Six days later, Ashley and I spoke with Sandoz at his lawyer's of-fice. He looked us in the eye and said that everything he had told the grand jury was true.

In the ATF photo, there is a young-looking officer, Joshua Burns, wearing baggy jeans and a T-shirt with an AK-47 casually slung over his shoulder. He looked like a cross between an Afghan fighter and a teenager who'd wandered over from a nearby basket-ball court. Burns, despite his youthful appearance, had been with NOPD for seven years at the time of Katrina and had transferred to SOD shortly after the storm hit.

When I first met Burns, he was a federal inmate at Coleman Federal Penitentiary in Florida. We had him transferred to a local jail in St. Charles Parish, Louisiana, so we could talk to him more easily. The jail was upriver from New Orleans, about a forty-five drive through the lowland boonies, in the vicinity of the Mau-repas Swamp Wildlife Management Area and Cajun Pride Swamp

Tours. The closer we got to the jail, the more lost we felt, no businesses or houses nearby, just dense swampland.

When we arrived, the jail staff said we could visit Burns in one of the "attorney-client" rooms. The "room" was tiny, enough space for two lawyers to sit pressed close together, with a glass partition that separated visitors from the prisoner. However, we were three people: Ashley, me and an FBI temporary duty agent. It was so tight that we staggered who could lean back and who had to lean forward. When I tilted forward, my body almost touched the scratched glass divider that separated us from Burns.

Burns wasn't happy to see us. Clearly, this local parish jail was a few steps down from his federal accommodations. (Years later, I investigated a case in the federal prison where Burns was a prisoner. While I have found the conditions in jails and prisons around the US inherently inhumane, the federal facility was certainly "better" than the run-down jail in St. Charles.)

When we met him, Burns was about three years into a five-year federal sentence for conspiracy to commit robbery for his role in two armed robberies of an illicit erotic message parlor.

The Bangkok Spa was one of a score of seedy, barely veiled sex parlors that flourish in New Orleans, a city that, since the days of the Storyville red-light district, has marketed illicit sex as part of its civic charm. Typically, these massage parlors are dressed up in ticky-tacky pseudo-Asian decor, and they're staffed by mostly Southeast Asian women who occasionally attract the interest of either NOPD or federal law enforcement investigating sex trafficking. It was not uncommon for these establishments to pay off cops to protect their business.

In January 2006, four months after Katrina with the city still reeling from the storm, Burns and five other men, including a former NOPD officer who'd been fired for dereliction of duty, entered the spa. One man pointed a gun at the head of a female employee and told her to be quiet. Then all the women were herded into one area while the armed intruders ransacked the place, coming away with between $2,500 and $3,000.

Five months later, as the city struggled to regain some vestige of normalcy, Burns and two of his co-conspirators returned to the spa. Again, they herded up the employees at gunpoint and robbed the joint. One of the thieves attempted to shield his identity by draping a towel over his head; another wrapped his hands in a piece of clothing, trying not to leave fingerprints. It wasn't the most professional of jobs. Cameras, installed by the FBI after the previous robbery, captured most of the incident. Five hundred dollars of the money the men stole was "bait money," planted by NOPD's Public Integrity Bureau. It would be difficult to get caught any more red-handed. Burns pleaded guilty to his involvement in the conspiracy.

With Ashley, the temporary agent, and me sitting squashed together in the room, Burns told us about the day the car with Henry Glover arrived at the compound.

Burns had been asleep inside Habans when he heard lots of yelling coming from the front of the school. He quickly got dressed, grabbed his personal AK-47 from his car and ran towards the commotion. He found three Black civilians, facedown, handcuffed, and surrounded by cops.

"...[A] couple of [the Black men] were yelling and screaming. One was yelling, help my brother... The other was just being belligerent; and the third guy, he was somewhat quiet."

"When you say 'belligerent,' did you see them do anything violent?"

"Anything violent, no...cursing them out." In Burns's assessment, the men didn't pose any physical threat.

The police were yelling back, calling the men "looters" and cussing them out, although Burns denied any racial slurs were used. Offering up the usual disclaimer that he wasn't at the scene the whole time, Burns said he only saw one officer rough up anybody. Jeff Sandoz, with the large arm tattoo and massive memory issues, grabbed one of the men by the shirt and shoved him to the ground.

In general, Burns said, the police were hostile towards citizens who hadn't heeded the mandatory evacuation order. Burns did not hide his own disdain for the people he called "looters." The feeling of most cops—Burns included—was that if people had evacuated when they should have, this never would have taken place. Basically, *looters got what they deserved.*

It seemed only fair to Burns that looters received extra judicial punishment. There was no functioning jail, so there was no point in arresting them. Most were just let go, but some, he said, were "roughed up."

I was floored by this extended rant against "looters," given his extracurricular activities while on the force. I just looked at him. "Didn't you rob a brothel at gunpoint?"

He grimaced. "It's different."

Burns gave us the fullest account we'd heard to date of the role played by Dwayne Scheuermann, the SOD lieutenant in charge at Habans. Scheuermann yelled at the detainees, at one point telling them to "shut the fuck up." He didn't seem interested in asking them many questions, and he failed to separate them, standard procedure if he'd been trying to get a better understanding of what had happened to the dead man in the car. But according to Burns, Scheuermann worked the police radio to see if someone could tell him how it came to pass that a man who had been fatally shot had been driven into his compound.

Burns said that Scheuermann "was looking to send a couple of guys [SOD officers] to try to find out what happened…" That would be consistent with what Patrice Glover and officers Simmons and Bell had told us months before, that a group of intimidating cops in tactical gear had shown up at the spot where Henry had collapsed and been driven away. Possibly those SOD officers heard Patrice accuse cops of shooting her brother. Conceivably, they could have also learned something about the shooting from David Warren, on the mall second-floor breezeway. For all our efforts, Ashley and I never identified the heavily armed officers who had been at the mall.

Burns said the SOD cops at Habans searched the three men for weapons and drugs, but they didn't find anything. Eventually, the situation calmed down. At some point, he said, the two ranking officers from the Fourth District, Captain Kirsch and Lieutenant Italiano, showed up at the school, along with some other officers

from the precinct, probably, he figured, in response to Scheuermann's calls over the radio. Burns saw Italiano and Scheuermann
walk away from the others and have a conversation "out of view"
so as "not to be disturbed by other people."

Burns didn't know exactly what was said. Nor did he know what
happened to the car after it was driven out of the school. But later in
the evening, he had a conversation with "the tool guy." He pointed
to McRae in the ATF group photo. McRae told him he "got rid
of the car," although Burns didn't know exactly what that meant.
He figured they moved the body away for public health reasons.

"Did he tell you that he had burned the car?" I asked.

"No."

"But did you have the sense that McRae was acting alone, or
together with someone else?" I asked.

"Acting together with someone else."

CHAPTER 9

TOURIST ATTRACTION

September 2009 through January 2010

The most dramatic visual representation of Henry's remains was not a still photo, but rather a video taken by a retired corrections officer from Pittsburgh who worked with the fire department and FEMA after the storm. Ashley got a call from a Pittsburgh TV station that the ex-officer, Istvan Balogh, had given them the video, which they planned to run on the evening news.

The video, shot on September 9, a week after the incineration, didn't tell us much more than we already knew from the still photos we'd studied. Nevertheless, we watched with some astonishment as Balogh, a stocky figure in cargo pants, T-shirt, and wraparound sunglasses, played tour guide at the crime scene: "We found this completely burned-out vehicle. There's a dead body. There's a—looks like a femur right here. And from here you can—there's a skull. It looks like it was shot from the side. Absolutely amazing!" When his associate with the video camera zooms in, the tangle of riverine foliage gives way to the car back seat, washed-out grays and whites, flesh and bone. The skull with a hole in it is plainly front and center.

Balogh had come across the body while traveling around New Orleans documenting scenes of the storm's destruction. One afternoon, he went down to the river to get a better look at a barge that had smashed into the levee when he stumbled upon the burned-out car. Of all the dead bodies he had seen during his volunteer stint, mostly drowning victims, he said, "This was the most suspicious to me."

Balogh said he reported the burned body to multiple law enforcement authorities: federal agents, state police, the military, NOPD. Nevertheless, he told us the authorities didn't seem particularly interested in doing anything about it. Another week would pass before the body disposal team contracted by FEMA arrived to bag the remains and take them to the city morgue.

For Balogh, the existence of a charred body suggested something sinister. He later said, "The magnitude of the way it was destroyed. It was telling a story—'I don't want no one ever to find out what I did.'"

On the flooded east side of the river, it wasn't unusual to see bodies of the deceased lying by the side of the street, on a bridge, on rooftops. The most disturbing images were those of bodies that had been secured to streetlights or buildings during the flooding, only to be left dangling once the waters receded. In Algiers, which was spared most of the flooding, there were fewer bodies, so they attracted more attention.

Henry in death was different. Tanner's Chevy, tucked under heavy underbrush at the base of the levee, was hidden to anyone who didn't know where to look (or, like Balogh, happened to walk along the top of the levee).

But the cops, particularly those from the Fourth District and SOD, whose respective compounds were only blocks away, were well aware of the body's presence. NOPD officers may or may not have known Henry's name, but they knew his case was unusual. Of the over 1,800 people who died after the storm, his was the only corpse that was burned. For the two weeks the remains lay uncollected, cops would stop by to snap pictures. For them, Henry had become something like a post-apocalyptic tourist attraction.

The sheer volume of photographic evidence that came to light—almost all of it produced by members of law enforcement—was overwhelming. At the beginning of the investigation, the best I had hoped for was that we would locate the grainy photos that A.C. Thompson's police source showed him, but that were never published. Ultimately, however, we found photographic documentation of each phase of the violence committed against Henry, the shooting excepted, a crime timeline as it were.

We had photos taken shortly after Henry was shot, multiple sets of photographs taken during the roughly two hours that Henry's bloody, intact body lay in the back seat of the Chevy. Then, thanks to the border protection officers, we had a handful of photos of the car in flames at the levee, and of Henry's charred remains after the fire had burned out. And finally, during that two-week period when his remains sat at the levee, at least ten different law enforcement officers took photos that wound up in our investigation. We had scores of photos, both digital and film, especially remarkable considering that in 2005, few people had "smartphones" with built-in digital cameras. None of the photos we received were "official" photos from an "official" investigation.

Sifting through our photographs of Henry Glover, it was hard not to think about the legacy of lynching. Photography played a prominent role in the extrajudicial executions of thousands of Americans, mostly Black men, mostly in the Jim Crow South, from the late 1800s until the beginning of the 1960s civil rights movement. Lynching victims were murdered in a variety of ways—shot, burned, dismembered—anything that would sufficiently intimidate and terrorize the African American populace. But in the public imagination, lynching became synonymous with hanging, partly because a motionless body hanging from a tree or a lamppost was easier to photograph and made for a more striking image. Sometimes law enforcement officers could be seen standing by approvingly.

Photographs of lynchings had a second life as postcards, which enjoyed a durable regional popularity until the US Post Office banned them in 1908. Other images, published in newspapers and magazines, stirred a national revulsion against lynching, most famously the photograph that ran in *Jet* magazine of the mutilated body of Emmett Till, a fourteen-year-old boy murdered in Mississippi in 1956 for allegedly whistling at a White woman.

But the differences between Glover's death and a lynching seemed to me as instructive as the resonances. Henry was killed by a police officer who had assumed the prerogatives of judge, jury and executioner. But Warren pulled the trigger, not in front of a cheering crowd, but in a nearly deserted city. Henry's body was disposed of in secret, a secrecy we were still trying to crack. And yet the pictures of his dead body proliferated nonetheless.

Most of the photos we had were, as best we knew, taken by cops who played no role in the shooting or the cover-up but who were simply drawn to dramatic, morbid subjects.

I don't know if police are, on average, more drawn to murder and death than the rest of us. It seems that "morbid curiosity" is hardwired into the human psyche. What I know for certain is that police have far more access to gruesome scenes than ordinary civilians. That regular exposure leaves its mark. One of the greatest predictors of "adverse events" for police—from suicide and divorce to use of deadly force—is repeated exposure to traumatic events.

During the course of our investigation, I met many officers who took photographs of Katrina's devastation, including dead bodies, trying to document a once-in-a-lifetime event. But for some of the cops, I sensed, taking photos of dead bodies was a way of keeping the death and destruction they encountered at arm's length. It's a coping mechanism that comes with a price—desensitization. In more extreme cases, cops taking and collecting grisly photos was a part of a macho, locker-room culture that could turn sadistic.

During our investigation, Ashley connected with an FBI agent temporarily dispatched to New Orleans in September 2005 to assist SOD with guarding supplies. One day, he was at Habans making small talk with an SOD officer when the cop whipped out a couple of Polaroids of Henry, dead, lying in the back seat of the Chevy, similar to others we had received. According to the agent, the cop boasted, "Fuck it, he is dead, so we took him behind the levee and burned the car with his body in it." Then, perhaps worried he had said too much to a federal agent, he backpedaled: "Oh, I'm just kidding."

Bragging about Henry's demise seemed a not uncommon occurrence. There were other rumors circulating around the department that SOD officers had boasted of giving Henry a "Viking funeral." In other words, they incinerated him the way the medieval Vikings practiced "ship burials," cremating their dead on boats they set on fire. The Viking imagery was particularly jarring given the racial composition of this case. In recent years, White supremacist groups have appropriated language and symbols from a romanticized Northern European warrior past. While I had no reason to doubt the authenticity of these rumors, once again, we had difficulty finding anyone willing to admit they heard them firsthand.

For Ashley and me, one element of the case that refused to fall into place was Henry's skull. By the time his remains were collected and autopsied, his skull was missing. And yet, as was clear from the photographs and video taken before the federal Disaster Mortuary Relief Team (DMORT) arrived on September 16 to collect the remains, a skull is plainly visible. A skull that appeared to have a bullet hole in the forehead. A skull that disappeared about two days before DMORT showed up to collect it.

This was confounding, because all of the evidence suggested that Warren shot Henry with a single high-caliber round, "center mass," in his torso. The pre-burning photos had no visible trauma to Henry's head.

The more we looked, the more we kept finding evidence that suggested Henry was shot a second time before he was incinerated. Two of the CBP officers had told us that just before they saw the flames and smoke spewing up from behind the levee, they had heard several loud sounds that could have been gunshots.

It seemed highly plausible that whoever had burned Henry's body—and for weeks now, SOD officers Scheuermann and McRae were our leading suspects—had put a bullet in his skull immediately before lighting the car on fire. We hoped that if we could find a bullet, we could test it against our subjects' weapons, and perhaps link them to the burning that way.

Ashley and I tried to figure out why someone would shoot Henry again, when he was almost certainly already dead. Perhaps that person wanted to be absolutely sure. Perhaps Henry's dead body had moved because of travel. Or maybe it was just the coup de grâce, a final gesture of contempt. If an officer *had* shot him in the head, perhaps the shooter later returned to collect the skull and any other physical evidence that might implicate him.

We kicked around other theories. Perhaps the skull was taken by a cop as a grisly trophy. Conceivably, a feral animal made off with it. And this being New Orleans, we considered the possibility that it was taken for use in a voodoo ritual. (I recalled walking into one voodoo shop in the French Quarter, popular with tourists and locals alike, that featured a profusion of gris-gris dolls, talismans, potions, and skull models.) Much later, I looked into this further and was disabused of the notion that theft-by-voodoo was a plausible scenario. While it's true that human bones are sometimes used in vodoun rituals in Haiti and that Haitian emigres first brought the seeds of vodoun to the US, the New Orleans voodoo offshoot generally steers clear of human remains. But we were grasping at straws.

There were moments during the investigation when I worried that I was being affected, even somewhat traumatized, by regular exposure to the graphic images I was seeing every day. Henry's skull became a regular fixture in my dreams.

I had one recurring dream, always in black-and-white, as if I had stepped into a crime movie from the '40s or '50s. In the dream, Ashley and I exit a shotgun-style house; it was never clear whose home it was. Ashley is carrying a large plastic evidence bag with a skull inside it. As she and I step on to the front porch, an old-timey reporter snaps a picture with a massive flashbulb camera. The cracking sound and flashing light always woke me up. I found myself lying in bed, combing through the dream for clues that never materialized.

Ashley and I met a young Fourth District officer as we slowly and methodically worked our way through our list of potential witnesses.

In the days after Katrina, the district officers had a barbecue grill set up behind the police station where they frequently cooked up meals, including food they had taken from the local Walmart. During one such cookout, our officer first learned about the burned car.

"Did you hear they found a car burned out over by levee?" another officer asked. "It had bones in it."

"Where do you think the ribs come from?" a different officer joked.

I left the interview thinking that we had received a disturbing peek into the NOPD post-Katrina psyche, nothing more. Ashley was convinced he had more information. She sensed there was something off about this guy. The officer had distanced himself from the barbecue talk, but he seemed giddy when he talked about the burning of the car and the body.

As usual, Ashley was right. A few days later, she got a call from him. When we met him again, he showed us nine images of Henry's burned remains that he had saved on his cell phone.

The officer seemed particularly fixated on death and skulls. The backdrop of his cell phone was Red Skull, a power-hungry and manipulative character from the Captain America comic books, whose face is, indeed, a red skull. When Ashley later visited the officer's house, she couldn't fail to notice two realistic-looking skulls sitting on his mantelpiece.

During a later interview, Ashley laid out all the photos he had turned over. It was clear from the series that Henry's skull had been moved. The officer's tone got more animated as he admitted to poking the skull with a stick so he could get better angles for his photos. This was hardly unknown in battlefield photography (the images of dead soldiers captured by Mathew Brady's team during the Civil War were often somewhat staged). But it was highly unusual for a police officer to be "improving" a crime scene for artistic reasons.

We wondered if he had done more with Henry's remains than simply moving them a few inches—he seemed like the type of person who might take a skull as a souvenir. He denied it.

We never solved the mystery of Henry's missing skull.

If, as Istvan Balogh said, the levee crime scene was telling a story, we had to decipher it with the limited physical evidence we had.

One of our first steps was taking possession of Tanner's Chevy. When I first arrived in New Orleans in February 2009, Ashley and I drove out to the Patterson Road levee to get a better feel for the area. We were still in Orleans Parish—the city of New Orleans—but it didn't look that way: hardly any people or buildings in sight, just a smattering of river commerce on the banks of the brown, sluggish Mississippi. Much to our surprise, what was left of the car still remained behind the levee, three and a half years after it had gone up in flames. The car now looked ashen-gray, windows completely shattered, with red spray paint marking it as having been cleared by ICE on September 10.

Not long after our investigation began, NOPD moved the car to a department impound lot. But as the department evinced no interest in the car, Ashley and I filled out the paperwork to take possession of it.

When the FBI's Evidence Recovery Team (ERT) picked up the car, it had no tires, no trunk, no seats, and no steering wheel. The car's roof was smashed in, suggesting the car had been upside down at the impound yard, then flipped upright.

We worried that three years and half years of exposure would likely mean we wouldn't find much. But ERT recovered some useful evidence. Mixed in with the debris, it found a flare pin—an inch and a half piece of metal used to ignite a flare—and two blackish blobs of copper metal. Though the FBI would not conclusively call the blobs "bullets," they knew of no other objects with similar metallurgic qualities. This lent credence to our theory that McRae had ignited the car with the road flares Tanner had seen him holding, improbable as that had always seemed. The blobs suggested that at least two shots were fired into the car. Unfortunately, neither the blobs nor the flare pin could be traced back to any specific officer.

Our early reviews of autopsy evidence were similarly unfruitful: a skimpy report, and a few blurry pictures of the charred remains. We suspected that there had to be more, so in late 2009, Tracey and Ashley headed to the coroner's office to examine their files in person. The coroner's office was run by genial, silver-haired, trumpet-playing Frank Minyard, known to some as Dr. Jazz. As in many jurisdictions, coroner in New Orleans is an elected position that does not require any experience conducting autopsies. Minyard was trained in gynecology, not forensic pathology, and yet the law gave him the final authority to determine the cause of death. Initially, Minyard just left the cause of death blank, and later changed the determination to "unclassified."

In later interviews on the topic, he seemed to throw up his hands as to what happened to Henry, "Was he shot, was he hit on the head, did he shoot himself, did he catch himself on fire? All of those kind of things, we can't say."

When Dr. Dana Troxclair, a pathologist in Minyard's office, performed Henry's autopsy in late October '05, she had no idea whose body she was working on. The morgue would not conclusively identify the body through DNA until April 2006, seven months after Henry was killed.

But Troxclair had been told by her superiors that the body had been removed from a car. The radiology department of her office, having observed metallic spots on the X-ray, had told her to be on the lookout for any metal fragments that might indicate a "projectile," i.e., a bullet. Troxclair sifted through the bags by hand. "All we could find was little metal fragments of what appeared to be the car," she said. "As soon as you picked it up, it broke into smaller pieces."

In '05, Dr. Troxclair was a trainee who had been on the job for only two and a half months when the storm hit. She was almost certainly overwhelmed by the post-Katrina combat conditions. She estimated that she personally performed about 155 autopsies in the three months after Katrina, a pace more than double what the National Association of Medical Examiners believes can be performed competently.

But of all the autopsies she performed, this one stood out. Tracey asked her how many of those bodies had been burned. "Just that one," she replied.

Dr. Kevin Whaley, an experienced out-of-state pathologist who had volunteered to help at the besieged coroner's office, had come to the same conclusion as Troxclair. The metal fragments were so deformed by the extreme heat, far in excess of a typical car fire, they couldn't be ID'd as coming from a bullet. If more of Henry's remains had been available for analysis, that likely would have allowed for more definitive conclusions.

"When I heard he was found in a burned car, I thought that was a classic homicide scenario: you kill someone and burn the body to get rid of the evidence," he had said. "This state of all that being gone, that's just really out of the ordinary. That's like Roswell, New Mexico out of the ordinary."

When Tracey was reviewing the coroner's files with Troxclair on the pathologist's computer, a photograph of an almost perfectly preserved 9-mm slug, labeled with Henry's autopsy number, seemed to justify the Roswell comparison.

A 9-mm would validate our theory that Henry had been shot a second time—after all, Warren had killed him with a .223 round. But it seemed improbable that this bullet could have emerged from an estimated two-thousand-degree blaze in such pristine condition.

The coroner's office couldn't explain where this bullet came from, or, perhaps more disturbingly, where it was now. Was it possible the bullet was buried along with Henry Glover?

The condition of the bullet was such that, unlike the blackish balls, we might be able to link the bullet to a gun, and perhaps finally bring more conclusive evidence against the person who burned Henry's body. That is, if we found the bullet.

We reached out to the Glovers to explain the situation. With the family's agreement, we exhumed Henry's body.

The taxi dropped me off at the Carrollton Cemetery one afternoon in mid-December. Located in the Uptown District, home to some of New Orleans's larger, high-priced homes, it seemed an odd place to find a crumbling public cemetery.

The winter air was cool, and the sky appropriately gray. I had assumed that exhuming a body would require a large backhoe violently tearing into the earth. But because so much of the city lies below sea level—a major reason for the extensive flooding after Katrina—people in New Orleans are buried above ground. In this cemetery, most of the dead rest in concrete rectangle structures made of cinder block filled with earth, resembling low-budget flower boxes. Because burial space is at a premium, these graves accommodate multiple bodies. Henry was buried in a crypt at the corner of the cemetery.

I worried the scene would be chaotic. Ashley and I had heard that news of the exhumation was circulating around NOPD, and if that information were leaked to the media, this sad, grim moment might turn into a media circus.

But the only people in attendance were six FBI agents in jeans and Bureau windbreakers and an assorted cast of locals assisting with the job. The cemetery caretaker, a graying Black man in overalls, sat to the side with a rusty shovel, next to his assistant, who looked to be in his teens. A hearse driver stood nearby, a White man outfitted per New Orleans tradition in a tuxedo complete with top hat and tails. He would drive Henry's remains to the Jef-

ferson Parish Medical Examiner's Office, where an FBI pathologist would conduct a second autopsy.

The lead agent from the FBI's evidence recovery team nodded
to the caretaker, who, in turn, looked at the boy and told him to
dig. I stood by uncomfortably.

I have never been particularly good at handling death. I'm never
quite sure how I'm supposed to feel or how I really do feel. I'm
skeptical about the existence of an afterlife, and yet am not quite
prepared to write it off entirely. Working in conflict zones in the
midst of so much religion-inspired violence had caused my own
faith to dwindle. And yet here, the only thing that felt right was
to go back to the traditions of my childhood.

I lowered my head and quietly recited the traditional Jewish
prayer of mourning, the *Kaddish*. Written in the ancient language
of Aramaic, the *Kaddish* makes no mention of death. Instead, it is
a prayer of exaltation to a higher spirit that ends with the request
that the maker of peace in heaven also make peace for those of
us down here on earth. It was the prayer I said when my mother
died two years earlier, and the prayer I said when I visited Asel's
grave a decade before.

After the Or Commission found Asel's shooting unjustified, it
fell to the Israeli attorney general's office to determine whether
anyone could be prosecuted. As a part of its investigation, the AG
asked the Asleh family to exhume Asel's body to perform a much-
after-the-fact autopsy. Because Islamic religious tradition forbids
disturbing the dead, and lacking any confidence in the Israeli investigation, the family denied the government's request. In closing
its investigation, the AG cited the lack of an autopsy as a key reason for not bringing charges, though this same office never made
any real effort to pressure Asel's presumed killer to give an explanation for his actions.

As I stood next to the grave, I thought about Henry's family.
So much violence had been done to their son and to his body, and
yet they trusted us to disturb him one more time, with the hope
of holding someone accountable for what had happened.

We didn't find the pristine bullet that day, or any bullet. The bullet from the photo, labeled with Henry's autopsy number, most likely was misnumbered and placed in Henry's file by mistake. Where it actually came from was anyone's guess. I worried that we had let the Glover family down.

CHAPTER 10

WRONG PLACE, WRONG TIME

September 2009 through March 2010

Early in our investigation, Ashley and I interviewed Fourth District homicide detective Sergeant Ronald Ruiz. Keyalah Bell had seen him at Habans on September 2. She told us he had looked inside the Chevy and callously pronounced Henry "a good 30," NOPD lingo for a clear-cut homicide case. Ruiz was in his early thirties, chatty, cocksure, and working his way up the ranks.

On September 2, 2005, Ruiz was patrolling the streets of Algiers in his squad car with his partner. When he heard a call over the radio about a gunshot victim arriving at Habans, he headed over there.

Ruiz denied saying anything about "a good 30" because he claimed he never saw anything that looked like a homicide. He hadn't seen the white Chevy or the body in the back seat. All he noticed during his visit to the school were some Black men on their knees in handcuffs surrounded by a bunch of SOD officers. The scene looked under control, no yelling or violence, so he left after five minutes (naturally).

The interview yielded little new information, but then the next day, Ruiz called Ashley and said he wanted to speak again. Ashley seemed to have a knack for winning the trust of witnesses who were on the fence about coming clean. Unfortunately, our next interview with Ruiz wasn't much different than the first. The only encouraging thing was that he seemed perfectly willing to keep talking to us.

Lots of prosecutors and investigators don't like taking multiple statements from witnesses. Generally, more interviews mean more inconsistent statements, which in turn makes these witnesses more vulnerable later at trial. Overall, I've found the trade-off is usually worth it. Sometimes witnesses will remember new things that hadn't seemed important before; sometimes, as you build rapport, witnesses become more forthcoming.

Gaining trust is especially crucial in police misconduct investigations. It's hard to make a successful police prosecution without cooperating police witnesses, and in my experience, few police officers tell the whole story the first time around. Getting to the truth often requires keeping a witness talking, which often means being lied to multiple times. Ashley and I kept setting up meetings with Ruiz, and Ruiz kept accepting. We figured he had something he wanted to get off his chest. Either that or he just enjoyed our company.

In mid-September 2009, Ruiz called Ashley up to arrange for yet another interview, this time accompanied by a lawyer. In this, our fourth meeting, the sergeant owned up to making the "good 30" comment. He said it was pretty obvious: there was a dead gunshot victim in the car.

More instructive was Ruiz telling us in more detail all the things he *didn't* do that day. He said that there were obvious steps he could have taken had he been asked to investigate. He would have interviewed the three men at the school separately to get their stories. He would have gone over to the mall to collect physical evidence, take photographs, and document the crime scene. However, Ruiz said, "I was advised that SOD was handling it and…was going to generate whatever report that they needed to generate…"

It was hard to understand why SOD, a tactical unit, would investigate a homicide. Ruiz, like Josh Burns before him, confirmed that at Habans, Italiano and Scheuermann walked away from the scene together to have a conversation. Also, like Burns, Ruiz didn't know what exactly was said. Whatever was said, it didn't involve having a homicide investigator investigate a homicide, so Ruiz got back in his squad car and resumed patrolling Algiers.

This interview with Ruiz was a rambling, repetitive multi-hour affair. But the lawyer regularly stopped to take smoke breaks, which allowed Ashley and I to recalibrate our strategy. We zeroed in on the burning, since previously Ruiz had told us he had seen the smoke coming from the levee not long after he left the school.

"Walk us through what happened after you left Habans," Ashley asked.

Ruiz shifted in his seat and laughed nervously, suggesting he was about to tell us something he knew we desperately wanted to know. He said that after leaving Habans, he drove towards the Fourth District station. On the way, he passed Dwayne Scheuermann and Greg McRae driving a truck coming from the direction of the Patterson Road levee.

Five or ten minutes later, Ruiz saw smoke rising from the levee. Shortly thereafter, he heard rumors Scheuermann and McRae had burned the car with a road flare.

Though hardly conclusive, Ruiz's testimony was the best admissible evidence we had to establish who set fire to the car and Henry's body.

February 2010 marked the one-year anniversary of our investigation. Things were changing. New Orleans was slowly pulling itself out of its post-Katrina despond—I was sharing my favorite bars with more out-of-town visitors and, something not to be underestimated in a sports-mad town, the New Orleans Saints won the 2010 Super Bowl.

One thing hadn't changed. Even though we'd devoted much of the past six months to solving the burning, I wasn't convinced we had a winnable case against Dwayne Scheuermann and Greg McRae.

We certainly had a *chargeable* case. William Tanner had seen McRae drive off with the Chevy with Henry inside, and the ATF photo confirmed Tanner's assertion that the officer had been carrying road flares. A flare pin had been found in the burned car. When Alex Brandon, the *Times-Pic* photographer, asked what happened to the body, McRae replied, "NAT," or "Necessary Action Taken." And according to Josh Burns, our ex-SOD brothel robber, McRae had told him that he had helped another officer "get rid of the car." Most persuasive of all, Ruiz had seen Scheuermann and McRae driving together in a truck away from the levee area just minutes before he'd seen the plume of smoke.

It was a decent circumstantial case, but I had reservations that it would convince a New Orleans jury to convict two NOPD officers. After all, no one had actually seen McRae or Scheuermann burn the car, and McRae's comments to Brandon were arguably open to interpretation. I anticipated the two officers would likely testify in court that they had left the car by the levee because they didn't know what else to do with the body, and they had no idea what happened to it after that. That story, however unlikely on its face, might easily constitute reasonable doubt in jurors' minds. Only one juror needed to entertain such doubt for a hung jury, and a mistrial.

I felt we needed more, but time was not on our side. There was no statute of limitations for the charges against Warren for killing Henry. For any other crimes, the statute of limitations clock ran out after five years, which was only six months away.

I couldn't even conceive of what new evidence would pull the case over the finish line. I had hoped that some SOD officer who had talked to McRae and Scheuermann after the fact would give us something incriminating. But a year in, and hundreds of police officer interviews completed, nothing had popped. Then we stumbled on Lieutenant Joseph Meisch.

Meisch had been on our list of people to interview since one of the SOD officers we talked to during our quest to find Alec Brown had dropped his name the previous summer. (At the time, we only knew him as "FNU Meisch," FBI shorthand for "first name unknown.") When we finally connected with Meisch's lawyer, he told us that his client would only speak to us if we granted him immunity. That startled us. We had no reason to think Meisch had any criminal exposure in this case. What was he worried about? Perhaps he knew something useful.

Meisch ultimately received "use" immunity, which meant that we could not use his own words against him, nor could we use new evidence derived from him against him, but would compel him to testify about what he knew. This immunity required complete honesty—he could neither exaggerate or minimize—and if he did, he could be prosecuted for perjury or obstruction of justice. Meisch accepted, and towards the end of February 2010, Ashley, Tracey and I met him at his attorney's office.

Meisch was my age, early thirties, with the look of a Boy Scout troop leader. He was rising up NOPD's ranks, making lieutenant while still in his twenties. A month before Katrina hit, he transferred to the Fourth District at Major Kirsch's request with the expectation that he would head up its DIU after Italiano's impending retirement.

After the storm hit, Meisch took on a random assortment of odd jobs. He set up a medical aid station, and helped secure and later manage a Walmart that had been commandeered by the police as a de facto supply depot. He was one of the officers who responded to the Kevin Thomas shooting.

On September 2, Meisch sweated in the late summer heat, part of a thrown-together work detail of Fourth District officers and border protection agents clearing brush outside the CBP compound, attempting to level a helicopter landing pad so much needed supplies could arrive by air. The Fourth District officers had recently confiscated a bulldozer from civilians who had been joyriding it through the streets of Algiers.

That morning, things were not going well. A border patrol of-

ficer, inexperienced with heavy machinery, ran the bulldozer over
a water pipe that was connected to a fire hydrant, sending water
gushing into the sky, flooding into the street, and cutting off water
to the station. According to Meisch, "…[W]ater was about the only
thing we did have at that point, and we lost it."

The young lieutenant now had to deal with a crisis on top of
a crisis. Around this time, he told us, he noticed a white car, followed by a small pickup truck, driving along the gravel road that
tops the Patterson Road levee. Then the car suddenly disappeared
off the back side of the levee. "I looked up and saw the car actually drove towards the river and off the edge of the levee and dip
down out of my sight," Meisch said, "like driving off a cliff." A
truck pulled up and parked next to where the car had disappeared.

Meisch worried about the safety of whoever was in the car and
jogged over to investigate. "It definitely piqued my curiosity." As
he got closer, he noticed smoke rising from behind the levee. He
said he saw a person running down from the top of it. Then from
the corner of his eye, he saw another person coming down the
levee diagonally from the direction of the truck.

As they got closer, he identified the two men as Greg McRae
and Dwayne Scheuermann. Meisch had known McRae casually, a
fellow officer, for about a decade. He had once worked for Scheuermann on a task force, and off and on since then, and considered
him a friend.

With the smoke billowing behind them, the two officers trot-
ted up to him. Meisch asked if they were all right and whether
they needed any help.

"Don't worry about it," McRae told him. McRae seemed to
be laughing.

"Laughing like someone had just played a joke?" Tracey asked.

Meisch explained, "…[L]ike a humorous or a nervous laugh,
laughter. I mean, it wasn't like…an all-out roar laughter like you
had just watched a comedy show, but…I guess as much as you
could laugh after having just run down a levee."

Scheuermann, he said, had a "blank, like, nonchalant look about
his face, just expressionless." Neither man seemed concerned about

the fire behind them. The lieutenant reassured him: "It's all right. I'm handling it. I got it."

For the moment, that was good enough for Meisch. Another more senior lieutenant had taken responsibility for the situation. Meisch already had more than enough on his hands as the water main break flooded Richland Street, which ran alongside the station. While Scheuermann and McRae hung out for a few minutes to talk with the Border agents at the nearby CBP compound, Meisch headed back to the station and met up with the district commander, Major Kirsch.

Meisch told us that within days after the storm, his relationship with Kirsch had deteriorated under the stress of Katrina conditions. He broke the news about the water main break, and Kirsch chewed him out for loaning CBP the bulldozer. Meisch didn't mention the fire behind the levee, or the SOD cops who were supposedly taking care of it.

Four or five nights later, Meisch climbed up to the levee to try to get better cell reception on higher ground. He held his phone in the air trying to find a signal. It was pitch-black dark—the city's power was still out—but looking down through the foliage, he saw the outline of the car that had disappeared from the levee road. The smell of burned metal and rubber still hung in the air.

Meisch scrambled down the embankment to get a better look at the car. He flipped on his flashlight, and the beam of light struck what appeared to be a human rib cage. He recoiled from the horror movie image and fled back to the station. He didn't tell anyone what he had seen for four-plus years when he confided in his attorney, and then us.

We pressed him on why he chose to remain silent when he had had nothing to do with whatever crime had been committed on his turf.

"My basic thought process was that even if it was a rib cage...I had a lieutenant [Scheuermann] who I know very well and have a great amount of respect for say he was dealing with it. So my assumption was basically whatever paperwork or investigation that had to be done, he was handling it."

★ ★ ★

Meisch's testimony, however late, substantially narrowed down possible SOD defenses. No longer could McRae and Scheuermann claim that they didn't know what happened to the car after they moved it. They would have to admit to burning the car and somehow justify it. Their best defense, I assumed, would be to say they made a difficult "public health" decision. If that were true, why was McRae laughing?

We would need to persuade a jury that a man had been fatally shot by a police officer without justification, that this man's body had been the only one burned in New Orleans after Katrina, and *that* couldn't be a coincidence.

A few days after our first sit-down with Meisch, we got a call from his attorney asking for a meeting. I drove to his attorney's office with Tracey. As we turned onto Canal Street, we noticed a blue pickup truck trailing us. As we pulled into the attorney's parking lot, the truck entered an adjacent lot. We walked into the office, unable to make out the driver.

We encountered Meisch in the attorney's conference room, clearly shaken up. The day after our first interview, Scheuermann had shown up at Meisch's office and asked about our meeting. Meisch was spooked. He insisted that he hadn't told anybody he had met with us.

Before that day, Meisch had had ten or fifteen run-ins with Scheuermann during the course of the federal investigation. Meisch told us he had always thought those encounters were random. During those interactions, Scheuermann would bring up the Glover investigation, and tell Meisch, "Just tell the truth." Scheuermann would also say things like, "We're not going to deny what happened." He would often throw in a comment like, "Greg made a stupid mistake."

After the most recent interaction, Meisch had to reconsider that these previous interactions were random.

Scheuermann had asked Meisch about our recent interview. Meisch told Scheuermann he was surprised by a question we asked about hearing gunshots at the levee. Meisch told Scheuermann he hadn't heard any shots, but that could have been because of the bulldozer.

Scheuermann then looked at Meisch, lowered his head, and "made a gun motion, like he was simulating a pistol, and said, 'Well, Greg did shoot out the window to ventilate the car.'"

Meisch was unnerved by what he felt were Scheuermann's attempts to manipulate him. Given the high-stakes nature of the investigation and the lieutenant's history of misconduct allegations, Meisch worried about harm to himself or his family.

We were nervous too. How *did* Scheuermann know about our meeting with Meisch? By now, we were used to leaks. Grand jury appearances, for instance, were supposed to be secret, and yet which NOPD officers had testified seemed to become common knowledge, sometimes even appearing in the newspaper. We assumed information leaked out from the attorneys representing NOPD officer witnesses, or from courthouse security, most of whom were retired cops.

But this breach of security was of a different order. I worried that it had to have come from inside one of the law enforcement organizations that was working the case: the DOJ, the New Orleans US Attorney's Office, or the New Orleans FBI. All I knew for sure was that it didn't come from my team. No one ever established the source of the leak.

When the meeting concluded, Tracey and I headed back to her car. The blue truck was still there in the adjacent parking lot. As we drove off, so did the truck.

Meisch wasn't our only witness having unplanned encounters with Dwayne Scheuermann.

In an interview with Simmons later in the investigation, she told us about a supposedly chance run-in she had with Scheuermann at a local supermarket. The lieutenant told her that he had in his possession, somehow, a copy of her original Signal 21 report.

This was exciting, the possibility of documentary proof that her report had been doctored. We even had a very nervous Simmons make a recorded phone call to see if we could catch Scheuermann on tape referring to her "original" report. He never used that word on the call but he did say he had "both" reports and implied that he would send her a copy of her original report. He didn't. We doubted Scheuermann ever had such a thing.

A final witness offered up a late-in-the-game revelation.

We continued meeting with Linda Howard throughout the winter and spring, as we inched closer to an indictment. Over time, she grew more comfortable with our team, particularly Ashley and Tracey, two fellow Black women in law enforcement.

Ashley arranged a meeting with Howard to go over the case. This time, she offered some new information. Howard told us that when she and Warren first arrived at the mall, they engaged in small talk, when, abruptly changing tack, Warren asked her, "Did you know, we are under martial law?"

Howard responded, "Well, I don't know anything about martial law, but I do know the same laws that you have to follow as a police officer before the storm are the same laws that you have to follow now."

Warren didn't say anything. He just nodded his head, as in, "whatever." From time to time, he got up from his chair and casually strolled the balcony. He kept lifting his gun, peeking through the scope, and scanning the horizon.

Howard noticed a Black man walking across the mall's front parking lot about 150 yards away. As far as she could tell, this was a regular civilian going about his business. The man didn't seem threatening and stood out only because the neighborhood was so empty.

She pointed him out to Warren. Warren lifted his rifle and pointed it at the Black man at the far end of the parking lot. He fired one shot.

The man crouched down, looked around, and then started running towards the main street.

Howard was shocked, and yelled at her partner, *what the hell are you doing?* Warren was blasé. "Don't worry about it." Then he added, "I just wanted to see something. What's the big deal?"

Howard explained the obvious, that even though there were only a few people around, a bullet could ricochet off a building and hit somebody. Warning shots were expressly prohibited by NOPD.

He shrugged. "I didn't hit him."

Not long after that, Henry Glover and Bernard Calloway pulled up behind the mall in the Firestone truck, and Warren fired the shot that killed Henry Glover.

We knew Howard's fuller account could significantly bolster our case against Warren. A jury would have a much easier time believing that Warren shot Henry without justification knowing that earlier that morning, he'd used potentially lethal force against a different unarmed, unthreatening civilian.

We believed Howard's story was true. Tracey, Ashley and I had come to know her over the course of a year's worth of conversations, and we trusted her. But how could we ever independently corroborate it? I couldn't imagine we'd ever find the man who had been shot at, and I didn't think there was any way Warren would ever admit to firing his weapon at an unarmed civilian hundreds of feet away.

We asked Howard why it had taken her so long to tell us about this event. She didn't have much of an answer other than to say she hadn't thought about it before.

Ashley and Tracey believed they had a line into some of what Howard had gone through as a member of that first generation of Black women hired by the NOPD.

"I could just imagine what it was like to be a Black female in NOPD in the '80s," Ashley told me later. "I felt that for years and years, she just suppressed her emotions. You never want to come off as 'the angry Black female.' And so she never spoke up for herself. Even when Italiano asked her whether it was a 'good shot,' she didn't say anything, just sort of shrugged her shoulders and shook her head, 'no.'"

As summer got nearer, we had sufficient evidence to indict five officers for their involvement in this case: David Warren for killing Henry Glover; Dwayne Scheuermann and Greg McRae for burning Henry's body and Tanner's car; and Robert Italiano and Travis McCabe for the false report following the shooting.

The closer we got to indictment day, the more the potential threat to our team and our witnesses seemed to escalate. Meisch and Simmons were still unnerved that Scheuermann had been following them, even though he had since receded into the woodwork. One civilian witness believed he was being tailed by Fourth District police officers, who seemed to be nearby whenever he left his home.

Even more alarming, one night Tracey got a call from her home security company that her alarm had gone off and that her house was being broken into. She rushed home to find a handful of NOPD officers hanging out on her porch, her house wide open, having presumably been searched by the cops. "I lived in Algiers, right in the Fourth District, so I felt I couldn't call the police if something really did happen," Tracey told me later.

To top it off, an attorney who represented key witnesses in both the Glover and Danziger Bridge cases received a death threat.

I had been worried about my own safety since November 2009 when FBI agents caught an officer on tape using violent language to describe a prosecutor handling a different case. The FBI assumed that the officers involved in our case were likely saying similar things about me.

By then, Ashley's boss, Kelly, learned of my after-work music habit. Kelly didn't like the idea of me wandering around New Orleans at night by myself, so she assigned an armed agent to accompany me whenever I went out at night.

For a few weeks, that task fell to a temporary duty agent named Nathan, a former Seattle tech guy turned rookie FBI agent. When he wasn't looking out for me, he was helping Ashley chase down case leads.

Nathan was about my height, five-foot-nine, and slim, certainly not my image of an imposing bodyguard. The first night I went out with him, I noticed the edge of his bulletproof vest protruding from under his short-sleeved button-down shirt. Not reassuring.

One night, early in our partnership, Nathan and I had dinner

on Frenchmen Street, and then we went to listen to some traditional jazz at the Spotted Cat, a standing-room-only dive bar. The
sizable eclectic crowd—mixed races, ages, and genders—danced
together in celebration, the embodiment of New Orleans's *laissez
les bon ton rouler* ("let the good times roll") spirit.

However, there is nothing like having a bodyguard to make
you aware of your own mortality. I realized how easily someone
could kill me if they wanted to. I found my mind drifting to the
logistics. If someone wanted to kill me, how would they do it?

It seemed unlikely that my hit man would want to shoot up a
crowded bar. Most likely, he'd stab me, and there would be no way
for Nathan to stop it in time. But I was betting that he would catch
my killer, and that might help Ashley find the evidence we needed
to secure some convictions. I went back to enjoying the music.

As we got closer to indictments, I stopped going out at night,
even with a bodyguard. There just seemed to be too many suspicious happenings connected to NOPD and the case. All of us on
the prosecution team were on edge, even though it was impossible to know just how worried we should be. But we were dealing
with a police department that had two of its former members sitting on death row. It didn't feel right to risk Nathan's life to satisfy
my appetite for music.

So instead, I found myself regularly sitting at the hotel bar at
night and watching whatever was on TV. For three months, that
meant watching crude oil spill into the Gulf of Mexico after BP's
oil rig, the Deepwater Horizon, exploded, killing eleven workers, dumping an estimated 1.5 million gallons of crude oil *per day*
into the Gulf, and decimating Louisiana's fishing and tourism in-
dustries just as they were beginning to come back from Katrina.
Even on the rebound, this city couldn't catch a break.

PART II

PRE-TRIAL

CHAPTER 11

CHARGED

June through July 2010

On a warm Friday afternoon, June 10, Ashley, Tracey and I stood on the steps of the federal courthouse in the center of downtown, behind the US Attorney for the Eastern District of Louisiana. James "Jim" Letten, DOJ's chief law enforcement officer in the district, announced the indictment of five New Orleans Police Department officers in the Glover case. Facing us on the plaza was a small army of about twenty local media, TV and print journalists, cameras and microphones aimed in our direction, ready to capture the moment for the evening news.

"We are absolutely committed to bring those who have violated the sacred rights of our citizens to justice," Letten told the assembled reporters, "in the hope that our pursuit will give the people of New Orleans confidence in the protection of honest and professional law enforcement."

Normally, I don't feel much emotion over an indictment. Getting a grand jury to return an indictment is generally a low bar, the whole "ham sandwich" thing. Generally, indictments just mean we've reached the legal starting line.

And yet I felt overwhelmed by the significance of the moment, that our team managed to unearth evidence of serious misconduct by the police. When Ashley and I first met Patrice Glover sixteen months earlier, she told us, "We just want to know what happened." While there was a lot we still didn't know, we had identified the police officers who killed Henry Glover and burned his body, something few people within the DOJ or FBI had thought was possible. That alone felt like a victory. I've learned as a civil rights lawyer, victories can be few and far between, so when they arrive, celebrate them.

But Patrice had also told us that her family wanted justice. That, I knew, was the tougher challenge. I wondered whether any jury would be willing to second-guess the decisions of police officers in those fraught days after Katrina. Would a jury find that we had sufficiently proven that the police burned Henry's body to cover up an unjustified shooting?

And even if a jury returned convictions, would that give the Glover family, and the larger community, a sense of "justice"? Perhaps "retribution." Maybe even "vindication." But "justice," in these circumstances, seemed like an almost impossibly lofty goal.

In the two years I had spent, off and on, in New Orleans, I'd fallen for the city—its culture, the food, the music, especially the music. I loved that a city some had written off as not worth saving had come back from the brink. Still, I had to wonder whether this city was ready to reckon with its disturbing racial history.

The indictment unsealed that morning brought eleven charges against five different officers. Our case against the indicted officers was, in a word, complicated. The allegations covered a period of four years, starting with the events of September 2 (the killing, the beating, the burning), through the false police documentation in December 2005, and continuing all the way through the lies and evasions of NOPD after we'd begun our federal investigation in 2009.

In essence, the indictment could be divided into three different sections: the shooting at the mall; the beating at Habans and the burning at the levee; and the false reporting that followed.

The first two charges in the indictment covered David Warren's killing of Henry Glover.

Count one was a "civil rights" charge that accused Warren of depriving Henry Glover of his constitutional rights. The statute—18 USC section 242—prohibits police officers or anyone acting "under the color of law" from "willfully" depriving individuals of constitutional rights spelled out in the Bill of Rights and subsequent constitutional amendments.

Most people don't think of murder as a civil rights violation, but Henry's killing was also a grievous abuse of state power, violating the Fourth Amendment's prohibition against "unreasonable search and seizure." The courts have found that officers who use "unreasonable force" against an arrestee have, in the language of the amendment, "seized" that person.

On its own, a violation of the Fourth Amendment is only a misdemeanor, punishable by up to a year in prison. However, the statute provides for increasing penalties, depending on the nature of the crime. In this case, we alleged that Warren used a dangerous weapon, that the shooting resulted in Henry's death, and that Warren intended to kill Glover. The last "enhancement," "intent to kill," might seem superfluous, but given uncertainties on the timing of Glover's death and the fact that he might have been shot in the head by someone other than Warren, we gave the jury multiple options for finding Warren guilty. Charged in this way, he faced up to life in prison or the death penalty. (Not long after indictment, the attorney general opted not to seek the death penalty in this case.)

The second charge against Warren was a weapons charge that piggybacked onto the civil rights charge. The statute prohibits the use of a weapon during a crime of violence, in this case, the shooting of Henry. Because Warren used a weapon, if the jury agreed that Warren had indeed violated Henry's civil rights, it would set off a mandatory ten-year sentence, on top of whatever sentence he received for the civil rights charge. Additionally, the count alleged that the circumstances surrounding that shooting constituted "murder." If a jury found that Warren acted "deliberately and intentionally" or with "callous and wanton disregard for human life," then Warren would likely receive an even more severe sentence. But to me, more important than the sentence itself was the acknowledgment that when law enforcement intentionally takes the life of a person without justification, it's murder, and we should call it such.

The second set of charges, five separate counts, covered the conduct of McRae and Scheuermann, in two separate events: the beating of Henry's three handcuffed allies at the school and the subsequent burning of Tanner's car and Henry's body at the levee.

Like the first count against Warren, the beating at Habans was charged as a violation of the Fourth Amendment, though since no one died, the maximum penalty was ten years' imprisonment. The supporting evidence came wholly from the testimony of Calloway, Tanner and King since, up to this point, we hadn't gotten a single officer to admit to seeing the beating. Normally, I would be reluctant to charge an excessive force case on the word of the victims alone. Of all the charges against McRae and Scheuermann, I felt this would be the most difficult to win. But Tanner, Calloway, and King had proven to be reliable witnesses, and I believed that a jury would find them credible as well. At the very least, charging the beating signaled that we believed the three men.

We charged the burning in multiple ways to maximize our chances of securing a conviction. The most straightforward charge was another civil rights violation, asserting that McRae and Scheuermann deprived Tanner of his constitutional rights to his property by destroying his car. This was probably the easiest charge to prove, even in the context of Katrina, an almost textbook case of "unreasonable search and seizure." Police aren't allowed to confiscate your possessions, much less burn them, just because they are the police.

We also charged the two SOD officers with obstruction of justice. For a jury to convict, we'd have to establish that the defendants destroyed evidence with "the intent to impede, obstruct or influence" an investigation into the shooting of Henry Glover. The burning of the car and Henry's body certainly had impeded an investigation, so much so, it wasn't until A.C. Thompson wrote his article three and a half years after the fact that anyone seriously looked into what happened. Did we have enough to overcome "reasonable doubt" about the cops consciously trying to cover up the shooting? The case against McRae and Scheuermann was circumstantial; we never found a witness who said the officers knew about Warren's shooting.

I also wanted the indictment to address the impact the burning of Henry's body had on his family. So, we charged a civil rights violation in a way that, to my knowledge, had never been done before.

In a handful of conversations Tracey and I had at the courthouse with McRae's attorney, Frank DeSalvo, he said something to the effect that "dead people don't have civil rights." Generally speaking, that's true. But Henry's surviving family members did.

American jurisprudence allows a victim's survivors to bring civil lawsuits to recover damages in cases of police misconduct. This is known as the right of "access to courts." We alleged that by burning Henry's body, the police prevented Henry's survivors from finding out what had happened to him and to receive financial compensation for the harm done to him.

"Access to the courts" had been firmly established in civil cases—that is, plaintiffs suing for damages—but, as best I could tell, never as the basis for a criminal charge. It seemed to me that this novel legal theory fit perfectly in this case, and my DOJ supervisors authorized us to charge it for the first time.

Finally, we charged McRae and Scheuermann with a "fire enhancement"—using fire during the commission of a federal offense. If the jury found the two officers guilty of any of the federal crimes committed at the levee, and that fire was used, it would trigger a mandatory ten-year sentence. The rationale for these "mandatory minimums"—which Warren's weapons charge also carried—is that their severity deters future crime.

The truth is, I've grown to hate mandatory minimums. They've been a major contributor to America's mass incarceration problem. In many jurisdictions, there are massive racial disparities in how they are used. They remove a judge's ability to fashion a fair sentence that considers the totality of a defendant's circumstances. Because the penalties are often so extreme, these mandatory minimums force guilty pleas, leading to excessively punitive sentences and, sometimes, people pleading to crimes they did not commit. Moreover, there is ample research that they don't actually deter crime. Fifteen years inside the criminal legal system has convinced me that we should significantly limit the use of mandatory minimums.

But as a young prosecutor, I used all the tools at my disposal. My hope was that the big hammer of the fire charge would push McRae to take a guilty plea, which in turn would lead us up the NOPD chain of command.

Last, we charged Italiano and McCabe with aiding and abetting each other, creating a false narrative of the Warren shooting. Italiano was charged with intentionally giving the FBI false information about the missing persons report, the police report, and the connection between the shooting and the burning; McCabe with making false statements both to the FBI and the grand jury about his sanitized Signal 21 incident report.

In all, eleven charges, against five defendants. My fourth jury trial—the third took place during the Glover investigation—would be the most complex case I would ever handle.

One person not named in the indictments was Gerard Dugue, a malign, though mostly unseen, presence throughout our investigation. Officer Linda Howard told us that Detective Sergeant Dugue had pressured her to give a statement implying she didn't see the shooting. Sergeant Nina Simmons told us Dugue showed her the sanitized narrative of the Glover shooting before her grand jury appearance and implied she should testify in line with the official report. His investigation into the Glover case seemed designed to hobble ours. But Dugue was a loose end that we didn't need to tie up. By the time of the Glover indictments, he was entangled in a different Katrina-era police shooting, on the Danziger Bridge.

Two days after Glover was killed, NOPD officers responded to a call of "shots fired" at the Danziger Bridge, a nearly mile-long bridge that crosses the Industrial Canal in the eastern part of the city. The officers arrived at the call armed with assault rifles and shotguns, storming the bridge and killing two unarmed people, a teenager and a man with intellectual disabilities, seriously wounding four others. The bloodbath notwithstanding, after the shooting, the officers were hailed as heroes who had defended the city against armed criminals.

A year later, it was the official narrative that was under attack. Civil lawsuits filed on behalf of the victims who crossed the bridge that day alleged that the police had opened fire on civilians for no apparent reason, falsely arrested one of them, and then covered up the entire affair. One family was walking across the bridge trying to escape the city on foot; the other family was trying to find supplies for a diabetic grandmother.

What exactly precipitated the shooting may never be entirely known. An NOPD officer had put out a radio call that two Black males fired their weapons near the bridge, and that an officer's life was in danger. In response, a group of officers from NOPD's Seventh District, which had set up a base nearby, piled into the back of a Budget rental truck and sped off to the bridge. Upon arrival, the officer driving the truck fired "warning shots" out his window. Another officer fired his rifle at the Black civilians. The other officers followed suit, bombarding the civilians with gunfire until the bridge was littered with bodies, the bleeding, and the dead. One officer ran up to the mortally wounded Ronald Madison, the man with intellectual disabilities, and stomped the remaining life out of him with his heavy boots.

The official report justified the shooting, stating that the officers had come under fire from civilians, and had fired back in self-defense. But glaring inconsistencies began to turn up in the NOPD account of the incident, first unearthed by the legal team representing the older brother of one of the men who had been murdered, who had himself been initially, and falsely, charged with attempted murder for firing at the police. Seven officers were charged with murder in state court, but the process of getting at the truth was short-circuited before it could begin. In August 2008, the judge slated to hear the state criminal case against the officers threw out all the charges, ruling that the prosecution had improperly used immunized statements to get the state grand jury indictment.

Following the collapse of the state case, Bobbi Bernstein, the DOJ supervisor who had assigned me the Glover case, came to New Orleans to lead an investigation into the shooting and the cover-up that followed. Bobbi and her team did what Ashley and I were never able to do in Glover. They flipped some of the cops who were in on the conspiracy, and one even wore a wire. And whereas our case was challenging owing to the absence of evidence, Bobbi and her team had to sort through an abundance of the fake variety.

Search warrants of NOPD computers revealed the existence of multiple, and very different, versions of what ultimately became the official fifty-four-page NOPD report of the incident at the bridge. Journalist Ronnie Greene, in his *Shots on the Bridge*, captures the creative process behind the elaborate cover-up.

"The police story that began to emerge in black and white was more like an airbrushed Hollywood screenplay than an official recounting of that devastating morning… And like a screenplay going up the line in the studio for notes…the police reports went up the line to supervisors, who sent back comments, wrote through confusing passages, and strove to craft a Hollywood ending."

Detective Dugue was accused of playing a key role in this cover-up. Detective Jeffrey Lehrman, one of the first officers to cooperate in the federal investigation, later testified at trial that in January 2006, he and the two co-authors of the official NOPD report, Dugue and Sergeant Arthur "Archie" Kaufman, met with the shooters to rehearse them. "I call it a secret meeting," Lehrman said, "because Dugue told us in the meeting, he said, 'Look, this never happened. I'll never admit this meeting occurred.' And what the meeting was, it was, basically, 'Okay, this is the story, everybody read the report, everybody know what you're going to say, so we can put it on tape and take the statements.'"

That was the Dugue we were familiar with, a company man, a "cleaner," who could tidy up after a questionable police shooting. His report co-author, Kaufman, played more of a lead role in the cover-up. In the pressurized "writer's room" atmosphere at the Seventh District, Kaufman hollered out, "Give me a name!" (To flesh out an invented witness to the shooting, Lehrman came up with "Lakeisha," which eventually became make-believe witness Lakeisha Smith.)

Kaufman also devised a solution to a major problem in the police narrative: no gun had ever been found on either of the two men who allegedly fired on the cops. Six weeks after the shooting, Kaufman drove a handful of NOPD colleagues to his house and emerged from his garage holding a paper bag. When asked what was inside, Kaufman told the officers it was a "ham sandwich," which, in this case, meant a "clean" or untraceable gun. (Not the apocryphal ham sandwich that a grand jury would be willing to indict.) He placed the Colt .357 Magnum into evidence, claiming that he found it under the bridge the day after the shooting, but forgot to log it in for a month and a half.

The racial dynamics of the Glover and Danziger cases differed. Glover was a black-and-white case: the implicated cops were White and the victims were Black. Danziger was more complicated. While the NOPD investigators who initially cleared the shootings, with the exception of Dugue, were White, four of the seven NOPD shooters were Black. (In the first fabricated report, only the Black officers were alleged to have struck civilians with gunfire.)

But in broad outline, the cases were similar. In both, the NOPD maintained that officers shouldn't be blamed for errors in judgment, or for the absence of a conventional police investigation, because after all, it was Katrina. Some passages in the official report ("It should be noted that after Hurricane Katrina passed, the city of New Orleans was in a state of chaos and confusion") seemed like a carbon copy of the language used in the official Signal 21 report of the Warren shooting. In both cases, the indifference to Black lives was breathtaking. It would be difficult for me to imagine comparable carnage if the families crossing the bridge that morning had been White.

Frankly, I was relieved that both Danziger and Glover were breaking at the same time. Although the local papers and news channels were packed with news about both cases, Danziger definitely had a higher profile. I felt that took some of the pressure off me. Plus, it was a bonus having Bobbi in town. I could bounce ideas off her and not feel like I was, within the DOJ, completely on my own.

Dugue would be prosecuted as a part of the Danziger case, though his portion of the case eventually would be severed from the other defendants.

I only met Dugue the one time in the FBI lobby. Ashley went back to see him once more, still in the early months of the investigation when we were trying to make sense of his taped interview with Linda Howard. Ashley remembers that more was said with looks than with words.

Ashley was usually polite, almost deferential, in our interviews, one reason why our interviewees seemed more willing to confide in her than me. But this time, she recalls, her body language and her tone were angry. She says it communicated something like, "You know what happened…and you're covering it up for them. You're selling out Linda Howard and you're selling out Henry Glover."

He must have read her clearly. Ashley says he gave her a look appealing for racial solidarity and went so far as to say something like, "You get it, don't you?" In other words, *This is what I, a Black person in a position of authority, have to do to survive.*

Six days after the Glover indictment, I returned to the courthouse for arraignment, where defendants appear for a formal reading of the criminal charges, a process typically wrapped up in about five minutes. This arraignment was an event. As I exited the elevator on the fourth floor of the courthouse and headed towards the courtroom, I waded through a throng of people lined up to enter the already packed room. Never had I seen this many people at a trial, much less a pro forma procedural hearing. (Among the crowd, I recognized the journalist A.C. Thompson, whose investigative reporting had sparked our investigation.)

I walked down the center aisle of the large cherrywood courtroom to take my place with Tracey and Ashley in the front. On the prosecution side of the room sat the Glover family and their friends and allies from Algiers. On the opposite side of the courtroom sat the defendants, and behind them were their families and a phalanx of NOPD police officers, some in uniform, some familiar from our investigation. Warren's wife and five young children sat quietly in the front row.

My first thought was that this was like attending a tense wedding where the bride's and groom's families hated each other. The second, more disturbing feeling was that I was stepping back fifty or a hundred years into the Jim Crow South, strictly segregated by custom and law.

One side of the courtroom was predominantly Black; the other was predominantly White. One side prayed for our success in bringing the cops who killed and burned Henry to justice. The other side of the room just glared at my team. I studied the faces of the scores of people on the defendants' side, hoping I would remember them. If I encountered any of them outside the courtroom, I wanted to know who they were. They certainly would know who I was.

The courtroom clerk called the case to order, and Judge Lance Africk, a George H. W. Bush appointee, took the bench. I stood up and introduced myself to the court, "Jared Fishman for the United States." Over the course of my career, I introduced myself that way more times than I can count. It always felt a little presumptuous to pretend I spoke on behalf of the entire country. And yet I loved fighting for principles enshrined in the Constitution that protect even the most vulnerable among us, even though I also recognized that as a country we often fail to live up to those ideals.

The judge summarized the charges against the five defendants, who all pleaded not guilty. The attorneys for McRae, Scheuermann, Italiano, and McCabe readily persuaded the judge to grant bail to their clients, a foregone conclusion. They would all go home to their families that night.

At least in theory, the legal system doesn't want to imprison people who have not yet been convicted of crime. Indicted individuals are presumed innocent, and thus cannot be "punished" prior to their conviction. However, a court may detain defendants who are deemed a flight risk or a danger to the community. In lieu of detention, courts will often set bail amounts, where a defendant secures release by putting up a portion of money, known as bond.

Over the course of a typical year, approximately 10 million arrestees cycle through the criminal legal system, often for low-level and nonviolent offenses. Every one of them faces detention hearings. Many economically disadvantaged defendants, often people of color, can't afford to pay even meager bail amounts, and will spend months or even years incarcerated before receiving a trial, a fact that virtually ensures a conviction. Many plead guilty to charges simply to get released with "time served" sentences, creating an Alice in Wonderland outcome: people are detained while they are "presumed innocent," only to be freed once they admit their guilt.

Warren, the lone defendant arrested upon indictment, had been held in a local jail for the previous six days, awaiting this hearing. He faced the most severe penalties, including the weapons charge in count two that carried "the presumption of detention," that is, no bail, unless he could establish he was neither a flight risk nor a danger to the community. But police officers, even those facing murder charges, usually get the benefit of the doubt and have an opportunity for release.

I figured Warren's lead attorney, Joe Albe, would call a parade of witnesses in support of Warren, and that the judge would likely release him on a high bond secured with his house. But unexpectedly, Albe waived the right to the detention hearing and reserved the right to call witnesses later. I thought to myself, what the hell has this guy been doing for the last six days, if not trying to put together a case to have Warren released?

Warren was remanded to custody and would spend at least the weekend in jail, perhaps longer, depending on when Albe got his ducks in a row. As I exited the courtroom, I glanced over at the defendants' side of the courtroom. Warren's family members, it seemed, were just as surprised as I was that he wasn't going home that night.

Joe Albe continued to demonstrate that he had no business handling a high-profile murder case. Days after the botched detention hearing, he appeared on an obscure right-wing Christian radio show, *Politically Correct*. (The two hosts of the show liked to remind listeners that "God is always politically correct.")

The radio show helped clear up one mystery for me. Warren, evidently a devout Christian, had hired a civil attorney on the strength of his religious, not legal, credentials. Later, a consultant on Warren's legal team told me that Albe had been chosen because he was a "good Christian" who would not "kowtow" to the government. Fine, I thought, but if I was facing a potential life sentence, I'd probably want someone who knew something about criminal law.

In the version that Albe presented to the listeners of *Politically Correct*, two looters charged at Warren. The problem with the looters, Albe explained, "is that most of them were armed and most of them were desperate," and they stood a good chance of "overcoming and overpowering a policeman, and that the chance of backup and reinforcements coming was very slim."

He then offered up a glimpse at how he planned to defend his client. Warren's shot "stop[ped] the attack" and "the attacker turned around and ran off," Albe said. In his estimation, Warren's single shot "in all probability didn't kill Glover." He was wrong—everything we knew about September 2 told us that Henry had died en route to Habans or shortly after his arrival at the school. But it was a startling claim.

While Albe's command of the facts of the case was shaky at best, he seemed familiar with the video and photos we'd turned over to the defense that suggested a bullet hole in Henry's skull. "…[T]his is the main part of our defense," he declared. "…[A]ssuming that Dave's shot hit Glover and he was one of the people that charged the building, Glover didn't die from the gunshot wound."

One of the hosts asked Albe, "There are a lot of people in this country that think this is a racial issue that a White man from the US Government has come down to New Orleans, Louisiana and he is hell-bent on indicting a White police officer for killing a Black looter. Is there anything to that?"

Albe suggested that "Aaron Fishman" (me) was aggressively pursuing his client to pressure him to testify against the "real" killers, the NOPD officers who shot Glover in the head (presumably, he meant McRae and Scheuermann). "They usually go after the small fish," he hinted darkly. "…I think that the Civil Rights division in Washington was specifically brought down here through political forces."

One of the hosts was outraged: "This is the United States of America. I'm sorry, that doesn't work for me."

Albe pressed on. "I think the US Attorney would make a deal with the devil if it accomplished their goal." But it wasn't enough that his client was a fall guy. He was positively Jesus-like.

"The people who were responsible for the death of Glover have made Dave the patsy, keeping him under a lull of protection, saying well, 'We're covering your back' where it is actually they're holding him out as the sacrificial lamb, just like Jesus. And Jesus was crucified for something that he didn't do. Dave is being crucified for something he didn't do. He did his job and he did it well and this is the thanks that he is getting."

Of all the defenses I had foreseen, I had not imagined Warren claiming that someone else had actually killed Henry. I had not anticipated him alleging a grand conspiracy in which he was the victim. And I had certainly not expected him to be likened to Jesus. This promised to be a very interesting trial.

Two weeks later, Joe Albe finally called witnesses in support of Warren's release. It was a half-hearted showing that resulted in a magistrate judge, below the trial judge in the legal pecking order, affirming the detention order. Warren would remain in jail pending trial.

Perhaps that was the nail in the coffin for Joe Albe. Evidently, Warren realized that his attorney was out of his depth, and shortly after the hearing, he replaced Albe with a new team headed by Julian Murray, a well-known New Orleans attorney. Earlier in his career, Murray had been the number two in the New Orleans US Attorney's Office, leaving to join a firm that specialized in federal criminal defense.

Murray turned his attention to a different issue. In a series of pre-trial legal briefs, he attempted to separate the trial of David Warren, the shooter, from the other four defendants who had covered up that shooting. The legal term for separating the trials is "severance."

In their briefs, Murray and his team argued that trying all five defendants together would deprive Warren of his right to a fair trial. They noted that the indictment hadn't alleged Warren's involvement in the burning of Glover's body or of submitting false reports. They argued that trying Warren with the others implied his guilt since there would be no reason for the other officers to cover up a justifiable shooting. Forcing Warren to sit through the trials of the other four officers, "which, for the most part, has absolutely nothing to do with him," would represent "prejudice in the extreme."

The defense argument wasn't unreasonable. In some ways, this case would have the feel of three separate trials merged into one. However, as we highlighted in our opposing brief, because there were so many overlapping witnesses and facts, extensive legal precedent suggested the defendants should be tried together. That makes the judicial process more efficient and helps preclude the possibility of different juries arriving at inconsistent verdicts.

As a practical matter, the shooting and the burning were so intertwined that we couldn't readily explain one crime to the jury without explaining the others. Proving that McRae, Scheuermann, Italiano, and McCabe had, in their different ways, covered up a crime, we had to prove that Warren had, in fact committed, one. To convict Warren of killing Henry, we didn't need to prove the other officers had engaged in a cover-up, but it would be hard to make our case if we couldn't explain the absence of the usual forensic evidence, missing because the other defendants destroyed it or simply failed to investigate.

Our brief argued that this case had to be viewed as a "chain of events," set in motion by Warren pulling the trigger. Had there been no shooting, there would have been no burning and no fraudulent departmental paperwork. Because no one could say definitively when Henry died, to establish his death in a legal sense, we needed to take the jury from the shooting to Habans to the burning at the levee to, months later, the identification of his body via DNA sample at the morgue. This was particularly vital if the defense intended to allege, as Albe had, that the other officers, not Warren, had actually killed Henry.

When Judge Africk ruled on the motion, he sided with the prosecution. We would be able to tell the full story of Henry Glover's last day in a single trial. It would not be the last word.

Around the same time Warren's attorneys tried to separate him from the other defendants at trial, we tried to get McRae's attorney removed from the case.

I had been alarmed about the question of McRae's representation from the early months of our investigation. Everything we knew about the burning suggested that McRae had done the dirty work. He grabbed the flares at Habans, he drove off with Henry, and he burned him by the levee.

But I was convinced that McRae acted in concert with Scheuermann, possibly under his direct orders. Scheuermann drove McRae back to Habans after the burning, and, as far as we knew, he never reported the burning to anyone else at NOPD. Strange behavior even for Katrina. We also suspected that this cover-up rose higher in the chain of command than just the two officers at the levee.

However, proving a deeper conspiracy would require cooperation on the inside that we didn't yet have. McRae was the obvious candidate. Not only was he the lowest on the NOPD food chain, he faced a mandatory minimum sentence of ten years unless he cooperated in exchange for a reduced charge.

When we approached McRae to talk, we learned that he had changed attorneys and was now being represented by Frank De-Salvo, the legal powerbroker who served as the attorney on retainer for PANO, the NOPD police union in which Scheuermann acted as vice-president. Small in stature, DeSalvo was an oversize presence in the courtroom, quick with a witty one-liner and well-versed in sharp-elbowed tactics.

But early in the investigation, DeSalvo represented Scheuermann. It was highly suspect for an attorney to switch clients during an investigation, particularly when one could readily implicate the other.

In the months leading up to the indictment, Scheuermann appeared to be setting up McRae to take the fall. According to Lieutenant Meisch, during their "chance" meetings, Scheuermann sidled up to him and said things like, "Greg made a mistake." According to Sergeant Ron Ruiz, Scheuermann told him, "McRae really has us in a pickle." Perhaps more concerning, DeSalvo seemed to echo the SOD lieutenant's party line. One day, Tracey ran into DeSalvo at the courthouse, and he said something to the effect of, "Greg acted stupidly." This was in marked contrast to McRae's alleged admission to officer Josh Burns not long after the burning, that he had helped another officer get rid of the car. When DeSalvo declined to let McRae speak with us, we took action. DeSalvo's representation of McRae reeked of conflict of interest.

Three months before the indictments, in March of 2010, we raised the issue with Judge Africk, who scheduled a hearing. It was the first time I'd face off against three major players in the case: McRae, Scheuermann, and DeSalvo. DeSalvo introduced himself to the court, acknowledging his unusual double role, attorney for McRae and the subject of this hearing: "Frank DeSalvo, Your Honor, for—I am not sure, for me I guess. And for Officer McRae."

DeSalvo argued both that he had not really represented Scheuermann and, in any event, no real conflict of interest existed. In his opinion, neither McRae nor Scheuermann had committed a crime. "I saw [a] lot of maybe not the best decisions that were made, but I didn't see any criminality... And I am still convinced that there's no criminality, that nobody really needs a lawyer, other than the fact that the government has decided that people did things they didn't do... I gave them advice, I said, I don't think y'all did anything wrong."

He was happy to claim that case-specific legal advice didn't constitute representation. In his capacity as PANO's attorney on retainer, he said, officers came to him for advice all the time: "They come to me for personal advice like they think I'm the priest."

DeSalvo said he told McRae that he was free to discuss a plea deal with the government. "He's [said] emphatically, I don't want to speak with them. [I said,] 'Do you understand that they say if you come in and speak with them, they will help you?' And he said, 'I know they'll help me go to jail.'"

McRae testified next that he wanted DeSalvo as his lawyer, regardless of any conflict of interest. I got a chance to cross-examine him, a thick, balding guy who looked out of place in a suit. There was a lot I would have liked to ask. I wanted to push him on the connection between the shooting and burning. I wanted to know if he had been one of the SOD officers who had responded to the shooting scene at the mall. Who had ordered the burning of the car? What type of accelerant had he used for the car to catch fire so quickly? What about Henry's missing skull?

Instead, I was limited to asking him about his knowledge of DeSalvo's attorney-client relationship with Scheuermann, which wasn't much. McRae was polite but evidently didn't feel the need to do much explaining.

Dwayne Scheuermann testified next, and similarly waived conflict of interest that arose from having his former attorney representing an officer under his command who could (and would) become his codefendant. Scheuermann seemed pleased to have DeSalvo representing the man who could most easily incriminate him. (I got the flavor of the DeSalvo-Scheuermann connection when I had earlier cross-examined DeSalvo about the legal advice he'd given the SOD lieutenant: "Probably went in one ear and out the other because Mr. Scheuermann's been looked at [by investigators] so many times. It's kind of like one of the things we laugh about.")

It was my first taste of Scheuermann on the stand. He went out of his way to smile and address me as "Mr. Fishman," as he would every time I saw him from then on. In one breath, he would say that he was "only a high school graduate, not a lawyer." Then in the next, he let you know he could hold his own in an investigation of his conduct. "But I can tell you this, as a police officer for twenty-six years, as a lieutenant and also as a first vice-president of the Police Association, I didn't need Mr. DeSalvo, or any other attorney, telling me not to waive my rights..." His style felt oily and insincere, and yet I worried that his Eddie-Haskell-with-a-badge routine might play with some of the jurors.

Judge Africk ultimately found that while DeSalvo had represented both Scheuermann and McRae, they both could—and had—waived the conflict of interest. His reasoning rested, in no small part, on the fact that neither man had yet been charged with a crime.

In July, after the indictments, we asked the court to reconsider its earlier ruling. Now that the two men were codefendants charged with the same crimes, much of Africk's earlier rationale no longer held.

Besides undercutting McRae's right to effective counsel at trial, a conflict of interest could make any convictions we were able to win vulnerable to reversal on appeal. Appellate courts had made it clear that defendants cannot waive a conflict of interest unless they are informed of all the ways that conflict could undermine their defense.

My hope, even expectation, was that the conflicts, exhaustively laid out, would seem so egregious that Africk would reject McRae's waiver "in the interest of justice" and remove DeSalvo as his attorney.

The judge instructed me to come up with a list of all the ways a conflict could manifest at trial. It was a huge ask, given all that we didn't know: What trial strategies the defendants would pursue; which defendants would testify; which witnesses? The possible pitfalls were mind-boggling.

I came up with a list of twenty-some-odd possible conflicts. I played out every scenario I could think of, but in the end, they all basically came down to DeSalvo throwing McRae under the bus to save Scheuermann or the police department.

For the hearing, I had hoped that McRae's wife, Gail, would show up, so she could hear about the risks her husband faced and perhaps convince him to change attorneys. But Judge Africk had set the hearing for 7:30 a.m., so as not to disrupt the rest of his docket. (As I was learning, the judge was always on the clock and expected the same of the lawyers in his court.) In marked contrast to the scene at the arraignment, the courtroom gallery was completely empty. McRae's wife didn't show.

Africk laid out the possible conflicts to the defendants, quoting almost verbatim from my brief. With each question, McRae said he understood the conflict and still wanted DeSalvo as his attorney. The court wasn't required to accept this waiver, but in the end, Judge Africk did. I feared DeSalvo's continued representation of McRae might come back to haunt us.

CHAPTER 12

ON THE THRESHOLD

July through October 2010

I understood why my office assigned a novice attorney to look into the suspicions raised in A.C. Thompson's article. It was a low-probability investigation that required time-consuming investigative digging. I doubt that anyone thought we would be able to make the case.

But after we identified the officer who shot Henry, and then the two officers we believed had been involved in the burning of his body, I was sure that I would be replaced as the lead in the investigation. It didn't happen.

Following the indictment, the five defendants put together their legal teams. Warren was represented by three lawyers: Julian Murray, Rick Simmons, and Mike Ellis. Scheuermann retained a high-priced criminal defense lawyer out of Fort Worth, Texas,

Jeff Kearney, and New Orleans lawyer Roger Kitchens. McRae continued to be represented by DeSalvo. Italiano was represented by Steve Lemoine, a solo practitioner based in New Orleans. And McCabe was represented by Mike Small and Alan Stroud, out of Alexandria and Shreveport, Louisiana, respectively.

There were a lot of lawyers. Tracey and I definitely needed help.

With only two months to go before the November trial, we needed someone seasoned, who wouldn't need a lot of hand-holding. But we worried that a senior attorney might try to hijack the case that we had meticulously built over sixteen months, mostly by sheer doggedness. Tracey, Ashley and I had meshed beautifully over the course of the investigation, and I wondered how adding a new person this late in the game would alter the team chemistry. The team had become like family.

The US Attorney's Office added a third attorney to the team, Michael Magner, a senior Assistant US Attorney. Mike brought twenty-five years of litigation experience to the table and lots of high-profile trial experience. He had led a team that racked up seventeen corruption convictions, including against several Jefferson Parish judges and sheriff's deputies, and he'd been part of the prosecution team that had put the former governor of Louisiana, Edwin Edwards, in prison for extortion and bribery.

I had a nightmare vision of Mike struggling to get up to speed on the case while trying to call the shots on witnesses and strategy. But Magner, whose full head of white hair resembled Phil Donahue's, also had something of the daytime talk show host's genial, easygoing manner. A day after he joined the team, Mike took me aside and said, "I know this is your and Tracey's case. Just let me know how I can help." And he meant it. Initially, we gave him witnesses to prep for trial, like the border protection officers, that didn't require him to understand the entire five-defendant case. As Mike gained command of the case, we sent more responsibilities his way.

From the beginning, he provided us with a valuable asset: local credibility. Mike grew up in Long Island, New York, the son of a police officer, but he'd gone to Tulane Law School, married a local woman and made New Orleans his home. He'd worked at the US Attorney's Office for close to two decades, developing a friendly rapport with Judge Africk. When Katrina hit, he briefly fled the city but returned within days to help out with post-storm law enforcement. He was stationed for a time at the Royal Sonesta Hotel, the makeshift headquarters where the NOPD, FBI, and other local and federal agencies worked. He participated in the very first federal trial after Hurricane Katrina, prosecuting two men for shooting at a coast guard helicopter. If anyone ever asked him if he had "been here after Katrina," he could definitively answer "yes." With sixty witnesses to prepare for and countless motions to file, I was relieved to have an extra set of experienced hands on the team.

I have come to think of trials as battles between two sides trying to tell the most compelling story under a set of tightly regulated rules. While the federal rules of evidence include detailed provisions regarding what generally should or shouldn't be admitted in court, at the end of the day, the judge has enormous discretion when deciding the evidence that a jury will hear.

Much of that determination comes down to a balancing test where the judge weighs the "probative" value of any potential evidence—does it speak to the guilt or the innocence of the defendants?—against any undue "prejudice"—would it play to the emotions of the jurors and interfere with their ability to rationally apply the law?

In our case, the prosecution and the defense filed dueling sets of motions—hundreds of pages in all—known as *in limine*, Latin for "on the threshold." We argued about which evidence was within the threshold and which was out of bounds. In a case rife with emotion, how the court ruled on these motions would shape the course of the trial and quite possibly its outcome.

Katrina would inevitably cast its shadow over the proceedings, but the last thing we wanted was for the defense to put the hurricane on trial. If their attorneys could replay every terrible thing that happened, a jury might be persuaded that the normal rules of police conduct simply didn't apply, and grant blanket absolution.

Warren's attorneys wanted to introduce a whole slew of "Katrina conditions" to establish the "circumstances and environment" that informed his use of deadly force, including Mayor Nagin's unsubstantiated claims of mass rapes at the Superdome and an unexplained fire that burned down much of the Oakwood mall, not far from Algiers.

Italiano's attorney planned to bring up the Kevin Thomas shooting, including having Italiano explain that "a quantity of Officer Thomas's brain cells ended up on the pavement of the location where he was shot."

In our briefs, we countered that if the defendants were allowed to testify about Thomas's brain cells, or instances of violent looting not related to the case, the jury should also hear about bad police conduct, like the shootings on the Danziger Bridge.

In the end, Judge Africk set reasonable limitations. Any evidence of Katrina conditions would have to be tightly tethered to the perceptions of the witnesses, plausibly influencing their state of mind and their subsequent actions. Though mention of mass rapes and Kevin Thomas's brain matter would be excluded, over the four weeks of trial, plenty of Katrina's worst moments would find a way to seep in.

Another flurry of motions moved to exclude any defense asserting that officers were "just following orders." We suspected that any of the five defendants could assert this type of defense. I styled my brief as a motion to exclude "the authorization defense and any reference to orders from superiors." Informally, we called it the "Nuremberg Defense" motion.

The motion drew its name from the tribunal established at Nuremberg following World War II, to prosecute top Nazi leaders for their roles in committing war crimes and crimes against humanity. Many on trial defended themselves against these charges by asserting that they were just "following orders."

The Nuremberg Tribunal uniformly rejected this defense, setting precedent for all the postwar war crime tribunals that followed. They included the International Criminal Tribunal for Rwanda (ICTR), where I interned during law school, working on the prosecution of the former Rwandan finance minister for his role in mass killings of Tutsis. The Nuremberg trials, and the global justice system that evolved after it, legally established the principle that it was a crime to follow illegal orders. American law has embraced this principle ever since.

Throughout our long investigation of NOPD, the assertion periodically surfaced that someone—it was often unclear who that someone was—had authorized police officers "to shoot looters." Officers Linda Howard and Alec Brown had told us that David Warren had suggested as much when he had said to them that he understood the city to be operating under martial law.

In the summer of 2010, the PBS *Frontline* series aired the episode "Law & Disorder," which investigated incidents of police abuse after Katrina. The episode correspondent—once again, A.C. Thompson—dug into this issue of official sanction. On air, Warren Riley, who served as NOPD chief for most of the Katrina aftermath, denied making any statements about martial law or shooting looters. "I may have said, 'We need to take control of the city.'" Several of his police colleagues have gone on the record to say that he did in fact give a "shoot looters" command.

But there was no doubt that members of the political leadership— from Mayor Nagin to Governor Kathleen Blanco—had suggested that because of Katrina, new rules of force were permitted. In a radio interview, following the Kevin Thomas shooting, Nagin claimed, "I've already called for martial law in the city of New Orleans." He hadn't.

Martial law, when the US military assumes control of the government and normal judicial process is suspended, can only be declared by the President or the Congress, certainly not the mayor. What Nagin seems to have meant was that the police should get tough on the widespread looting that had broken out, and they shouldn't feel shy about commandeering whatever matériel they needed—boats, cars, food, and water—to get the job done. (In other words, actions that would be considered looting done by anyone other than the police.)

Blanco wasn't averse to tough talk herself. In response to the widespread looting, and the national media's representation of New Orleans as a city on the verge of lawless collapse, she called in the

National Guard. A day before Henry was shot, she announced at a press conference, "These troops know how to shoot and kill and they are more than willing to do so if necessary and I expect they will." (Blanco later estimated that troop levels in New Orleans, a combination of National Guard and federal troops, exceeded 40,000.)

With these kinds of directives hanging in the air, it was easy to imagine how a "following orders" defense might play out, not only for Warren, but for the other defendants as well. We knew SOD commander Jeff Winn had been at Habans talking to Scheuermann before the burning. Would it be a stretch for Scheuermann and McRae to claim he told them to burn the car? Italiano and McCabe might claim they'd been ordered to cover up the shooting by their superiors.

However, a Nuremberg Defense, by itself, was not likely to be a winning defense strategy. (After all, it failed at Nuremberg.) The defense would have to admit that their clients had committed the acts we'd charged them with, while arguing that they had reason to believe the orders they were following were legal ones. And they would, of course, be putting the defendants' commanding officers in legal jeopardy.

More likely, I thought, was that the cops' attorneys would tack on Nuremberg to their core defense: self-defense for Warren; outright denial for Italiano and McCabe; and whatever McRae and Scheuermann came up with to justify the burning. Martial law rumor and innuendo would be a way to muddy the waters, to get closer to reasonable doubt in the minds of the jurors.

The other side responded to our motion by asserting they would not advance a "following orders" defense, giving us a nice tactical advantage. We wouldn't have to waste any more of our limited time trying to uncover what was or wasn't said within NOPD circles. Evidence concerning possible illegal NOPD orders was outside the "threshold."

But the larger question that was raised at Nuremberg—how do you hold individuals accountable when the entire society around them is falling apart?—wasn't going to leave me anytime soon. And I suspected it would be in the thoughts of the jurors as well.

I'd spent a good part of my twenties wrestling with these issues. After Asel was killed, despite the Israeli government's own commission finding the shooting unjustified, no individual was ever held responsible for his death. When I worked in Bosnia during two summers in law school, the participants in the reconciliation program I ran pointed out known participants in wartime rapes who walked the streets freely.

Justice seemed to me an elusive concept even when people were prosecuted and jailed for their conduct. In my first job after law school, working in postwar Kosovo for the State Department as a police and justice advisor, I witnessed a selective application of justice, with the losers of the war incarcerated and charged, while most of those on the winning side had their conduct glossed over, with some of the most notorious war criminals rising to the upper echelons of government.

Rwanda was home to perhaps the speediest mass killing in world history, over half a million people killed in a hundred days. I visited the prisons there where over a hundred thousand alleged participants in the genocide—many accused of hacking their neighbors to death with machetes—lived in overcrowded, deplorable conditions, still awaiting trials over nine years later, many being held on questionable evidence. Within a year of my time there, the nation launched a process called *gacaca*, where participants who "accepted responsibility" for their actions at a local tribunal hearing could have their sentences cut in half. Most of the people I saw in prison were released by the tribunals with "time served." It was, at least, a pragmatic approach. (The *gacaca*, like most postwar courts, did not focus on crimes committed by the victors.)

Of all the attempts to achieve justice after societal collapse, none of them, I think, hit the mark. Honestly, I'm not sure any ever could. If we won convictions, I wanted to believe that we had contributed to "justice." But I had my doubts.

In every police misconduct case that I ever tried, the parties battle over the issue of character. The defendants, not surprisingly, are keen to introduce "good character" evidence—jurors are more reluctant to convict "good people," and most jurors are inclined to see the police as protectors anyway. Defense attorneys usually try to bolster their case with litanies of commendations, acts of bravery and the absence of prior misconduct. But the rules of evidence generally limit this kind of evidence, to keep the focus on whether a defendant actually committed a crime, not on whether they're a good or bad person.

Dwayne Scheuermann wanted to present specific acts of heroism, with photos and stories of him piloting his boat through the flooded city, plucking citizens from the water or from their roofs. Warren wanted to introduce his lack of prior complaints, notwithstanding that he had only been a cop for less than a year when he shot Henry. Italiano wanted to bring in his time working in internal affairs, to suggest that he would never cover up police misconduct.

In our countervailing motions, we argued that the introduction of such evidence would open the door to bad character evidence. In addition to Scheuermann's ample history of abuse complaints, we sought to present evidence that McRae had threatened a Black man who was looking for help at Habans School after the storm. He allegedly pointed a handgun at the man and said, "Get back before I shoot your Black ass."

In the end, the court limited such evidence, on both sides.

Character evidence rules play an even more important role when it comes to the victim. The defense's goal often strives to "dirty up" the victim so that the jury feels he merely "got what he deserved." It is, sadly, an effective strategy.

Offering up evidence of any negative interaction a victim ever had with the police—particularly any arrests or convictions—the defense attempts to present the victim as undeserving of the law's protection. I've seen defense attorneys try to bring up prior drug or alcohol use, nonpayment of child support, twenty-plus-year-old arrests, illegal immigration status, prior gang affiliation, or the fact that they lived in a "dangerous" neighborhood.

But the federal rules are strict. Prior arrests, generally, are not allowed, if they don't result in convictions. Prior convictions are not allowed if they are over ten years old.

In Henry's case, he had been arrested in his late teens, though not convicted, for possessing a handgun and battery. He had two minor convictions, for simple burglary and drug possession, both over ten years old, the first one when he was a minor. In the final twelve years of his life, Henry hadn't entered the criminal justice system. He worked two jobs and cared for his children as best he could. Judge Africk ruled that Henry's prior encounters with the police were not admissible.

That didn't stop the defense from trying. Italiano's attorney, Steve Lemoine, filed a motion that oozed with disdain, describing Henry as "a thug with a substantial criminal record." Warren's attorney, Julian Murray, used more legal-sounding language to paint an equally damning picture. He wrote, "At the present time the defense is aware that in this very district Henry Glover pleaded guilty to the distribution of cocaine and was sentenced to three years in prison and five years of supervised release upon completing his sentence. He was still under supervised release at the time he was killed while attempting to illegally enter the shopping mall."

The only problem: Murray had the wrong Henry Glover. Reading the briefs, I wondered whether officer Jeff Sandoz also had had the wrong Henry Glover in mind when, at Habans, he called Henry "a piece of shit," the remark that so wounded Bernard.

I had to wonder if, for the defense, any Henry Glover would do.

With the rules of the trial more or less settled a few weeks before its start, Tracey, Mike and I refined the narrative that we would present to the jury. We needed to tell the story of what happened to Henry Glover in a way that that made him seem like a real person, someone whose murder and immolation demanded that the officers who did it be held accountable.

As I write these words, I'm struck again by the thought: How could this not be a given? How could it be possible that a jury might give the cops a Katrina pass, or worse, conclude that Henry, defined by that all-purpose term "looter," simply got what was coming to him?

And yet that was always a possibility. One of the biggest reasons for this disconnect between crime and punishment was, there was no doubt in my mind, race.

One day, Tracey and I worked on the opening statement she would give to the jury at the outset of the trial. I'm not sure what caused me to blurt out, "Henry Glover wouldn't have been killed if he were White."

Tracey looked surprised: "How do you know that?"

I was confused by her question. I assumed Tracey would feel the same way. "You don't think so?" I asked.

"No. I know so. How do *you* know that?"

Tracey wanted to know how I, a White guy, had come to this conclusion that for most White people was not self-evident.

I paused to find the words to describe what I had learned in my short time working in the criminal legal system. Traveling to different cities and towns across America as a civil rights prosecutor had opened my eyes to the dynamic between police and communities of color, something very different from what I'd experienced in the mostly White, relatively affluent communities where I'd lived. It was inescapable. Black people, particularly Black men, are policed differently.

At the beginning of my prosecutorial career, I handled misdemeanor cases at the US Attorney's Office in DC and saw firsthand the high volume of Black and Brown men being funneled through the criminal legal system, often for minor offenses, for which White people, in my experience, rarely seemed to get charged. I never saw any students from DC's numerous universities, where there is likely the highest per capita drug use in the city.

In an effort to combat violence, police often target low-level offenses that they can see with their own eyes, things like public intoxication, prostitution, and drug use. Most of the people who get caught are lower-income people of color. There is little evidence this approach reduces serious crime. Recent research suggests the opposite is true: that incarcerating people for low-level crimes has a "criminogenic" effect, increasing future crime.

When I worked as prosecutor in DC, I observed a common policing strategy known as the "look-see" that the city's Metropolitan Police Department regularly deployed. A team of cops known as "jump out squads" would pull up on groups of Black residents and wait for people to run away. The police would "look" to "see" who tossed drugs, then arrest them on low-level drug charges. People would be arrested, and often charged with felonies, which, in turn, curtailed their ability to get a decent job. I was thankful that these types of cases were not on my docket. I don't think I could have prosecuted them.

While I had seen racial inequalities in the system firsthand, as I spoke to Tracey, I didn't yet grasp the magnitude of the problems. Black people are arrested at grossly disproportionate rates, on average receive longer sentences for similar conduct, and are seven times more likely to be wrongly convicted of a felony. Officers, both White and Black, are 2.5 times more likely to respond with deadly force when the person they encounter is African American, according to the latest stats.

Over the course of fourteen years at DOJ, I kept encountering ineffective policing strategies leading to terrible outcomes. I investigated the deaths of two people during the execution of a no-knock warrant, where a police officer had fabricated evidence of a drug deal. This unit routinely busted down the doors of suspects' homes looking for incredibly small amounts of drugs. (High-risk raids of this type resulted in Breonna Taylor's death in 2020, but hers was hardly exceptional.)

I reviewed many, many instances of cops killing Black civilians, usually Black men, in episodes that began on a flimsy or suspicious pretext, such as a broken taillight or expired tags. The most soul-crushing cases were the ones we couldn't go forward with —"lawful but awful" deaths that should never have occurred, but were nonetheless deemed justified under current law.

In many Black neighborhoods across America, police serve as a constant, disruptive, humiliating presence in the lives of the community they are supposed to serve. Walk into most court-rooms or prisons in America and you can see the downstream consequences—policing reinforcing inequality.

In my opinion, the clearest window into Warren's mind when he pulled the trigger was what he had heard from Officer Alec Brown: Warren's comment that looters were animals who de-served to be shot.

"Looters," as it was being used at the time by both the police and the media, was a term mostly reserved for those who were low-income, Black, and desperate.

We had no evidence to suggest that Warren targeted Henry "because of" his race. That's why we didn't charge him with a ra-cially motivated hate crime. Legally speaking, federal hate crimes require proof that "but for" a protected characteristic (such as race, religion, national origin, or sexual orientation), the person would not have been targeted.

This almost impossibly high standard of proof partly explains why so few federal hate crimes are prosecuted. Absent obvious slurs, or a racist manifesto, most people don't telegraph their feel-ings so plainly. (In 2010, this type of evidence was exceedingly rare. In recent years, spurred on by Donald Trump, and Fox News among other right-wing media outlets, it's become more socially acceptable to air racial bias.)

Nevertheless, I was certain that the perception of race influenced the speed with which Warren resorted to using deadly force. Race operated as a kind of distortion lens. In his mind, Black men were "thugs," inherently more dangerous, and deserving of a maximal response.

If I had some clue about the differences between White and Black America in 2010, I was only just beginning to get my head around why it might be so. Growing up in Atlanta in the '80s and '90s, I wasn't exposed to much in the way of critique about race or the history of slavery or Jim Crow. Without irony, my schools took class trips to both The King Center for Nonviolent Social Change and Stone Mountain Park, a granite mountain carved with images of Confederate leaders that once served as the spiritual home of the Ku Klux Klan.

What was dawning on me as a young civil rights prosecutor was that the ending of the most obvious, in-your-face forms of racism—like explicitly mandated separate facilities for Black and White people—simply obscured more complicated, and subtle, forms of racial bias. Growing up, I knew nothing about the covenants that restricted who could live in which neighborhoods, or "redlining," where mortgage lenders or insurance companies simply choose not to do business in communities of color, perpetuating segregation and reducing access to wealth.

I never learned about how our public education system—which purportedly had ended "separate but equal" four decades before I attended a public school—remained incredibly unequal, thanks to how counties fund public schools, generally with property taxes. The system ensured that those who had historically benefited from racism could send their children to better-funded schools, while those who endured its ravages could not, perpetuating a generational cycle of poverty and lack of opportunity. It's why the Black students in my high school had to bus in from over an hour away to receive a quality education. These were intentional decisions, designed to perpetuate existing (predominately White) power structures.

Nowhere was the historical legacy of racism easier to discern than in the criminal legal system. The links between slavery, Jim Crow, and the legal system I operated in were becoming more obvious to me by the day.

Algiers Point, where the Glover family decamped to catch a bus to escape New Orleans after Henry's murder, was the site where many enslaved Africans first arrived in America. In the early 1700s, the surrounding area served, one scholar wrote, as "a jail-like compound for those captive Africans who survived the wretched Middle Passage and arrived in New Orleans in chains."

The earliest policing structures in America were the "slave patrols" of the pre-Emancipation era, mini-militias organized by the states to hunt down runaway enslaved people.

After the Civil War, the Thirteenth Amendment to the US Constitution ended traditional forms of slavery, although slavery continues to be permitted "as a punishment for crime whereof the party shall have been duly convicted." Almost immediately following the ratification of the Thirteenth Amendment, lawmakers passed an assortment of "Black Codes" that criminalized conduct such as walking "without purpose," "vagrancy," walking next to railroad tracks, "loitering," or "assembling after dark." These "crimes," race-neutral only on their face, were nearly uniformly enforced against newly freed Black citizens, who, in turn, were sent to jails and penitentiaries, where they were "leased" back to plantations and businesses and forced to work. In Alabama, by 1898, 73 percent of state income was generated through these leases.

While "convict leasing" in its most abusive forms gradually faded out by the early twentieth century, the policing of Black people for low-level crimes never stopped. It has been perpetuated as a part of the "war on drugs," "stop and frisk," and "broken windows policing," a theory of law enforcement that relies heavily on arrests for low-level infractions. Many who are incarcerated work jobs in prison, often producing items like government desks and license plates, being paid pennies per hour. When the arrestees return to society after incarceration, their criminal records serve as a bar to future employment. People with felonies are nearly ten times more likely to experience homelessness and have a significantly decreased life expectancy.

Law and order is an easy concept to get behind. Practically everyone I have ever met wants to live in a secure and stable environment, and societies have a natural inclination to establish rules to maintain that order. But while violence in lower-income communities is real—and that violence disproportionately affects people of color—what's often glossed over are the lives ruined by aggressive, racially biased enforcement of those rules. Henry Glover—and David Warren—were both products of that system.

While race and racial dehumanization turned up everywhere you looked in our case, Tracey, Mike and I knew without even discussing it that we couldn't tackle it head-on at trial. For one,

Judge Africk would most likely prevent us from discussing the racialized history of American policing.

But we also recognized that highlighting race would not be a winning strategy. If we took it upon ourselves to try to challenge the entrenched belief systems of what presumably would be a mostly White Southern jury, we were going to lose. The most we could hope for was to persuade a jury to put aside any prejudices they might harbor and, as much as humanly possible, evaluate the evidence with an open mind. We would have to tell a story that would move them.

"It was frustrating not to be able to talk about race directly," Tracey admitted to me later. "But when I gave my opening statement to the jury, I tried to figure out ways to talk about race without talking about it, like, 'Henry was a human being,' or 'he mattered.'" (Even in our current era, more sensitized to "systematic racism" and awash in video evidence of police abuse, prosecutors dance the same dance. The prosecutors in the George Floyd trial used similar neutral language.)

In the end, we wanted the jury to care about Henry regardless of his race. And yet race would repeatedly insert itself in our case. Probably the most obvious instance was when we picked a jury.

CHAPTER 13

SPEAK THE TRUTH

October and November 2010

Depending on where one is in the US, *voir dire* sometimes receives the French pronunciation ("voah deer"). The state's French colonial heritage notwithstanding, many in Louisiana opt from the Southern pronunciation, "vor dire," as in "dire straits."

Voir dire, from Old French and Latin, literally means "that which is true," and is what people colloquially call "jury selection." Prospective jurors are supposed to "speak the truth" about their ability to be fair and impartial in weighing the evidence to reach a verdict. If they can't, *voir dire* is supposed to root them out. Whatever you call it, jury "selection" is something of a misnomer. The judge and the attorneys on both sides don't "select" a jury as much as eliminate one.

Jury selection in the Glover trial began in earnest on November 8, but the winnowing process started months earlier, in a series of conferences with the judge and the attorneys. Our team developed a twenty-seven-page questionnaire, modestly modified by the defense, that went out to hundreds of prospective jurors across Louisiana. We asked about anything that might be germane, from their feelings about NOPD or gun ownership to their knowledge of the case.

Some five hundred questionnaires came back, loaded with an oppressive amount of biographical information. The attorneys for both sides went through them, one by one, flagging candidates who couldn't or didn't want to present even the pretense of objectivity. These people the judge dismissed "with cause."

Some of the candidates asked to be excused from jury service because of some hardship or logistical conflict, a difficult home or work situation or a prepaid vacation, for instance. The judge granted some of the requests. Others would have to come to court to plead their case. The man who served as the mascot for New Orleans Hornets, the city's then-professional basketball team, wrote that the team would suffer hardship without him. The judge rejected the request. I imagined him showing up in court in his bulbous, blue-striped hornet costume, like in one of those signature ESPN *SportsCenter* commercials. (He didn't.)

On the first day of *voir dire*, the 110 potential jurors who had made it through the questionnaire culling crowded into an ornate courtroom on the fifth floor of the Hale Boggs Federal Courthouse. The room, much larger than Judge Africk's usual courtroom, felt appropriately ceremonial—massively high ceilings, oak wood paneling, and, behind the judge, the golden seal of the federal courts. Black-and-white photos of deceased judges from the Eastern District of Louisiana—at that time, overwhelmingly White men—hung on the wall behind the jury box.

Over the course of two days, the judge, with input from the attorneys, further culled the jury pool down to the "magic number" of thirty-six eligible jurors required to seat a jury. From this thirty-six, the attorneys would exercise peremptory "strikes," reducing the panel to twelve jurors and four alternates. The attorneys don't have to justify their choices. They simply remove panelists they think will be the least sympathetic to their case.

In theory, the system seems stacked in favor of someone accused of a crime—it only takes one juror to "hang" a jury, preventing it from reaching the unanimous decision necessary to convict. A hung jury, or a "mistrial," can result in another trial for the defendants, though many times, the prosecutors will elect not to re-try the case. The underlying philosophy here dates back to English common law of the eighteenth century, the famous dictum, "It is better that ten guilty persons escape than that one innocent suffer."

In practice, in this country, only 2 percent of federal criminal cases go to trial. The vast majority of cases are resolved by plea agreement. If everyone went to trial, the entire system would come crashing down. (This is beginning to happen in some jurisdictions now, after pandemic-related closures limited the number of cases that would be resolved, exacerbating case backlogs.)

When a Black person requests a jury trial, he's unlikely to be tried by a "jury of his peers." Communities of color are often underrepresented in jury pools, which typically are assembled from voter rolls or driver's license data. And juries in a typical criminal case might be selected in less than an hour, hardly enough time to ferret out bias. No impartial jury, no chance of a truly fair trial. The odds of prevailing against the government in court are dismal—and the consequences of losing high. (This is known as the "trial penalty," where defendants who have gone to trial and lost typically get higher sentences than those who plead guilty.) For many defendants, waiving the right to a jury and pleading guilty is the only practical option, regardless of their guilt or innocence.

While the *voir dire* process in our case was painstaking—the sheer amount of time, effort and money that went into selecting a jury was astonishing—I didn't begrudge the protections it afforded. Every defendant should have access to a fair and impartial jury. What our defendants received should be the rule, not the exception.

The five cops we were prosecuting were doubly fortunate. They would be judged not only by a meticulously chosen jury but also one that would, most likely, be open to the possibility that they were innocent, given the trust that society places in the police, even a department as tarnished as the NOPD.

More often than not, case outcomes hinge on the composition of the jury. If this were a trial under state law, that jury would come solely from Orleans Parish, that is, New Orleans proper. Given the demographics of the city, the jury would necessarily be racially diverse and likely intimately familiar with local conditions after Katrina. The only way a trial could wind up with an all-White jury would be if the attorneys struck all the Black juror candidates, something lawyers are *not* allowed to do. According to the 1986 Supreme Court decision in *Batson v. Kentucky*, as well as subsequent decisions, peremptory strikes cannot be exercised on the basis of race, or other protected characteristics, such as gender, national origin and sexual orientation.

In federal court, however, potential jurors are drawn from the entire judicial district of the Eastern District of Louisiana, which includes parishes (the Louisiana equivalent of counties) as far as eighty miles away, places like Terrebonne and Tangipahoa Parishes. The farther one goes away from New Orleans, the more rural, whiter and more conservative it gets, with plenty of people with friends or family serving in law enforcement. A more David-Warren-friendly part of the state.

In many federal trials, the questioning of jurors is handled by the judge. This would be the first case where I would have an opportunity to put questions directly to jurors.

I'd absorbed from more senior colleagues that the opportunity to speak to jurors was an ultra-important opportunity to shape the jury (and hence the trial). My mentor and friend Barry Kowalski told me that there were only three things you could hope to accomplish in *voir dire*: Educate. Ingratiate. Eliminate.

Try to educate the jurors about the themes of the case and begin framing the facts in a favorable light. Ingratiate yourself to the jurors. Show that you are competent and fair. If they trust you, they'll be more likely to trust the case you present. And most importantly, eliminate as many of the obviously biased jurors as you can.

The judge asked his first question to the assembled prospective jurors (known as the *venire*): "Will you accept and apply the law as given to you by the court and disregard any ideas, beliefs, or notions you may have as to what the law should or should not be in reaching your verdict? Is there anybody who will not do that?"

A smattering of hands shot up. The judge called a middle-aged White woman, Juror 26, to the bench, so as not to have her answers influence the other potential jurors. Eleven lawyers—ten White men and Tracey, who was three months pregnant—huddled around the bench, crammed into the small space between the judge and the court clerk. The judge flipped the switch on the courtroom "husher" to drown out the juror's answer. The husher blasted white noise around the bench while the court's sound system pumped country music throughout the courtroom. We strained to hear what the juror said.

"If I understand you correctly, you want for me to have a fair and unbiased understanding of the law during that time," Juror 26 said.

"What I want you to do is…to apply the law as I give it to you, not what you think it should be or was," Judge Africk answered.

"That's what I'm trying to tell you…I don't believe there were any laws in effect during that time… It was a difficult time. It was a lawless time. It's an emotional time. And it's my belief that if you lived through that time and you have family that remained behind, it's very difficult to believe that there was an opportunity to have the law be enforced during that time." Africk struck her for cause.

Juror 21, the next juror called to the bench, a Black man, had the opposite perspective. "My preconceived notion is that the police department defendants are guilty. I think it was a horrible time for all of us…and these kinds of things that are going on are just preposterous… Somebody getting burned in a car. I mean, this is not what the police are supposed to do… I don't know for sure, but I feel as if…they're guilty." When the judge tried to draw out a specific opinion about the police, Juror 21 replied, "...[I]t's just an overall kind of guilty for me." The juror was also removed for cause.

Often, during jury selection, jurors will come up with myriad reasons why they cannot serve. Remarkably, few jurors on this panel actively tried to get released from service, thanks at least in part to Judge Africk's paean to the virtues of civic duty, his reminder that trial by jury is one of the only rights mentioned in both the Constitution and the Declaration of Independence. Then he went for the jugular.

At the time of the trial in 2010, the US had been fighting two wars in Iraq and Afghanistan that were costing the lives of thousands of American soldiers (and many more thousands of Iraqis and Afghans). Africk asked the jurors to think about the soldiers who died: "Presumably, one of the reasons [they] made the sacrifice they did was that they thought they were fighting on behalf of a country worth fighting for... I am not going to dishonor their memory by doing less than their best today, and I certainly hope you share that goal."

When Judge Africk asked who needed to be dismissed for hardship, few hands went up.

Listening to juror candidates talk about their experiences with the criminal legal system is a window into a lot of American trauma. Our panel included people who were friends with police officers killed in the line of duty; a juror with a family member in jail for molesting children; and people whose friends had been beaten by the police. Being able to understand the lived experiences of our potential jurors was key to identifying who would be more likely to hold the police accountable and who would not.

A Black man, Juror 42, described being randomly stopped a couple of times by NOPD, once when they removed him from his car at gunpoint and searched his car without a warrant. He felt he was being targeted because of his dreadlocks. A Black woman, Juror 10, told the court about a traffic stop in Nevada endured by four male friends, pulled over and hog-tied by the side of the road in a case of mistaken identity.

A White man, Juror 57, had a brother-in-law who was murdered in his home, along with his mother, in Jefferson Parish. The juror had been responsible for cleaning up the bloody crime scene after the investigation concluded. The killers—both Black men—were ultimately convicted of the crime; one was on death row, and the other received a life sentence.

The judge asked Juror 57 whether he would be able to evaluate the Glover case based only on the evidence and the law. The juror said he couldn't. "I wish we had the luxury of what's taking place with Mr. Glover. I mean, these people murdered my…brother-in-law and his seventy-six-year-old mother, and we continue to live this and fight this."

Judge Africk seemed as perplexed as I was by what the juror meant by "luxury of what's taking place with Mr. Glover."

"Well, I mean, had those two individuals suffered the fate of Mr. Glover, my family would not be living through…appeal after appeal."

The judge replied, "So…you believe standing here that Mr. Glover deserved to get shot?"

"I am not sure I can segregate Mr. Glover's activities from what these people did. I doubt one of those officers over there picked Mr. Glover out and said I am going to shoot him." The judge removed him for cause too.

A day and a half later, with the lawyers having exhausted all of their questions of the prospective jurors, each party then got the chance to exercise its strikes. The defense team huddled together around their table. Tracey, Mike, Ashley, our paralegal Gina, and I gathered around our table to compare notes. Bobbi Bernstein, who happened to be in New Orleans, contributed her thoughts.

Of the thirty-six potential jurors available, twenty-four identified as White, seven as Black, and one was of South Asian/Indian descent. They ranged in age from twenty to sixty-five and had an eclectic mix of jobs that included a man who ran a GED program at a local prison, a manager at a Domino's Pizza franchise, an accountant, a gutter installer, a nurse, and a taxi driver. It was a reasonably diverse cross-section of working and middle-class Eastern Louisiana. It looked like we'd get a jury we could live with.

The court clerk handed us a form to document our strikes. We wrote down the numbers of two jurors to strike, then passed it to the defense, who would strike three names. We passed the paper back and forth four times, until we had struck eight jurors, and the defense twelve. (Typically the defense gets more strikes than the prosecution.)

When the final tally returned to our desk, one thing immediately leaped out. The defense had struck every one of the seven Black potential jurors.

I was enraged. It was a transparent maneuver to solidify an all-White jury that the defense figured was most likely to acquit their clients, a tactic expressly barred by *Batson*. But I feared we were probably hamstrung. *Batson* challenges are rarely sustained, and in the rare case where the harm is remedied, it only happens after a review of a conviction on appeal.

Because the prosecution cannot appeal a not-guilty verdict, my only hope was if Judge Africk granted our *Batson* challenge. I figured the odds of a Southern trial judge doing such a thing were close to nil. With a twenty-seven-page questionnaire to hide behind—and ample information from our day and a half of *voir dire*, I assumed the defense could easily put forward race-neutral-sounding reasons to justify their strikes that the judge would accept.

I asked the court if we could approach. The judge had already sized up the situation: "This has to do with the *Batson* issues?"

I responded, probably too flippantly, "You know it, your honor." I was pissed off.

After looking closely at the strikes on the list, an angry Africk agreed that we had met the threshold of discrimination, a *"prima facie"* case. "I want to know why that happened," he demanded.

The burden shifted to the defense to explain, juror-by-juror, why it had exercised each strike. The first Black juror to have been struck was Juror 9, a fifty-six-year-old Black man from New Orleans, who worked as a road manager for a blues band and a parking valet. His wife was a schoolteacher.

Two defense attorneys put forward unconvincing justifications for their strikes. Then, Frank DeSalvo, typically the best of the bunch on his feet, stepped in to try to save the day. "I did not like his demeanor; not just what he said, the way he said it. Quite frankly, I think the description we gave of him was that he appeared like a hipster, and we didn't think he should be on the jury."

"What is a *hipster*?" Africk asked, seeming truly confused.

"Just a guy that's a cool cat or something."

My first thought was: *Did he really just say "cool cat"?* What I should have said was, "I think that is just a code word for 'Black.'" Instead, I ranted about the defense's post hoc rationalization for their strikes. "They struck every single African American, and if you look at them from one to one, they are the most diverse group of seven individuals you could get... The only thing those seven people have in common is their race."

The defense made more half-hearted efforts to justify the strikes. It wasn't much of a performance, but most of the time, this sort of lawyerly prevarication passes muster in courts all over America, not just in the South. (A few years ago, a video surfaced from a district attorney's office in Philadelphia training prosecutors to use coded language about "demeanor" to circumvent *Batson*.)

Africk wasn't having it: "I find the responses are not credible."

In the end, to my amazement, and I'm sure the amazement of the defense team, Judge Africk reseated, in total, three of the struck Black jurors: Jurors 9, 33, and 66.

With that, we had a jury. The twelve jurors and four alternates took a new oath as actual trial jurors, and I had gone from despair to guarded optimism. The system seemed to have actually worked like it was supposed to. We had what appeared to be a persuadable jury. Now we just needed to persuade them. Court would resume at 8:30 a.m. the next morning for opening statements.

PART III

TRIAL

CHAPTER 14

TELLING STORIES

November 10, 2010

The week before trial began, I hunkered down in my DC house, working on a draft of the opening statement, surrounded by binders of transcripts and trial exhibits, legal pads and scattered photos of Henry Glover. My two-year-old daughter fluttered around in her green fairy outfit, constantly demanding that I "play!" I thought back to Keyalah Bell's tutu-clad daughter dancing across our first interview, and the challenges that parents often face managing work and family responsibilities.

When the trial started, my routine of shuttling back and forth between DC and New Orleans would be upended, and I would remain in New Orleans for the duration of the trial. I knew this would put a huge strain on my wife, Fiona, who, in addition to solo parenting while three months pregnant with our second child, was managing rapid growth of the social enterprise she had founded ten years earlier. During my extended absence, all the household responsibilities would fall on her. While I was still around, I wanted to log as much family time as possible.

Back in New Orleans, Tracey worked through her edits to the opening. We traded draft files back and forth until we had something that felt right to both of us. The challenge was to tell a coherent, compelling narrative that explained separate crimes that were both distinct and overlapping, without bogging the jury down in minutiae or the nuances of civil rights law.

A lot of trial lawyers fail to articulate a clear narrative of the case in their opening statement, defaulting to witness-by-witness summaries of the evidence (usually in chronological order) and a bland recitation of legal statutes. That's a missed opportunity. Though Judge Africk would remind the jurors that the lawyers' arguments "are not evidence," opening statements inform—both explicitly and subconsciously—how jurors digest everything that follows.

On the morning of November 10, Tracey slowly walked to the podium, placed her notes on the rostrum, and stepped to one side to stand face-to-face with the jurors without a barrier between them. She delivered her opening remarks, which we had finalized only the day before, from memory.

"Four days after Hurricane Katrina, Henry Glover was simply trying to get his family out of New Orleans, but you will hear that he never made it out."

Most trial attorneys have big egos and big voices, and they appreciate an audience. That was true of most of the defense attorneys. Even though Magner and I had our stylistic differences—I was overtly intense and Mike was tactically folksy—it was true enough for us too.

Tracey was different. She sounded calm and unassuming, and most importantly, credible, as she delivered the lines for maximum impact. "Instead, he was shot as he was running away. He was left to bleed to death in a stranger's car, and his body was burned so that no one would ever know what happened to him." She continued: "The [defendants] believed that after the storm, no one was watching. They were convinced that no one would ever care about Henry Glover and how he died and that no one would ever care about the inhumane, criminal acts that they committed."

Piece by piece, Tracey told the story of Henry's last day, explaining how the shooting by Warren at the mall connected to the beatings at Habans School and then the burning of Henry's body by the levee. She detailed the many acts by police officers—some by the defendants on trial, others by witnesses who would testify— to hide the truth. And she used the opening to address the biggest vulnerabilities in our case, and as best we could, inoculate the jury against the defense attacks to come.

One challenge we faced was that many key prosecution witnesses had lied at some point during the investigation, or at best, had remained silent for years about the crimes they witnessed. We knew Linda Howard would be confronted with her first ambiguous interview with the NOPD investigator, Gerard Dugue. We expected that Sergeant Nina Simmons would be branded a liar after she had perjured herself multiple times in her testimony before the grand jury. And we anticipated that the defense would question the motives of Lieutenant Joe Meisch, who agreed to testify that he'd witnessed the burning only after receiving immunity.

Tracey explained the mindset of officers who'd witnessed wrongdoing but felt muzzled by the culture of the NOPD. "Some [officers] will tell you that they were afraid. They were afraid because they didn't want to be considered 'a rat'; they were afraid that other police officers, if they told the truth, they wouldn't back them up on the street later on."

She tried to predict likely defenses and tackle them head-on. We assumed that for David Warren, self-defense would be his core defense, so she emphasized that Warren, perched on the second-floor balcony, behind locked gates, was never in danger. Our case against McCabe, for doctoring the shooting report and lying about it, and against Italiano, for denying the existence of both that report and the missing persons report, was circumstantial. So Tracey meticulously explained how each small piece of evidence contributed to the larger picture of obstruction.

We were uncertain how the SOD officers Greg McRae and Dwayne Scheuermann would defend the decision to burn the body. It's hard to counter a defense argument when you don't know what it is. Tracey took her best shot: "The defense may suggest to you that the car was burned for health and safety reasons, but you will hear evidence that no bodies in the New Orleans area were being burned for health and safety reasons or any other reason."

At the end of the opening, she cut through the eleven charges to land on some simple truths. "The days that followed Hurricane Katrina were difficult for anyone who stayed in New Orleans. But as hard as the storm was for the defendants, it was even harder for the Glover family. They left New Orleans that day without Henry; their father, their brother, their son... There is no disaster grave enough to permit a police officer to shoot an unarmed man as he is running away, to allow a man to bleed to death in a stranger's car, to set a man's car on fire, to burn a human being's body, or to lie to cover these things up.

"That is exactly what these defendants did," Tracey concluded. "At the end of this trial, we are going to ask you to find each and every one of them guilty as charged."

I doubted Tracey's opening revealed anything new to the defense attorneys. Our theory of the case already had been laid out in multiple ways through the indictment and pre-trial motions. The defense openings were a different story. Over the course of nineteen months, we had struggled to nail down exactly how the defendants would defend their conduct. Our team listened intently as each attorney gave a separate argument on behalf of their clients.

Warren's attorney, silver-haired Julian Murray, stepped up to the podium, his baritone voice broadcasting indignation: "What you have heard from counsel for the government is not the way it happened. It's not even close to the way it happened." He began by painting a picture of David Warren as the good Christian family man, pausing to look at Warren's wife and his five young children, all under the age of sixteen, sitting silently near the front of the courtroom, as if at church.

He explained how this forty-year-old father of five became a police officer. He arrived in New Orleans after selling his share of the family business in Wisconsin, and looked for new business opportunities. But he was nudged towards police work by a mentor, a Tulane criminology professor who ran a shooting range in the city. The mentor suggested, "You always wanted to be a policeman. You have always been into guns. You have belonged to NRA. You have taken courses on shooting. Why don't you go into the police department? You're not too old." And Warren responded, "Well, I think I'm going to do that... I can do this. I can make a career of being a policeman."

"Wait," I thought to myself, "he became a cop because he liked guns?" Reason enough to open a shooting range, but it was an odd way to explain the career aspirations of a man accused of lawlessly firing his prized sniper rifle at a man who was running away. It was a disquieting insight on how Warren viewed his role as a police officer.

As expected, Murray gave us an alternate narrative for the shooting that cast Warren as a good cop protecting his life and the life of his partner, Officer Howard.

"He hollered at them [Glover and Calloway] twice, 'Police, get back. Police, get back,' and they kept running [towards him]. And he had about a second to decide whether to let them get in there or whether to fire his weapon, and he had that second to do it. He knew if they got in there that there was no way that he and his partner could protect [themselves]. He did not see a gun. He saw him reach in his waistband for what he perceived to be a weapon."

This was a telling way to phrase it, that "a weapon" had merely been "perceived," as the only threat that could justify lethal force against a man sixty-plus feet away is possession of a gun. Murray claimed this didn't matter: "What was compelling was not so much seeing the weapon, but he was in plain view in uniform with a rifle in his hand, and Henry Glover looks right up at him as he is running towards that gate and doesn't break stride." In this retelling, Henry and Bernard's efforts to pick up two suitcases morphed into a full-scale assault on the police substation.

Murray offered up some evidence to the jury that his client felt vulnerable on that second-floor breezeway. Earlier that morning, before Henry Glover approached the strip mall, Warren encountered a different Black man.

Not long after Warren and Howard arrived, they noticed "a person on a bicycle who was circling the substation." Murray explained that this was unusual four days after Katrina. "There was nothing out there, nothing moving, nothing at all. It was absolutely dead silence.

"So about the fifth time [the man on the bike] comes around, [Warren] takes his rifle out that he had taken from home... So he fires a warning shot at this guy." Murray dismisses the gravity of this, "not close to him, it's into the grass behind him—but the guy just hears it and he quit circling."

It was a startling admission. Just weeks before trial, Linda Howard had told us about how Warren fired at a man—in Howard's account, on foot, not bicycle—who was, she estimated, about a football field and a half away.

We wanted to introduce this earlier shooting incident as evidence of Warren's state of mind, which seemed to be to shoot at anything that moved, whether it presented any immediate danger or not. However, Judge Africk deferred ruling on admissibility, and did not allow Tracey to mention this earlier shooting during her opening.

But now Murray had "opened the door" by introducing the earlier shooting, thinking—why, I'm not sure—that it helped Warren's defense.

Up to this point, Murray's rather disjointed opening only seemed to bolster our case against his client, the gun-loving rookie cop willing to use lethal force whenever he felt like it. But then he slipped into attack mode, with his first line of attack coming from a direction I'd never anticipated: the "boy on the bike."

For much of the investigation, Ashley and I had tried to find "the boy on the bike," whom we had heard witnessed the shooting. Late in the investigation, we finally found him.

The boy was twelve when he saw Henry get shot. I was somewhat leery about putting him on the stand. Memory, credibility, and reliability are always issues with a juvenile witness, especially one asked to recall events that happened five years earlier. On top of that, the temporary duty FBI agents who located him ignored Ashley's instructions and interviewed him without us. They produced a mangled version of the facts in their report of the interview.

When Ashley and I re-interviewed the boy, he clarified his statement and corrected misunderstandings. The inconsistencies, I thought, would probably preclude us from calling him as a witness, but we weren't ready to write him off completely, and so we kept him on the witness list.

But it wasn't so much the boy's version of events that was under attack. It was me.

Murray flagged differences in the two FBI reports.

"What's going on here?" Murray's ruddy complexion got redder as he got excited. "I'll tell you what's going on. Twelve days later, two different FBI agents go to interview [the boy on a bike], and they go together with *Mr. Fishman*." Murray emphasized my name as if the sound of it was distasteful. "...[Y]ou will find [he] is not only the prosecutor here, but he investigates also."

After noting that there is "nothing illegal or improper about that," Murray pounced. "But what about going out twelve days later? They don't like what the other agent said. Do they go out with the same two agents again? No. They go out with two different agents...

"Think about it and be careful because that's what happens by reconstruction. I'm not going to say anybody is lying. I'm saying four years later, when people try and come up and tell you what happened, they're reconstructing it."

I felt my heart drop into my stomach. I realized for the first time that our nineteen-month investigation would also be on trial. Murray was accusing Ashley and me of pressuring a witness to change his story to comport with our theory of the case.

Murray then doubled down on his theme of "reconstructed memories," turning his attack on Linda Howard, our most important witness against his client. "Linda Howard was seeing zombies. She was seeing shadows at the time." He rolled his eyes, mocking her. Murray twisted her evocative description from her first Dugue interview—that the lifeless expressions of the residents after Katrina reminded her of "zombies"—to paint her as unstable, even delusional.

Murray stressed how Howard's account of the shooting expanded over time. But instead of merely targeting Howard for her inconsistencies, he again directed his ire against our prosecution team.

"Now, of course, when the FBI goes to interview her [after Dugue], the statement is different. When she goes before the grand jury, the statement is different again... And you know what she says? 'Well, it was *revealed* to me what happened.' Revealed to her? By whom? Not by the Lord. Who revealed it to her? The government!

"...Why is it these things keep changing? They keep changing to fit the way the government wants it to be, and that's dangerous, ladies and gentlemen."

I worried that there was at least one juror, quite possibly more, who might believe that the prosecution of these police officers was political. Magner, Tracey and I had a hasty *sotto voce* conversation at the prosecution desk. Mike then addressed the court. "We have an objection to make to Mr. Murray's opening statement. We believe that he unfairly and improperly maligned Mr. Fishman..."

At the bench, Murray adopted a casual, "can't you take a joke?" tone: "Judge, they can't put him out there as an investigator, as he has been throughout the trial, and be so sensitive."

Africk wasn't amused. "I don't want any other mention of Mr. Fishman unless you come to the bench." Frank DeSalvo, always on the lookout for an opening to get in a jab, reassured the judge. "I won't have anything bad to say…" he turned to me with a smile "…about Tracey or Mr. Magner."

I was anxious to hear DeSalvo's statement in defense of McRae. Ever since DeSalvo testified at the conflict of interest hearing that he was "convinced that there's no criminality," and "that nobody really needs a lawyer," I puzzled over his trial strategy. Throughout the investigation, DeSalvo had repeatedly told us that we had "got it all wrong." Now it was time for him to show his cards.

DeSalvo didn't waste any time.

"On September [2], 2005, my client Greg McRae drove William Tanner's car from the Habans School to the levee… In that car was the dead body of Henry Glover. He drove over the levee, parked the car in a green space so a fire wouldn't spread, he lit a flare, threw it in the car, closed the door, walked away. As he was walking away, he turned around and fired one shot into the rear glass of the car.…

"Nobody asked him to set that car on fire with the body in it. No one ordered him to set that car on fire with the body in it. No one knew he was going to set that car on fire with the body in it. He just set that car on fire."

There it was, just what I had wanted to forestall in that pre-trial hearing to remove DeSalvo from the case. By taking full responsibility for the burning, McRae insulated the rest of the police department, including DeSalvo's former client, the higher-ranking Lieutenant Dwayne Scheuermann.

But, DeSalvo continued, his client's actions, while solely his responsibility, should be viewed in a compassionate light. "…[I]t's not under today's standards or the thinking of a person who sleeps at night or who has normal stress, who gets to eat and drink, that Greg McRae should be judged by. You need to look at what Greg McRae knew, look at what he didn't know, measure his intent when he did what he did."

DeSalvo was asserting a full-blown "Katrina defense," which the judge had explicitly disallowed in his pre-trial ruling. Magner jumped from his seat to lodge an objection, which Africk sustained.

DeSalvo wasn't left with much of a defense. He wasn't presenting any medical experts to support his contention that Katrina had altered McRae's sense of reality. Essentially, he was asking the jury to sympathize with his client. DeSalvo argued that McRae's actions were irrational, and therefore they couldn't be "willful." He also claimed that McRae didn't know that Glover had been shot by a fellow police officer, and therefore his actions could not constitute obstruction of justice.

"Greg McRae didn't know that Henry Glover had been shot by a policeman. He didn't know David Warren. He didn't think about denying anyone access to a court system. He didn't fathom that he was violating anybody's civil rights… He just dealt with another body. He was emotionally drained when he did what he did. And he wishes today he hadn't done it, but he did it."

DeSalvo's opening statement seemed to concede that McRae acted unreasonably by burning Tanner's car. I felt confident, before a single witness had testified, that we would walk away with at least one or two convictions against him.

I glanced over at the stone-faced, stoic-looking SOD officer. I'm a big believer in loyalty but this was a level that I couldn't fathom.

Ashley leaned closer to me and whispered in my ear. "You know I love you, but I would never fall on my sword like that for you."

McRae got a partial reprieve at the conclusion of the openings when Judge Africk reversed himself. He said he would allow the officer to testify about seeing dead bodies in the water in the course of SOD rescue missions, a gruesome detail that DeSalvo tried to emphasize in his opening argument, but that the judge excluded. As the attorney put it, "It's extremely relevant to him [McRae] because it was the rotting bodies that just had him totally depressed and emotionally unstable and that's what caused him to do what he did."

★ ★ ★

Jeff Kearney, a well-seasoned defense lawyer from Fort Worth, Texas, strode to the podium. He looked like a lawyer for Big Oil—slicked back hair, dark suit, cowboy boots—although his practice represented an eclectic mix of criminal defendants from corporate fraudsters to a member of the Branch Davidians. DeSalvo had gotten to know Kearney when they had worked together on a case in Kentucky, and he'd brought him on board to represent Scheuermann.

DeSalvo certainly made Kearney's job easier, teeing up Scheuermann's defense and letting the Texan swing away. "[Scheuermann] did not knowingly or willfully or in any manner participate in the burning of William Tanner's vehicle that contained the body of Henry Glover," Kearney announced, almost the first words out of his mouth.

"It was a total surprise to him. He did not have any idea that Greg McRae was going to throw a flare into that car and set that body on fire... It was never discussed with Mr. Scheuermann." Kearney paused for emphasis. "Greg McRae acted on his own."

During those days after Katrina hit, he said, his client had been working at the limits of human endurance. "From Monday morning till Friday morning, when this happened, Dwayne Scheuermann had about six or eight hours of sleep, had eaten a couple of Tootsie Rolls in that four-day period of time and one can of soup."

According to his attorney, Scheuermann was in the wrong place at the wrong time. "...[A]ll he was doing was following Greg McRae. McRae drove the vehicle...parked it where Commander Winn had told him to park it. Dwayne Scheuermann was waiting to pick him up to drive him back to the Habans School, and shockingly and surprisingly Greg McRae burns the car and shoots the window out.

"When he gets back to Mr. Scheuermann's vehicle, Mr. Scheuermann asked him, 'What in the F have you done? Why did you do that?' He gets a response something to the effect that, 'I wasn't going to let a body rot'… And Lieutenant Scheuermann tells Greg McRae, 'You need to go get some sleep.'"

We didn't believe Kearney's story, but we were intrigued nonetheless. It directly implicated Captain Jeff Winn, the head of SOD.

Kearney asserted that while there was plenty of blame to go around for what transpired at the Patterson levee, none of it should attach to Dwayne Scheuermann. According to his attorney, Scheuermann didn't know that Glover had been shot by the police, and investigating the shooting wasn't his job.

Investigating a homicide in the Fourth District, Kearney told the jury, correctly, was the job of the Fourth District Investigative Unit, which had been headed up by Scheuermann's codefendant, Robert Italiano.

Italiano's attorney, Steve Lemoine, had a small local practice and seemed to pick up cases through the police union. He wasn't an eloquent speaker, but listening to his less than scintillating opening, it seemed that his averageness might work to Italiano's advantage, minimizing his importance in the case.

And Italiano was undeniably at the center of the case. The shooting took place at the substation he commanded. He responded to the Habans call. He was there while Glover lay dying or dead in Tanner's car. He reportedly spoke with Dwayne Scheuermann shortly before the car and the body were burned. And his name appeared on the two key documents in the case—the missing persons report and the Signal 21 report on the shooting.

Lemoine appreciated that the jury wasn't going to be riveted by accounts of missing or misremembered paperwork. The more Italiano's contribution to the crimes against Henry could be made to seem uninteresting or incidental, the better for Italiano. In a case with five defendants, getting lost in the crowd wasn't a bad thing.

Lemoine provided lots of excuses. Italiano didn't connect the shooting at the mall and the shooting victim at Habans because he'd heard over the police radio that the victim had been driven away from the mall in a white truck, not a white sedan. The lapses in memory and the failure to make obvious connections could be explained away by Katrina. And besides, a police-involved homicide should have been investigated by Dugue's homicide unit, not Italiano's Fourth District DIU, shifting blame to yet another part of the NOPD.

Any one of those claims might be plausible. It was our job to demonstrate to the jury that in the aggregate, they defied belief. Lemoine saw it differently.

"Now, ladies and gentlemen, I know that it's possible to take facts, put them all together, and weave them in a way that looks like someone had to know, but that's simply not what happened... The evidence will show that it's a tragedy that Mr. Glover died, it's a tragedy that his body was burned on the levee, but that doesn't mean that it's a tragedy that...was involved with an intentional police cover-up of the facts, because the evidence will show that that's not what occurred."

To my mind, Sergeant Travis McCabe, the officer charged with writing a false report of the shooting and lying about it to the FBI, was the least significant defendant in the case. I had hoped he would come clean and help us build our case against more senior officers. Instead, McCabe had assembled some top-notch legal talent to handle his defense, two accomplished trial lawyers, Allyn Stroud and Mike Small.

Stroud opened for Team McCabe. Aiming for the head, not the heart, Stroud laid out a methodical ten-point presentation dissecting our case against his client, corporate PowerPoint style.

He began by painting McCabe as the world's most unlikely cover-up artist, just a regular guy trying to do his best in irregular circumstances. On September 2, McCabe had been pumping gas at a makeshift gas station that fueled emergency vehicles. Stroud told the jury, "...[A]s you listen to the alleged evidence that the government says it will present in support of this supposed super-duper cover-up by Officer McCabe...at the end of the day, that evidence is going to be very anticlimactic and unconvincing."

Stroud's ten-point defense landed a few damaging blows that we'd have to parry when our witnesses testified. His core argument was our charges against McCabe—that he lied and that he perjured himself—relied on witnesses who themselves had lied.

"You'll be able to judge the credibility of those witnesses. You will be able to decide if someone takes that stand and admits to having previously lied under oath whether anything they say is worthy of belief."

With close to five hours of opening statements concluded, we were ready to present testimony. Judge Africk declared, "The government...will call its first witness."

CHAPTER 15

CASE-IN-CHIEF

November 10 through 12, 2010

In any criminal trial, the prosecution presents its "case-in-chief" first, calling its witnesses to prove guilt "beyond a reasonable doubt." We planned to call thirty witnesses to build our case, and all five defense attorneys would do their best to tear what they had to say apart.

Similar to the impact of the opening statement, choosing the first witness for trial has an outsize importance. Jurors, like most humans, are heavily influenced by what they learn first—the so-called "primacy effect." That first witness frames the way jurors remember all the details that follow.

Whenever possible, I want the first witness to speak to the emotional heart of the case, why this case matters. For me, that was Henry's sister, Patrice Glover.

Patrice could set the stage by viscerally describing what had been done to her brother—Henry bleeding to death on the street; Bernard and Edward dejected and bruised after a police beating; the family torn apart by uncertainty.

Just as important, she could humanize Henry in the jurors' minds. Opening statements demonstrated that the defense would characterize Henry as a "looter" and a "thug." It was our job to counteract that, but without asking questions that might "open the door" to the "criminal history" that we managed to exclude, like Henry's more than a decade old arrest record as a teenager and young adult.

Though her testimony spoke to many of the charges in the case, nothing she said directly implicated any of the defendants, which, I hoped, meant their attorneys wouldn't beat her up on cross-examination. There is no point in scoring some early points on direct, only to have them snatched away on cross.

In the months leading up to trial, Patrice and I spent many hours together, often in the living room of her mother's house. We rehashed the events of 2005 again and again, to help her tell a coherent, forceful narrative. Once she was on the stand, it would be harder for me to fill in the gaps. According to the rules of evidence, I could only ask open-ended questions, like, "Tell me what happened," and hope she responded in a way that sounded natural and unrehearsed, no matter how many times we'd gone over it.

In the almost two years I'd known Patrice, I'd grown to appreciate her warmth and her perseverance, qualities that had kept her extended family together through innumerable hard times. But as strong as she was, she was clearly nervous about testifying. "Just look at me when I'm asking you questions," I told her. "Let's just try to have a conversation like we always do."

From the podium, I could see the terror in her eyes. The courtroom was obviously nothing like her mother's living room. Staring down at her was the robed judge from his raised desk. A courtroom packed with people watched her, including, less than thirty feet away, the five men who, between them, were accused of killing and burning her brother and covering up those crimes. Three of them were still employed by the NOPD, "serving and protecting" the city of New Orleans.

Patrice's voice was shaky, and the answers to my questions were clipped and staccato. I struggled to elicit from her the kind of conversation we'd had so many times in the past.

I wanted her to paint the picture of those first days after the storm, trapped in a mostly deserted Algiers, huddled together in a dark, roofless apartment with two young kids, without the basics of urban survival, like water or electricity. But her descriptions lacked the detail that typically brought her story to life.

"It was very scary at nighttime."

"Why was that?"

"Because you just was frightened. You know, anybody could have come in your house or—you know, you couldn't see. It was very dark. It was very scary."

Patrice explained why her family would stay in these miserable conditions, several days after the levees had breached and most of the city was underwater. I wanted the jury to consider the precariousness of living through Katrina without emergency cash or a way out of the city.

"[Henry] didn't want to leave because, you know, he didn't have any resources or, you know, any finance or no transportation."

The morning of September 2, Henry and Bernard left the apartment complex together, looking for a way to get the family out of New Orleans. A half hour passed, but only Bernard came back.

"He was screaming, hysterical, and telling me my brother had been shot." She testified that she and Bernard then ran out to the corner of Texas and Seine, near the mall.

Before she could tell the court about finding her brother lying bloody in the street, Patrice began to sob. I told her to take her time and offered her a glass of water. The courtroom was silent as I waited for her to recover her composure.

I was nervous too. Patrice was the first witness in the biggest trial of my career. I was rushing through questions, sticking to my prepared script, and not being flexible enough to adjust to Patrice's new reticence. I had a sinking feeling that I was not doing a very good job "humanizing Henry." Instinctively, I didn't want to push Patrice too hard. I worried about her completely falling apart on the stand.

When she recovered, I asked her, "Now, when you got there, was your brother still alive?"

"Yes, he was."

"What did you tell Henry?"

"I said, 'You all right? Blink your eyes.'" Henry blinked his eyes. He was alive but desperately needed help.

That's when a stranger, William Tanner, showed up with a white sedan. Edward and Bernard loaded Henry in the car and disappeared, looking for help. Patrice and others from the neighborhood lingered on the street where Henry had fallen.

About two hours later, Tanner, who had been released from Habans first, told her what had transpired. Patrice walked to the school looking for Bernard and Edward, only to be told by an officer there that they had "let the motherfuckers go." She returned home to find her boyfriend and her brother bruised and desperate to get out of town as fast as possible.

Her first time back in New Orleans was in 2006 for Henry's funeral.

"So why had it taken eight months to have a funeral for your brother?"

"Because my mother and the kids had to do dental work and try to identify, you know, the body."

"What sort of funeral did you have for Henry?"

"We had a closed casket."

"Why was that?"

"Because they said his body was burnt beyond recognition." Patrice began to sob again.

It's impossible to truly prepare a witness for cross-examination. My advice to Patrice was the same I have for all witnesses: "Listen closely to the questions. Answer the question that was asked. And just tell the truth."

Though Patrice's testimony did not incriminate Warren directly,

Julian Murray came out swinging. As stiff as Patrice had been on direct, on cross she simply froze up. At times, she seemed genuinely confused by Murray's sometimes sloppily worded questions. His intent, it seemed to me, was less to discredit her for any substantive inconsistencies than to establish his intellectual superiority over a lower-income woman with only a high school education. That came across most clearly when Murray, a White septuagenarian, started referring to her brother Edward King by his nickname, "Dirty Red," which sounded like dog-whistle racism, a way to "ghettoize" Patrice, and by extension, Henry. I thought he came off as a bully, and I hoped the jurors would see it that way too.

Jeff Kearney, Scheuermann's attorney, must have thought Murray's line of attack yielded results, taking it one step further, calling Edward only "Dirty."

"So Dirty went back, you say, and got Mr. Tanner, who I guess he knew?"

Patrice, it appeared, had heard enough.

"His name is Edward King," she said. "And we didn't know Tanner."

The defense had scored points on cross. But the party that calls a witness is allowed a "redirect examination." I could parry the most damaging blows and remind the jurors what mattered most about her testimony.

When Frank DeSalvo had crossed Patrice, he'd asked her questions about where she'd seen the blood seeping from her brother's body. DeSalvo didn't represent Warren, but he nonetheless wanted to plant the idea in the jury's mind that Henry had been shot in the chest—not the back—which would bolster Warren's self-defense claim.

I took issue with that on my "redirect" that followed DeSalvo's cross-examination. I asked her about the blood she had seen "…[W]hat were you focused on at that time?"

"I was focused on, you know, him—you know, talking to him, making sure, you know, he is all right and trying to get him some help."

I had planned to wait until William Tanner testified to introduce the photos of Henry lying bloodied in the back seat of the Chevy. I had not wanted to put them up enlarged on the courtroom's overhead screen when Patrice was on the stand. Testifying for her was already emotional enough, and I didn't want it to look like I was trying to manufacture a tearful moment.

But my redirect provided a good opportunity to rebut the notion that Henry was shot in the chest. The photos also served as visual corroboration for our next witness, Linda Howard, who would describe how Henry was shot in the back while running away.

Certainly, the image would bring anyone up short: Henry facedown, as if in deep sleep, a cherry-red entrance wound visible in the center of the back of his white T-shirt. He must have lost a lot of blood from what we were sure was the chest exit wound—the sides of the T-shirt are soaking it up.

I placed the photo on the overhead screen. "Who is that in that picture?"

"That's my brother."

Patrice, once again, broke down in tears.

When I next saw Patrice that evening, she was abject. "I'm sorry, Jared, I messed up." She felt like she had disappointed me, that her emotions, and her nerves, had gotten the better of her. I tried to reassure her: "You didn't mess up. Were you honest?" She nodded yes. "Then everything is good."

But truthfully, I *was* a little disappointed. I was disappointed that the jury didn't get to see the same Patrice that I knew. I was frustrated at myself for not being flexible enough to adapt to the changed circumstances.

With hindsight, I realize I was being too hard on both of us. Patrice had done exactly what she needed to do. However dissimilar her life may have been to some of the jurors, they couldn't listen to Patrice's testimony and not come away with a feeling that Henry was deeply loved.

Linda Howard was our most important witnesses in the murder case against David Warren. She was certain she had seen her partner-for-the-day shoot at two unarmed Black men with a sniper rifle, killing one with a shot through the back from about sixty feet away.

But she had her own baggage. Though she now clearly described a police assassination, just as clearly, she had not said as much to Sergeant Dugue when he interviewed her only days before we had. Her explanation for the discrepancy—that she had been on medication and that she had repressed her memories—had never felt to us like the whole story.

Murray had made it clear in his opening that he would attack the "reconstructed memories" of a woman who was "seeing zombies." We needed the jury to see a different Linda Howard, a traumatized woman who had witnessed a murder, and then, after the indifferent reaction of the department higher-ups who were supposed to investigate it, had retreated into silence.

Howard had a distinctly different persona from the stereotype of the macho, rule-skirting New Orleans cop. She projected a sweetness at odds with an often gritty job. She told Tracey that she was inspired to join the police force by watching two gender-norm-busting cop shows of the 1970s, *Police Woman*, starring Angie Dickinson, and *Get Christie Love!*, starring Teresa Graves. "I always wanted to be just like them when I grew up," she said.

She seemed happiest performing jobs not typically thought of as "policing." Working with the Police Athletic League, she coached young girls, mostly lower-income Black girls, in sports like basketball and volleyball. It was the type of "community policing" that most police departments pay lip service to and yet underfund.

Tracey handled the direct of Linda Howard. My sense was, Tracey's calm, empathetic presence helped Howard come to terms with memories and feelings that she had bottled up since Katrina.

Tracey's job on direct was to guide Howard through the shooting and, almost as importantly, the Dugue statement, in a way that helped the jurors understand just how traumatic the shooting had been for her and why she hadn't told Dugue the whole story, even if, as we suspected, she herself hadn't yet fully acknowledged the reasons.

Howard's affect on the stand was completely different from her emotional reliving of events that Ashley and I had experienced during our first interview with her a year and a half earlier. Though the words she used were similar this time, she recounted the events of the shooting in a flat, neutral tone, almost matter-of-factly.

Howard testified that she and Warren entered the mall by the front entrance. When they explored the back side of the mall, they discovered the only access point to the mall from the back parking lot was chained and locked.

Things went downhill when he spotted a young man across the parking lot over 100 yards away. Warren scanned the scene through the scope of his high-powered rifle and fired a single shot. The man crouched down and then ran off. Howard yelled at Warren. *Why had he just fired his rifle?*

"I just want to see something," he replied.

Not long after, she and Warren saw two women in the parking lot pushing a shopping cart containing what the officers assumed were stolen goods from one of the mall stores. Warren shooed them away while brandishing his gun.

Shortly after, a Firestone truck, making loud gear-grinding noises, pulled into the rear lot. She said that "two young Black males" jumped out of the truck, making their way to a shopping cart with the two suitcases the women had left there. Before the men could load the suitcases in the truck, Howard said, Warren yelled out a brief command. She couldn't remember the exact words, "but it was a loud command…telling them to get away from there."

It seemed to take the two men by surprise. "You know, like they were, like, startled… [T]hey didn't know someone was at that location. So when the loud voice rang out, they were scared, and then they ran off."

To get a better look at the fleeing men, she moved towards the rear of the mall, right up to the locked gate that overlooked the back parking lot.

"And out of the corner of my eye I could see [Warren] coming [forward] and leveling his weapon at that time, and then a shot rang out."

Tracey pressed for the details to demonstrate that Warren was unjustified in taking that single, fatal shot. Howard testified that she saw the back of the man whom Warren shot, as he was running away. She did not see a gun in either man's hands, or for that matter, any type of weapon. Neither man had tried to enter through the downstairs gate, which they couldn't have done even if they'd wanted to. It was locked, and the only entrance was at the front of the mall.

Howard said she didn't even reach for her weapon. "I didn't feel threatened."

After firing his rifle, Warren informed Howard that he hadn't hit the man in the parking lot. She said he did.

"I said, 'Well, I got to call the rank,'" meaning, alert a superior officer. "He said, 'Why?' I said, 'Because you shot somebody!'"

Howard testified that maybe three to five minutes after the shooting, she saw a white sedan drive up and spirit the wounded man away. She was in tears, stunned by what she had just witnessed. When the "rank" arrived shortly afterwards, Sergeant Nina Simmons with her rookie partner, Keyalah Bell, Howard was still near-hysterical.

At the end of shift, Warren drove her back to the Fourth District precinct, where Italiano asked her if it was a good shooting. She said she shook her head and indicated it wasn't.

Save for her brief conversation with Simmons, who was preparing the Signal 21 report three months later, this was the only conversation about the shooting she had within the department until 2009. Howard got the message, wordlessly but unmistakably, that she should bury what she'd seen.

"…[N]obody came to me and asked me anything about it. I just didn't know who to trust or who to believe or who could you— who could you talk to. So what I did was I just kept it inside because you had to show that you were strong."

This self-preservation instinct provided context for Howard's interview with Detective Sergeant Gerard Dugue, the first person to ask her about the shooting in three and a half years. According to Howard, she and the detective spoke in total three times, just days before she spoke to Ashley and me for the first time in the spring of 2009. It was the first Dugue interview, the only one that he had recorded or even documented in the investigative record, that the defense attorneys would use to attack her.

Howard testified that Dugue had called her on her cell and insisted they talk that day, even though, as she explained, she was home sick, drowsy from taking prescription-strength Benadryl three times a day for a severe allergic reaction.

"He said, 'Just do the best that you can, but I need to get this done.'"

Dugue arrived at her house that day, she said, and before turning on his tape recorder, he explained the interview ground rules.

"Well, he ran through it, and he told me the questions that he was going to be asking. He told me that he had to get it done because they [the federal investigators] was trying...to railroad Officer Warren."

I twitched in my seat. This was the clearest explanation I had heard of Dugue's corrupt influence. In so many words, "Give me what I need to protect Warren and hold off the feds."

The defense made a "hearsay" objection concerning what Dugue had told her. "Hearsay" is a legal term of art for an out-of-court statement introduced "for the truth of the matter asserted." With some exceptions, hearsay is inadmissible. This statement about what Dugue told her wasn't technically "hearsay," because it was being used to show how it impacted what Howard did next, and not for its "truth." (We disputed any suggestion that the federal investigation hoped to "railroad" Warren.)

Before she could describe her conversation with Dugue, Judge Africk interjected himself and quizzed her about whether Dugue's pre-interview comments had "influenced" what she told him in the taped interview. He was asking her, without spelling it out, whether she had lied to Dugue about what she had and hadn't seen on September 2.

It seemed like an opportune moment for Howard to admit that

she had felt pressured to not tell the full truth. But if she admitted to lying to Dugue, she'd likely lose her job. The NOPD's new chief of police had committed to firing anyone who lied during investigations. "You lie, you die," was the ominous-sounding name given to the new policy.

The judge queried, "…[D]id what he tell you in any way influence the substance of what you told him?"

Howard seemed confused by the question. "Well, he told me that he needed to get—" She seemed to want Dugue's words to speak for themselves, rather than to perform a retrospective psychological assessment of her thought process. The judge cut her off once more.

"No, no, don't tell me *what* he said… He gave you a reason why he said he needed to get this done, right?… Did it make a difference that he told you that, to you?"

"No, not really," she responded. As a result, Judge Africk wouldn't allow her to testify about what Dugue had told her. On such rulings, the fates of trials can turn.

Guided by Tracey's questioning, Howard gave her account of how her memories of September 2 had evolved from the original taped interview. At his request, she said, she returned with Dugue to the DeGaulle mall breezeway several days later.

"And once I was able to go to that location, it started—I started having flashbacks in reference to some of the—the incident that took place at that time. And it stopped me from sleeping and so forth. It's like in the movies, like when you see an incident that took place and then they start asking about—the movie and they start showing different flashbacks or different keys to the story, that's how it was."

I feared that Murray would be dissecting that one on cross.

"Ms. Howard, you seem to be tired today. Are you?" Murray's condescending first question out of the box set the stage for an attack on her mental health.

"I'm fine, sir."

"On any medication?"

"No, sir," she calmly responded.

"Are you taking any therapy?" he asked. Howard denied that she was.

"Have you recently?" he continued.

Howard acknowledged speaking to a social worker about her feelings testifying in this case.

"A *board-certified* social worker, correct?" He was insinuating there was something suspicious about seeking help to deal with a painful experience. His goal of making Howard seem "crazy," and hence unworthy of belief, infuriated me, but it didn't seem to be working.

Murray introduced the recording of her twelve-minute statement to Dugue. I had listened to the recording many times, and Howard, admittedly, didn't sound impaired, although I'm not sure that there is any uniform way that people sound when they're cognitively slowed down by a medication. She didn't slur her words. Her tone was neutral, similar to how she sounded on the stand.

Listening once again to the remarkably short interview, I hoped the jurors noted that Dugue seemed to make every effort *not* to get clear answers about what she had seen from the mall breezeway. Howard only answered the questions in front of her, and Dugue deliberately asked for as little as possible.

The harder Murray attacked her, the more clearly she described the pressure Dugue had applied.

"[Dugue] also told me that, 'I *know* you didn't see the incident, and they are trying to railroad Officer Warren.'" She testified that Dugue said, "'You can't testify to what you didn't see, can you?'"

Murray was furious. "This is hearsay testimony. She well knows it and so does the government."

This time around, Judge Africk allowed the testimony.

Mike Small, the lawyer representing Sergeant Travis McCabe, was generally the most effective attorney on cross-examination. He now took his shot at exposing the contradictions between what Howard had told Dugue and what she testified at trial.

"You admit that that statement [to Dugue] and what you have said today cannot be reconciled? They just don't fit, do they?"

Linda wouldn't be cowed: "It's according to how you look at it."

Linda Howard had walked a fine line. She had given us an account of Henry's murder that was impactful and credible, and she'd somehow managed to avoid admitting that her statements to Dugue were knowingly false, thereby saving her pension and the remainder of her long NOPD career. She had withstood the determined attacks of five high-powered defense attorneys. We didn't ask any follow-up questions.

Fiona had come to New Orleans to support me during the first two days of trial. We headed out to grab dinner when Day 1 concluded. I was eager to compare notes with her about how the day had gone. As we were leaving the courthouse, some of the defendants and their lawyers joined us for what felt like the world's longest elevator ride. What was the protocol? Do I introduce my pregnant wife? I opted for awkward silence.

We left the courthouse and headed to dinner. For months, Fiona had listened patiently as I expressed frustrations about the challenges that witnesses like Linda Howard presented: the inconsistent statements and late-appearing revelations. Now, I worried whether these issues would cloud how jurors understood the facts of the case. Fiona, for one, found her credible. She noted how courageous Howard had been in coming forward at great personal risk. Fiona had thought the jury had seen that too. I hoped she was right.

The next morning, I woke up early after only four hours of sleep. As I would find out over the next few weeks, no matter how late I worked the night before, I couldn't sleep past 4:30 a.m. It was only day two of the trial, and I was already exhausted.

I opened my hotel room door to find a copy of *The Times-Picayune*, beginning what would become my daily ritual. In this era before around-the-clock news on my phone, the print newspaper was the only way to get feedback on how we and our witnesses performed the previous day. At the end of each day in court, our team would deconstruct the highs and lows. But often, the best insights we gleaned came from the local paper.

That morning, the Glover case was the lead story, appearing above the fold, as it would virtually every day that we were in trial.

Officer Fires at Fleeing Man, Cop Says, read the headline. It seemed our narrative was holding, at least for the *Times-Pic* reporters.

William Tanner was arguably *the* pivotal figure in bringing the case of Henry Glover out of the shadows. An NOPD officer drove off with his Chevy Malibu, with Henry in the back seat, and he was determined not to let anybody forget it. He pursued multiple avenues, alerting everyone from a small local nonprofit organization, Safe Streets/Strong Communities, to US Immigration and Customs Enforcement (ICE), which ultimately found his burned car by the levee.

It took three and a half years for his story to gain any traction. By this time, he had paid off his car loan, and made a full-force attempt to get restitution, taking his story to NOPD's Public Integrity Bureau, and most significantly, to investigative journalist A.C. Thompson, whose article in *The Nation* got the attention of my office.

Tanner's role at trial was more limited. He was our first, and likely best, witness to describe the beatings that took place at Habans, and how the police ignored Henry in the back seat of the car. Unlike Edward or Bernard, both close to Henry, Tanner was an impartial third party, which we hoped bolstered his credibility. The news media had taken to calling him "the Good Samaritan," a role that he seemed to relish.

Tanner was Magner's witness. Magner had a disarming "everyman" style that meshed well with his witness. Unlike Patrice, whose nervousness was palpable, Tanner beamed from the stand with his lopsided smile. He wore an ill-fitting taupe suit, with Mardi Gras beads dangling from his neck, a tribute, he said, to his father, who encouraged him to pursue justice in this case and had died on "Fat Tuesday," Mardi Gras day, two years before. He was eccentric, yes, but winning. It was like he'd been waiting all his life to tell his story to the right audience.

"My mother-in-law—her name I will not reveal—she always said I do crazy things. I stayed and videotaped the situation before and aftereffects of the hurricane."...

"Are you going to do that for the next one?" Mike asked.

"No, sir. I won't be here. I guarantee it."

Magner prompted Tanner, never hard to do, to explain how he had tried to save Henry. After Edward King had flagged him down in the street, Tanner could see how gravely Henry was injured. He wasn't concerned about loading a bleeding man into his car: "When you are dealing with somebody's life, you have got more importance." He made the executive decision to drive him to the closest place where he thought they could find medical assistance, the SOD compound at Habans School.

When Tanner drove into Habans's semicircular driveway, he, Bernard Calloway, and Edward King were pulled out of the car and handcuffed.

Tanner identified Greg McRae as the officer who ultimately drove off with his Chevy, flares in hand. Before doing so, McRae had rifled through the car, removing a toolbox and some jumper cables. McRae also snatched away Tanner's neck lanyard that held his driver's license, a credit card and $60 in cash. Tanner asked for it back.

Magner pushed Tanner for specific details. "I know you're not particularly comfortable doing this, okay, but I'm going to ask you to tell us exactly what Defendant McRae told you…"

Tanner reluctantly answered: "'Nigga, it's with your car. That's where it's at.'"

Tanner's weakness as a witness was that he sometimes came across as overconfident. He would double down on some of his less likely assertions to keep the story rolling. It made for a better story but undercut his credibility.

Magner introduced into evidence a photo of the burned-out Chevy taken after US Immigration Customs and Enforcement (ICE) had ID'd the car. On the car's trunk, in red spray paint, was the shorthand used across the city to document where the dead had been found. The car was marked with a large red X, the date, 9-10, and ICE, identifying the agency that "cleared" it.

These markings were so ubiquitous after the storm that Mike assumed Tanner knew what they meant, although they hadn't discussed it in any of their prep sessions. Magner asked Tanner about the markings on the car.

"You're talking about somebody's graffiti?" Tanner asked back.

"Do you think that's graffiti?" Mike replied, surprised by the response.

"Yeah, that's—everybody has a logo for their graffiti. That's a logo. The dude that did it, his name is Mike Ice, and that's his logo."

It was classic Tanner. But I knew that "Mike Ice" was definitely going to make a return appearance on cross.

"Did you ever learn that law enforcement put those marks on your car?" Kearney asked him on cross.

"Probably did." But Tanner stuck to his story, "But I know a dude named Mike Ice, and that's how he autographs stuff sometimes too." (Much later, it occurred to me that Tanner may have been thinking of the well-known New Orleans graffiti artist Bmike. Like I said, Tanner was terrible with names.)

One of our biggest challenges throughout the investigation was identifying who hit whom at Habans. In Tanner's earliest statements, he said that the man who assaulted him had a large tattoo similar to "The Rock," Hollywood action star Dwayne Johnson.

When we first received the ATF photograph showing six officers guarding the three men at Habans, we expected Tanner would confirm the barrel-chested officer with large tattoos and a gun slung over his shoulder was the officer who beat him.

However, when we showed Tanner the ATF photo, he had told us that that man hadn't beat him. Tanner picked out McRae from the same picture and insisted that McRae had kicked him and hit him with a rifle. Nonetheless, Tanner insisted that McRae bore some resemblance to "The Rock," which, admittedly, was a stretch.

When DeSalvo began his cross-examination smiling, I could see the train wreck coming. "Do Mr. McRae and The Rock look alike?"

"Well, if you want to be suggestive, yes. He is built like The Rock because you see the chest area and how his neck and his head look."

DeSalvo pointed out that the basis for Tanner's comparison between the SOD officer and The Rock was the tattoo, not the muscles. So Tanner doubled down, suggesting that McRae and Dwayne Johnson both had similar tattoos. "Like McRae has one [tattoo] on his arm, too, if you look right there, the bottom of his arm."

"You think?"

DeSalvo turned back towards McRae and leaned in for his Perry Mason moment: "Okay. Get undressed."

McRae stood up, removed his jacket and tie, and then, in what felt like a dystopian strip show, he slowly unbuttoned his dress shirt. He was now down to his white undershirt, and his arms, it was clear, lacked any tattoos.

McRae seemed to want to go totally shirtless: "T-shirt, also, Your Honor?"

"Hold on a second!" Africk jumped in. I certainly didn't need to see McRae bare-chested, and likely no one else in the courtroom did either. "No, sir, it's not necessary for you to take your shirt off. Thank you, Mr. McRae."

Steve Lemoine, Italiano's attorney, tried to weaken Tanner's credibility even further. Lemoine had taken note of an odd statement Tanner had made during his grand jury appearance.

"Do you recall making a comment…to the grand jury about a preparation that you had undertaken so that you could be better in your grand jury appearance?"

"There's no preparation you can take for the grand jury," Tanner replied, almost solemnly.

Lemoine seemed to think that Tanner was evading the question, so he quoted directly from the grand jury transcript. "Do you remember saying, 'But I did do a special thing yesterday that made me be more better and all, not a joke or nothing like that'? Do you remember saying that?"

I tried to suppress a laugh. Lemoine must have suspected Tanner of taking some sort of court-performance-enhancing drug.

The day before grand jury, Tanner had shown up uncharacteristically late for our prep session, with a big grin on his face. Yet again in Good Samaritan mode, he had driven his neighbor to the hospital after she had unexpectedly gone into labor. When he testified before the grand jury, he had been eager to tell the jurors about the birth, but I wouldn't let him. Here was his chance.

"What it was, the preparation I did." Tanner paused, seemingly for dramatic effect. "I delivered a baby. That's what that was about. That was the preparation you're trying to speak of in this courtroom. I delivered my friend's baby."

Lemoine seemed genuinely confused. "So in delivering the baby, that prepared you for your grand jury testimony...?"

"I had a chance to see life," Tanner concluded. "I missed my little girl being born, so my friend gave me a chance to deliver her baby. And I was there, and I cut the umbilical cord."

Tanner's confusion about the identity of the officer with the tattoo added to the already difficult challenge of proving the beating case against Scheuermann and McRae. We felt like we had to call the tattooed Sergeant Jeff Sandoz to testify, to corroborate that the men were, in fact, beaten.

When we first received the ATF photograph, I assumed that one of Henry's three allies would confirm that Sandoz had assaulted them. But although the three men said he called them "looters," and called Henry "a piece of shit," none recalled him actually hitting anyone. Josh Burns, the cop turned brothel thief turned prosecution witness, told us that Sandoz slammed one man to the ground, but that wasn't enough to charge him with a civil rights violation.

Sandoz lied shamelessly and unconvincingly when he testified before the grand jury, about not knowing what happened at Habans, leaving him exposed to a perjury charge. After the indictment of the five officers, we approached Sandoz again, and this time, he had a change of heart. He admitted that his prior statements were false, and in exchange for immunity, he agreed to testify against the two officers he had seen assault the three men: Scheuermann and McRae.

Sandoz had been in the school's cafeteria when he heard a loud commotion outside. When he stepped out, he saw three Black men surrounded by fifteen to twenty officers. He saw a bleeding man in the back seat of the car, whom he presumed was dead, though he never saw anyone check his pulse. He called the mood at the school "tense" and described the officers as "agitated" and "aggressive." Though he wouldn't admit to hearing or using racial slurs, he acknowledged thinking that the Black men "had gotten what they deserved," because he "felt like these people shouldn't have even been in the city."

Lieutenant Scheuermann had been in charge, barking orders at the SWAT cops milling around. "Well, while we were standing out there, at some point I observed Lieutenant Scheuermann approach one of the individuals and strike that individual in and about the head area with the butt of his rifle."

"And what prompted Scheuermann to do that at that time?" I asked.

"Nothing that I could see."

Sandoz said that the three men began asking questions about Henry in the back seat, which seemed to enrage the officers. "I observed Officer McRae approach one of the subjects and kick the subject and punch him with his fist."

Finally, Sandoz saw McRae drive off with Tanner's car, followed by Scheuermann in a truck. There had been no conversation, at least none that he claimed to be privy to, about what would happen to the car or the body inside it.

McRae and Scheuermann left the school with the car, and when they returned, they seemed calmer. "…[T]hey weren't agitated, as I had previously described them," Sandoz testified, "but there was nothing that stood out about their demeanor." There was no mention of burning the car or the body. Scheuermann didn't evince any concern about anything that had happened by the levee.

Sandoz explained that he had lied to the grand jury because he had been afraid of what his police colleagues might do to him if he cooperated with us. "Well, [I was concerned] that if I encountered a situation where I needed backup from other officers, that, you know, other officers may not show up, they may say, well, 'He's on his own.'"

I asked why he would risk criminal penalties to protect cops whom he had seen break the law.

"Well, it wasn't necessarily to protect them, it was more about me. I mean, I didn't want to be in that situation. I didn't want to be labeled a rat... I'll be looking over my shoulder for the rest of my life."

Judge Africk cut Sandoz off. "So what's changed that now you decided to tell the truth, according to your testimony?"

"Well, because I felt like, you know, once they were indicted, I felt like I had to come clean, I had to tell the truth, because naturally, I didn't want to be in that position either. I have a son that I am raising, my mother is sick with cancer, I need to be there for those people."

"Well, let's be clear," I jumped in. "When you decided to tell the truth, you had been confronted with your lies. Is that correct?"

"Yeah."

"And it was only at that point that you decided to come clean?" I asked. "Is that correct?"

"Yeah, that's true."

To me, Sandoz came across as an aggressive bully and an unrepentant liar who likely knew far more about the abuse at Habans than he admitted even after taking our immunity deal. The reality of prosecuting police misconduct is that to prove a case, you often have to rely on cops who themselves have violated their oaths.

Over the course of multiple interviews, I grew to really like Bernard Calloway. His stocky, imposing-looking appearance belied a sensitive makeup. The emotional scars incurred in 2005 were far from healed, and he was still anxious that testifying at trial posed a grave risk, given that the last NOPD cop he had seen told him that he'd be killed if he came back to town.

Bernard's vivid description of the days immediately after the storm laid bare the fear and uncertainty facing the lower-income people who were trapped in the city. He described what it felt like to be stripped of food, water, and communication with the world outside his Algiers neighborhood: "It was like the end of the world inside my city."

One thing that struck me about Bernard was that he never tried to hide or minimize what were arguably "bad facts," like stealing to survive. He said he didn't know how Henry came into possession of the Firestone truck but, as he freely acknowledged, "I know he didn't work for Firestone, so I got to safely assume that he stole the truck."

Bernard effectively made the point that he and Henry were simply trying to leave New Orleans. Their trip to the mall was a detour—one that Bernard hadn't wanted to make—at the behest of two women in their travel party who had left stolen goods in two suitcases in the mall parking lot.

When they arrived at the mall, they found the shopping cart with the suitcases near the edge of the lot, exactly where the women said they had left them. Henry hopped out of the front for a brief smoke break while Bernard struggled with one of the suitcases.

"So I was, like, 'Man, this is heavy.' And I looked at Henry, and he was about to light a cigarette. And I went back down again to get the bag. When I reached down again to get it, I heard a 'pow,' just like that, and then I heard the voice, 'Leave now.'... Right behind each other. I heard the sound first... And then as the echo faded, you heard, 'Leave now,' in an authoritative like voice, like that."

Bernard played out the story. The two men took off running; Henry collapsed, sprawled out on his back near the corner of Texas and Seine. Bernard dragged his best friend to the shady side of the street, and ran back to the Skyview apartments to get Edward and Patrice. When the three made it back to Henry in the street, Bernard testified, Edward leaned over the prostrate body of his brother, willing him to survive. "...Edward was on the top of him talking to him saying, 'Hold on, little brother. Be strong. You're going to live. You're going to live.' And I could hear [Henry] breathing hard. And [Edward] kept telling him, 'Fight. Fight.'"

260 JARED FISHMAN with JOSEPH HOOPER

Bernard's account of what transpired at the school helped round out the picture that Tanner had described earlier in the day. "When we got there, they drew all them automatic weapons on us and threw us on the ground, handcuffed us real rough. And I remember right after I got slammed on the ground, I got handcuffed... I got hit in the back of the head." One of the officers "grabbed [King] on his neck and started choking him." Henry was "in the back seat dying."

Bernard described how deeply Scheuermann—the man he called Schumacher—had been involved throughout. Bernard painted a picture of Scheuermann calling the shots at Habans, which suggested that he also was involved with what happened afterwards.

"Schumacher" had participated in the beatdown. Bernard, like Tanner, recalled the officer throttling Edward by the neck. But the lieutenant also seemed to be investigating how Henry wound up bleeding out in his compound, which, we suggested, is how Scheuermann knew about the Warren shooting.

Bernard said he told Scheuermann that Henry had been shot at the DeGaulle mall, between the police substation and the Tuesday Morning store, precisely where Warren had fired his weapon. Bernard didn't recall telling Scheuermann a cop had pulled the trigger, although that was his assumption. Scheuermann told him he'd look into it and left the school.

Later in the day, after Tanner's car had been driven away, and Bernard and Edward had been moved behind the school and handcuffed to a picnic table, the lieutenant returned with information. "Oh, he came back and he told us that—he said, 'Man, your brother and your brother-in-law had been shot for looting.' And he said that we can get the body from the coroner's. And he instructed them guys to give us a bottle of water." There was no mention that an officer had just burned Henry's body behind the levee.

Eventually, and unexpectedly, the police released them. "They made us go around the school. And I remember me and Edward had came up with what we thought was a good plan about running like that, crisscrossed." Bernard made crossing motions with his hands.

"And why did you think you needed to run crisscrossed?"

"Because we didn't want to get shot in the back."

Bernard and the rest of the family fled New Orleans that day, heading to Texas.

"Did you ever come back to New Orleans to live?" I asked. Bernard said no.

"Why not?" I asked.

Bernard responded with conviction: "I fear for my life."

Murray's cross of Bernard was telling. Murray seemed so convinced of his client's innate righteousness, and of the unworthiness of the Black man from low-income housing, that he figured he could badger Bernard about almost anything and score points with the jury. From the get-go, it was obvious to me that Murray underestimated Bernard's intelligence.

Responding to Murray's question, Bernard said that he hadn't asked Henry if the Firestone truck was stolen; he assumed that it was. Murray was snide: "It was so routine that you didn't feel the need to discuss it with him, correct?"

I objected to what felt like a gratuitous and improper attempt to criminalize Henry and Bernard. The judge told Bernard to answer.

Bernard was unfazed. "No, it was not a routine, sir. We was just trying to evacuate and survive. Like I said, we had very little food. My kids, his kids, his brother's kids, my girlfriend, his girlfriend, his brother's girlfriend, we was just trying to get out of town."

Given Bernard's centrality as a witness to an unjustified shooting, Murray seemed fixated on relatively small details, one thing in particular.

Bernard had testified on direct that the last time he saw Henry, his best friend was preparing to light a cigarette. In Ashley's 302 report of our first interview with Bernard back in Tulsa, she wrote that Henry was "smoking" a cigarette. This didn't seem inconsistent to me, but it became almost the heart of Murray's cross-examination.

"It's your testimony that as you were picking up this bag, you saw Henry Glover—did you see him lighting a cigarette or was it already lit when you looked at him?"

"When I looked at him, he was about to light the cigarette."

"Light the cigarette?"

"Yeah. He had just got out of the car, and he was about to light the cigarette."

"Did you tell the FBI that he actually was smoking the cigarette?"

"I said he was about to light a cigarette, smoking a cigarette."

And then, as if Murray had just gotten a confession, he smacked the podium and joyfully exclaimed, "Well, you can't smoke it till you light it!"

The rest of the cross-examination continued in a similar vein. Bernard was a thug, case closed. Not for the first time, and certainly not for the last, it struck me how casually our society simply writes off people like Bernard Calloway.

Magner took the direct examination of Brandi Williams. Williams, along with Katherine "Cooler" Short, had asked Henry to drive back for the suitcases they had been forced to leave behind the mall. Williams was a close friend of Henry's girlfriend.

Henry protected Williams after the storm. "Henry provided for us... Anything he could do to make us comfortable in his home he did. He fed us. Whatever we need to clothe ourselves, bathe ourselves, he gave it to us." Though Williams was not a blood relation, she said Henry was "like my brother."

Williams and Short took suitcases from the Tuesday Morning store in preparation for their exodus from the city. "I feel it was necessary, but also unnecessary... I know it was illegal, because it did not belong to us."

As they walked away, they saw two armed police, including a White cop with a long gun. "They told us we could not take other people's property and to leave it there," which they did, abandoning the items by the back curb of the parking lot.

Williams testified that they ran into Henry, driving the truck, and asked him to go back and pick up the suitcases. They failed to mention that they had just been run off by the police.

"Do you feel badly about that now after the fact?"

"Of course, I do."

But, Williams said, by the time they realized they made a mistake, they figured it was too late to run back and warn Henry and Bernard: "Before we could take another five or six steps, we heard gunshots. I kind of went into shock." And then she heard a man "coming up the street saying Henry had been shot…" She still felt the guilt keenly. "If we hadn't asked him to go back, he would probably still be here."

CHAPTER 16

SPEAKING UP

November 17 through 23, 2010

In 2005, Keyalah Bell was a twenty-six-year-old patrol officer who found herself in a near-impossible situation. She and her senior partner, Sergeant Nina Simmons, arrived at the DeGaulle mall minutes after Warren shot a man whom the officer's partner had described as defenseless. By the time she had arrived at the Habans School, she suspected that the shooting victim and the man bleeding out in the white Chevy were one and the same. But as a young Black female rookie, she assumed, correctly, I'm sure, that no one in the NOPD rank wanted to receive that message, certainly not from her. She kept her mouth shut.

By the time she testified at trial, five years had passed since the storm. She had decided that police work was probably not for her, and enrolled in night classes in nursing as a way out of law enforcement. But before she departed NOPD, she wanted to make right what she couldn't as a rookie cop, to help expose the truth about what happened to Henry. Bell's sleuthing uncovered the allegedly whitewashed Signal 21 report.

Tracey's direct examination keyed in on the information Bell relayed from Henry's family and allies to the NOPD. Within an hour or so of the shooting, she had encountered his sister Patrice, at the spot where Henry had collapsed. Patrice told her that her brother had been shot and driven away in a car. A month or so later, in October 2005, Henry's mother Edna showed up at the Fourth District, and Bell passed on her information to Lieutenant Italiano: this mother was looking for her son, whom she knew had been shot by the mall.

"And what was Italiano's response?" Tracey asked.

"He told me to tell them to check the morgue."

When Henry's brother Reginald later made the same trip to the Fourth District and asked the same questions, Bell felt more confident that she knew what had happened to Henry Glover.

"I knew at that point that he was no longer living."

"And how did you know that?" Tracey asked.

"Because I saw his body in the car."

Once again, Bell didn't share her suspicions with the Glovers. But she took down Reginald's phone number in case she ever did feel ready to tell the family what she knew.

"Did you keep those numbers?" Tracey inquired.

"Yes… They're in my pocket right now." Bell had kept the piece of paper as a kind of talisman. Tracey asked her why she hadn't been able to tell Reginald on that day what she knew about the case.

"Just fear of everything," Bell responded. "If the investigation wasn't going the way it was supposed to, and it was like no one cared…or me to say, oh, you know, I have this information, but I didn't know how to tell you because of fear of what may happen to me."

"What did you think would happen to you?" Tracey asked.

"Anything. Bull's-eye… Like a target or something."

By drawing Bell out about the pressure she felt to stay quiet, we hoped the jury could understand her passivity back in 2005. Fear permeated her entire involvement in the case—from her initial silence in 2005 to her denial to Ashley and me at our first meeting in 2009 that she'd seen the body in the car. We knew that her withholding information from us, however briefly, would be used against her.

Rick Simmons, Warren's co-counsel with Murray, handled the first cross. Simmons was an aggressive, analytically minded New Orleans attorney. He had successfully represented Dr. Anna Pou, a doctor accused of euthanizing patients in the city's flooded and abandoned Memorial Medical Center, a morally ambiguous Katrina episode recounted in the highly regarded bestseller *Five Days at Memorial*. Early in his career, in the mid-1970s, Simmons was on the team that successfully appealed Lieutenant William Calley's conviction for murdering 109 South Vietnamese civilians in the My Lai massacre, an event we had referenced in our Nuremberg Defense motion.

The heart of Warren's defense was that Glover had charged the back gate. If he'd gotten past the gate, Simmons argued, Warren would have been a sitting duck. But if that gate had been locked, as both Bell and Howard had testified, Warren's self-defense argument would become tenuous. Unless, perhaps, there was another way into the strip mall.

Simmons tried to trip Bell up with the schematics of the mall. "As you sit on the stand right now, you're telling us that if those gates are locked, there is no other way to get in that complex, is that what you're telling me? That's your recollection?"

"Correct."

Simmons rolled an injection-molded styrene scale model of the strip mall towards Bell. He pointed out a stairwell on the side of the building—far from both the back parking lot and the front of the strip mall.

"If you walk up that stairwell and go to the balcony, can you get in the premises?"

"I've never seen that."

Simmons was trying to stump Bell with our own exhibit, a model of the shooting scene that we had custom-made by an elite design unit at Quantico. We thought it would be useful to re-create, at scale, the features of the DeGaulle mall to help the jury visualize how far away Henry had been when he was shot. It even included a scaled-down Firestone truck and wooden human figures, which I had intended to use with witnesses to demonstrate who was standing where at any given moment.

The FBI shipped its creation to New Orleans. The next time I was in town, I couldn't wait to see the model. I asked Laura Orth, our legal assistant, to show it to me. "It looks great," she told me, "But why is it so...*little*?"

It wasn't that the model itself was small—it barely fit through the courtroom doors. But the scale, however, was miniature, shrinking the portion that we cared about—the police substation, the breezeway, and the back parking lot—to distressingly minute dimensions. The Firestone truck was smaller than a Matchbox car—*Spinal Tap!* had come to New Orleans.

The charges against Robert Italiano only required proof that he knowingly signed and submitted a false report about the Glover shooting, and then lied to the FBI about what he knew.

Ashley and I spent close to two years assembling a parade of law enforcement officers, inside and outside of the NOPD, who informed Italiano about the connection between the shooting at the mall, the gunshot victim at Habans, and the burned car behind the levee. We hoped the jury would believe that it was beyond-a-reasonable-doubt impossible for Italiano *not* to have known that Warren had fatally shot Henry and that SOD had burned Henry's body.

Marlon Defillo was chief of detectives during Katrina, and at trial, a deputy chief of the NOPD. He testified that after learning about Tanner's allegations against NOPD, he contacted Robert Italiano. The call occurred at least a month before Ashley and I spoke with Italiano. Defillo asked him if there was a connection between the David Warren shooting and the body found by the levee.

"What I asked him was that, I have information that Mr. Glover may have been shot by Officer David Warren of the Fourth District and his body was found burned on the levee. Can you confirm that this is, in fact, information, valid information? He said, 'Yeah.' So we didn't get into a tremendous dialogue in terms of the specifics of it because I wasn't trying to do a full interview with him."

Defillo then directed a senior cold case homicide detective, Gerard Dugue, to begin an official NOPD investigation into Glover's death. Ashley and I had been pushing back against Dugue's investigation ever since.

The most damning evidence against Italiano came from John Schmidt, an Immigration and Customs Enforcement (ICE) supervisory agent, who worked closely with the Fourth District after Katrina.

During the period Tanner searched for his car, he connected with Schmidt who was helping patrol the Fourth District. Schmidt interviewed Tanner in October 2005, and took meticulous notes. The following day, Schmidt debriefed Italiano about what he had learned. As Schmidt testified, we projected his contemporaneous notes on the courtroom wall.

Schmidt told Italiano that "a husky, White male police officer… with some flares" drove off with Tanner's car and the gunshot victim. He told Italiano that Tanner's car was found burned behind the levee. Italiano said he would "take care of it."

When Ashley testified, we tried to finish the job of burying Italiano in incriminating paperwork. Calling Ashley as a witness was a curiously formal exercise given that we'd spent the better part of two years joined at the hip. In the courtroom, she was "Agent Johnson," and I was "Attorney Fishman," as we ticked through some of the choice documents in the Italiano paper trail.

When Ashley and I interviewed Italiano in April 2009—before the NOPD had turned over any reports related to the Glover case— we tried to figure out whether it was possible, as the ex-lieutenant alleged, that no documentation existed because of the storm. These were not normal times, he had told us. His tone and body language had strongly suggested that we were idiots to think otherwise.

But as disruptive as Katrina had been, we didn't believe that the department stopped documenting things like shootings and missing people.

The evidence suggested Italiano was lying. In the weeks after we talked to him, we found the missing persons report and the Signal 21 report documenting the Warren shooting. Both had Italiano's name on them.

But we also uncovered numerous other reports out of the Fourth District, most of which came from Italiano's DIU unit. In all, the NOPD provided us with approximately 450 reports, from the time Katrina made landfall until October 31, 2005. The reports of serious crimes—like rapes and aggravated batteries—were assigned to DIU investigators for follow-up. The less significant incidents were documented as Signal 21 reports, just like the report of Warren's weapon discharge.

Two of these other documents stood out. With Ashley on the stand, I projected a report about an event that occurred on the same day Henry was shot. The subject: a police officer losing his radio. That had seemed important enough for officers to document.

Then I flashed another such report, this one from mid-October, documenting an abandoned car found on Woodland Highway, not far from the Patterson Road levee.

"And this particular abandoned car, was it burned?" I asked.

"No, it was not," Ashley replied.

"Were there human remains found inside?"

"No, there were not."

Lieutenant Joe Meisch was an indispensable figure in the Glover investigation. Meisch gave us the most conclusive evidence that McRae and Scheuermann had burned Glover's body. With McRae now admitting he burned the car, Meisch's value shifted from proving who burned the car, to why, and to what degree Scheuermann was involved. Meisch's testimony suggested Scheuermann either knew what McRae was going to do and didn't stop it, or, more likely, that they acted in concert.

Meisch had been standing downhill from the raised-earth levee, maybe fifty yards away, when he saw the two SOD officers running towards him. Behind them, billows of smoke rose from the side of the levee that dropped down to the Mississippi.

Meisch looked over to Scheuermann, the veteran officer, for guidance, "and Lieutenant Scheuermann said, 'It's all right, I'm handling it, I got it.'" He said McRae was laughing and Scheuermann appeared almost nonchalant.

"Did either man appear to be concerned about what had just happened?" Tracey asked.

"No, not that, not that I saw, ma'am."

A few days later, while walking on the levee searching for cell phone reception to call his wife, Meisch stumbled upon Henry's skeletal remains.

"Again, I mean, it did raise some suspicion in my mind, but it was still, you know, Lieutenant Scheuermann had said that he's got it."

Meisch testified that he had no further dealings with Scheuermann until 2009 when the SOD lieutenant began to bump into him, supposedly by accident. Scheuermann would often bring up the incident at the levee.

"And I can't remember the specific words that were used, but it was something to the effect that, you know, it was always, 'We're not going to deny what happened; we're not going to deny that Greg and I burned the car.'"

It was a strong admission that Scheuermann had been involved in the decision to burn the car even though Scheuermann took care to deflect the responsibility onto McRae. "...[G]enerally it would be followed up with, you know, Greg made a stupid mistake, or Greg did something stupid."

Kearney challenged Meisch about the conversations he had with Scheuermann. On cross, Meisch allowed that Scheuermann might have said something like, "We're not going to deny the car was burned," a passive-voice construction that suggested a less active participation by Scheuermann. Kearney made sure to highlight that, in each of these conversations, Scheuermann had told Meisch to "tell the truth." (The SOD lieutenant had no problem with the truth, we figured, as long as it could be shaded so it didn't implicate him.)

DeSalvo, I thought, had the most effective cross, highlighting that Meisch hadn't passed what he knew up the chain of command. Meisch admitted he hadn't told his commanding officer, David Kirsch, about the burning car at the levee.

"So during Katrina, you felt like this was nothing, so you didn't have to bother to tell him; is that correct?" DeSalvo asked.

"Not that I necessarily didn't have to bother telling him. It's just that when I say that nothing was *normal*, I'm meaning that there was so much *abnormal*...it would be impossible to sit there and go back to him every time something [unusual] happened..."

Maybe the biggest point DeSalvo scored was that Meisch had never connected the burned body behind the levee to a shooting by David Warren. He said he never even knew about the shooting until after our federal investigation made the papers in 2009.

"You never connected the dots, did you?" DeSalvo asked.

"No, sir," Meisch responded.

The implication being, if the heir apparent to the Fourth District Investigation Unit hadn't connected the shooting and burning, there would be no reason to think anyone else would either.

Sergeant Purnella "Nina" Simmons was, hands-down, our most vulnerable witness in the case.

I knew enough about Judge Africk—possessed of a near-religious reverence for the oath "to tell the truth, the whole truth and nothing but the truth"—to know that Simmons's perjured grand jury performance probably put her beyond redemption in his eyes.

But that was only one of our challenges. Simmons's testimony was all over the map, which put me in a bind. Ethically, I could not elicit testimony I knew to be false. But I didn't know for certain that any of her statements were false; I just knew that they couldn't all be true, because some of her assertions contradicted each other.

And yet, so much of the case ran through her. For better or worse, she offered evidence that implicated all five defendants. I had to focus my examination on the parts of her testimony I believed were reliable.

Standing behind the podium with my three-ring binder of files, I guided her through the immediate aftermath of the shooting. Her language got vaguer as she described driving to Habans to inform, or try to inform, the Fourth District rank that Warren's shot and the shooting victim in the Chevy in the school lot were probably related.

"He [Captain David Kirsch] was on the telephone, and I said, well, I proceeded to tell him that David Warren had discharged his firearm over on DeGaulle and that he could have possibly shot someone and this could be the victim. And they [Kirsch and Lieutenant Italiano] said no, it wasn't the same, they're two separate incidents."

Simmons testified that she was cut off so quickly that she wasn't able to tell the commanding officers everything she had learned at DIU. As Simmons left Habans, she suggested to Italiano that she document the discharge at DIU. "As I walked away...I said, 'Well, okay. I'll go and write the report.' [Italiano] said, 'No.'"

Simmons testified that when she and Bell returned to the mall, she had slightly longer and more coherent conversations with both Warren and Howard. Warren told her that he didn't think he had hit the man he'd shot at. Howard, no longer crying, had a different take: "He shot him for nothing."

Simmons said, as best she could tell, no one from the Fourth District, certainly not Kirsch or Italiano, had shown up at the mall that day to take a closer look at what had transpired. Normally, few things grab a department's attention like an officer shooting a civilian. I trusted that the jury would see that even Katrina conditions didn't adequately explain the department's strangely hands-off attitude towards the Warren shooting.

I wish I could have explained to the jury how the Fourth District leadership knew to treat it as a nonevent. Had Warren somehow communicated with Kirsch or Italiano, perhaps by cell phone? Did they decide that if they didn't visit the mall, they could maintain plausible deniability? Perhaps the whole thing might simply blow over, an unknown Black male shot by an unknown gunman—just another casualty of the storm? I couldn't explain it to the jury because I didn't know myself.

As best we could figure, with the creation of the report and the entry of Henry Glover into a national missing persons database, the calculus changed. It became necessary to put out an official story about the mall shooting that de-linked the firearm "discharge" from the shooting victim who had turned up at Habans that same morning.

It was only in late November or early December—three months after the shooting—that Italiano ordered Simmons to write a report, though he didn't give her any specific instructions. Simmons spoke with Linda Howard and David Warren, and produced a report, classified by the department as a Signal 21, a catch-all category for less important police matters that didn't automatically trigger an investigation.

In my direct, I tried to zero in on the most damning elements of the report. Simmons testified that she had handwritten the six-line "Resisting Arrest Report" (a label then used by the NOPD for all uses of force, regardless of whether anyone actually "resisted"), but the fuller one-and-a-half-page typed "narrative" had been "fabricated" by someone else.

Perhaps the biggest hole in this part of the case was that we never recovered Simmons's "original" typed narrative, so we could never establish what was, or wasn't, included in it.

Further muddying the waters, Simmons testified that the only documentation that had turned up in her old files was a single page from the McCabe narrative. She had no idea how that came to be in her possession. She assumed someone planted it, but had no evidence to support that claim, a point the defense would exploit on cross.

The only independent corroboration that Simmons's original report ever existed was Dwayne Scheuermann's comment, captured in a surreptitious recording, that he had a copy of "both" reports, although he never provided her with the original.

Without the actual report, it was impossible to prove what, exactly, it had said. Simmons's own description didn't inspire confidence. She claimed that she had written that Howard "didn't agree" with the shooting. My guess was that her original report was hardly more incriminating than the fake report, though it likely acknowledged, possibly obliquely, that a man was shot and that the shooting may not have been justified.

"Did you write anything in your report that Linda Howard did believe that David Warren had hit this man?"

"No, I didn't."

"And why didn't you put that in your report?"

"Because I was scared," she said. "I was afraid. I was afraid of losing myself, losing my life and Linda's life. It was not a happy time, a good time there. It was—when these things were going—so many things were going on that we were just hearing of, and I was scared. It was eerie."

But Simmons was clear about what she had hoped her original report, however inadequate, would accomplish. "It served the purpose that it would bring to somebody else's attention that there should be another investigation." Simmons hadn't done all she could have done, far from it, but just as Bell had testified, she thought she had done enough to cue the NOPD to do its job.

Before I turned Simmons over to the defense attorneys, I addressed her perjured performance at the first grand jury hearing. It wasn't her finest hour. Nor, in retrospect, was it mine. But we couldn't hide from this episode. Otherwise, we would lose credibility with the jurors.

"You went into the grand jury, and you said this was your report, did you not?"

"That was a lie," she admitted.

"And why did you go into the grand jury and take responsibility for this report if it wasn't, in fact, yours?"

"Because my name was on it. My name was in that report, on that report and typed in that report."

Judge Africk interjected: "So it was better to lie under oath because your name was on the report, is that your testimony?"

"No, sir, it wasn't better. That's why…"

Africk interrupted. "That's what you did, though." Simmons lowered her head in contrition. "That's what I did, but it wasn't better."

The defense made short work of Simmons on cross. They had so much ammunition to destroy her credibility and wasted no time in using it.

Representing McCabe, Mike Small, the silver-maned attorney from Alexandria, Louisiana, had the demeanor of an elegant Southern statesman, with the aristocratic drawl to match. He took pains to emphasize every time Simmons had lied to the grand jury, claiming ownership of the Signal 21 report language that she would later disown. "…[W]ould I be correct if I just estimated that you swore under oath twenty-five or thirty times in response to a specific question that every word in those narratives that you say were fabricated were, in fact, your words; did you do that time and time again?"

"On the first grand jury hearing, yes," she responded meekly.

Simmons was nothing if not malleable. She certainly hadn't tallied up the number of times she lied; she just seemed ready to go along with whatever Small said. Small's theory of the case was that Simmons had, in fact, written the report with McCabe, and only changed her story because we had accused her of lying. By holding a perjury charge over her head, he argued, we pressured her into bringing her testimony in line with our theory. In other words, Simmons had committed perjury (by claiming the report was fraudulent) to avoid a perjury charge.

In the middle of Small's cross-examination of Simmons, I heard a clicking sound coming from the defense side of the courtroom. I looked over to find Warren's attorney Julian Murray clipping his fingernails. Evidently, he wasn't too worried about what Simmons had to say.

In the end, what was the most detrimental to our case was Simmons's own uncertainty about what she had told the NOPD command in real time. Frank DeSalvo quizzed her again about what she had told the rank after she showed up at the Habans School. Simmons said that she began to tell the senior officers about "further information" she had concerning the shooting but Italiano cut her off, because, he said, the shooting and the shooting victim at Habans were not related.

"What was the further information you were going to tell him?" he asked.

"Telling him about the sister, the towel and the other things that I had encountered."

"But you didn't tell him?"

"I didn't get a chance to."

Italiano's attorney, Steve Lemoine, in my estimation, not much of an orator or a storyteller, but tenacious on cross, picked up the baton.

"And you never informed Bob Italiano that anyone was shot at DeGaulle, did you?"

"I didn't say it in those words, no, sir."

"You did not. Now, ma'am, and that means, that means ever; you never did, did you?"

"No, sir."

Nina Simmons got off the stand. I could only hope that the jury saw her more or less the same way I did—not someone you wanted to trust with the details but not someone intentionally lying to bring down other cops either. I didn't doubt that her heart was in the right place. I just wished she were a better witness.

On November 23, we called our thirtieth and final witness, Kawan McIntyre, Henry's first cousin. After two weeks of trial, I was exhausted. We'd been in court ten or eleven hours a day, and I'd been averaging less than five hours of sleep a night. Thanksgiving recess was only a day away, and I desperately needed a break.

Our case presentation had gone as well as we could have hoped. I had worried at some point during our case-in-chief there would be a major revelation—a piece of evidence that we had missed that made the cops' behavior less sinister. Twenty-nine witnesses into the case, I had the opposite thought: the cover-up was likely deeper than we could ever prove.

I ended our presentation much as we had started it—by tapping into the emotion that suffused Henry's murder. The legal system, of course, pretends that trials are exercises in impartial weighing of evidence. That logic and reason should always prevail.

But jurors—like all humans—are rarely dispassionate, rational beings. Modern cognitive science suggests that people do not merely think with their "heads." Consciously or not, humans tend to rationalize their feelings after the fact, coming up with logical-sounding reasons to justify what they "feel" to be true.

As we brought our case-in-chief to a close, I wanted the jurors to feel, to whatever degree they could, the loss of Henry Glover as experienced by those who loved him. To my mind, no witness did this better than Kawan McIntyre, who described her relationship with Henry as "best cousins." Henry was three years her senior, and the two had grown up spending time together in the Fischer Projects. Kawan was soft-spoken and thoughtful.

I met Kawan for the first time late in the investigation, after we had already indicted the five defendants. I worried about calling Edna Glover as a witness. The murder of her son had taken a toll on her mental and physical health, and testifying at a high-profile trial would only exacerbate the problems. Kawan had been with Edna on some of the visits to the police station, and she could speak to the efforts the Glovers made to get answers and the deliberate obstruction they encountered.

I prompted Kawan to talk about the last time she had seen Henry, a day after the storm. Kawan had decided to leave town, and she wanted to bring Henry with her, but he chose to stay with his family and protect his home.

"He said that he was okay, that he was going to stay back in

New Orleans." Henry told her not to worry, joking that he could swim. "I said, well, I can't swim." They both laughed.

Henry "stretched his arms out to me, gave me a hug, told me that he loved me, and I said 'love you, too.'"

In our prep sessions, Kawan always underscored what a caring, compassionate man Henry was. He didn't own a gun, she had told me, and he certainly wasn't carrying one in the days after Katrina. I wanted to erase the portrait the defense was trying to paint of Henry as an armed thug who would charge at a police officer.

I asked two questions, perhaps overly broad, to drive home the point.

"Did you know Henry Glover to carry a weapon?"

"No, sir."

"Did you know Henry Glover to be a violent man?"

"No, sir."

Kawan recalled the shock of learning that Henry had been shot. She and her family had relocated to an evacuation center in Gonzales, Louisiana, west of the city. She was settling into her new, uncertain life when she received the call with the news.

"Who would want to shoot Henry?" she asked herself. "I was in disbelief, denial, a lot of pain and agony."

"I left the building where I was registering my children [for school], went over to the shelter where the rest of my family members were, and we embraced one another."

Kawan and her family members went into overdrive seeking information.

"We then got on the phone making phone calls trying to find out, you know, what exactly happened to Henry." She called missing persons hotlines, the Public Integrity Bureau, the coroner's office—anyone and anywhere she could think of to locate Henry. The long-distance effort proved to be an utter failure.

A month or so later, Kawan returned to New Orleans, joining her aunt Edna in the search. Their first unsuccessful stop was the Fourth District police station, less than a hundred yards from where Henry's charred remains sat in Tanner's car. Kawan said that Edna had a feeling, a premonition. She began to cry, "He's around here, he's around here somewhere."

A few weeks later, Kawan and Edna returned to the police station, but this time, a police officer took a missing persons report. By now, the odds that Henry might turn up alive had dwindled, though Kawan tried to remain optimistic. "I didn't want her to get discouraged and give up on finding Henry because I knew that one day, you know, we were going to find out [what happened] and there was hope." At the very least, she wanted to locate his body to have a proper funeral.

Two more weeks passed with no response from the police. Kawan returned to the station for a third time, alone. This time, she brought a new piece of information she had gleaned from William Tanner: Henry's body had been burned behind the Patterson Road levee.

Faced once again with the indifference of a desk officer, Kawan grew agitated. Eventually, an older, more senior officer came out from the back of the station. She described him as a "medium build, White guy with a scar under his eye with a goatee."

Kawan told the officer where Henry was shot, that he was last seen with the police at Habans, and that his burned body had been found by the levee. Her voice grew louder. "I said the police must have killed him. They're not giving us any information. When we come here, they're giving us the runaround...and no one ever returns a call."

The senior officer pushed back, raising his voice and thrusting his finger at her. "'We didn't kill Henry Glover,'" he said. "He just looked at me, stared me straight in my face and told me that no one killed Henry Glover."

Kawan's description of this senior officer sounded a lot like Robert Italiano. When she first told us about the encounter, I asked her if she thought she could identify the officer if she saw him again. She said she thought she could. If Kawan could identify Italiano, she'd be one more in a long line of witnesses who put the case together for him, further evidence of his central role in a cover-up.

But I was leery. It had been a long time since she'd seen him, and cross-racial identifications are notoriously unreliable. (They play an outsize role in wrongful convictions.)

Ethically, I played it by the book. Not wanting to prejudice any in-court ID, I didn't let her know where he would be sitting in court. Then I violated the trial attorney's maxim: "Never ask a question if you don't know the answer."

I asked Kawan, "Now, do you think you would recognize the older White officer if you saw him today?" If she could identify Italiano, we'd score a point, and if she said she couldn't, we would simply move on.

Kawan's answer was ambiguous. "There's a possibility." It was the worst answer she could have given. Now I had no choice other than to play it out.

"Do you see him today in court?" I asked, uncertain what would happen next.

Kawan's gaze slowly traveled around the packed courtroom. She glanced at the prosecution table, then at the two defendant tables, briefly looking at Italiano, and then continued to scan. The courtroom was silent.

Her eyes came to rest on Judge Africk, whom, I realized for the first time, had recently grown his facial hair. Africk was an older White man with a goatee. Was Kawan going to identify the judge? I was going to end our case-in-chief with that?

Kawan stared at the judge for what felt like forever. The silence was growing oppressive. I knew I had to give her "adequate" time to make up her mind, a plausible minimum anyway, otherwise it would look suspicious to the jury. I finally intervened, "If you're not certain, you can say that."

"I am not certain. I am not sure," she said.

I let myself exhale. Crisis averted.

I closed out the examination by contrasting two photographs on the large overhead screen. The first was of Henry with his young daughter, smiling broadly. "That's the Henry that I know," Kawan said.

The second showed Henry's remains that Kawan collected from the morgue.

"And what did you see when you went to Davis Mortuary?" I asked.

"A bag of bones," Kawan replied.

I projected onto the screen photos of Henry's remains, or rather, the five red biohazard bags containing charred bone and ash. Kawan was in tears.

Steve Lemoine jumped out of his seat with an objection: "Your Honor, may that be taken down, please?"

Africk didn't pause. "Let the witness identify it. Go ahead."

"Is this the Henry Glover that you buried?" I asked.

"Yes, sir," Kawan answered in a soft voice.

"All right. Take it down," Africk ordered.

"No further questions for this witness," I concluded.

As I returned to the prosecution table, the relief flooded through me. The trial was far from over—the defense would be calling over thirty of its own witnesses—but I was feeling good about where things stood.

Jeff Kearney, Scheuermann's attorney, rose to his feet. "May we approach?" We gathered around the bench with the white noise machine whirring and the country music blaring in the courtroom.

"The witness has testified that she has never known Mr. Glover to ever carry a gun and that he was not even a violent person." Kearney began listing all of Henry's run-ins with law enforcement—including arrests for carrying a concealed firearm illegally and simple battery—all of which we had managed to exclude through our pre-trial character motions. "I think we're entitled to ask her about that," he said.

At that moment, I realized how badly I had screwed up. With two poorly worded, overly generic questions—"Did you know Henry Glover to carry a weapon?" and "Did you know Henry Glover to be a violent man?"—I had "opened the door." I had made Henry's character an issue.

The look of shock on my face must have been obvious. "I don't know why you asked about the violence," Judge Africk said to me. Kearney piled on. "I couldn't believe he asked it."

I couldn't believe I asked it either.

I had been keen to combat the image of Henry "the thug," but my brain was so clouded by weeks of stress and sleep deprivation, I simply hadn't thought through the implications of my questions about weapons and violence.

Now, depending on how the judge ruled, the defense attorneys might be able to cross Kawan about those past arrests, previously ruled off-limits. I had given the defense ammunition to portray Henry as a violent criminal. All our efforts to humanize Henry could come undone.

Judge Africk knew the serious implications of my mistake. He deferred making a ruling, opting to review Henry's criminal record and the relevant case law.

Since we didn't have further witnesses, the defense began its case-in-chief, with David Warren as the first witness. I was glad Magner was handling that cross. I was too distracted and upset.

Making matters worse, this was the last court day before the Thanksgiving recess. Africk wasn't going to decide until after the trial resumed the following week. I had hoped to spend the break recharging, catching up on sleep, and celebrating with my family.

Instead, I spent the holiday with everything left hanging in the air, increasingly convinced that with two stupid questions, I had destroyed everything we had worked to create.

CHAPTER 17

NOT A FRIENDLY PLACE

November 23 through 29, 2010

My Thanksgiving vacation was terrible. The Kawan debacle was only part of the problem.

I spent the holiday in Atlanta with my dad and siblings, failing to make up for lost sleep. Thanksgiving was a big deal in my family. It's the holiday when my siblings, typically spread out in four different states, come together. My mom passed away eighteen months earlier, and this was the first Thanksgiving we would all be together since she had died.

I had been looking forward to seeing Fiona again, and reuniting with my daughter, whom I hadn't seen since the start of the trial. After I landed in Atlanta, Fiona called me and told me she wasn't making the trip. She had been solo parenting and battling morning sickness while still working full-time. She was exhausted. She couldn't fathom an airplane ride with a toddler during the busiest travel day of the year, spending nights in a damp basement, and managing a toddler in an unfamiliar environment. Instead, she asked me to come home. I couldn't bring myself to get on another plane, and so I stayed put in Atlanta and tried to prepare for my upcoming cross-examinations.

We exchanged harsh words and hung up the phone angry. The only way I could stay focused on the trial was to ignore the hurt that I was causing my own family.

Growing up, I had a working dad and stay-at-home mom, their responsibilities split along traditional gender lines. Fiona grew up with two professional parents, but her mother, a physician, assumed all the household duties, cutting back to part-time when her kids were young. Neither Fiona nor I had good role models for how to navigate the world of two working parents, especially ones experiencing a simultaneous surge in their careers. Nor did we yet have the skills to do so.

In addition to the Kawan episode and the family stress, I was mulling over the testimony of David Warren, who had testified the day before the recess.

I had spent much of the trial watching Warren sit quietly at the defense table. He was deeply engaged, taking notes and regularly consulting with his attorneys. His face rarely betrayed any emotion, regardless of who testified or which exhibit was shown. I found his neutral affect unsettling.

His five young children sat in court every day as photos of Henry Glover, from the exsanguinated shooting victim to bags of ashes, were projected on the courtroom's overhead screen. It was hard to know what to make of a person who brings his kids to court to hear, over and over again, the story of how he killed a man, in graphic detail.

I had wondered why he pulled the trigger for close to two years. Now I would find out. His delivery was careful and cerebral. He projected a confidence that I imagined came with his extensive formal education and his apparent belief that he had done nothing wrong.

Warren had been scheduled for vacation as Katrina approached. Instead, he packed up his wife and kids, the youngest of whom was only four months old, and sent them out of the city to wait out the storm. He remained behind in New Orleans to do whatever needed to be done. "I knew that I had a responsibility, that that was part of the job that…I had signed up for."

According to Warren, he worked twenty-four hours straight on the first day after the storm and then rarely got more than two hours of sleep a night. Because of the flooding on the East Bank, he couldn't get to his usual post in the Seventh District, so he reported to the Fourth District, only a mile from his home. When he wasn't working, he assumed the role of neighborhood security guard. "If I wasn't doing duty and I wasn't patrolling…I was in my own neighborhood just trying to walk around and try to keep an eye on things." Three of the eleven homes in his neighborhood had been looted, he noted.

There were "a number of things that made me feel more vulnerable after the hurricane," he testified. The first was the lack of a central lockup to put people who had committed crimes, New Orleans's main jail having flooded. (Jefferson Parish jailed the men involved in the shooting of Officer Kevin Thomas, but Warren's impression was that those were exceptional circumstances.)

"One of the determining facts of being a police officer is the ability to be able to incarcerate somebody, the ability to say if I catch you doing this, I can take you to jail," he explained. "Without that ability to be able to do that…it raises the boldness or the ability for somebody to be able to say, 'I don't care. There's no jail to take me to.'"

The shooting of Officer Kevin Thomas, in particular, weighed on Warren, who had responded to the scene. The next day, as he guarded one of Thomas's alleged attackers at the hospital, Warren could see the nearby Oakwood mall on fire. It seemed to him that his city was collapsing.

By September 2, after four days of very limited sleep, Warren sensed that law enforcement backup wasn't coming. Even in Algiers, which was in significantly better shape than the rest of the city, the local police were on their own.

On the morning of September 2, Warren reported with Linda Howard to the mall, and he felt the eerie un-city-like quietness that she had described. That isolation was broken by a man on a bicycle who "was kind of riding around the shopping center…and he kept looking back at us.

"Probably about the fifth loop around I said, you know, I said something to Linda like, Linda, I don't like this guy doing this. I am getting the feeling I am being set up, I get the feeling he's scouting. Something isn't right."

Warren testified he leveled his gun and "fired it out towards the neutral ground." He called it a "warning shot."

"I wanted the noise out there. I wanted him to realize this is not a friendly place. Go away. You don't want to be coming here."

Later that morning, they observed two women pushing a shopping cart loaded with what the officers assumed were stolen mall goods, and he had successfully run them off. "I asked them what they were doing. And I said, 'Is that your property?' And they were like, 'Well, no.' I said, 'Well, then leave it, go on, get out of here.'"

Time passed and Warren settled into the silence. Then he was startled by the sound of an over-revving truck. "…[I]t immediately drew my attention to the back of the building." He noticed the Firestone logo, which indicated to him that the truck was stolen.

"After it came in and came to a hard, fast stop, both doors opened immediately and I saw the passenger, I saw both his feet hit the ground at the same time."

Warren explained: "I was very concerned. To have somebody come up that quickly in a stolen vehicle, you know, and stop that quickly, both doors open, both jump out at basically the instant that those doors opened, and they jumped out, I screamed at them…" He demonstrated how loud he yelled, his booming voice startling the courtroom: "Police, get back! Police, get back!"

In Warren's retelling, the men charged forward. Even though he occupied the high ground one floor up and was armed with a high-powered rifle, he said he still felt vulnerable. Contrary to the testimonies of Howard, Bell, and Simmons, he said that the gate separating him from the Black men was unlocked. "Once they're [through the gate]…they can get underneath and get behind me, one can get in front of me and one can get behind me, and it becomes a difficult situation for me to be able to manage."

The command didn't deter the charging man. "And as he continued to come towards the gate, I was concerned that he had a weapon." Interestingly, Warren did not say that he perceived this weapon to be a gun.

"…I had about a second to react to it… My reaction was to fire a shot at the man in the lead." He wanted the jury to understand he had cause to take the shot. "Yeah, let me just be very plain. I mean, I was concerned for my life, I was concerned for my partner's life. You know, I was concerned about going home to my family." Because Warren's affect was so flat, it was hard to know if this professed emotion was real or whether he was just using code words to make the shooting sound "reasonable."

Warren said that Linda Howard couldn't have seen what happened. According to him, she was behind him, so her view of the two men would have been obstructed by the building. Warren said that Howard did not raise any objection to his shot. She was quiet afterwards, without the tears or hysterics described by Nina Simmons or Keyalah Bell.

Warren thought he should have hit his target. "You know, I didn't see how I could have missed at that range…" However, "[the two men] immediately broke off, they veered off and they proceeded toward Texas [Street]… [That] left me with the conclusion that I missed."

Warren heard the call over the radio that a gunshot victim had arrived at Habans. "Yeah, I thought maybe the two are related…" But he made no effort to find out and did not notify other officers that he had just fired his weapon.

While he initially thought he missed, over time, he began to reconsider. He referred to two conversations that changed his mind. Both were news to me.

In late November, around the same time that the Signal 21 report was being written up, Warren said he was interviewed by Lieutenant Joseph Waguespack, an investigator with the Public Integrity Bureau (PIB), NOPD's equivalent of internal affairs. Waguespack, according to Warren, had shown him a photo of a Black man and asked him if that had been the person he'd shot at.

Warren didn't recognize the man in the photo, and he said nothing came out of the brief conversation. Interestingly, the NOPD claimed it had no records of Waguespack conducting any investigation. And Waguespack, who testified later at trial on behalf of Italiano, denied conducting any investigation or discussing the shooting with Warren. But Warren's account was certainly plausible, though rather than exonerating him, it seemed to indicate that the shooting cover-up went higher up the chain of command than we would ever know.

The second conversation that made him think his shot may have hit was a mysterious phone call that he received in November 2005.

"Did you get a telephone call of any significance relative to what we're here about?"

"Yes. There was a lady that called, I don't remember her name, I don't. But she called and said that—"

Magner objected. The statement was hearsay and thus was technically inadmissible. Africk didn't allow Warren to finish his thought.

As our team conferred before cross, we decided that it might be useful to hear more about this call. Any evidence suggesting Warren believed he had hit his target would indicate his "I thought I missed" account in the Signal 21 report was a lie. Magner would circle back on that point on cross.

As we moved into the defense case, our team roles had shifted. Tracey and I, who had the deepest knowledge of the case and the closest relationships with our witnesses, handled the most significant direct examinations. But Mike had significantly more experience cross-examining witnesses than either Tracey or me. In the defense case, he and I divided up the crosses of the five defendants between us.

Magner had a casual, shoot-from-the-hip style that, at times, reminded me of DeSalvo. But he was also a formidable legal technician, steeped in the federal rules and relevant case law. He was often ready to go to the mat with the defense, and sometimes the judge, when he felt it mattered. If he thought the jury needed to hear it, he wasn't afraid to get in a defense witness's face.

But Magner's approach to crossing David Warren was non-confrontational by design. We assumed the jury found Warren at least somewhat sympathetic—a mild-mannered, well-educated man with his wife and five kids in the courtroom. We were not expecting Warren to back off his self-defense claim, just because Mike pushed his buttons.

Mike wanted to get Warren talking about his interest, bordering on obsession, with guns, which might help the jury understand how he shot at two different unarmed Black men that day. Murray's direct played into our strategy, as he made an explicit connection between Warren's gun hobby and his becoming a police officer. In his opening, Murray even said that Warren became a police officer because he liked guns.

Mike's cross sought to push this line of inquiry to the limit. Mike was not a "gun guy." He didn't hunt and he didn't hang out at the gun range. But like many great lawyers I know, he could digest a lot of research in a short time, and then skillfully deploy it on cross. What resulted was an oddly collegial and discomfiting conversation about guns between two White men, one of whom was facing a murder charge.

"…[Y]ou told me you would read up on these different firearms?"

"I've read about different firearms over time. I mean, I found it something interesting to do."

"And there's nothing wrong with that," Mike replied. "You belong to the NRA, you're a gun enthusiast, correct?"

"Yes."

"And you collect firearms?"

"Uh-huh."

"At the time of September 2, approximately how many firearms did you have?"

"I am not sure exactly, two dozen."

Mike locked down the specifics of the shooting. Warren had been thoughtful in choosing his most expensive and deadly weapon when he went to guard the DIU. "...[Y]ou know, I just looked at it and said what am I comfortable with and what have I shot and that was what I grabbed."

Mike produced the magnification scope that Warren had on his weapon. When I first looked through the scope at the FBI, I was struck by how zoomed-in and precise it allowed the shooter to be. Looking through the scope at a person sixty-six feet away, the distance between Warren and Henry, all you see is body.

Mike then asked Warren about the difference between the two types of ammunition he typically used, the 5.56 versus the .223. "From what I understand," Warren explained, "the caliber itself is the same, meaning the bullet diameter is the same. The difference has to do with the operating pressure of the cartridge, I believe one is a military specification and the other is a civilian or sporting arms specification." On September 2, Warren chose the military round.

Mike's discussion of guns went on for well over an hour and a half, so long that I worried it was losing its impact. I was amazed the defense hadn't objected yet. As time passed, Mike hit closer to home regarding what Warren knew about his ammunition, particularly how it "yaws" and "tumbles" once it enters the body, creating "temporary wound cavities" and "hydrostatic shock." Warren's answers helped bolster the argument that the wound to Glover's back was an entrance wound.

The photo of Henry bleeding out in the back seat of the Chevy suggested this was the case. High-velocity rifle rounds typically leave small entrance wounds and significantly larger exit wounds. The copious bleeding at the front of his torso, we believed, indicated the bullet's exit. And yet, because pathologists could not inspect Henry's body, none of them could draw a definitive conclusion based on the photo alone.

As Mike invited Warren to analyze the component parts of a bullet, Murray finally lodged an objection. The judge put some limitations on Magner's cross but still permitted him to ask questions about the general physics of bullets penetrating bodies, such as what is meant by the term "permanent wound cavity."

"That would be after the area that has been stretched collapses," Warren explained. "...I guess you would call it the destructive path of the round. The amount of tissue that's damaged."

"So you want to affect as many vital organs as possible with your shot, correct?" Mike asked.

"I would think that would be the logic. I mean, you're causing disruption."

"And that is exactly what you did with Henry Glover, correct?"

"That would seem to be."

Mike moved on to Warren's "warning shot" that violated every bit of his training. "There was no law that said that somebody could not walk through that parking lot on September 2, was there?" Mike asked.

Warren sounded matter-of-fact. "No," he answered.

"You shot in that man's direction because he was looking at you?"

"After a number of repeated runs past, yes."

Mike noted that Warren never even attempted to communicate verbally with that man on the bicycle. If Warren could so readily justify the use of lethal force against someone over a football field away because he looked at him funny, it was also easy to see how that same person could shoot a man who was running away.

Magner's crossing style was leisurely, almost circular in approach. He'd cover a topic, move on and then return to it from a slightly different angle. He came back to the shooting, this time focusing on the weapon that Warren thought he might have seen at about Henry's waist level. Warren's descriptions to Murray on direct had been maddeningly vague, and for a man who taught classes on guns, borderline ridiculous: "Whether we're talking rifle or we're talking revolver or small semi-automatic, I don't know."

In his opening, Murray specifically said, "He did not see a gun. He saw him reach in his waistband for what he perceived to be a weapon." On direct, Warren didn't mention seeing a gun. Now Warren was claiming he *had* seen a gun, albeit a nondescript gun of indeterminate size. Magner called him out on it, and Warren sounded defensive. "Sir, his hands were down in the area of his waistband.... I can't tell you that it *was* a gun. I perceived it to be a gun."

Magner noted how different Warren's testimony was from Linda Howard's. Warren admitted to Magner that if the shooting had occurred as Howard testified, he would have no defense.

"...[I]f you had shot Mr. Glover with his back towards you leaning up on that car...that would have been unreasonable and unconstitutional, correct?"

"Yes, sir."

Magner also noted that Warren's perception of the shooting differed from that of every other police witness, fellow officers who had had no obvious reason to frame him.

"So when Linda Howard said that the gate on the first level was locked, you're saying that she is lying, correct?"

"Incorrect, I am saying that she is wrong."

"And when Keyalah Bell said that this gate was locked, she's lying, too, huh?"

"She is wrong."

Warren denied having a conversation with Linda Howard that morning about martial law.

"So is she's making that up, too?" Mike asked.

"I think Linda has some problems."

Mike's sarcasm could be withering. "You, however, are looking at a potential prison sentence. Wouldn't you agree that you might have some problems yourself?"

"Yes, sir."

Magner looped Alec Brown into the picture. Briefly Warren's NOPD partner after the storm, Brown had testified that Warren had told him that looters were "animals" who "deserved to be shot." Warren, not surprisingly, denied saying such a thing.

"So Alec Brown's lying too?"

"I don't know what to say about Alec Brown. I don't know what's motivating him."

"Did you do something to Nina Simmons or Keyalah Bell or Alec Brown to make them come in here and tell stories about you?"

"Not that I am aware of."

To close out his cross, Magner returned to the phone call Warren had received from "a lady" that had made him think his shot had hit. Warren explained that in November 2005, two months after Katrina, he worked a shift at the temporary police headquarters at the Royal Sonesta Hotel in the French Quarter, where each NOPD precinct and several federal agencies had desks and phones.

Warren testified he received an unusual phone call from, judging, he said, by the voice, an older Black woman. "...I don't remember how she identified herself," he said. "It might have been, you know, Mrs. Glover or somebody like that, I just am not sure... [S]he mentioned Mr. Glover and she mentioned that she thought he was shot by [the mall]...and that he was taken to Habans Elementary School by somebody, that there were some problems at Habans, and that subsequently, you know, that he was in a car that was over the levee and the car had been burned or something like that."

This we had *not* been expecting. According to Warren, Edna Glover, or at any rate, someone he believed to be Edna Glover, had called the Fourth District to get information about her son and, unbeknownst to her, her son's killer answered the phone.

Warren understood that the woman was talking about his shooting, but declined to identify himself on the phone. On the stand, he recognized how extraordinary this incident was. "...[W]hen I heard all of that it seemed fantastic to me," he told Magner. What he didn't seem to grasp was that learning he had likely killed a man, from that man's mother no less, conferred on him a responsibility to share that information, if not with the victim's family, then with the NOPD rank.

Instead, Warren testified, "I explained that this was not the Fourth District station that she had reached... I sent her to the district station at 1348 Richland. I told her that she could go in there and address the questions and that kind of thing."

And that was the last he spoke of the incident until the trial. He didn't mention it to anyone at the NOPD.

We appreciated that Warren's silence, and the information he had provided in the Signal 21 report about believing he had missed, implicated him in a cover-up.

Magner finished off with a question for Warren, if you could call it a question. "But in any event, by that point you were part of this Fourth District fraternity, and you knew to keep your mouth shut about what Ms. Glover had told you?"

My stomach sank. This felt close to the line. Throughout the proceedings, Murray had pushed hard for Warren to be tried separately. Murray had argued that being included in a trial about the cover-up, which we had no evidence Warren knew anything about, unfairly prejudiced a jury, whose job it was to determine Warren's innocence or guilt on the merits of his case alone. At the suggestion of a "Fourth District fraternity," Murray erupted.

"On behalf of David Warren, we move for mistrial," he decried at a hastily called conference at the bench. "The government did exactly what you told them that they were not allowed to do and they kept pushing it, kept pushing it, and kept pushing it, and this jury now has a distinct impression that there is some conspiracy going on and our client is a part of it."

Judge Africk denied the mistrial request. He was going to let the case play out and let the jury reach a verdict.

To shore up Warren's testimony, Murray brought in a "use of force" expert, Alan Baxter, who testified the first day back from the Thanksgiving break. He testified that the officer's actions had been "objectively reasonable." Baxter had the unenviable job of overturning a few thousand years of settled military tactics, arguing that Warren, occupying the high ground with a high-powered rifle, was in a more vulnerable position than Henry and Bernard on the ground. Baxter did not have a résumé that inspired confidence.

Before Baxter was allowed to opine on the shooting, Magner, who had done his usual thorough job of research, challenged his expert status. Baxter boasted holding a full professorship in criminology at Tulane, though his actual academic credentials consisted of a BA in psychology. He had never served as an American police officer. His only policing experience, he said, came from having commanded UN police forces in hot spots around the globe in the '70s and '80s.

Magner inquired, "Yet the United Nations has no record of your having worked for them, do they?"

"No, they sure don't."

"You have claimed that any record of your employment with the United Nations has been destroyed; isn't that right?"

"The odd thing about that is that the United Nations sent me my Nobel Prize medal this year, which I have at home, and the documents that go with it, yet they can't find any record of my employment. I find that highly irregular."

"So you have won a Nobel Prize too?" Mike sounded genuinely puzzled.

"General recipient in 1988, yes."

"I see. I must not have heard about that."

Baxter, it turned out, had never testified in a federal case and had in fact been rejected multiple times as an expert witness over the years. On top of that, he had sustained a head injury from being stomped in the head by a horse.

Magner moved to have him tossed. "I think there's a serious issue as to his credibility, his reliability, and I think the man is simply a flake… I think the [head] injury raises some very, very serious questions."

Africk responded, "Nothing I have been provided with indicates that he is in any way cognitively impaired as a result of being hit by a horse."

"Other than that he received the Nobel Prize…" was Mike's snarky response.

In the end, Africk allowed Baxter to testify. The result was not persuasive. Though he had interviewed Warren, he failed to take notes, causing him to get facts wrong. I hoped the jury got the sense that Warren's justification for using lethal force was so weak, no reputable expert would touch it.

CHAPTER 18

A SOCIETY FOR
THE LIVING

November 29 and 30, 2010

Frank DeSalvo began his defense of Greg McRae with a grab bag of witnesses who did little to advance his client's cause. He even recalled Tanner to the stand, to rehash the long-since straightened-out tattoo confusion. Tanner was fine with that. As he walked off the witness stand, he gave the courtroom version of a short Oscar acceptance speech: "Thank you, Jury. Thank you, Judge. Thank you, people in the room."

It was all a sideshow. The witness everyone wanted to hear from was Greg McRae. DeSalvo didn't linger over his client's professional bio. McRae, forty-nine, was a twenty-seven-year veteran of the NOPD who hadn't risen above the rank of "officer." Early in his career, he sustained serious injuries in a car crash during a high-speed chase and never returned to street duty. He spent much of his time at the NOPD in the crime lab, processing evidence like shell casings. DeSalvo had described McRae in his opening as a "desk jockey," though he might as well have added "motorhead." McRae's real value to the SOD team was his ability to fix vehicles and engines. His hobby was building and restoring cars, and he'd even raced at the Bonneville Salt Flats in Utah.

Just days before Katrina hit, McRae transferred to SOD, where his mechanical skills were in high demand. While his immediate superior, Lieutenant Scheuermann, piloted his boat around the flooded streets, McRae functioned like a one-man pit crew, repairing two-stroke outboard motors when they fouled or swapping parts when a propeller sheared, unglamorous but essential work.

Whenever equipment failed, McRae was the go-to guy. "I would normally go out to rescue the rescuers when those engines would poop out or quit running or shatter... At times I would get in water up to my chest... Water that was...contaminated with fuel, contaminated with oil, floating bodies."

McRae also served as a go-between, passing information from people searching for missing family and friends to the SOD cops in the boats who were looking for them, a particularly wrenching part of the job. "I set up, basically, a dispatch system," he testified. "I took a basic yellow notepad and began to record the addresses of homes in the Lower Ninth Ward. Most via the radio. We had people calling in, mostly family members of policemen. Cell phone usage was sporadic, so we had a lot of police officers calling up saying they had family members or neighbors or what have you trapped in their homes in the Lower Ninth Ward. McRae had given the list of addresses to the SOD boat units. They couldn't find the houses.

"And they said, 'Could you call them back and get a description of the roof of the house?'" McRae then realized, "All those people were dead."

He continued: "Nobody was coming to help us. Nobody seemed to care, but we kept rescuing the people."

McRae said that everywhere he went, he found overwhelming human suffering. "We would take those people and we would put them on the interstate. We had nothing to give them, no water to give them. Most of the elderly were dead by that night."

I objected multiple times. At one point, Africk agreed that the testimony was getting far afield from the fact of McRae setting a man's body on fire. "What does it have to do with Officer McRae and September 2?" the judge asked. "I don't understand."

But as the testimony progressed, Africk seemed more and more persuaded that all these incidents impacted McRae's state of mind in the aftermath of the storm. Any bad thing that McRae experienced now seemed evidentiary fair game.

Finally, McRae described being at Habans when Tanner's Chevy pulled in. Tanner's car, he said, was followed by a patrol car with the lights and sirens on: "It got my attention." The scene, as the officer sketched it, was chaotic—"[a] lot of yelling, a lot of screaming"—but things calmed down when Scheuermann, the ranking SOD officer on the premises, walked out from the school to take control. By that point, the men in the car, all save the one who was dead or dying in the back seat, were handcuffed on the ground.

McRae steadfastly denied that he, or Scheuermann or Jeff Sandoz, had abused the detainees in any way. He said he overheard Scheuermann on the radio requesting SOD commander Captain Jeff Winn to come to the school and inquiring over the radio whether any of the officers in the Algiers area were working "a possible shooting involving a white vehicle." Officer David Warren, McRae said, was not on anyone's mind.

"Have you ever had a conversation with him?" DeSalvo asked.

"No, sir, I have not, other than saying hello and shaking his hand in this courtroom."

McRae then explained how it came to pass that he burned the car.

"I remember hearing a conversation by Captain Winn and Lieutenant Scheuermann," McRae testified. "Captain Winn had said, 'We have to get it out of here.' They had exhausted all of their means of, I guess, investigation." Winn, Scheuermann, and McRae agreed that they would bring the car to "a spot on the other side of the levee." McRae turned to Scheuermann and said, 'I'll meet you behind the levee.'"

He continued, "I drove the car to…the river side of the levee. I drove it into the woods as far as I could drive it. I left the car running. I opened the driver's side door. I lit one flare and threw it into the vehicle."

Leaving the Chevy, McRae started walking back up the levee and saw Scheuermann parked in the truck at the top. He turned his attention back to the car below. He intended to burn the car and its contents, but the flame had smoldered out.

"Apparently, when I had driven the car to the levee, I had used the air conditioner and put all the windows up…" (It seemed unlikely that McRae would manually roll up the windows when moving a dead body.) "Apparently, the fire had exhausted itself out or was trying to go out, I guess, because of the [lack of] oxygen in the vehicle." It seemed to me that the word "apparently" might be McRae's "tell" that he wasn't being truthful.

McRae got close enough to Scheuermann that they could hear each other. "I don't remember if I told Lieutenant Scheuermann, 'Give me a second,' or, 'Wait a second.' I may have made a motion. He looked back at me. I walked back toward the vehicle… I…stood directly behind the vehicle, fired one shot into the rear glass [window], at which time the car began to burn.

"I turned and walked up, got into the silver truck with Lieutenant Scheuermann. I believe he had words with me…something along the lines of, 'What are you doing?' or something like that. And I remember telling him, again, something along the lines of, 'I wasn't going to let it rot.' He seemed kind of shocked."

McRae had just admitted to the unlawful seizure and destruction of Tanner's car and, far worse, the incineration of Henry's body. The rest of DeSalvo's direct tried to establish that McRae lacked the requisite intent for his actions to be "willful."

"What was your state of mind at that time?" his attorney asked.

"I couldn't explain my state of mind at that time."

"Were you thinking about Mr. Glover's family and whether or not they could file a lawsuit?"

"Not at all." Similarly, McRae said he wasn't thinking about covering up evidence.

DeSalvo might have mounted an affirmative mental health defense by arguing that his client suffered from temporary insanity or diminished capacity, but that would have required psychiatric experts and pre-trial hearings, which didn't seem like DeSalvo's style. In this case, his strategy, as best I could tell, was to let McRae talk about Katrina, for as long as Judge Africk would let him, to win the sympathy of the jury. McRae had a remarkable ability to allow the courtroom audience to feel something of the desperation of Katrina.

"...[I]t was in the high nineties, ninety-seven, ninety-eight degrees, and it was 98 percent humidity," he said. "Exposure was beyond belief. Water—if you took a sip of hot water you would throw it up." At night, he said, he foraged around Algiers for gas, siphoning it out of gas tanks of parked or abandoned cars, and removing parts for the SOD motor pool, which required constant repair.

But, McRae said, it was the sight of the dead bodies that shook him.

"I had seen enough bodies, I had seen enough rot... The bodies I had seen, bodies I knew that were trapped in the peaks of the roofs of houses, bodies that I saw when I was on boat missions."

I objected once again that DeSalvo and McRae had wandered into an impermissible "Katrina defense," but I was overruled. DeSalvo went for the emotional payoff.

"How were you feeling at this time?"

"Helpless, lonely."

"Where was your family?"

"I sent them up north."

"Do you know if they got there?"

"I had no idea. At that point in time, I had no idea."

"How did that make you feel?"

"Scared."

That might have seemed like a good place to stop—McRae had been traumatized by the storm and its aftermath; point taken. But DeSalvo elicited yet another war story, this one about a barbecue at Habans that McRae had said had pushed him to the breaking point. One of the SOD officers had killed a deer, which the officers grilled outside the school. McRae said that while he was speaking to another officer, distraught and on suicide watch, "I observed this cook attempt to light a fire with one of my commandeered five-gallon jugs of gasoline, and it blew up... It almost burned down Habans School. We kept it a secret, but I was watching the men deteriorate, and I was watching them fatigue and begin to fail." McRae broke down. (Strange, it seemed to us, that after being so undone by this incident, he would set fire to Tanner's car.)

Judge Africk seemed spellbound by the officer's account. The sight of McRae, this beefy middle-aged guy, choking back tears made, I'm sure, an impression on the jury. I wasn't devoid of sympathy. I accepted that McRae was probably traumatized by Katrina. But he was also the loyal company man, willing to do the NOPD's dirty work.

To close out his direct, DeSalvo returned to the crime and the near-impossible job of explaining how the suffering that McRae had endured had somehow put him in a state of mind to inflict pain on others.

The attorney opted for brevity. "You realize now the pain that you may have caused the Glover family?"

"Yes, I have."

"If you had to do it again today, would you do it?"

"No. No, sir."

"When did you first realize that this was something you shouldn't have done?"

"I remember Lieutenant Scheuermann telling me to get some sleep. I remember sleeping for four or five days. The first day I remember, I believe it was the fifth, that I could tell you the day. And I believe, at that point in time, I knew what I had done."

"Did you believe that there was any legitimate law enforcement reason for doing what you did?"

"No, sir."

"Did you ever pick up the phone and go visit anybody from the Glover family and say, 'I'm sorry'?"

McRae said he didn't. "I had done a wrong and I couldn't do it."

DeSalvo asked McRae whether Scheuermann or Winn or anyone else told McRae to burn Glover's body. The officer ended his testimony with one final falling on his sword.

"Nobody told me to do it."

The burning of Henry's body set the Glover case apart from other notorious cases of unjustified police killings over the past few decades. And yet it remained somewhat mysterious, which is not a good thing when it's your job to hold someone accountable. Greg McRae was taking sole responsibility for the burning, and yet it seemed highly unlikely to me that a low-ranking SOD officer, an unstinting team player, would take such drastic action on his own say-so.

On cross, you don't expect the defendant to break down on the stand and tell you they did it. That happens on television and almost nowhere else. Typically, you want to poke holes in the defendant's story, why it shouldn't be believed, or why the witness himself was unreliable and shouldn't be trusted.

But McRae had already admitted to most of the charges against him. I wanted to do more. On cross, might he possibly say something that would implicate Scheuermann, or one of the other officers on trial, or perhaps even one of the ranking officers we had never been able to charge?

I asked, "You had no intention, when you left that day, of bringing this car or this body back to Habans School?"

"I had made a decision before I left Habans that I was going to burn the body in the vehicle."

I was surprised by that answer. I had assumed he would say that burning the body, as opposed to simply moving it, was a spontaneous decision. "So before you even left Habans School, you had a plan in your mind?" I asked.

"That's correct."

"And so just so that we are clear," I continued, "when the car went up on fire, that wasn't a mistake."

"No, sir. That was definitely not a mistake."

In a short series of answers, Greg McRae had just admitted to crimes that could send him to prison for at least ten years, the mandatory minimum penalty for the use of fire in the commission of a federal crime.

In any normal prosecution, that should have been a victory. The problem was, I didn't believe he'd acted alone on some strange whim.

"Why did you burn the body?" Africk asked him point-blank. The judge was puzzled as well.

"I had reached a point, Your Honor, I was tired of smelling putrefied human rotten flesh. The [West] Bank was at that point clean. It was the first body we had come across…"

A few minutes later, he tried to clarify his point. "…[T]he factor, to me, was the point that the West Bank was still safe, it was still dry. We were living there, it was inhabited. The East Bank was completely uninhabitable, it was unsafe, and it was dangerous." By contrast, the West Bank was still "a society of the living."

"Because of those situations on the East Bank, you thought it made sense to burn Henry Glover's body on the West Bank?" I asked, unable to follow the logic.

"Sir, I was exposed to so much death, so many bodies, that's what I did."

McRae's account of the moment he set Tanner's car on fire raised yet more flags. Scheuermann remained at the top of the levee in the truck when McRae was downhill at the base of the batture. McRae threw the flare into the Chevy and then walked up towards Scheuermann, close enough so they could communicate. "I believe I made a gesture of one minute, or one second." And then, he said, after observing the Chevy was smoldering, not burning, he waited "a minute or so" and walked back down the hill to send a bullet through the rear window of the car.

On direct, McRae had been quite clear that he had waited longer for the car to catch fire. I quizzed him about the discrepancy. "Is it not your testimony that you said that you waited four to five minutes with Dwayne Scheuermann before you shot into that car?"

I had been struck by the length of time. It was hard to imagine the lieutenant watching the commission of a crime in slow motion, over the course of four or five minutes, and being unaware of what was going on. At a minimum, it signaled that McRae had Scheuermann's approval.

"I can't judge time, sir. I mean I don't remember how long," McRae replied.

But according to McRae's testimony, Scheuermann was an innocent bystander. When McRae rejoined Scheuermann after lighting the car on fire, he said, the two men drove the truck down from the levee, where they encountered the Fourth District Lieutenant Joe Meisch near the Customs and Border Protection headquarters. McRae said he didn't know Meisch and let his senior partner do the talking: "Lieutenant Scheuermann had a small word about along the lines that 'We'll handle this later.'" McRae denied that he had been laughing.

"I remember the disheartening feeling of him telling him what had just occurred. I believe he mentioned something, 'This was the body we had at the school, or the corpse from the school.'"

I finished my cross of McRae the following morning. I kept asking questions, and McRae kept responding politely without implicating anyone else. I hammered away at him that his story didn't make any sense.

"Again, sir," he replied, "I don't expect you to understand how I felt at that time, and I hope you never will. But I did what I did." He remained adamant that he acted alone. "Before I left the school my mind had been made up. I didn't want to go to sleep that night. I couldn't sleep. I couldn't eat. I kept myself busy by working. I stayed awake for four days."

"You didn't think it was a good idea to run this idea, 'I'm going to burn this man's body,' by someone who outranked you?"

"Never crossed my mind, unfortunately, sir."

"Four to five minutes passed from the point that you put the flare in the car to the point that you fired into the back of the car; is that correct?" I remained incredulous.

"I can't give you a time frame, sir... I guess what I'm trying to say, sir, is we didn't do this hurriedly. We didn't do it with an intent to escape, you know, 'Let's get out of here.'"

His use of the word *we* was telling. The same word Lieutenant Meisch testified that Scheuermann had used when he said, "We are not going to deny that Greg and I burned the car."

I didn't push McRae about his word choice at that moment. I didn't want to give him the chance to take the "we" back, or to claim that he hadn't meant what it sounded like he had meant, namely that he and Scheuermann committed this crime together. "We" would come in handy for my closing argument.

I finished the cross by underscoring an understanding between the officers about the need to cover up their crimes—how much of it was communicated and how much was simply understood, I never knew for sure. My sense was that the NOPD protected its own, and everyone knew to fall in line.

McRae helped me make this point when I asked him about his conversation with an officer whom the jury knew well by now, though he wasn't on trial: Sergeant Detective Gerard Dugue.

When I first read Dugue's draft investigative report, I immediately suspected that he had authored it in a way that would protect the officers suspected of misconduct. Public employees can be required to participate in investigative interviews or risk losing their jobs. However, when public employees are "compelled" to give a statement, those statements cannot be used against them in any future criminal proceedings. These are known as *Garrity* rights, after the 1967 Supreme Court case, *Garrity v. New Jersey*.

Throughout the report, Dugue claimed that his interviewees were "compelled" to speak to him. By making this claim, the statements would be kept from the federal investigative team. Not only could we not *use* what his interview subjects told him in court, we couldn't even *see* these compelled statements. Otherwise, they'd risk "tainting" the entire investigation, resulting in the entire case being dismissed. (This happened in the prosecution of Blackwater personnel accused of killing seventeen Iraqi civilians in 2007.)

That potential risk was so great that a DOJ "taint team," unconnected to the investigation, reviewed all police statements and redacted any arguably compelled statements of anyone who might conceivably be charged in our case. Dugue had interviewed McRae, but I had been walled off from the summary, putting me at a distinct disadvantage.

But I never believed that Dugue actually "compelled" any of the witnesses. We had spoken to many of his police witnesses, who told us their interviews were voluntary. I could only surmise that Dugue wrote his report this way to keep information away from the federal prosecutors.

Before I began my cross-examination, I asked the judge to question McRae without the jury present. If I could establish that the statement he gave to Dugue was not compelled, I could use it against McRae, if I found anything useful.

McRae described his conversation with Dugue as "very casual," "informal," and "voluntary." That did it. I extracted McRae's earlier statement from a sealed yellow envelope.

What I found surprised me, although by now, it probably shouldn't have. Dugue interviewed McRae in February 2009, just as our investigation was getting underway. McRae had told Dugue that he drove Glover's body to the levee and was followed by Scheuermann.

But the interview abruptly stops at the point where McRae parks the car. Dugue—just like in his interview with Linda Howard—doesn't ask the obvious question: "Did you burn the car?" McRae knew better than to answer any unasked questions.

"…[A]t no point in your conversations with Sergeant Dugue did you tell him that you knew who burned the car; is that correct?" I asked McRae.

"He never asked me, and I never told it to him. That's correct."

I pointed out that Dugue's investigation was purportedly trying to discover who burned the car and, more importantly,

Henry's body. It was an odd thing for an investigator *not* to be curious about.

"I don't know what his reasoning was," McRae said. "He basically said, 'Let's stop talking about this. I'm coming back. I need to keep talking to some other people.'"

McRae and Dugue never spoke again.

The head of SOD, Captain Jeff Winn was a twenty-seven-year NOPD veteran, a former marine gunnery sergeant who had fought in Iraq in 2003. After Katrina, Winn was put forward as a hero— "no one stood stronger" than the captain, intoned Ed Bradley on *60 Minutes*. He was a hard-nosed, take-charge kind of guy who, from what we had learned, had the respect of his men. "I'm not proud of it," he told the court with evident pride, "but I tend to be a very demanding commander. When I want something done, I want it done now."

Winn had been the senior officer at Habans, but his involvement in the events of September 2 remained somewhat mysterious. In anticipation of being indicted, Winn and Scheuermann raised money for their defense, selling an arm patch that featured a caricature of Winn holding a Glock and talking on a cell phone. Below the image were the stitched letters *WWJWD*, short for "What Would Jeff Winn Do?" (a cheeky rip-off of WWJD, "What Would Jesus Do?"). I had been asking myself the same question for months.

DeSalvo called Winn as a witness to help establish that McRae had been under tremendous strain, keeping the SOD vehicles up and running in the days after the storm: "I didn't have another guy to fix a boat at 2:00 in the morning." How that stress translated to the burning the body of a homicide victim went unaddressed.

Winn arrived at the school, after the three men had already been removed from the car. They were calm and didn't complain about their treatment, he said. Then he told McRae to drive the car and the body to the levee.

"I couldn't have a decomposing body inside my compound. Secondly, I thought that if I told him to put it on the other side of the levee behind the Fourth District station and the US Border Patrol office right there, it would be somewhat secure."

"Did you tell him to burn the body?"

"No, sir, I didn't."

During his questioning of Winn, Scheuermann's attorney Kearney emphasized that McRae had gone rogue all on his own. "If you had had any idea that Greg McRae was going to burn that body, you would never have let him drive away in that car, would you?"

"Absolutely not."

Though called as a witness for McRae, Winn's testimony was far more consequential for our case against Scheuermann. Winn testified that, in no uncertain terms, he did not know about the burning until after Dugue's investigation began in 2009. Scheuermann had never told him, he said.

On cross, Magner immediately attacked the idea that McRae, his "go-to guy," burned a man's body, and he didn't know about it. Winn said he only learned about the burning as Scheuermann was preparing to give his statement to Dugue, as a part of the NOPD investigation. (In the end, Scheuermann never spoke to the detective, opting to plead the Fifth.)

"Well, after Lieutenant Scheuermann was to make his statement, we were talking about the case and the things that were going on. I told him basically that, you know, 'Well, I don't know who burned the body but, you know, I mean, we didn't do it.'

"[Scheuermann] said, 'No, that's not correct.' He said that Officer McRae did it. And I remember him telling me, you know, 'I thought I told you.' And I said, 'No, you never told me that.'"

Magner repeated the answer as if he couldn't quite believe what he was hearing. "Scheuermann said, 'Oh, I thought I had mentioned it'? Is that what you are saying?"

It was. If Winn was telling the truth about being kept in the dark, perhaps Scheuermann had wanted to insulate his commanding officer from the criminal act. If he wasn't, perhaps Winn had set the whole thing in motion himself. Winn testified that when he had learned of McRae's involvement in the burning, he never shared that information with either the NOPD higher-ups or the federal investigation. "You never came forward to tell what you knew until today, correct?" Magner asked.

"That's correct."

Throughout the investigation, the only motive we could deduce for why police officers would burn Glover's body was to cover up the shooting. Winn's testimony suggested an additional possible motivation, corrupt in a totally different way. Testimony at trial revealed strong discord between the commanders of the Fourth District and SOD. The history of distrust between Winn and Captain David Kirsch went back a long way, exacerbated after the storm, when SOD operated on Fourth District territory.

"You hate Kirsch, don't you?" Magner asked Winn.

"I don't hate anybody, but I don't get along with him very well."

Winn had testified on direct that he'd sent his men to a nearby Walgreens to forage for antibiotics. He elaborated: "I broke into a pharmacy, and I took everything with 'cillin on it... I took every kind of antibiotic I could find because I had five and six officers going down because they were getting sick from being in dirty water."

Kirsch, who had himself turned a local Walmart into the Fourth District commissary, evidently regarded this as poaching on his precinct's turf, and the two captains were barely on speaking terms.

"Look, I hope this doesn't come out sounding bad," Winn explained, "but you know what? I had enough other stuff going on. I still had people in attics. I had people on rooftops. If this was Captain Kirsch's responsibility, then he needed to handle it." Winn suggested that if he knew a Fourth District officer had shot the man, then he would have "delivered it" to Kirsch.

I considered, for the first time, if Henry's body had gotten mixed up in a pissing match between two commanders with big egos. By driving Tanner's car to the levee, directly behind the Fourth District station, SOD had, in fact, "delivered" the body back to Kirsch and then burned it in his backyard. Fourth District officers saw the smoke from the district station. Could the burning have been merely a big "fuck you" to the Fourth District, and its commander Captain Kirsch, for a corpse having wound up in Winn's compound? Winn denied, however, knowing that the man had been shot by a Fourth District officer, and he claimed at trial that he still wasn't convinced about that fact.

"I mean, I know what I read in the newspapers," he had testified on direct, "and I know what I have seen in the news media. But to this date, no one has ever asked me or informed me that this guy might have been shot by a New Orleans police officer."

It was a ridiculous claim given that there was no longer any dispute that Warren had shot Henry. Additionally, NOPD deputy chief Martin Defillo testified that he spoke to Winn in February 2009, and the captain confirmed that a cop had shot Henry Glover and another had burned his body. Winn denied it.

Magner attempted to bring in material that might suggest to the jury, however loosely, that Winn knew, or could have known, that the man in the back seat had been shot in the back by a police officer. Mike asked Winn about the wounds he had seen when checking Glover's pulse and quizzed him about the "NATO round" ammunition that Warren had used. Magner tried to use Winn's combat experience to suggest that Winn knew Henry had been shot in the back by a high-powered rifle.

Murray erupted. "They tried to get some type of agent or expert to come in and testify regarding this, which was not allowed, and now they are bringing it up and trying to get it in when it's not even part of the scope of direct examination… I think it's improper and we move for a mistrial."

Magner pled his case. "There's no other way I can do it if these defendants have burned the body. Judge, you have to be able to give me some opportunity to cross-examine these men when they are charged with obstruction of justice and destroying this body."

Africk ruled, once again, against us. Mike decided to go to war with the judge. "If I can't do that, Your Honor, I'm going to have to seek writs…" Mike was telling the judge, in somewhat arcane legal language, that he would appeal the decision, mid-trial, an exceedingly rare move that would end the trial and could possibly preclude us from retrying the case. Of all the adverse rulings we endured, this one seemed like an odd hill to die on.

Africk, clearly not accustomed to being challenged in open court, blew up. "Well, you know what?" he thundered, "Seek writs. Get back. The objection is sustained." Mike protested, and Africk raised his voice even louder. "Get back. If you threaten me with that one more time, you will sit down. Okay? Get back. Let's go."

Even though we were at the bench with the "husher" on and the country music pumping, Africk's loud voice prompted a few shocked looks from jurors. Mike had crossed a line with the judge, and he knew it. At the end of the Winn cross, we approached the bench, and Magner was contrite. "Your Honor, I simply want to apologize to the court."

Africk himself seemed a little abashed at his judicial outburst. He apologized to the jury, if not to Magner, for losing his cool. "To the extent that I did that in a way which was louder than usual, you know, I need to sit back and take a deep breath."

Judge Africk explained that he'd been up most of the night sorting through some evidentiary matters that had to be settled. One of those matters had been keeping me up at night as well: what to do about Kawan McIntyre and Henry's arrest record?

Africk decided that two of Henry's four past arrests, including the one juvenile arrest, were off-limits. The other two arrests, both of which occurred in a five-month period over a decade before he was killed, could be admitted, but only if Kawan knew about them. Otherwise, he ruled, "that will end it."

I had no idea whether Kawan knew about Henry's prior arrests. I hoped, for the good of the case, she did not. Kawan approached the witness stand, nervous to be back in the courtroom. Kearney handled the examination.

"I believe that you told us in your earlier testimony that you and Henry Glover were cousins, right?"

"Yes."

"I think you used the term 'best cousins,' is that right?"

"Yes."

Kearney was setting the stage for the conclusion that Kawan had to know about Henry's run-ins with the law. "When you weren't with Henry, would you keep up with him through talking to friends and family members about what Henry was up to, what he was doing, that type of thing?"

"Yes. We kept in close communication, yes."

"So you probably knew most of everything that was going on in his life as y'all were growing up together; is that right?"

"Yes, sir."

I was getting anxious. Just ask the damn question already.

"I'm going to ask you a very specific question. Between December of 1991 and April of 1992, have you heard ever, from any source whatsoever—family members, friends, Henry, or anything—that Henry was ever arrested during that period of time?"

"No, sir."

"You never heard that?"

"No, sir."

That ended it. The arrests were not coming in. And with that, I could finally exhale.

After a week in purgatory, I should have felt more relaxed, but now I had something else to worry about.

Dwayne Scheuermann testified next. Once McRae claimed that he had acted alone, the odds of convicting the lieutenant sank. For Scheuermann, McRae was, as Magner put it later, "walking reasonable doubt." My only chance of salvaging a conviction was breaking down Scheuermann's story on cross.

The night before the lieutenant testified, I returned to the hotel after a long day in court to pore over my notes for the cross. When I got to my room, I found the door ajar. I knew I had locked the door when I last left the room. Hadn't I? I was prosecuting cops, so I was extremely conscious about my personal safety. But I was also exhausted. Could housekeeping staff have failed to properly lock up after cleaning my room?

Fearing that someone had tampered with my room, I immediately called down to hotel security. "Do you know who I am?" I asked the head of security, the first and only time in my life I've ever used that line.

"Yes, Mr. Fishman, I know who you are," the head of security replied.

"Then you can appreciate why this is so concerning," I said.

Hotel security ran tests on the locks that showed that the door had been properly secured after housekeeping left. There was no indication that the door had been opened again.

We entered the room, and nothing was obviously amiss. I kept all of my case files at the US Attorney's Office, so I wasn't worried about any missing documents. But with security unable to explain what had happened, I was moved to a different room, requiring me to pack up a month's worth of belongings when I should have been working on my cross.

I checked into my new room under an assumed name. If my room had, in fact, been broken into by someone connected with the case, the name I chose was probably not the smartest: Mike Ice, Tanner's renowned graffiti artist.

I had absolutely no evidence that Scheuermann had anything to do with my unlocked door, but it was the only explanation that made sense to me. I could only assume that he, or someone at the NOPD, was trying to send me a message.

After a particularly fitful sleep, I faced Scheuermann at trial the next afternoon. But first, the lieutenant justified his actions to his attorney on direct examination. "Did you know [McRae] was going to throw a flare into that vehicle?" Kearney inquired.

"No, sir, absolutely not. We had no clue. None whatsoever." His was the voice of injured sincerity.

Scheuermann said that he had done his best to get a straight story from the three men pulled from the Chevy about what had happened to the fourth man in the back seat. "You know, [Edward King] kept saying multiple times, 'I am going back to kill the person who killed my brother.' ...I took him seriously. There was no reason not to take him seriously. He knew who he was going to kill and I didn't.

"When he refused to start giving us detailed information on how his brother was killed, I began to think that, obviously, he was not being truthful with me. And that somehow, with all the looting going on, maybe it was a homeowner, a shop owner, business owner that had maybe shot this gentleman during some kind of looting event.

"I couldn't even go warn this person who he was threatening, because he wouldn't tell us anything about it. So having no jails, having no detectives, the best thing we could do was hold him for a little while. And we didn't really have any place to hold him other than the bench in the back of the school."

Like most plausible-sounding, self-serving accounts, this one was grounded in some truth. We knew that Edward had uttered that exact threat. We also knew that the men did not initially tell their story to the police, having been, they said, assaulted on arrival. (Bernard testified that he later told the officers where Henry was shot at the mall.)

Even if we didn't know exactly how much Scheuermann had known about the Glover shooting on September 2, we were confident it was considerably more than he was letting on to the jurors.

Scheuermann, I believed, had ample opportunities to piece together what happened, but also plenty of room to obfuscate by blaming it on Katrina. "Katrina was such a massive disaster, and it was so many human lives that were lost and so many that were at risk of being lost that, like in anything in law enforcement or rescue, you have to deal with the living before the dead. And it's just what we had to do, to do our best to save the people who were still alive."

The lieutenant's version made sure to emphasize how considerate he had been. He had checked to see if Henry was alive, but he had no pulse. Then, he made sure to park Henry's body away from any residential neighborhood, because "some poor family may come home and see a horrible sight… So this gave us a good place for the safety of the scene and the safety of citizens."

After McRae burned Glover's body, the lieutenant's first concern was his officer's emotional health. "And I knew it was obvious the way Greg was talking and what he just did that…he had, I guess, serious issues with the storm. And I knew—he looked exhausted. He looked like he was just having problems. I said—the only thing I could do with him at the time was I sent him to bed. I said, 'Go to sleep. I don't want to see you for a while.'"

And he said he had done the proper thing, reporting the incident to Joe Meisch when he was exiting the levee. "I drove up to him and... I said, 'Joe, there is a body in the back of that car.' I said, 'We are going to have to deal with this when things settle down.' ...I mean you couldn't avoid seeing it. It was black smoke billowing up over the levee."

Scheuermann explained away other instances when he had allegedly used the *we* word. "...I couldn't say 'we burned the vehicle' because 'we' didn't burn the vehicle. I was aware that the vehicle was burned, but 'we' didn't [do it]."

Kearney asked if the lieutenant had ever mentioned to other people that "Greg did something stupid."

"Oh, I probably did. But amongst policemen, it was probably a little bit different language."

Scheuermann was smooth. I hoped the jury would be able to tell the difference between slick and honest.

Facing Scheuermann on cross, I don't think I sounded shaky, though my mind drifted to that open hotel door. Throughout the trial, I wrestled with this weird disconnect between what I saw—an outwardly respectful, intelligent middle-aged man; what I had read about him—his laundry list of alleged aggressions that included extreme brutality; and what I feared—the things he might be capable of doing to me or my team. The fact that so many police officers were afraid of him made an impression.

There was no dispute that Scheuermann was present when McRae lit the fire, but I needed to show that Scheuermann was complicit in the burning. I homed in on the length of time between McRae tossing the flare in the car and the car going up in flames. If McRae's estimate was correct—that it took four or five minutes for the car to catch on fire—it was simply impossible to believe that the lieutenant wasn't in on the plan.

Scheuermann chalked it up to McRae having had a case of Katrina memory.

"Well, you would agree that it would be a problem for you if Mr. McRae was down by that car with the flare for four to five minutes?" I asked.

"It would be a problem if it was true."

"Your testimony is that Mr. McRae's memory is just wrong?"

"A lot of people's memory is wrong. ...I always say I can't give you time, because under those conditions...it was day and night. That's what it was. There was no time in Katrina."

Explaining how his junior officer burned a body and he didn't see fit to report it to anybody required more effort. On direct, he had testified that he told Meisch that when things calmed down, "we" would take care of it.

But, I pointed out, that day never arrived. Scheuermann protested: "Sir, we went back to doing rescues, to try and save people's lives, saving people's property. We were still working nonstop."

Scheuermann said he never told any ranking NOPD officers about the burning. Somehow, it was all Meisch's responsibility.

"...[Y]ou never told anyone other than Joe Meisch?" I asked.

"You are saying anyone other than Joe Meisch, like Joe Meisch is insignificant in this. And Joe Meisch is absolutely not insignificant in this. He is a ranking member of the department on the staff of the Fourth District who is being groomed to take over the investigative unit. And so it's very important to tell Lieutenant Meisch."

I moved on to the key elements of the civil rights charges he faced. "...[G]iven the circumstances under Katrina, it would be unreasonable to destroy that car?"

"Again, I wouldn't have destroyed it. I wouldn't have thought to destroy it. But under Katrina conditions, again—again, not justifying it, but you have to take into consideration the stress factors with officers... You can't take Katrina out of some of the mental issues officers suffered from, and still suffer from."

The strongest part of the cross was my going after the lieutenant on his selective recall. Both Josh Burns and Ronald Ruiz had seen Scheuermann and Italiano, the SOD lieutenant and the Fourth District lieutenant, conversing away from the swarm of officers at Habans. This hardly proved they'd conspired to burn Henry's body, but at least it suggested that the ranking officers on the scene conferred about how to handle the most pressing problem of the morning: the dead man at the school.

"You don't recall having a conversation with Lieutenant Italiano?"

"I don't recall. It is very possible. It is very, very possible… I'm not saying I didn't talk to him. I just don't have a recollection."

I also pushed Scheuermann on the most glaring implausibility in his testimony, that he'd somehow neglected to tell his commanding officer, Jeff Winn, about what had happened at the levee. The lieutenant's response was underwhelming.

"…Captain Winn is a very good friend of mine.… If he says I didn't, then maybe I didn't. But it wasn't intentional, because I wouldn't let him get blindsided by somebody he really doesn't get along with, especially Captain Kirsch."

CHAPTER 19

HANDLE THE TRUTH

December 1 through 3, 2010

Our prosecution of retired NOPD lieutenant Robert "Bobby" Italiano felt more like a white-collar crime case than a typical police case, resting as it did on a bunch of potentially incriminating documents. We had assembled what we thought was a convincing paper trail: the missing persons report, the Signal 21 incident report on Warren's weapon discharge, and ICE agent Schmidt's logs that documented his debriefing to Italiano about Tanner's account. They made, we thought, a strong argument that the lieutenant connected Warren's shooting and the burning that followed not long after they happened.

In addition to the paper trail, we elicited testimony from various witnesses who said they had linked the two incidents for Italiano, before he signed the Signal 21 report or spoke with Ashley and me at the FBI. It wasn't the sexiest case, but it was hard to believe that Italiano did not know that Glover had been shot and burned by the police.

Italiano claimed he simply hadn't put the pieces together. He said that, in addition to the stress caused by the storm, he was distracted by his wife's and mother's medical issues.

Italiano's attorney, Steve Lemoine, called Beverly Italiano, the ex-lieutenant's wife of forty-one years, a frail woman who had suffered a stroke six months before Katrina. At the time the storm hit, Italiano was burdened with her health problems as well as those of his ninety-year-old mother, steadily succumbing to dementia.

"He was very close to his mother," Beverly Italiano testified. "He would go to see her every Sunday. And she had Alzheimer's and didn't know who he was, but every Sunday he went to church and then went straight to see her. We would go with him in the beginning—"

Tracey objected, and Africk interceded: "Ma'am, I understand your pain. I understand that, but we need to get to the meat of the matter."

Lemoine tried to focus her testimony. "During the period while Ms. Italiano was dying, your mother-in-law was dying, did that have an effect on your husband's state of mind?"

"Yes, it did. Again, during that period, he was—you know, he was depressed. You know, he didn't sleep well."

However this bid for sympathy might play with the jury, it didn't wash with Africk. He instructed the jurors: "Any verdict that you render should not be based on any bias, sympathy, or prejudice."

Italiano's defense would depend mostly on his own testimony. On direct, his attorney couldn't have been more direct. Not wasting time with getting-to-know-you biographical details, Lemoine went through the list of charges against Italiano and registered his client's blanket denials.

"Bobby, did you aid and abet Travis McCabe in knowingly altering, concealing, covering up, falsifying, and making false entries in documents with the intent to impede, obstruct, and influence the investigation and proper administration of a matter within federal jurisdiction?"

"No, sir. Absolutely not."

Italiano denied "knowingly or willfully" telling the FBI that no report was written after the Warren shooting. He denied intending to "make a false statement" when he said that missing persons reports were filed after Katrina. He denied intending to deceive when he claimed not to have been aware of a connection between the September 2 shooting and the burning.

Italiano explained that when he was interviewed at the FBI office in April '09, he had said there was no incident report concerning David Warren discharging his firearm because he had forgotten about the December 2, 2005 report. He remembered only after having lunch with some NOPD colleagues several months after the FBI interview and one of them mentioned it, the Glover case being much in the news by then.

"I said, 'There's a report on it?'"

"He said, 'Yes.' He said, 'You signed it.'"

"I said, 'I signed it?' I said, 'Can you fax me a copy of that report so I can see that?'"

Italiano's sense of shock was less than convincing.

Lemoine asked about the definitive-sounding statement Italiano made to Ashley and me (and the ASAC) that no reports were being generated after Katrina. On the stand, he explained that he had meant that only serious crimes were being documented in the first two months after the storm, although that was certainly not what he had told us. And that the discharge of an officer's firearm, with no evidence of anyone being hit, did not rise to the level of a serious crime.

Then Lemoine directed his client's attention to the missing persons report, with Italiano's name on it, the document that clearly connects the shooting to the shooting victim at Habans.

Italiano said he didn't see the missing persons report on November 16, 2005.

"How do you know you didn't?" Lemoine asked.

"Because I had left work in the morning, because my mother had died, and this is in the afternoon." Italiano said he didn't return to work for two or three days.

This was the first time we'd heard about this remarkable timing, corroborated by his mother's death certificate. For us, it was "a bad fact," but not conclusively so, since Italiano would likely have seen the report after he returned to work only days later.

After this "win" with the report, Lemoine had an uphill battle. Italiano needed to explain how it came to pass that he had talked, however briefly, to both Sergeant Nina Simmons and Officer Linda Howard about the shooting, knew about the shooting victim in the car at the school, and yet had failed to consider there might be a connection, or report this apparent homicide to anyone in the chain of command.

We heard some familiar excuses, such as the police radio call saying that the vehicle carrying the shooting victim was a truck, not a car. Italiano said he heard that the victim had been shot in the nearby low-income apartments, with no mention of a police shooting. And, he testified, had it been a police shooting, why in the world would the rescuers go to Habans? "I didn't think it was logical if the police shot him that they would bring him back to a police compound."

Italiano's strategy was to deny every incriminating detail that, by itself, couldn't be corroborated. If he sounded confident that he'd never seen the missing persons report until 2009, he was less so in rejecting the possibility that he and Captain Kirsch had met Sergeant Simmons at night in the dark at the mall, a creepy proxy for an actual inspection of the shooting scene.

"…[D]o you know that you didn't do that or do you just not recall?" Lemoine asked.

"I'm pretty sure we didn't go there to meet with her, no."

"Would there be a reason to go there in the dark?" Lemoine inquired.

"Certainly wouldn't be a reason to go there in the dark, no."

Italiano claimed Deputy Chief Marlon Defillo was mistaken

when he testified that Italiano confirmed to him a connection between the shooting and burning, months before our interview at the FBI. "I heard him testify, but…it didn't resemble any phone call I had with him."

According to Italiano, Defillo had raised the question of the connection, and Italiano had said only, "Well, it's possible. I can't discount that now," and that only because he had read the news reports.

And so it went. Bell and Simmons had, contrary to their direct testimony, never told him about Glover family members who came to the Fourth District with accounts of their relative having disappeared under suspicious circumstances.

It seemed to me that Italiano's most useful ally was the NOPD bureaucracy itself. For a medium-sized police force, responsibility for investigating an officer-involved shooting was spread over a couple of different departments. Depending on whether anyone was wounded or killed or not, such a shooting might properly be the responsibility of either Dugue's office or the Public Integrity Bureau. If an officer hadn't been involved, then it fell to Major Crimes Homicide, but possibly the districts' individual Investigative Units might have a say. And, of course, in the months after Katrina, assignment responsibilities were scrambled.

Italiano was the ranking investigator at the scene at Habans that morning, but he could plausibly argue, so he hoped, that the dead man in the back seat of the car was someone else's problem. After all, it was Katrina, and "[n]obody was investigating anything. There were bodies all over the city, and that's what the policy was."

And when he eventually inquired through an intermediary about the burned body recovered at the levee, he was told by the coroner's office that it had not been ruled a homicide—too much of the body had been destroyed to allow the cause of death to be pinpointed. It was hard to say whether the coroner's office was good at covering up suspicious shootings or just bad at doing its job. Either way, Italiano felt he was off the hook.

The bigger problem, as Italiano understood it, was that so many of the officers he worked with had failed to give him the information he needed to understand what really had happened at the mall and the school and the levee. He blamed Lieutenant Joe Meisch and Sergeant Nina Simmons by name.

It was a fair point. Meisch didn't tell him about what he saw at the levee, and it was unclear exactly what information Simmons passed on to Italiano the day of the shooting. But even after ICE agent Schmidt connected all the pieces for him, the lieutenant had seemed remarkably resistant to getting the message.

The testimony, and the written logs, of ICE agent John Schmidt were a problem for the defense, a very "bad fact." It was a piece of evidence, from an unimpeached witness, that documented Italiano should have known that the man Warren shot was brought to Habans and later burned behind the levee.

"Did you hear him tell you those things?" Lemoine inquired.

"It's possible he—he told me some things about the...the burned car and that. But I—I didn't hear any of the other stuff about Mr. Tanner or anything. I—I don't know. Like I say, I had several conversations with ICE supervisors."

The Schmidt episode elicited the smallest of mea culpas. "And if—if he said all of that to me and I didn't, then that's my mistake. But that's what it is, a mistake. I missed something. But that's it."

There were, he admitted, on reflection, "a number of things that maybe I should have done differently." He could have himself talked to "those three subjects"—Calloway, King, and Tanner—instead of relying on SOD to figure out what had happened to them. Instead of relying on Sergeant Simmons's uncertain-sounding account, he could have driven over to DIU to look for evidence that someone had been shot.

"Have you thought about that very much?" Lemoine asked him.

"Yeah, I think about it, because it's something I didn't get right. You can always learn from your mistakes." While I agreed with the sentiment, it certainly sounded like self-exculpatory bullshit to me.

The Italiano glowering at me from the witness chair was the same guy I remembered from our interview at the FBI a year and a half earlier. Then I was trying not to sound out of my depth, trying to figure out how hard to press as I was just beginning to get my head around the case. After amassing a year's worth of evidence against him, I felt significantly more sure of myself.

On cross, Italiano conceded as little as possible, to show that he wasn't going to let me push him around.

"You were never told to stop investigating homicides after the hurricane, were you?"

Italiano was seething. "They took my detectives away from me. How am I going to have them investigate if they are not working for me?"

I contrasted Italiano's laissez-faire attitude towards the body at Habans with NOPD's hands-on response to the shooting of Officer Kevin Thomas. Within minutes, officers from different police divisions, including Italiano, converged on the scene. Cops made arrests, collected physical evidence, and processed the weapons in the neighboring Jefferson Parish crime lab.

But the shooting at the mall and the victim at Habans hardly received that kind of red-alert attention. The only explanation, Italiano maintained, was that he did not believe that the wounded man at Habans had been shot by a police officer.

"If you suspected that this man had, in fact, been shot by David Warren, would you agree you would have had an obligation to preserve the evidence?" I asked.

"If I suspected that David Warren had shot him, I would have preserved the evidence and I would have had it—taken action to the top as far as I could."

The more I dug into the conversations that Italiano had with Sergeant Simmons, when she arrived at Habans soon after Warren's "discharge," and with Officer Howard at the end of the day, the more frankly pathetic his story sounded. Italiano testified that Simmons had not told him that Warren's shot had hit.

"She said he thought he missed," Italiano said. "...Nina Simmons told me that Linda Howard could not see what was happening. That's what she told me at Habans right off the bat."

But the next exchange was telling. "But she also told you that she thought the man at the school was connected to the David Warren shooting, correct?"

"She told me that. I told her that we thought it was connected too. That's the reason we went over there. But after we spoke to the Tac unit [SOD], we didn't—I didn't think it was."

I trusted the jurors were asking themselves the same question I was. How could Simmons think that the firearm discharge at DIU was possibly connected to the shooting victim at the school unless there was a good chance that Warren's shot had struck someone?

"And you never went back to the DIU after you left Habans Elementary School?"

His response was oddly equivocal. "Not that I remember, no, sir."

"Even though you knew about the discharge at the scene?"

"Certainly I knew about the discharge, but it was a discharge. I didn't know that somebody was hit."

Italiano also had little recollection of his conversation with Linda Howard the evening of the shooting, though he claimed he never asked her if it was "a good shoot." Italiano said he relied on Simmons's account of what Howard had witnessed. "Nina Simmons told me that Linda Howard didn't see anything."

"And you didn't ask her anything about the circumstances surrounding the discharge?" I asked.

"No. I just—and this could be wrong on my part, but I assumed that if she had seen anything contrary to what Nina Simmons said, she would have told me what she saw." It was hard to believe that he wouldn't ask her if Warren had hit anyone unless he already knew the answer.

Before I returned to the documentary evidence, the strongest part of our case, I asked about the communication between him and Scheuermann in the minutes before Henry's body was driven away. We thought this conversation was the key to understanding what happened next.

"I heard a couple people say that, so I probably did. But I don't remember it."

Scheuermann and Italiano had a long history together, and considered each other friends. When Italiano worked at PIB, he once cleared Scheuermann of misconduct. I wanted to explore their relationship on cross, but the judge wouldn't allow me to ask about past accusations of misconduct against Scheuermann.

I had always assumed the missing persons report was our strongest documentary evidence against Italiano (at least I did before I learned about the timing of his mother's death). The missing persons report helped explain why there was suddenly a need, three months after the fact, to write a report about Warren's shooting. Once Henry Glover's name was entered into the national enforcement database, there was a need to disconnect him from a police shooting.

"That report came after the Glover family filed the missing persons report on November 16, 2005, correct?"

"I can see that now. I didn't know that then."

"Right, because you claim you never saw the missing persons report, correct?"

Italiano was indignant. "I don't claim it," he replied, voice raised. "I didn't see the missing person report." He had a harder time explaining the Schmidt logs. "Maybe he spoke to me, maybe I didn't hear him say everything that he says he told me. I don't—I don't know... I might have connected it. If I had had all the information, I might have connected everything."

I had to point out that there seemed to be a pattern of Italiano not hearing information connected to Henry Glover.

Attempting to take advantage of his contempt for me, I tried to push him into a Jack Nicholson "you can't handle the truth" moment from *A Few Good Men*, where Italiano unwittingly would admit to his role in the coverup.

I didn't get it, but I hoped the jury might think he was hiding something.

When my cross-examination resumed the next morning, I returned to Italiano's conversation with ICE agent Schmidt. Italiano was absorbing a lot of punishment, and he was beginning to sound beaten.

"You don't recall that he gave you the information that would have connected all of this together, correct?"

"I was working eighteen, nineteen hours a day," was the weary reply. "...I was not a hundred percent. Okay? I was physically beat from all of these hours. If he told me that, I didn't hear that." The Signal 21 report was, if anything, worse for him. He ordered the report and signed it.

"Is this the narrative that was attached when you signed off on the report?" I asked him, that one-and-a-half-page document now up on the court's big screen.

"I can't really say that," Italiano said, an admission that lent credence to Simmons's contention that the narrative section had been switched out. "It was five years ago. I don't remember. I was working eighteen hours a day for a couple months, so there's a couple of things in the narrative that I don't think I would have approved. But maybe because of working eighteen hours a day for a couple of months, maybe I missed that."

I zeroed in on some of these things in the report that Italiano said he didn't agree with.

Italiano admitted, contrary to the report, that neither he nor Captain Kirsch had done an investigation that concluded Warren's discharge had been "reasonable."

When I pushed him on this, some of his old fight came back. "Things changed when the hurricane hit... I had no detectives.... I was not investigating. Everything changed for the hurricane."

The ex-lieutenant was left to defend the position that his conversation with Simmons, a person whom he claimed to have barely spoken to, had persuaded him to clear the Warren shooting.

"I spoke to Nina Simmons. She could not list any violation of any departmental rule that he did. Later on, I spoke to David Warren and...when he told his story, there was no violation of any rule of the department.... There was no sign of anyone hit. It was a discharge. Now, since somebody lost their life, it is a big deal, but at the time a simple discharge is not a big deal."

I questioned his assertion that no one was injured, given that

near the end of the narrative section, the report says that bystanders near the mall had seen a shooting victim being driven away.

"That would indicate that David Warren did, in fact, hit someone, correct?"

"No, that's not what it indicates."

"That would not be evidence that he perhaps hit someone with
his shot?" I asked incredulously.

"It may be perhaps he hit someone with his shot, but it could
be another shooting."

"About a block away, right?"

"Yes."

"On the same day?"

"Yes."

"At the same time?"

"I don't know about the time."

Italiano sounded defeated.

I closed the cross on the emphatic note I wanted.

"Now, you would agree that an allegation that the police shot a
man and burned his body is a pretty memorable allegation, correct?"

"Yes. I believe it's barbaric."

His response stopped me. It seemed to convey a genuine horror. I wondered if Italiano truly hadn't known what McRae and
Scheuermann were up to when they drove off from the school.
Likely, I'd never know. In any event, the word *barbaric* would get
a lot of use for the rest of the case.

"You would agree that it would look pretty suspicious if [the
allegation that the police burned the body] was not investigated,
correct?"

"Yes."

"You would agree that it looks even more suspicious if it turns
out that those allegations were actually true?"

"Yes, it does look suspicious."

The final defense witness of real consequence was Lieutenant
Travis McCabe. To my mind, he was the least interesting of the
five defendants. He had admitted to helping write the narrative of

the Signal 21, allegedly at Simmons's request. I wished he'd come clean and implicated higher-ups in the cover-up, but he didn't.

Allyn Stroud, who had impressed us with his PowerPoint-style point-by-point defense of McCabe in his opening argument, handled the direct.

"Did you, as charged in count eight of the indictment, author and submit a false and misleading report with intent to obstruct the investigation of the death of Henry Glover?"

"Absolutely not," he said, mimicking the emphatic tone of Scheuermann and Italiano.

He denied lying to the FBI or in grand jury. "I told the absolute truth."

He had no memory of having a conversation with Keyalah Bell in which he suggested she tell Tanner to check with SOD about his car. Likewise, he claimed to have never spoken with Alec Brown about Tanner's burned car. Brown had testified that McCabe upbraided him for asking about the burned body behind the levee, telling him to be quiet because "Police officers need to stick together." The lieutenant testified this conversation never happened, and suggested that Brown held a grudge because McCabe once scolded him for botching an arrest.

As for actually producing the Signal 21 incident report, McCabe portrayed himself as something of a Good Samaritan, helping out Sergeant Simmons, who was "stressed" about doing it herself. "I thought it was a fire and miss," he said. "If I had known anybody was actually shot, I would have referred her to Cold Case Homicide. I would not have gotten involved in that."

The division of labor was elaborate for a three-page report. McCabe tried to make it sound unforced, collegial. He said that Simmons had provided most of the information—she was, after all, the officer who responded to the scene—but that he had also had brief conversations with both Warren and Linda Howard to clarify certain points.

"As we discussed it, we typed these paragraphs. I'm pretty sure that I physically typed a large majority of this. After we were through, we discussed it in great length. We typed it. After we were through, she did the final proofreading."

"Officer McCabe," Stroud asked, "was there ever some other typewritten narrative that existed that you swapped out and re-placed [with] the narrative that we are looking at?"

"Absolutely not."

McCabe struck me as an odd duck. The guy who had the least reason to be on trial seemed to relish it the most, wearing the in-dictment as a badge of honor. Whenever I saw him in the court-room, he would try to stare me down with his best tough-guy look, an effect more comedic than intimidating. (His wife, on the other hand, an assistant district attorney in next-door Jefferson Parish, had a far more chilling stare.)

On cross, Magner didn't have many blanks to fill. We had al-ready played the jurors McCabe's recorded grand jury testimony in our case-in-chief, and he had pretty much eviscerated himself. Magner made sure to highlight the inconsistencies in his earlier testimony concerning his alleged collaboration with Simmons.

"Can Simmons not type?" Mike asked. "Is she incapable of typing?"

"I'm sure she can. I have no personal knowledge of her typing."

"But you have never seen her type?"

"I don't think so."

"So that means you typed every word in that typewritten nar-rative, correct?"

"All I can say is I'm pretty sure I did. It's a long time ago," Mc-Cabe said.

The defense rested its case, and we had a chance to rebut some of the witnesses they had called. Most significantly, we called a use of force expert to rebut the conclusions offered by Warren's expert, Alan Baxter.

Charles Key, a retired police officer who had developed and taught the use of force guidelines used by the Baltimore police department, spoke to the relevant logistics, tactics, and ballistics of Warren firing on Henry. The use of lethal force, he explained, required a police officer to have a reasonable belief that the person he was shooting at posed a mortal risk to the officer or to others in the vicinity.

Magner gave Key a hypothetical. Suppose everything that Warren had said at trial was true, and that Henry and Bernard really had rushed the rear gate of the mall.

"…[G]iving Mr. Warren every benefit of the doubt of his story," Mike asked, was Warren's conduct justifiable, that is, "consistent with accepted standards of police policies, practices, or training?"

"It was not," Key answered. Even under those circumstances, he testified, Henry Glover did not pose a serious or mortal physical threat. "…[T]he absolute necessity is that the officer have…a reasonable belief that the individual poses a threat of serious injury or death. There is nothing…that would indicate that an objectively reasonable officer would believe that."

Mike gathered himself for the big finish.

"Now, I'm going to give you another factual scenario, Mr. Key. And I would like you to assume a couple things: that Mr. Glover drove that same truck to the rear of the shopping center, and he parked the car and backed up to that same shopping cart with the two suitcases in it. That Mr. Glover…had his butt on the bumper, sitting up here towards the front of the truck, and was either lighting or smoking a cigarette. And after being warned to leave the area, he was shot in the back while running away. Assuming those facts, do you have an opinion as to whether that shooting would be consistent with police policies, practices, and procedures?"

"I do."

Mike leaned in for his zinger: "It would be murder?"

"It would not be consistent with…police training, practices, and policy," Key replied.

That didn't land with quite the force that Mike hoped for. Key wouldn't opine on whether or not it was "murder." That would be a decision for the jury.

CHAPTER 20

THE LAST WORD

December 6, 2010

After four weeks of presenting evidence, the parties made their final appeals to the jury. The judge turned to me. "Let's begin with the government. Mr. Fishman."

I approached the podium in front of the jury. I took slow, careful breaths to calm myself down. This was the most important argument I had ever made, and the courtroom was packed to full capacity. I looked back at the Glovers, who nodded at me in support.

I had been sketching out my arguments for months. Too many lawyers wait to write their summations until near the end of the trial, but I had been developing mine ever since we had indicted the case six months earlier, keeping a notebook filled with points and phrases that I thought would be most convincing. As I watched the trial play out, I reshaped them into what I hoped would be the most compelling case for conviction.

To get a conviction on any count, we needed to win over every single juror. Throughout the trial, I angled my chair at the prosecution table towards the jury box, keeping an eye on the twelve jurors without seeming too obvious. Their facial expressions and body language gave me clues about which parts of the case spoke to them, and which didn't.

My closing included an assortment of different arguments that might appeal to different kinds of jurors drawn from all over Eastern Louisiana. I knew some jurors would be moved by "rights" arguments: that humans are imbued with inalienable rights, and that the law must protect the rights of its most vulnerable members.

But I knew that conservative-minded jurors responded more favorably to arguments emphasizing the importance of institutions, social stability, and order. For them, I stressed that the defendants had violated the norms that keep our society from crumbling—by going rogue, breaking rules, and abusing their authority.

I looked into the eyes of the jurors, one by one. I took one last deep breath.

"Henry Glover only wanted to leave New Orleans. It was the morning of September 2, 2005, and Henry had survived Hurricane Katrina. For four days he managed to keep his family safe. But that morning, Henry decided it was time to gather up his family and leave.

"Henry Glover never got that chance. Instead, Henry was shot in the back and left to die in the back seat of a stranger's car. His body was set on fire and left as a pile of ash. And then in the days and months and years that followed, all of this was covered up."

I front-loaded my appeal to the conservatives and the traditionalists: the five officers betrayed their oath, and they'd let their police force and their city down. "The defendants were officers of the New Orleans Police Department, they had sworn to uphold the Constitution, they had promised to protect and serve. Yet the people responsible for upholding the law were the very people who committed these unthinkable crimes."

Katrina was no excuse. "Hurricane Katrina did not *cause* these crimes. These crimes occurred because each of these defendants, these five officers, abandoned their commitment to their oath."

Then I emphasized the harm done by the powerful to the powerless. "These crimes happened because they saw their victims as unworthy of the law's protection. And when police see the citizens this way, their oath becomes meaningless. They stop protecting and serving and they begin to abuse the public trust. What happened to Henry Glover was a flagrant abuse of power, and each of these defendants must be held responsible for their actions."

I turned to the shooting that started the chain reaction that led to all the subsequent crimes. I needed to demonstrate that Warren's shot was unjustified and unconstitutional. If the jury believed that Warren had feared for his life on that second-floor breezeway, or if they believed he had made a panicky mistake, he would be acquitted. Our legal burden was to prove, not only that the shot *was unreasonable*, but that he fired that shot *knowing* that it was unreasonable.

In determining this, the law uses an imaginary "reasonable officer" standard. How would a "reasonable officer" have acted in those circumstances? I reminded the jury that we had such an officer. Linda Howard, a quarter-century veteran, had testified that she had felt so unthreatened by the two men in the Firestone truck that she hadn't even drawn her service weapon. That's why the defense attorneys were so intent on impugning Howard's mental health. Unfortunately, her inconsistent statements and evocative language about "zombies" and "flashbacks" gave the defense more ammunition than I would have liked.

But, I told the jurors, even if they did not take the testimony of Howard, or Bernard Calloway, for that matter, completely at face value, common sense demonstrated that Henry didn't pose a mortal threat. The mere fact that Warren was sixty-six feet away and a level above demonstrated unreasonableness.

And the scenario laid out by Warren and his defense team was borderline absurd. Henry and Bernard were supposedly rushing towards the strip mall. To what end? "...[Y]ou heard that Henry and Bernard had one reason for being at the DIU strip mall that day, to pick up the suitcase and leave... Henry Glover had absolutely no reason to run towards that strip mall. He certainly had no reason to charge at a bulletproof-vested, assault-rifle-toting police officer who was in a sniper position... That would have been a suicide wish, [and] Henry Glover needed to get home to his family."

Henry Glover could only have posed a serious threat if he had been wielding a gun. On the stand, Warren had parroted the language of the Signal 21 report, that the man he shot had on him an "object" that he "perceived" to be a "weapon." Only on cross did he claim he saw a gun, though he could not describe it.

I argued that Warren never felt threatened, ticking off the things he would have done if his life were in jeopardy. "...[Y]ou know he didn't fear for his life because if he did, he never would have taken his eye off the man he shot. He would have made sure to have warned his partner of the danger... He would have made sure that this man couldn't hurt civilians. He would have made sure that backup would have responded immediately. David Warren did none of those things.

"And if he was really afraid of two charging men, he would have...kept on firing until he made sure that he had hit. He would have made sure that he had neutralized that threat."

What did he actually do? "He told Linda Howard, I missed, and that was it. Now, that's not the reaction of someone who just feared for his safety, that is not someone who believed his life was in danger... That is the reaction of someone who shot a man just because he could. It was Hurricane Katrina and David Warren thought no one would care." I reminded the jury, "Katrina did not turn petty theft into a capital offense."

What Warren did and did not do, I told the jury, met the legal requirements of the most serious criminal charge he was facing. "You need not find the killing was premeditated or motivated by ill will. Defendant Warren used his assault rifle with magnification scope to pick off an unarmed civilian who was running away and who posed no threat to anyone. Defendant Warren knew there was no threat. He acted like a sniper picking off a target. And though his actions were swift, they were deliberate, and they were intentional. They showed callous disregard for human life. Ladies and gentlemen, that is the definition of murder."

Though we didn't have to prove *why* Warren shot Henry, jurors feel more comfortable convicting when they can grasp the motivation behind the crime. But Warren remained a cipher—a smart, controlled, rather beige guy on the stand who evinced no remorse, nor any strong emotion. We could only offer up clues about what made Warren tick and let the jurors sort it out as best they could.

He regarded the Black citizens left behind in Algiers as uniformly dangerous, "other." He saw them as "Them."

"You heard from Alec Brown that defendant Warren had that irrational hatred of all looters," I told the jury, "He believed they were destroying the community. He believed they were animals."

I moved on to Warren's fixation with guns. "...[I]t's the obsession with guns, the obsession with shooting that helps explain why Henry Glover was shot in the back.

"...[H]e told you he became a cop because he liked guns. That is no reason to become a police officer. He might as well have told you that he became a cop so he would have a chance to shoot a gun.... When Hurricane Katrina hit, David Warren had an opportunity to take out his arsenal of assault rifles. He had the opportunity to take out the gem of his collection, the most expensive gun he owned, that $7,500 SIG .223 assault rifle topped off with that $800 magnification scope. Defendant Warren wanted to shoot his gun."

I opened the case that contained Exhibit 1, the murder weapon, Warren's SIG .223. It's a big, heavy, ungainly rifle, a sniper's weapon beyond out of place in a commercial strip mall.

I carefully removed the gun from its case, making sure the muzzle pointed downward. I didn't just want to show the gun. I wanted to hold it, in ready position, just as Warren had when he pulled the trigger. I wanted to show the jury that this was a weapon designed to be fired with the utmost deliberation. Before firing, you had to set yourself, control your breathing, lock in your target with the scope.

Though the gun had been "made safe" for trial, courtroom security gets anxious anytime someone handles a firearm. I couldn't point it near any people, and in a room packed to capacity, that left me one sliver of the corner of the courtroom.

I felt nervous handling the weapon too, even though I had practiced this part of my closing many times. I knew I needed to look like I knew what I was doing, conscious not to have a Michael-Dukakis-in-a-tank moment that would cause me to lose credibility with any juror who knew their way around guns.

I lifted the SIG to my shoulder and looked through the scope. I took aim at that narrow sliver in the corner. "He brandished his gun that morning even when no one was around. He peered through that magnification red dot scope. He scanned the empty horizon."

I lowered the weapon. "Ladies and gentlemen, when you view the world through a scope, everything looks like a target."

I gathered myself for my close. "For Dave Warren, Katrina was the moment he had been waiting for, it was his chance, it was Katrina and he thought he could get away with it. For four years David Warren was right. It's now up to you to tell him that he was wrong."

David Warren benefited from two closing arguments, delivered by Julian Murray and Rick Simmons, an unusual arrangement that Africk allowed.

Murray began with a plea to the jury to separate Warren's case from the other defendants' cases, an echo of all the times he asked the judge to sever his case. "Mr. Warren is only charged in those first two counts. The other nine counts have nothing to do with him."

Then he gave the jury a rather vague, open-ended version of the "Katrina defense": the jury should "take into consideration" the special conditions that obtained that first week after the storm.

Warren worked eighteen hours a day, guarded one of Kevin Thomas's assailants at the hospital, and watched the Oakwood mall burn.

"But by God," Murray pleaded, "when you look at somebody's state of mind, when you determine what is reasonable and what is not reasonable as His Honor will tell you [that] you have to do, you cannot cut out Hurricane Katrina... Is there a heightened sense of vulnerability under those circumstances? Absolutely. But when you determine what is reasonable and what is not reasonable, you have to take into consideration the conditions under which he was living."

Then Murray got down to the business of character assassination, essential to Warren's defense—if the jury believed the gist of what Linda Howard and Bernard Calloway had said on the stand, Warren was guilty of murder. Howard and Bernard, according to Murray, "reconstructed" what happened on September 2 with delusions and lies.

Murray presented Howard as mentally ill. "And I'm glad Ms. Howard told you that she's getting therapy from a professional right now because of all that she went through," he offered up with mock compassion. "I think she needs therapy, and I hope the lady gets better. But when you start saying that that type of evidence is proof beyond a reasonable doubt, it's dangerous."

Murray cast Calloway as a ne'er-do-well thug from the 'hood. "Mr. Calloway, who had been the 'husband,' put in quotes—I don't think that he claimed to have been married, but...he had children together with Patrice, remember that? He was the one that decided to stay in Dallas, the one who left Patrice when she was pregnant with the third child, *that* Calloway."

Warren's sterling character, on the other hand, logically precluded him from having done the things he had been charged with. "This is a man that goes to church every week, you heard from his pastor... Never done a thing wrong in his life. He's lived a good life, worked hard, became a policeman because he thought it was a good thing to do.

"Does he really sound to you like the kind of man that just says, oh, these guys are making me mad, so I am just going to blow one of them away while he is sitting there smoking a cigarette? You don't believe that. In your heart you know that it didn't happen that way."

While Murray trucked in sweeping and, in my view, often offensive generalizations, Rick Simmons's closing put the prosecution case under the microscope, highlighting every inconsistency and discrepancy he could find.

"…[I]f we had tape recordings we wouldn't have all of this 'he said, she said' statements…" Simmons complained.

Our key witnesses were, indeed, imperfect. Their accounts of events often changed over time. Many had lied out of fear of retaliation. Over time, they told us more information as they came to trust us more, or as they remembered new details. None of this is unusual. Rick Simmons, not surprisingly, portrayed it differently. He likened our case to a giant game of what he called "Gossip," which I knew as "Telephone."

"If you had played the game of 'Gossip' and you do it with somebody in the row of six people who has a vendetta…and the story really gets turned around.

"One other variation [is]…guilt by gossip. What if you did the same thing, the game I referred to, you start out with Number One, you wait one year then you talk to her, then the next person waits another year. Memories fade, ladies and gentlemen of the jury… What you have is faded memories."

Simmons accused the government of playing an even more underhanded game that he called "Play Ball with the FBI," in which we coerced witnesses to say what we wanted to hear, either by offering immunity deals or by not charging them with perjury or lying to the FBI. "How do you get this grant or this forgiveness?" Simmons asked rhetorically. "To qualify, you have to have lied to the FBI or grand jury, you have to be able to provide additional evidence like locking gates or twisting conversations, and the third element to qualify is you have to have an agreement that you have no agreement… There is some understanding if not the belief by these people as long as they sing the same song and they please the government handlers, they will be okay. And they will get to go home."

The result, Simmons informed the jury, was a prosecution case "built on gossip, reconstructed memories, and it is not proof beyond a reasonable doubt.

"This is a tragedy and there are no winners here," he summed up. "If you, and I hope you do, find him not guilty, we will take no victory lap. Because as I say, there's no winners, there's only survivors of Katrina, that's all they are, including the Glover family, including some of the witnesses like Ms. Howard. She is damaged from Katrina. It's just a tragedy, but it's not my client's fault."

Frank DeSalvo, never afraid to make jokes at inappropriate times, tried to "inject a little levity" by telling a story about "the alcoholic and the worm."

"You see, there was this professor…who was standing before a group of alcoholics, and he was trying to explain to them about the ills of alcohol. He had two…glasses of clear liquid in front of him, and he reached in his pocket, and he pulled out a worm, held out the worm, and dropped it in the glass of water and that worm swam around in that glass of water, everything was fine. And the other glass where he had a clear liquid was pure alcohol. He reached in and got the worm out of the glass of water and dropped it in the glass of alcohol, and immediately that worm shriveled up and died.

"He said, 'Does everybody here understand the moral of the story?' Well, the little guy in front raised his hand and said, 'I do.' [The professor] said, 'Would you tell everybody what the moral of the story is?' and [the man] said, 'Well, if you drink you won't get worms.'

"He saw what he wanted to see," DeSalvo explained. "The evidence was clear that that alcohol is not good for you, but [the man] didn't want to quit drinking that alcohol."

DeSalvo managed to bring the tall tale back to our prosecution. "And that's what we have here in this case. The government's looking at this set of facts like that old guy. They just wanted to see it their way."

★ ★ ★

If the defense attorneys' mantra in their closings was "reconstructed memories," mine was, "connect the dots," especially as it applied to the cover-up. While our case against Warren mostly relied on eyewitness testimony and some undisputed logistics—the defendant was standing a floor above Henry armed with a high-powered sniper rifle—our cover-up case remained mostly circumstantial.

Unlike the Danziger case, we didn't have members of the conspiracy who "flipped" and incriminated their colleagues, or surreptitious recordings of the cops doing their dirty business. Instead, we had one incontrovertible fact: only one person's body was burned in the aftermath of Katrina, and that person was shot by a police officer. This, we argued, could not have been a coincidence.

In his instructions to the jury before its deliberation, Africk would explain to the jurors the difference between direct evidence, such as eyewitness testimony, and circumstantial evidence "that reason and common sense lead you to draw from the facts that have been established by the evidence." Both types, he assured them, were equally valid.

"When I was trying cases," he elaborated, "the example I used to give is if you go outside and it's raining, you see it raining, you have direct evidence that it's raining out. On the other hand, if you come into the building and it's sunny and the ground is dry and then you're in the courtroom with no windows, a couple of hours later you go outside and all of the ground is wet and the cars are wet, there's circumstantial evidence that it rained, although you have no direct evidence of that."

This case offered lots of wet ground.

The crux of our case against the four officers charged with the cover-up was that their actions constituted a conscious effort to cover up a "bad" police shooting. The chain began at Habans, when the officers made no real good faith effort to find out how and where Henry had been shot. Italiano, the district's chief criminal investigator, initially suspected that the shooting at the mall and the victim at Habans were likely connected. But then, without taking even the most basic investigative steps, he claimed to have decided they were not. Scheuermann said he conducted an "investigation," but claimed not to have learned about the mall shooting, even though he sent officers to investigate. At Habans, Italiano and Scheuermann discussed the matter privately.

I suggested that that is when the cover-up began. "Italiano knew about the shooting at the substation, Scheuermann knew about the [three] men at the school and the man in the car [Glover], and the two defendants did what lieutenants do, they told each other what they knew. Italiano had connected the dots and Scheuermann had connected the dots."

I asked the jury to hold Scheuermann accountable for the burning, just as much as McRae. "Defendant Scheuermann might not have tossed that flare into the car, he might not have fired his gun to make the car go up in flames, but he knew it was going to happen. He was the ranking officer on the scene when that decision was made. He knew the plan when McRae grabbed those road flares. He helped McRae get to the levee, and he transported him back." I reminded the jury about the slip-up in McRae's testimony when he had said that "we" weren't in a hurry. "They were taking their time to make sure that the evidence was destroyed."

I said the law was clear: "And when a person deliberately associates with someone to commit a crime, when they purposely participate in a crime and they take action to make that crime successful, then the law holds them every bit as responsible as the other participants."

Scheuermann had claimed he'd been "shocked" by McRae's act of burning the body, and yet he testified he never reported it to anyone, although he had waffled about his good friend, Captain Jeff Winn. "As an outraged law enforcement officer, surely he would want someone to know the truth," I reasoned with the jury.

The defense aimed to break apart individual links in my chain of events. Rick Simmons had warned the jury in his close: "Be aware of people connecting dots because sometimes they make false assumptions."

Scheuermann's attorney, Jeff Kearney, took issue with my representation of the conversation between the two lieutenants at Habans that morning. "There is not a scintilla, there is not a shred of evidence about what that conversation was about. This is one of those leaps of faith, this is one of these speculations, innuendo that I am talking about.

"The only way Mr. Scheuermann could be guilty is if he's joined in the venture with the same intent; in other words, joined the venture with the intent to do something illegally, willfully, against the law." At the levee, Kearney argued, the lieutenant had been caught unawares by McRae's "independent, unilateral, impulsive decision." As a matter of law, he elaborated, his client seeing a crime being committed and then not reporting it to NOPD command was not in itself a crime.

Frank DeSalvo picked up Kearney's line of attack to defend Greg McRae. His client had set the fire, no doubt about that, but, DeSalvo maintained, he hadn't acted "willfully," that is, per the statute, "with the specific intent to do something the law forbids."

"Did Greg McRae do that?" DeSalvo asked. He peppered the jury with questions: "Did he set that fire for a bad reason or was his judgment in doubt? Do you really believe that he even thought about what the law forbids?" As for the obstruction of justice count, "Is there an iota of evidence that a federal investigation ever entered the mind of Greg McRae?"

Then he took a broader swipe at our prosecution. "How many times in this case did you hear [the prosecution] ask a question like doesn't it or didn't it look suspicious? Well, I think it looks suspicious... Suspicion is what causes an investigator to seek evidence to prove whether or not the suspicions were true or whether they were merely suspicions." He capped the point with a flourish: "Standard of proof is not innocent until proven guilty by suspicious circumstances."

DeSalvo finished by defending McRae's character. "From the date this storm hit until the date of this incident... Greg McRae was about saving lives. Do you really believe that in the midst of all of this he decided 'I am going to violate some civil rights, I am going to go impede justice, and I am going to cover up a crime'? His tears weren't crocodile tears. This is a grown man, a big man, a big burly man who couldn't tell that story without crying."

In his defense of Italiano, Lemoine argued that Italiano never conspired to cover up the shooting. Real life is messier, he suggested, rarely so premeditated.

"Now, the prosecution would have you believe that when Bobby Italiano got to the Habans School that within a matter of minutes, never having gone to the DeGaulle shopping center, that he or he and somebody else decided that there had been a bad police shooting at DeGaulle and that it needed to be covered up by taking certain steps…

"I think one of the great American pastimes is hindsight," the attorney grandly offered up. Italiano's failure to make what in hindsight seem like an obvious connection between the shooting and the burning, he said, should be chalked up to the lieutenant's exhaustion and his feeling depressed about his mother and his wife.

In the final analysis, Lemoine said that a damaged Bobby Italiano just wasn't smart enough to be the criminal mastermind we had made him out to be, an unexpected defense for a veteran investigator. "A diligent man, an honest man, not a brilliant man," the attorney explained. "Sorry, Bob, I think you're a plodder, but the kind of man who could be trusted to investigate other police officers, and that's what he did. And would he change, would he change a couple of months away from retirement and become the kind of man who would cover up a crime committed by another police officer, would [he] do that? No, he would not."

The last of the defense lawyers to close, Mike Small, the attorney who reminded me of a Southern senator from a past era, effectively worked the room. "I am very well aware that you're tired," he addressed his fellow sufferers on the jury. "I'm bone-tired… I am going to reach down deep despite how tired I am, and I am going to ask you to do that for me as well."

For his defense of Travis McCabe, he used what was at hand, a pro forma trashing of Nina Simmons and Linda Howard, the key witnesses against his client. Howard was not to be believed for the old familiar reasons, the testimony about flashbacks and the taped interview with Dugue.

Small said that Nina Simmons had repeatedly lied and her testimony was too inconsistent to be trusted. Convicting a defendant, he told the jury, required the type of certainty that one would need to make the most important life decisions, such as investing one's life savings. "Now, I want you to imagine that the financial consultant is Nina Simmons. Would you find her word that she would properly invest your funds to be of such a convincing character that you would be willing to rely and act upon her representations without hesitation involving your children or your grandchildren's college funds knowing what you know about her right now? I don't think you would."

Defense attorneys make their living on "reasonable doubt." Small invoked it, in all its legal, constitutional, and even psychological ramifications, as well as any I've encountered. "The rule says unless you're so convinced that you have not one reasonable doubt, then your oaths require you to vote not guilty... And let me suggest to you in closing that the proof beyond a reasonable doubt rule has the effect of not helping only Travis McCabe, it helps you. The framers of our rules knew that jurors like you would take these decisions home with you and live with them for the rest of your lives. The framers of the rule didn't want...you to have to go home and wonder, 'Did I convict someone who perhaps didn't commit the crime he was charged with?' That's why our rule says if you're not convinced beyond a reasonable doubt, you don't have a choice, you must vote not guilty."

For four weeks, each attorney had entreated the jurors to exercise their powers of common sense. But in the end, we were asking them to make a moral choice.

Rick Simmons told the jury that all the officers on trial should be found not guilty because they had protected the citizens of New Orleans, as best they could, from a flood of biblical proportions and, the unsaid part, the predations of a criminal underclass. He let the courtroom know he was representing Warren *pro bono* and was honored to do so. "I'm a lifelong resident of New Orleans, grew up in the Ninth Ward, saw my city devastated, but am thankful for all of the NOPD people, even the border patrol agents, the doctors, the nurses, everybody that stayed behind. Each and every one of them, thank you. And I am glad to be able to pay back to my client for his service."

Rick Simmons had the buttoned-down look of a corporate accountant. But he could stretch for a very big finish. "When you go into your deliberations, I am going to ask you to think of two words. Whisper, say them out loud, think about them... Two words. It applies to all of these gentlemen: they stayed."

He paused, then raised his voice. "They stayed!"

I ended my closing with a different vision, of the law turning lawless, and a different moral reckoning. I acknowledged the challenges the officers faced during Katrina, but said that the jury must nonetheless hold the defendants accountable for the harm they had done.

"These five officers thought they could get away with their crimes because it was a disaster. They thought that because of Hurricane Katrina, no one was watching. They thought that no one would care. You will have an opportunity to let them know they were wrong. Hurricane Katrina was not the first hurricane to hit America, and it is most assuredly not the last. So, one of the many lessons that can be learned from all of this is that in times of trouble, the Constitution matters more than ever. It is abandoned with grave consequences.

"Henry Glover wasn't simply a casualty of the storm. He did not die in the hurricane. He did not drown in the floodwaters. He was murdered, and he was burned by police officers who violated the public trust. And when an officer shoots an unarmed man just because he can, it is the rule of law itself that dies. When an officer incinerates a human being and destroys evidence just because he can, it's our values and ideals that go up in flames." I hoped my vision of accountability and the mountain of evidence we unearthed would carry the day.

A four-week trial isn't a TV drama. It rarely ends on the dramatic high note. Though Magner, for his part, certainly tried.

The prosecution bears the burden of proof, and so always gets to make a second closing argument, a last chance to rebut the defense's case. Magner took the honors. I'd poured everything I had into my impassioned closing that had lasted for two hours. I didn't want the jurors to tune me out if I came back for an encore. Magner could play the part of the hometown lawyer to the hilt.

"I've known all of these attorneys, except for Mr. Kearney, who I have just had the pleasure of meeting recently, for a long time, and they're wonderful attorneys. And Mr. Kearney, who I've had the pleasure of working with in this case, certainly falls into that category."

That nod to the defense bar was, of course, tactical.

"...[T]hey're just fabulous attorneys," he continued, "and, you know, when I watched them practice their craft, I am just so impressed, because they can make white, black, and red, blue. But you've got to use your good common sense when you're evaluating this case and think of all of the evidence that you've been presented with."

DeSalvo came in for particular scorn. In his closing argument, he had pronounced Captain Winn as "the true hero of the storm." McRae was not far behind: "Ask yourself what would have happened to the city but for Greg McRae," his attorney had said.

"And it's been a long day," Mike countered, "and we have to sort of shake our heads every now and then, but all I could think of was, really? What would have happened? It could have been worse?"

Magner had a way of larding his arguments with language that I trusted the jury enjoyed. He called McRae a "gone pecan."

Mike explained why McRae would protect Scheuermann. "I think the answer really is pretty obvious. 'Police got to stick together.' ...

[McRae] knows that he's toast; he knows he is flambéed; he knows he is absolutely guilty as homemade sin, but there's still that loyalty that comes from, you know, falling on his sword…to try to protect Lieutenant Scheuermann, and Captain Winn for that matter. Because as we know, one of the immutable laws of physics and of life is that it rolls downhill."

Mike could certainly entertain. His weakness was that sometimes he didn't know when to stop.

In his close, Rick Simmons had suggested that the absence of forensic evidence—shell casings, a proper autopsy of the victim's body and so on—added up to "reasonable doubt." Mike had cooked up a snappy comeback.

"…[T]he defendants can't be like the Menendez brothers…who killed their parents and then kind of cried and whined that they were orphans… They can't say [we] don't have any forensic evidence and then go burn the body. That's ridiculous."

I cringed. I'm new at this, I thought, but questionable taste aside, this reference was pretty close to the line. Mike was explicitly linking Warren's shooting with the burning of the body.

Murray objected. "…I think it's improper argument and counsel knows it."

Mike responded, "Mr. Warren didn't have anything to do with the burning, okay, I am not suggesting that. But these defendants are suggesting that we should have all sorts of forensic evidence when they know full well that this body has been burned."

The judge addressed the jury: "I will instruct the jury as to how you're to undergo your deliberations, as you know you're to consider each defendant separately as to each count…"

I hoped that would be good enough for the court of appeals, if it ever came to that.

After four weeks of trial, the case would finally go to the jury.

CHAPTER 21

SENDING A MESSAGE

December 2010 through March 2011

As the twelve jurors hashed out the facts of the case in a small jury room adjacent to the courtroom, our prosecution team hunkered down in our war room on a different floor of the courthouse and waited for news. The judge ordered us to stay within fifteen minutes of the courthouse, so that we could quickly respond to the inevitable questions from the jury.

Waiting for a verdict is excruciating. There is nothing left to do, nowhere to go, and there is no telling how long it will take. My quickest verdict came in what I thought was a complicated case; it took about an hour. One of my longest waits came in a trial with just four witnesses and clear video evidence; the jury deliberated for three days. We settled in for what we imagined, given the length of the trial and the number of witnesses, would be a good long time. (For the defendants, their families and the families of the victims, this process is, I'm sure, far worse.)

The temptation was to fill that time with second-guessing: the witnesses we should (or should not) have called; the questions I should have asked on cross-examination; the arguments I should have made in closing. That was useless now, of course, so I tried my best to shut off that part of my brain. It helped that the adrenaline that had sustained me was ebbing, and my body was beginning to crash.

We set up a large TV and began watching season one of *The Wire*. It cut a little too close to home. Unanimously, we decided to switch to *30 Rock*.

For the entire first day, we heard nothing until we got the call from the courtroom clerk informing us that the jurors had ended deliberations for the day. The next day was more of the same. We watched more *30 Rock*. I constantly checked my cell phone to make sure I hadn't missed a call from the clerk. (I hadn't.)

Eventually, we got a call, a question. The jury sent a note that read, "We have received a CD of exhibits from the defense that do not look like items that were introduced in the courtroom, i.e., Edward King's statement to NOPD."

That might sound like a minor mix-up, but potentially, it was a disaster. Warren's defense team had provided a disk of their exhibits for the jury and included the King interview on the disk. King had not testified at trial, and his recorded statement (which would not have been admissible) implicated Scheuermann and McRae. If the jury listened to it, that could be grounds for a mistrial, and the last four weeks of trial would have been for nothing.

Fortunately, some jurors recognized that the recording hadn't been admitted, so the jury didn't listen to it. Potential crisis averted, we went back to waiting. Julian Murray was not, at this late date, going to get his mistrial. At the end of the day, we got another call from the clerk. The jurors had gone home for the night.

The third day of deliberations was remarkably quiet. No notes. No calls. I started to get antsy. It's hard to guess what is happening in the jury room, but the general thinking is that longer deliberations are less likely to result in convictions. As dinnertime rolled around, we prepared for another night without a decision. And then, unexpectedly at 6:00 p.m., we got the call. "We have a verdict," the voice on the other line told me.

I'm always amazed when a jury reaches a verdict. In our divided country, where people can't seem to agree on anything, twelve strangers are thrown together—different backgrounds, races, politics—and are asked to reach unanimous agreement, be it guilty or not guilty. I am surprised every time that it happens.

We gathered up our files and rushed over to the courtroom. Given the time of day, the rest of the building was empty, but our courtroom was packed with observers. Five armed guards (different from the usual unarmed court security) stood by the entrance. Members of the media filled the front two rows, as they had throughout the trial. The rest of the courtroom was filled to capacity with supporters of the Glovers and of the defendants. Edna and Patrice Glover greeted me with head nods and nervous looks on their faces.

Before the judge arrived, Steve Lemoine walked in and took his seat next to Italiano. Throughout the trial, I sat at the table adjacent to Italiano, our seats so close that we frequently bumped into each other, prompting some awkward moments.

Lemoine leaned in close to Italiano and whispered that "it" was "all good." Had I heard him right? Had Lemoine gotten the advance word on the verdict from court security, many of whom were retired NOPD? My first thought was, "Oh my God, are all of these guys going to walk?"

Judge Africk took his seat behind the bench. A few minutes later, the twelve jurors entered the courtroom, heads down, stone-faced, giving nothing away. I nervously doodled on a blank copy of the verdict form I would fill in when the verdicts were announced.

The clerk passed the jury's verdict to Africk, who shuffled through the eleven-page verdict form without visible emotion. "Madam foreperson, I understand that there's a verdict that the jury has returned as to all counts, all defendants; is that correct?"

The foreperson, a twenty-five-year-old Chartered Professional

Accountant (CPA) from the New Orleans suburb of Metairie, answered, "Yes, it is."

Africk briefly addressed the assembled: "I expect respect and decorum in this courtroom. Obviously, some people will be disappointed, some people will be pleased with the verdict. Anybody that cannot control themselves, leave now." Not a single person left the room.

The judge instructed the courtroom clerk. "Would you read the verdict, please. Nice and loud."

The words came out quickly as the clerk read the form, eager to get through the process. She began with count one: a civil rights violation—the use of force against Henry Glover. "We the jury unanimously find the defendant, David Warren: guilty." Count two: use of a firearm during a crime of violence. "We the jury unanimously find the defendant, David Warren: guilty."

By the time the clerk reached count three, she was speaking so fast, the verdicts sounded like a ping-pong match. Not guilty. Guilty. Not guilty. Guilty. The judge told her to slow down.

I could hear loud gasps behind me. The jurors steadfastly looked down, refusing to make eye contact with anyone in the room. Soon enough, the clerk reached the eleventh and final count—Travis McCabe, guilty of perjury—and it was over. Muffled sounds of crying—of joy and pain—came from both sides of the courtroom.

It took me a second to fully appreciate what had happened. David Warren, convicted on both counts, wore the same blank look that he'd had the whole trial. The jury acquitted Scheuermann and McRae of the beatings at Habans School, but convicted McRae on every count connected to the burning of the car and the body. McCabe was convicted on each of the three charges he faced: obstruction of justice, making false statements to the FBI, and perjury. McRae seemed unsurprised by the outcome; McCabe and his attorneys appeared shocked.

Italiano and Scheuermann, the two most senior officers charged, were found not guilty on all counts they faced. They both smiled and hugged their attorneys.

Judge Africk addressed the jury for the last time. "It's the court's hope that you now believe what I previously told you during *voir dire*, that is that the American jury system is the most powerful method yet devised for the ascertainment of truth."

Following the verdict, the prosecution team exited the courtroom and headed to a conference room where the Glovers and their friends had gathered. Family members cried and hugged. More than once I heard someone exclaim, "Thank you, Jesus."

In many ways, it was a huge victory. Three police officers were convicted, including the man who killed him and the man who set his body on fire.

But the victory also felt incomplete. The two most senior officers at the heart of the case walked out of the courtroom free— Scheuermann would be back policing the next day. "He's a police officer for the city of New Orleans," Kearney commented to the *Times-Pic.* "He'll be at work tomorrow doing what he does and what he's always done."

Even Warren's conviction came with an asterisk. Before deliberations began, Judge Africk gave the jury the option to find Warren guilty of the lesser manslaughter charge instead of murder. Manslaughter covers an unlawful taking of life where there is some mitigating circumstance, for instance, killing in the heat of passion. This allowed the jurors to find Warren guilty, while cutting him a break because of Katrina. They took that option.

I tried not to dwell on what we hadn't accomplished. I looked at the smiling faces of the Glover family for reassurance. To them, receiving any convictions at all must have seemed like a miracle.

And in truth, we had beaten some seriously bad odds. Approximately one thousand Americans lose their lives in police shootings every year, but between 2005 and 2020, only 121 officers were charged with murder or manslaughter in the entire country, and only 44 were convicted, often on lesser charges.

I reminded the assembled friends and family of how far we had come. I addressed Edna and Patrice. "When I first met you, I said I couldn't promise you what the result was going to be. But I promised you that we would work our hardest to figure out what happened to your son, your brother. I hope you feel a sense of closure and that justice was served."

Among the crowd that evening was Henry's aunt, Rebecca Glover, at trial a mainstay in the courtroom. She was a one-woman illustration of the high cost of being poor and Black in this corner of New Orleans. Four members of her family—a son, a grandson, a granddaughter, and nephew Henry—had been shot and killed in the city. Two of the cases were never solved, not that anyone tried very hard to solve them.

Aunt Rebecca's life experience served as an illustration of how Black communities can be both over-policed and under-policed at the same time. Police can lavish a remarkable amount of time and resources enforcing low-level crimes, like drug possession and shoplifting, while at the same time failing to solve the most important crimes impacting the community, like homicides.

Throughout the investigation and prosecution of our case, Rebecca Glover always looked at me suspiciously. While she would smile and joke with Ashley and Tracey, I think she saw me as a representative of the White establishment that had routinely ignored and caused her family's unimaginable suffering.

But as I talked with the family in a conference room after the verdicts had been read, Aunt Rebecca looked over at me and smiled. For the first time since he was killed, the system recognized that Henry Glover mattered.

On March 31, I returned to New Orleans for the sentencing of David Warren and Greg McRae, although not for Travis Mc-Cabe. After the verdict, McCabe's attorneys claimed to have discovered new evidence they asserted would prove his innocence, so the court held off sentencing him for a future date.

Prior to sentencing, there was, as there often is, a remarkable amount of legal briefing and argument. Warren received letters of support from members of his church and from his employer at the utility company. At the hearing, Murray chose not to address the court, relying on his written brief, though he called a character witness to speak on Warren's behalf. Warren sat in his usual chair, expressionless, at the defense table. He no longer wore a suit and tie but rather a baggy green jumpsuit from the local parish jail where he was being detained. Judge Africk offered Warren an opportunity to address the court, which he declined.

Edna and Patrice Glover came to the podium in front of the courtroom. Patrice addressed the court first. "Justice was served," she began. "My brother was a wonderful father, son, and brother, and we miss him dearly. The Glover family is devastated about Henry's death. That left the family feeling void, heartbroken, loneliness, and pain.

"We would ask the court to sentence these officers that was here to protect and serve this city to the maximum sentence. My brother didn't desire to die this horrible, gruesome death. We miss our brother. I miss my brother." As she often did when speaking about Henry, Patrice broke down in tears.

Edna, who did not testify at trial, followed her daughter. Her statement was just two sentences long: "I forgive these men, because if I don't forgive them, Jesus won't forgive me. And I would like justice to be served in Jesus's name."

I had extensively argued the government's position in sentencing briefs. I knew Judge Africk had already written his decision, so I kept my words short and to the point. "Nothing could be more true than that the sentence in this case will demonstrate the respect for the rule of law, that officers cannot abuse the public trust, and that if they do so, they will be held accountable for their actions." I was not convinced that any sentence the court imposed could or would accomplish these lofty goals, but at least it sounded good.

Finally, it came time for the court to hand down its sentence. Africk made plain the message that he hoped sentencing would send: that no one was above the law. He looked at Warren and said, "Your use of excessive force in this case is, at least in part, responsible for an erosion and deterioration of public confidence in law enforcement... You killed a man... Your testimony was contrived and fabricated... Henry Glover was gunned down because you believed he was a looter.

"Unfortunately, Mr. Warren, Henry Glover did not survive,

but thankfully for the rest of us, the Constitution of the United States did."

Africk ordered Warren to pay the Glover family $7,642.32 for funeral expenses. Otherwise, the only solace they received was knowing that David Warren would spend much of his adult life behind bars. The judge sentenced Warren to a prison term of 309 months (25.75 years).

McRae's sentence came next. DeSalvo spoke first, minimizing his client's conduct. "I know in my heart that everyone in this courtroom or everyone in this city prior to the time that this case was presented, thought it was way worse than what came out in the courtroom. They thought that Mr. McRae and everyone else involved in this case were the coming of the devil. I think they learned differently."

McRae seemed somewhat more contrite. "I acknowledge my mistakes. I came to our court. I told the truth. I never intended to impede justice or obstruct justice. I made a mistake... I apologize to all the people who I hurt. I pray for the Glover family daily. I also pray for all the victims of Katrina."

Africk was unmoved. "Your conduct was barbaric," he told McRae, using Italiano's adjective of choice. "Your purported reason for burning the body was nonsensical at best and pure fabrication at worst... There are certain things that we, as human beings, just know not to do.

"Your entire course of conduct has the stench of a cover-up... The Court cannot begin to imagine the despair that the Glover family endured not knowing what had become of their beloved Henry. The devastation caused by Hurricane Katrina was made uglier by your disturbing actions."

The court sentenced McRae to 207 months (17.25 years) of incarceration. As a part of the order, McRae had to pay Tanner $6,000 in restitution for his car, bringing an end to his quest for compensation.

At the end of the hearing, DeSalvo entreated the judge to reconsider McRae's lengthy sentence. To my mind, the attorney had not, until that moment, fully appreciated the legal risks his client had been facing, given the ten-year-mandatory sentence for using fire in the commission of a federal crime. Africk declined. McRae would take the fall—all seventeen years of it—for the cover-up.

If one measures "justice" by the severity of the prison time imposed, our prosecution had scored an unambiguous, even overwhelming, victory. Warren's sentence to this day represents one of the longest sentences ever given to a police officer, especially considering that in the federal system, defendants must serve at least 85 percent of their sentence before they are eligible for release.

McRae's sentence was even more remarkable. He received the longest sentence I've ever seen meted out for participating in the cover-up of a crime. Consider that eight years later, a state court judge sentenced a Chicago cop to less than seven years for fatally firing sixteen shots into the back of an African American teenager, Laquan McDonald. He ultimately served less than half of that sentence.

But as zealously as I prosecuted my cases, and as much as I wanted to hold individuals accountable for their misconduct, I generally felt ambivalent when it came to the length of sentences actually imposed. I loathed what Warren did, and I strongly believed that society needed to send a strong message that his conduct was intolerable. And yet, it seemed to me perverse that the prize for a hard-fought victory in court is another human winding up in a cage.

I cannot look at the defendant when the sentence is being read. It feels like a violation to watch someone's face when they receive what is often the worst news of their life. In the case of Warren, his face never revealed much, but I couldn't bear to watch the reactions of his wife and five kids as they learned that their husband and father wouldn't be coming home anytime soon. As much as I wanted Warren to be punished for what he did, I knew that when we incarcerate individuals, their families become collateral damage.

I looked over at the Glovers. I was pretty sure that a prison sentence alone was not likely to bring them whatever they needed to feel whole again.

I hated participating in sentencings, because it never seemed to me to have much to do with something that might meaningfully be called justice. Perhaps that was a terrible mindset for a prosecutor. Or perhaps, it is precisely the frame of mind that prosecutors should have.

PART IV

AFTERMATH

CHAPTER 22

IN BETWEEN

April 2011 through December 2012

With the Glover trial behind me, I was more than ready to get back home to my family. After six weeks away, I was ecstatic to be back with my wife and daughter. I walked through the door of our house in DC, and my toddler daughter yelled out a joyous, "Daddy!"

Though I tried my best to savor the reunion, I wouldn't have much time to make up for my extended absence. Over a two-month period, two other major trials would keep me away from my family, including a sex-trafficking trial on the other side of the world, in Guam. Once again, Fiona, now six months pregnant, was left managing the household by herself. Only now can I fully recognize the emotional toll it took on my family and the profound stress it put on my marriage.

In my office, the kind of travel I was doing was considered normal and expected and, without questioning, I fell into line. Fiona and I soldiered on. In retrospect, it is unfathomable to me that the attorneys in my office with caregiving responsibilities didn't get some kind of support from the Department of Justice, childcare subsidies for instance. It helps explain why the DOJ has serious problems retaining good attorneys, and more broadly, why few women with family responsibilities make it very long in jobs like mine. In the end, the government loses out on valuable perspectives and highly competent lawyers.

In April, four days after the Glover sentencing, I returned to New Orleans for trial, this time trying to get a measure of justice for yet another Black man killed by the NOPD.

In late July 2005, a month before Katrina hit, an NOPD officer fatally beat Raymond Robair, a forty-eight-year-old handyman and roofer, in the historic, mostly African American neighborhood of the Treme.

The Robair case further demonstrated that the crimes committed against Henry Glover, extreme as they were, were indicative of a broader NOPD institutional pathology.

Long before Katrina, the department had made itself infamous as a law unto itself. Katrina just made everything that much worse. In a 2010 interview, civil rights attorney Mary Howell, who frequently represented victims' families in civil rights suits brought against the NOPD, summed it up well: "By the time we came to Katrina, the department was, I would say, in as bad a shape as we had been in 1994 [when four NOPD officers were charged with murder in less than a year]. And the storm stripped bare any pretense that there was any structure, any accountability. It all vanished."

At one point in 2010, the FBI had at least nine open investigations into serious allegations of NOPD misconduct, six of which took place in the weeks immediately following Katrina. In each case, the police killed or injured unarmed civilians, all but one of whom were Black, under highly suspicious circumstances. Many of these cases came to light thanks to more investigative work by A.C. Thompson at *ProPublica* and his partners at *The Times-Picayune*, Brendan McCarthy and Laura Maggi.

Raymond Robair's death was only an outlier in that it happened less than a month *before* Katrina. The case quickly became what the *Times-Pic* would later describe as a "legend" within the tight-knit Treme community, prompting calls for a federal investigation. But the hurricane struck one month later, wiping out any chance the case would be seriously examined. People worried more about survival than righting past wrongs. The Robair investigation, it seemed, was yet another "casualty of the storm." NOPD, the FBI, and DOJ Civil Rights each shut down their cases.

When Howell observed federal investigators pouring resources into NOPD investigations, she saw an opportunity to breathe new life into the case. My DOJ colleague Forrest Christian was working on the Danziger Bridge case while I was investigating the Glover case. DOJ reopened the Robair investigation and teamed us up. Forrest was a friend and a talented and committed civil rights lawyer. We used whatever downtime we had when we were in New Orleans to see if we could build a case. We were almost certainly the last line of review.

Melvin Williams, a fifty-year-old Black senior officer, was a highly recognizable figure in the Treme, not only for his tall, rail-thin physique and trademark "flattop" haircut, but for his high volume of arrests and aggressive policing techniques. Members of the community said he was known for beating confessions out of suspects and planting drugs on them to make arrests. Some alleged worse.

Matthew Dean Moore, thirty-eight, was a White rookie officer from Winnipeg, Canada, who'd first come to New Orleans to play hockey for the city's minor-league team. He became a cop after an injury short-circuited his pro sports career. At the time of the incident, he had been on the job for all of seventy-seven days.

According to the police report filed by Williams and Moore, on the morning of July 30, 2005, the two officers patrolled the

Treme neighborhood, in an area they described, with some exaggeration, as being "known for high street level drug trafficking, prostitution, and where drug users frequent to purchase illegal contraband." The officers saw an unnamed man "stumbling and holding his upper chest" and in apparent "need of medical attention." When they stopped their patrol car to help the man, he tried to flee but slipped and fell to the ground.

The two officers brought the man to the hospital and told the medical staff they found a baggie with cocaine near his body and that he was a "known drug user." The ER doctors treated the man, later identified as Raymond Robair, for an overdose, before they discovered that he was bleeding internally. Robair died during an unsuccessful surgery. The police reported this event as a "medical incident." The subsequent coroner's autopsy saw nothing to contradict the officers' account, finding that the death was consistent with a street-level fall.

Howell wasn't buying it. The word on the street was that the police beat Robair to death. She commissioned a second autopsy from a respected out-of-state pathologist, Dr. Kris Sperry. Sperry determined that Robair died of internal injuries, consistent with a beating, his broken ribs and lacerated spleen the result of "severe blunt force trauma," with force comparable to a high-speed car crash.

The Robair case had much in common with the Glover case. The handyman's death had been ruled "unclassified" by the Orleans Parish Coroner's Office that made the same assessment of Henry's death. The elected coroner, Frank Minyard, the trumpet-playing gynecologist, ran the office for forty years, and had a long history of clearing police officers in in-custody death cases.

And the NOPD's criminal investigation into Robair's death had been led by our old nemesis, Detective Sergeant Gerard Dugue. Unsurprisingly, Dugue cleared both officers after a cursory investigation. Despite that damning second autopsy, he decided, "There was no physical evidence to corroborate the allegations of wrongdoing on the part of the officers..." Though his report included statements from three neighborhood residents who claimed to have witnessed the beatdown, he wrote that they were too unreliable to trust, describing them variously as "intoxicated," "under the influence of mind-altering drugs," and "argumentative." His report included an unsubstantiated claim by a person called "Keisha" (no last name, date of birth, or address) that someone other than the police may have beaten Robair. (In the Danziger case, Dugue faced conspiracy charges for co-authoring a report that included a make-believe witness named "Lakeisha.")

As with the Glover investigation, we figured the odds were stacked against us. There were no other cops who witnessed the alleged crime. I hoped Moore might come around and cooperate, but he evinced no interest.

That left us with the word of a handful of neighborhood residents who watched the scene unfold from their stoops and open windows. We got the feeling from the Dugue report, however unreliable it was, that many of these potential witnesses were unlikely to inspire a jury's confidence.

But before we could assess their credibility, we needed to find them. Witnesses were difficult to locate—many had fled New Orleans after the storm and hadn't returned. Plus, we only had nicknames for most of the people on the list. But over time, we collected the names of some fifteen people who might have seen the fatal beating.

Much of the investigative legwork fell to the lead FBI agent, Mike Dalide. (From time to time, Ashley would assist him with interviews.) Dalide couldn't have looked more out of place in the working-class, predominantly Black community. He was a white-haired White guy in his early sixties, nearing retirement, rarely seen in anything other than his FBI by-the-numbers dark suit, white shirt, and dark tie.

And yet Dalide managed to gain the community's trust. In the Treme, he was known affectionately as "Agent Mike." Early in the investigation, Dalide joined forces with Merlene Kimble, the Treme resident whose house Robair was supposed to work on that morning. Kimble stood out, a Black activist in her early sixties, with long, tightly wound dreadlocks and a huge smile. She was a one-woman force of nature committed to vindicating Robair's senseless death.

With Kimble's help, we tracked down some of the people who had watched the beating. Many had no interest in helping us. One man we spoke with put it bluntly: "This being a police case, I don't really want to testify."

We had better luck with Guy, a Treme resident in his fifties. He agreed to talk to us, and better yet, he said he would bring us another witness. All we needed to do was to show up at noon on Wednesday, "under the bridge."

At the designated hour, Dalide, Forrest and I drove to the underside of the Claiborne Overpass, on the edge of the Treme. The area was littered with broken glass and shopping carts filled with people's belongings. Groups of men, many who appeared to lack stable housing, milled about under the bridge, drinking beer. Guy was nowhere to be seen.

We cruised the neighborhood trying to spot him, heads craned out the window, when an older resident flagged us down. "Y'all boys looking for Willie Mae's Scotch House?" she enquired. Willie Mae's is an iconic New Orleans hole-in-the-wall restaurant. I'm sure this woman could think of no other reason why three White guys in suits would be driving so slowly through her neighborhood.

Not finding our witnesses, we took her up on her suggestion and grabbed some red beans and rice, fried okra and fried chicken. An hour after our scheduled meet time, we returned to the bridge, where we found Guy and another witness waiting for us.

All told, we found five Treme residents who agreed to testify, all Black men in their fifties and sixties. We had been hoping to find some women and younger people as well. "It will just be the old guys," Guy told me. "Everyone else is too afraid to testify."

I later asked him why he wasn't afraid. Guy had lived hard, scraping together an erratic career as a musician, with plenty of booze and drugs along the way. He said he'd lived a longer life than he had expected, and then he patted me on the shoulder and smiled. "I should be dead by now."

The fact that Guy and four of his neighbors were willing to testify at all was progress. In 2005, few neighbors wanted to come forward, and with good reason. The same week that Robair was killed, Len Davis, aka Robocop, was back on the front pages of the local paper, during his resentencing for executing a witness who had made a civil rights complaint against him. It was a chilling reminder of the worst-case consequences of accusing a police officer of misconduct.

We got the impression from talking with the men that the federal prosecutions of the officers involved in the Glover and Danziger cases had earned us some credibility. The feeling around the neighborhood seemed to be that bad cops might no longer be untouchable.

Over the course of 2009 and 2010, I spent a lot of time visiting the houses of our witnesses. I was a complete outsider, but I loved every minute of it. The Treme was certainly a gritty place, replete with the urban ills of crime and drugs that Williams, Moore, and Dugue took such pains to catalog in their reports. But the neighborhood was so much more than that.

The Treme, abutting the French Quarter on the East Bank of the Mississippi, overflowed with life, music, and history. As much as any single place in America can lay claim, it was the birthplace of jazz music, and it was one of the first places in America where "free persons of color" could own property.

Riding around the area, you might find roads closed for "second line" parades—marching brass bands, elaborate costumes, and ladies shimmying with their brightly colored parasols. (Watch the opening credits of David Simon's HBO series, *Treme*, and you'll get the idea.) These ubiquitous musical happenings—which might be held to mourn a death or celebrate just about anything—trace their origins to the early days after the abolition of slavery and evolved as jazz culture took root over a century ago.

Merlene Kimble's house on Dumaine Street was in the middle of all of this. Her home served as a kind of neighborhood meeting place, and we conducted some of our witness interviews there.

Her house was typical of the district, a modest wooden bungalow done up in traditional New Orleans style, painted in beige and light blue. Gus, another witness, lived across the street. Like a lot of the residents I met, they'd grown up in the district, and they owned their homes. These houses, carefully maintained, were important markers of their roots in the community.

It was easy to feel that history every time I visited the neighborhood.

The account of Raymond Robair's last day, pulled together from our five witnesses, wasn't pretty. At 9:00 a.m. on a bright Saturday morning, he set out to do roofing work on Merlene Kimble's house. When he arrived, she was still asleep, so he sat on the stoop of a nearby row house, eating an egg sandwich and chatting with friends.

He got up and had started to cross the street when the two NOPD officers drove up suddenly. For reasons that remain unclear, Moore, the former hockey enforcer, got out of the car and tackled Robair to the ground. Though the neighbors were all too familiar with "Flattop" Williams, they'd never seen the White rookie officer before. Some later called him "Patches" because the decals on his uniform were so new.

Moore struggled to handcuff Robair when Williams walked over. He kicked Robair once or twice in the torso. One witness described a "death scream" as a kick landed in the victim's ribs. Williams also struck Robair six to ten times with an expandable baton. It was hardly the worst beating the neighbors had seen dished out on the streets of New Orleans, but they could tell their neighbor on the receiving end was in a bad way.

The officers picked him off the ground, threw him in the back of the police cruiser and drove off. The entire encounter lasted less than two minutes.

Williams must have realized he'd injured the handyman more severely than he'd intended, and he needed to cover his tracks. He and Moore dumped Robair off at the Charity Hospital ER with a story about having found this known drug abuser collapsed in the street next to a baggie of cocaine.

Had the officers originally admitted to using force, we would have had an extremely difficult time bringing charges with the evidence we had. Because cops are permitted to use "reasonable force" in making an arrest, it would have been almost impossible to counter any claim by Williams and Moore that they had to physically subdue Robair because he had resisted.

But the officers said they hadn't used *any* force. If we could convince the jury that Robair was slammed, kicked, and struck with a baton by the police, we had a fighting chance.

When I returned to court in New Orleans for the April trial, sitting on the other side of the courtroom at the defense table was Frank DeSalvo, representing Melvin "Flattop" Williams. Matthew "Patches" Moore was represented by an attorney from the Fraternal Order of Police, the other major New Orleans police union.

Moore had, by now, put in five years on the job and had ambitions to move up, having applied for a position with the DEA. If he admitted to seeing the beating and signing off on a false report about Robair's death, he might avoid prison, but his career in law enforcement would be over. Moore seemed to think he had a good chance of beating the case. We later heard that he had told his soon-to-be ex-wife, "There are two types of people who don't go to jail: rock stars and police. I am both."

DeSalvo was joined at the defense team table by an unexpected addition: Dwayne Scheuermann. Following the Glover trial, Scheuermann retired early while under investigation for his actions in that case. DeSalvo, his former attorney, quickly picked him up as an investigator on other police misconduct cases.

Throughout the trial, I'd glance over at Scheuermann, who sat next to the defense table, to find him looking over at me with that polite smile of his. It seemed he took pleasure in my obvious discomfort at having to deal with him on an equal footing. It was a reminder, as if I needed one, of the implications of not getting convictions.

The defense strategy was similar to what I had encountered in the Glover trial and in other cases I would handle over the years:

blame and dehumanize the victim. Robair's autopsy provided the ammunition—he had a cirrhotic liver and he'd had cocaine in his system at the time of his death.

"Raymond Robair died because of his lifestyle," DeSalvo declared in his opening argument. "He died because of his alcohol and drug use. He died the way he lived."

The defense also blamed the community that had been angered and outraged by Robair's murder. DeSalvo attacked the neighbors who witnessed the beating, alleging a broad neighborhood conspiracy. "So the neighborhood, in this high-crime area, they decide they're going to have a little meeting at a neighborhood activist's house... They got together and they concocted their story."

For good measure, DeSalvo finished up by attacking the prosecution team and its witnesses, admittedly the most grab-bag assortment of characters I've ever presented to a jury. "You're going to be kind of surprised that your government, those people who say they are the United States of America—" he pointed over at the prosecution table "—will call lying people into a courtroom to try to send people to jail for life."

Our case-in-chief went relatively smoothly, which says something, given the challenges we faced. Three of the witnesses had criminal records, including one for assaulting a police officer. One witness had a stroke the weekend before his testimony but managed to make it to court with a walker. One witness showed up to court smelling of alcohol the day of jury selection. We sent him home and told him to come back the next day, but we never found him again.

One of our most important eyewitnesses, Karl, was incarcerated in Terrebonne Parish at the time of the trial. He was a Gulf War vet with PTSD who had self-medicated with various drugs, and had been prosecuted multiple times for drug possession. When we met with him in the court's holding cell the morning he was supposed to testify, he spit at the divider that separated him from us. "Fuck that shit," he said. "I ain't testifying."

We put him on the stand anyway. As Karl walked into court,

he recognized Robair's family, which seemed to put him more at ease. The defense, naturally, wasted no time attacking him on cross for his prior convictions and drug use. They even got him to admit that he may have been high at the time of the beating. "So, whatever drugs I was on that day, I don't remember," he acknowledged, "but I do remember Flattop kicking and beating that man to death... As far as you trying to drill me to make the situation change, it ain't ever gonna change: the man is dead. The cop kicked that man [and] hit him with a baton..."

It was some of the most powerful testimony I've ever heard. Other observers felt differently. As we left court that day, two court security officers mocked our witnesses. "Can you believe who they called today?" one laughed. Moore's mother accosted Forrest in the hallway and told him that our case was ridiculous and that he should be ashamed of himself for believing our witnesses. Her tone was not that different from her son's, who had belittled the neighbors as nothing more than "crackhead guys drinking."

Though we lacked law enforcement corroboration, the medical evidence bolstered our case. Two doctors and a nurse testified that the defendants' lies about Robair's condition cost them valuable time that they might have used to save his life. We played recordings from Williams's patrol car, in which you could hear Robair moaning in pain.

The defense called the pathologist in Minyard's office who conducted the initial autopsy. Dr. Paul McGarry testified that the injuries had resulted from a fall. The curmudgeonly octogenarian was a story in his own right. In my opening, I called McGarry a "fraud" who failed to follow routine protocols like photographing the body or having a peer review his conclusions. On cross, I impeached him with case after case where he had cleared law enforcement of wrongdoing, only to have subsequent autopsies identify numerous injuries he had failed to document.

Both defendants testified in their own defense. Williams, in the role of the seasoned, levelheaded veteran, presented himself as a model of constitutional policing and denied he'd ever assaulted

Robair. But Moore did himself no favors on the stand, especially on cross. He'd given multiple statements to investigators over the years, each with a slightly different version of what had happened, both at Dumaine Street and at Charity Hospital.

"Which one is accurate?" Forrest pushed.

"Both I guess… Sorry, I am confused with the statements I've given."

Forrest landed a quick jab: "Sure, I am too."

He attacked Moore's credibility so relentlessly, the judge called us to the bench. He advised that cross-examination should be "more like a guerilla raid than it is a Normandy invasion," and suggested my colleague wrap it up.

The highlight of the case was the defense calling Merlene Kimble as its own witness. As much as I wanted to call Merlene during our case-in-chief, she was a member of the local New Black Panthers chapter, and I didn't want to give the defense an opportunity to paint her as a dangerous agitator. DeSalvo's opening had cast her as the leader of a neighborhood conspiracy making up a story for money.

The night before she testified, I went to Merlene's house with Dalide to prepare her for what she would face the next day. We pulled up on Dumaine Street, and the neighborhood was thrumming with energy. Neighbors had set up folding chairs, tables, and a barbecue grill and were mingling with their friends. A few men were playing conga drums while others sang along.

As Dalide and I exited his car, the music came to an abrupt stop. I instantly felt like an unwelcome outsider, as all eyes turned to the two White guys in suits who had just interrupted the party.

Then, unexpectedly, the beat picked up again, with the drummer chanting, "Let's go get 'em Flattop…" The assembled neighbors responded in kind, "Go get 'em Flattop!" The call and response, cheering us on to get the man who terrorized them, had the whole neighborhood singing and clapping.

Merlene testified the next morning. Because the defense had called her as their witness, they could only ask direct questions, which she politely answered. When DeSalvo repeatedly tried to ask leading questions, the judge sustained my objections. Without the ability to suggest the answers he wanted, DeSalvo had an impossible time laying the foundation for his imaginary neighborhood conspiracy. He couldn't even extract a little innuendo.

Since Merlene was technically a defense witness, I had the opportunity to cross-examine her. She provided the raw emotion that had been lacking in the testimony of the world-weary older men. She described the immediate aftermath of the beating. "I saw people running up and down, I saw people hugging each other, I saw people crying. It was like total shock."

Knowing how the defense had tried to characterize her as a radical agitator, I tried to combat the suggestion that Merlene was anti-cop. "Ms. Kimble, do you hate the police?" I asked.

"No, I have a lot of police family, that's police narcotic agents and…homicide detectives. They're in my family. When I was growing up, my grandmother told me if I had a problem, find a police. He'll help me. But after all of this, I can't tell that to my grandchildren. We scared to death."

I asked her who called the Black Panthers. "I did," she said, but these weren't the only people she called. She also reached out to the NAACP, Safe Streets/Strong Communities, the Black Muslims, and a local organization called Stand.

I tossed her a softball: "Why?"

"Because Raymond was murdered in front of my house, and I called every Black organization that I have ever heard of, and they came…

"I felt that just the family and myself standing there wouldn't make such a big impact and we wouldn't have the attention we needed on it, so I figured if we come out in large numbers that it would help with the media to help us get justice for Raymond."

When we finished the presentation of evidence, the parties double-checked exhibits to make sure the record was complete. During the forensic testimony, Dr. Sperry, our pathologist, marked up a mannequin with a black Sharpie to indicate the locations of Robair's injuries. The court of appeals is not keen on receiving life-sized mannequins, so we needed to provide photographic substitutes.

The defense would take pictures, and I drew the job of making sure the photos were representative. When I entered the courtroom, I saw that Dwayne Scheuermann had been sent for the defense. "Good evening, Mr. Fishman," Scheuermann greeted me.

Being in the courtroom alone with Scheuermann made me cringe. I hated that he had escaped accountability in the Glover case, and I had trouble extending him my usual professional courtesy.

Scheuermann snapped the photos of the mannequin. He told me he'd send them to me. "What's your email address?" he asked with a slight smirk.

"Uh, that's okay," I replied. "Send them to Agent Dalide." I left the courtroom as quickly as I could.

After both sides rested, Forrest gave the first closing. He alluded to a 2001 Hollywood film about a flagrantly corrupt Los Angeles veteran cop, played by Denzel Washington, who tries to corrupt and victimize a rookie protégé. (If only "Patches" Moore had the conscience of Ethan Hawke in the movie.)

"July 30 was *Training Day*. Melvin Williams, a veteran cop and a field training officer, was supposed to show Matthew Dean Moore, a rookie just out of the academy, how to be an NOPD officer… Williams started the day by beating a man to death and finished it by turning in a false police report that covered up his crime."

I gave the rebuttal closing, explaining why this case was important. "The defendants want you to see a drug addict, and they want you to think that Raymond Robair somehow deserved to die. They told you those things because they want you to believe that Raymond Robair didn't deserve the law's protection… Ladies and gentlemen, despite every suggestion to the contrary, the Constitution does apply on Dumaine Street."

Two days later, the jury returned the verdict, guilty on all counts. We returned to Dumaine Street, where the neighbors greeted us with hugs, music, and spoken word poetry. Not only had the verdict demonstrated that Raymond Robair mattered, but it also showed that the community mattered too. Perhaps more than any moment I've experienced in my prosecutorial career, this *felt* like justice.

Over the next decade, Forrest and I would joke that we should have resigned from DOJ after the Robair verdict. It was the high point of my prosecutorial career. I had led successful prosecutions of five officers in two of New Orleans's most notorious killings by the police, in cases that looked far from promising when they first came to my office.

For his part, Forrest had assisted Bobbi Bernstein in getting convictions in the Danziger Bridge case.

Nine months after the guilty verdicts in the first Glover trial, Bobbi's team won convictions against all five of the Danziger defendants for fatally opening fire on families trying to escape the city on foot and for attempting to cover it up. Five other officers involved in the incident pleaded guilty and cooperated with the DOJ investigation. This case brought down more police officers than any single prosecution of police abuse in the history of New Orleans (and possibly the country). Tom Perez, then the Assistant Attorney General of Civil Rights at DOJ, called the Danziger prosecution "the most significant police misconduct prosecution since Rodney King."

But I didn't step down. I did make what was, by DOJ standards, an unconventional next move. In June 2011, Fiona gave birth to our second daughter. She temporarily stepped away as CEO of her company. I took a year off work, cobbling together various types of leave. I spent lots of time with my family, which now included a three-year-old and a newborn. This radical restructuring of our lives was temporary—we both returned to our careers full-time—but we proved to ourselves that we could slow down and just *be* with each other, and with our girls. It was a necessary reminder of the importance of family.

I came back to DOJ refreshed and recommitted to the work, and more thoughtful about how I would do it. I figured I'd be using my now more refined skills in brand-new cases in new places. But before I knew it, I was back in New Orleans.

The appellate decision came down on my birthday in 2012, about a year after I returned to DOJ. I knew from the first paragraph it wasn't good. Though it described the Glover case as "one of the nightmarish stories that arose from Hurricane Katrina," the court noted that the case demonstrated "the axiom that a cover-up, with its domino effect, begets more tragedy than the crime." While I certainly agreed that police obstruction extenuated the harm, I was perplexed and appalled how the court could reason that burning a dead body was worse than taking the person's life in the first place.

Most significantly, the appeals court found that Warren should have been tried separately from the officers involved in the cover-up. Including the other four officers in the same trial, the court said, signaled to the jury that the shooting was a criminal act that needed covering up. All of Murray's requests for a severance had finally borne fruit.

Though the court acknowledged that the initial decision to try the officers together was entirely appropriate, at some point, the appellate judges opined, the trial became unduly "prejudicial." As evidence for this claim, they cited Magner's cross-examination of Warren, about his knowing to "keep [his] mouth shut" because he was "a part of the Fourth District fraternity."

Magner's ill-timed quip comparing the defense attorneys to the Menendez brothers also came back to bite us. The Court found, "...[I]t was easy to confuse the allegations against the defendants... [I]f the government could so nonchalantly group the defendants together, then we cannot be reasonably confident that the jury could compartmentalize the evidence separately for each defendant." (The appeals court seemed to miss the fact that the jury had not lumped all the defendants together, meticulously parsing out the different charges, convicting some defendants and acquitting others.)

In some ways, this result wasn't entirely surprising. The Fifth

Circuit Court of Appeals is arguably the most conservative appeals court in the nation, the product of an increasingly politicized appointment process. It has historically gone out of its way to protect police officers. This opinion was no different.

We would have to try David Warren. Again. By himself. Could we salvage it?

Travis McCabe would also be getting a new trial.

Shortly before my sabbatical, Judge Africk vacated McCabe's verdict. While Africk had seemed persuaded by the prosecution's case against the other four defendants (including the two acquitted by the jury), he had never liked our case against McCabe, resting as it did on the testimony of Sergeant Nina Simmons, who had lied to a grand jury.

When McCabe's attorneys claimed to find "newly discovered evidence" in a post-trial motion for a new trial, they found the judge receptive. After his conviction, Warren asserted, for the first time, that he had received a draft of the Signal 21 from Nina Simmons back in December 2005. He produced a copy of this "draft," which was virtually identical to the report McCabe had been convicted of doctoring, with the exception of four typos that were corrected in the final report.

What made this "new" report supposedly significant was Warren's claim that he had received this version directly from Simmons herself, undercutting her claim that the narrative was "fabricated" by somebody else. Warren admitted that he had never told anyone else about having received this report from her, not until the last week of trial, nor did he have any corroboration to support the claim. At a hearing, Simmons denied she ever gave any version of the report to Warren.

I thought it was a pretty weak new trial claim, a "he said, she said" that pitted Warren, whose testimony Africk had recently described as "contrived and fabricated," against the scattered testimony of an officer who perjured herself in the grand jury. But in the end, Judge Africk was persuaded to grant McCabe a new trial.

David Warren would be the key witness in McCabe's stand-alone trial. If he remained convicted of unjustifiably killing Henry Glover, his testimony would be worthless. However, if Warren were acquitted in a retrial, McCabe would be a beneficiary.

Ironic, then, that the fates of Warren and McCabe should be so bound together, given that the rationale for Warren's new trial was that the shooting and the cover-up should be treated as unrelated acts.

McCabe's fate would be determined by the outcome of the Warren retrial. So would a lot of things.

CHAPTER 23

GROUNDHOG DAY

November and December 2013

One of my first mornings back in New Orleans, I popped into Mena's Palace, a diner where I frequently ate breakfast during the investigation and first trial. The waitress recognized me. "What did NOPD do this time?" she asked me, rolling her eyes. "Same old, same old," I said.

It was, and it wasn't.

Coming back for the December 2013 retrial had a *Groundhog Day* feeling. Same defendant, David Warren, same crime, same judge, and many of the same lawyers. Julian Murray and Rick Simmons once again defended Warren, and Tracey and I represented the government.

Mike Magner had retired from the New Orleans US Attorney's Office and entered private practice, so we picked up Julia Gegenheimer, a promising young Harvard law grad, who had interned in our office during the first Glover trial and had since become an entry-level prosecutor.

Though many of the characters were the same, the new trial felt decidedly different. Most obviously, we had four fewer defendants. And we would have entirely new ground rules on what evidence we could present.

In a series of pre-trial motions, Warren's attorneys, no surprise, argued for the broadest possible interpretation of the appellate court's decision. They contended that the prosecution should not be allowed to mention *anything* that implicated the other officers, not only the burning of Glover's body, but also the beating at Habans and the Signal 21 incident report that, in the first trial, we had successfully argued was fraudulent.

We countered that the jury couldn't fairly evaluate the shooting unless they knew *why* there was so little to go on. This paucity of evidence had been a main refrain of Rick Simmons's closing argument in the first trial, and we needed to be able to explain that the victim's body had been incinerated by an NOPD officer, precluding a proper autopsy, and that no real-time investigation of the shooting, or documentation of the crime scene, had been done.

At a minimum, we needed to introduce evidence that Glover's body was burned. While we agreed not to tell the jury that another officer was responsible, the civil rights charge required us to prove that "death resulted." We needed to be able to lay out the unusual chain of events that followed the shooting and concluded with the DNA confirmation of Henry's remains.

Much to my surprise, we lost. Big time. Africk prevented any mention of the burning, Habans School, or the Signal 21 report. In lieu of this forensic evidence, the judge required us to enter a convoluted stipulation that informed the jury that, "based on the known evidence…the remains of Mr. Glover were in such a condition that a full autopsy gathering additional ballistic or forensic evidence other than DNA identification was not possible." That certainly raised more questions than it answered.

Judge Africk generally made thoughtful, well-reasoned decisions, even if I sometimes disagreed with them. This one threw me.

Most judges hate being overturned on appeal. Judge Africk's strong words at sentencing told me that he was thoroughly convinced of Warren's guilt. I think the judge believed we could get a conviction on the shooting evidence alone—Warren had, after all, shot at two people that day for no good reason. By excluding all other evidence, my guess is that Africk hoped to "protect the record," so that a new conviction wouldn't be overturned.

The prosecution can't appeal a not-guilty finding, so the record wouldn't matter much if we lost.

We had one new card to play. During the Robair case, I had worked with Dr. Kris Sperry, the chief medical examiner for the state of Georgia, who had performed the second autopsy that was critical to winning convictions. I asked Dr. Sperry to take a second look at the Glover medical and autopsy evidence to see if we had missed anything. The pathologists we had consulted for the first trial were unwilling to offer opinions without examining Glover's intact body, an impossibility.

One piece of evidence jumped out at Sperry: a charred piece of Henry's left chest sufficiently intact to reveal, on X-ray, a pattern of small, tightly grouped white dots. The original pathologist who analyzed the X-rays, Dr. Dana Troxclair, at the time barely out of med school, had interpreted them as tiny pieces of burned metal from Tanner's car.

Dr. Sperry recognized the white dots as a manifestation of the "snowstorm" effect, produced when a high-velocity projectile enters a human body. The ammunition that Warren used makes a small hole upon entry. As it passes through the body, the projectile breaks apart, leaving behind hundreds of miniscule metal pieces along the wound track, some smaller than a grain of salt. The pathologist explained to us that you don't see this snowstorm pattern at the entry point; the pattern only forms after the bullet has penetrated about three inches. The "snowstorm" gets wider and more dispersed as the bullet travels through the body.

Sperry concluded that "to a reasonable degree of medical and scientific certainty," Henry had an entrance wound in the back and an exit wound in the front, indicating that Henry was shot from behind "facing completely away from the shooter." It was compelling corroboration of Linda Howard's and Bernard Calloway's testimonies.

Reasonable certainty, of course, is in the eyes of the beholder.

Over two days in August 2013, Judge Africk held a *Daubert* hearing (named after the US Supreme Court case that established standards for expert testimony) to decide whether Sperry could testify at trial. Rick Simmons aggressively crossed him about his conclusions. Sperry allowed that there were "obvious severe limitations" when dealing with incomplete, charred remains, but that the evidence was nevertheless "conclusive."

After the pathologist testified, Warren called four of his own experts, the most impressive of whom was Dr. Vincent J. DeMaio, who had literally written the book on wound ballistics. His *Gunshot Wounds* was a standard reference work on the subject. DeMaio had testified in numerous high-profile cases, including for the defense in the trial of George Zimmerman for killing Trayvon Martin, and had been retained by my office in the Danziger Bridge case. In preparation for his testimony, I checked out his book from the DOJ library and read it multiple times.

On direct exam, DeMaio took the conservative position that the available scientific evidence didn't allow for an opinion about entry or exit wounds. He went so far as to say, "You couldn't even say the person had been shot."

On cross-examination, I pulled fact after fact from my well-tabbed copy of DeMaio's book, harping on the left-chest location of the "snowstorm" particles. The doctor's hard line began to soften. He eventually agreed that there was a 75 percent chance that the X-rays indicated the exit wound. And he acknowledged that it was unlikely that the snowstorm pattern would appear inside Henry's chest if he had been charging at the gate when he was shot, as Warren had claimed. And yet he would not say that

Henry had been shot in the back. Of the wound to Henry's chest, he eventually conceded, "I'll accept it as an exit," but he would not recognize the blood spot on Henry's back as the entry wound. "I'm saying, you can't reach a conclusion."

My deep dive into his book seemed to have helped move the doctor off his original hard line. Africk joked that I must be a big fan of the pathologist's work. "Will you be happy to autograph Mr. Fishman's book for him?" the judge asked DeMaio as he left the witness stand.

He said he'd be pleased to. I had him sign my dog-eared copy with the inscription, "USDOJ: Keep on prosecuting. V.J. DeMaio."

A *Daubert* hearing requires that expert evidence be deemed sufficiently reliable to present to a jury. I figured, by any reasonable interpretation of the standard, Sperry should be allowed to testify in open court. After all, Africk had let the profoundly unpersuasive Alan Baxter testify in the first trial as a "use of force" expert.

But the judge deferred his ruling. Allowing Sperry to testify would require acknowledging that Glover's body had been burned, a Pandora's box that Africk wasn't yet willing to open. We would have to prepare for trial without knowing whether we could use the doctor as a witness.

At least the case would be tried in New Orleans, where we thought we would have a better chance at conviction than anywhere else in Louisiana. The defense argued that the trial should be moved out of the city because of publicity prejudicial to the NOPD, generated not only by the first trial but also by David Simon's HBO series, *Treme.* The show's third season wove the Glover case, by name, into the plotline. The fourth season would air the same month as the trial.

As I prepared for trial, I received a call from Simon, who offered to file an amicus or "friend of the court" brief in support of keeping the retrial in the city. (Mary Howell had given him my number. Mary served as a consultant on *Treme,* and the civil rights lawyer played by Melissa Leo in the series was loosely based on her.) That was certainly unexpected, and admittedly kind of a thrill. Like many people with firsthand experience in the criminal legal system, I regarded Simon's *The Wire* as a darkly on-the-money portrayal of our justice system. Ultimately, Africk sided with the prosecution (and, although he wasn't aware of it, with David Simon). The retrial would take place in New Orleans in December 2013.

Finding an impartial jury to hear the case was a different matter. We had narrowed down a pool of qualified candidates by removing jurors for "cause" based on their answers to the jury questionnaires. "Qualified" was a relative term. The judge had removed any juror candidate who knew *anything* about the incineration of Henry Glover, which, thanks to the extensive local news coverage, had become a well-known scandal within New Orleans. We selected a jury from some of the least informed people in the Eastern District of Louisiana.

On the second day of jury selection, we exercised our "peremptory strikes," removing potential jurors for purely tactical reasons, based on educated guesses about jurors' sympathies. The only caveat was that, according to the Supreme Court's *Batson* decision, no juror could be struck because of race. *Batson* had loomed large in the first trial when the defense had attempted to strike every single Black juror.

As we stood in the judge's chambers, moments before we exercised our strikes, Africk turned to Murray and Simmons and asked, "We are not going to have the same issue as last time, are we?" Murray replied, "No, Judge. We're going to leave *two of them* on this time."

I couldn't believe he had just said the quiet part out loud, openly acknowledging a race-based *voir dire* strategy.

After both parties made their strikes, I looked at the list. The defense had done it again, this time striking all but one of the potential Black jurors. That plus Murray's comments about leaving "two of them on" made it easy to establish a *prima facie* case for discriminatory strikes.

I objected, and Africk looked even angrier than he had in 2010. Simmons appeared flummoxed and said they must have made a mistake in their strikes. He ran back to his table to wildly shuffle through some papers.

When Simmons returned to the bench, he told the judge that the defense hadn't meant to strike one of the Black women, who was immediately seated on the jury.

By now, the defense's strike-by-race strategy was painfully obvious. Rather than trying to come up with some fig-leaf nonracial explanation for their *voir dire* maneuvers, Julian Murray just came right out and said it. "At the outset, generally speaking, it is foolish to not understand race is an integral part of this whole case," he explained. "…That's why we wanted to move to another jurisdiction, because the Blacks in New Orleans are marching in the streets, and for us to say we can't consider race at all when picking a jury just isn't fair." (No one was out "marching in the streets" in any significant numbers.) "…[A] lot of the African Americans say they don't trust the police, they think the Whites get preferential treatment, they say things like that, and we are supposed to take them on the jury?"

Africk challenged Murray: "You are telling me because of the fact you have a Black victim and a White defendant you feel like you need to keep the African Americans off the jury?"

Murray replied, "I'm not saying that, Judge. I'm saying when we use our peremptory challenges in this atmosphere, we have a right to think in terms of race and what it's going to do. And to say that race can't come in here is unrealistic…"

Race was the elephant in the room, and with the sudden exception of Julian Murray, everyone had danced around it. In some sense, I agreed with him. I strongly believe that if we are ever going to address inequities in policing and the justice system, we must talk about race and the legacy of racial discrimination in the US. But the defense was using race to stereotype and exclude jurors solely on the basis of the color of their skin. Ultimately the judge found the defense explanations "contrived and not credible," and he reseated two more struck Black jurors.

Going up against Julian Murray in court, it was easy enough for me to see him as a stereotypical Southern racist. Our paths never crossed again, and Murray died four years after the retrial. Years later, I came across a video clip of him, from 2004, accepting a distinguished service award from the Louisiana Bar Foundation. He tells the camera that his proudest moment as an attorney occurred when he represented, *pro bono*, Wilbert Rideau, a Black man who had been sentenced to death for the murder of a White woman. Rideau's convictions were overturned multiple times, and each time he was retried and convicted by all-White juries. Murray fought to have Rideau's last conviction overturned, because at the time of his indictment, Louisiana excluded all Black people from its grand juries. Murray won, and Rideau received one final trial, where he was convicted of the lesser charge of manslaughter and released from prison with a time served sentence. (There was no dispute that Rideau had killed the woman, but the defense argued it did not constitute murder.)

It was hard to reconcile the Murray in the video, who fought for years to overturn a conviction premised on racist laws and practice, with the attorney who used some of those same techniques to defend a White cop for killing an unarmed Black man. It is remarkable how humans can empathize with people we know, in Murray's case, Rideau, yet so easily fall back on cheap or ugly stereotypes when they're strangers. The adversarial nature of our criminal justice system seems designed to compound the problem.

By the end of *voir dire*, four Black jurors sat on the jury. It wouldn't be the final tally. The evening of the first day of testimony, we discovered that the lone Black male juror (the one Black person the defense had not struck initially) had referenced his jury service on his Facebook page, tagging it "#tokenblack." We were obliged to bring this to the attention of the judge, given that it violated the court's orders. Africk seethed. Murray looked smug, fueling my suspicion that the defense had known about the post and was holding it as an issue for appeal in case Warren was convicted a second time.

It seemed to me the juror had no malicious intent; he was a millennial for whom making "status updates" on the internet was almost a reflex. Nonetheless, Africk removed the juror and replaced him with an alternate, a White man.

I gave the opening statement. It was strange to talk about the case while leaving out so much of the story. No beatdown at Habans, no burning. But the streamlined nature of the trial made it easy to focus on the only two questions that now mattered: First, was the shooting of an unarmed man from sixty feet away and a level below "objectively unreasonable?" And second, did Warren act willfully—did he intentionally use impermissible force? The evidence would prove, I argued, that it was both: "This case is about how the deliberate choice to take a man's life, about how the defendant used [the fact that it was] Katrina to kill an unarmed man without any justification." I asked for the guilty verdict that would hold Warren accountable.

Murray began his opening with a backhanded compliment about my oratory skills: "Wow, what a story. Not true, but still quite a story."

The attorney had recalibrated his approach since the first trial. His opening was notably tighter, and he painted a more heroic version of his client. Warren no longer had chosen to become an officer because he liked guns. Now, Warren had become a cop so that he could serve the community, which he had done "honorably."

"Mr. Warren is a good, God-fearing man, who would never intentionally kill anybody unless he believes his life was in threat."

But Murray's rhetoric was even more combative at retrial, which was saying something. He took an approach that could best be described as "Trumpian," although in 2013, that adjective didn't yet exist. He came out swinging about "Flashback Linda" and "Looter Calloway."

And then he pushed the limits.

"Now, they have the burden of proving beyond a reasonable doubt that their theory is true, and yet they've got only two witnesses. No forensic evidence here. This is just two witnesses telling two different stories as to what happened at a crucial time, and they want to tell you, that's proof beyond a reasonable doubt.

"Linda Howard did not see any of this," he continued in this vein. "That's what she said when they made the report, that she didn't see it."

In those couple of sentences, Murray referenced both the absence of forensic evidence and the Signal 21 report that had been excluded from evidence. I argued that Murray had "opened the door" and opened it wide.

The judge looked like he was on our side this time. "There is forensic evidence which I was prepared to preclude… I'm going to reconsider my ruling, and I'll let you know how I'm going to handle that based on your opening statement to the jury."

This seemed like Murray's Kawan McIntyre moment. As with the Kawan incident, Judge Africk didn't rule on the spot. He wanted to mull it over and decide at a later, unspecified date, leaving us in the awkward position of starting our case presentation without knowing what could and could not come in.

Our case-in-chief commenced with some familiar faces. Once again, Bernard Calloway was strong on direct and more than held his own against Murray's cross. Amazingly, the defense attorney was still trying, and failing, to get traction on the cigarette question—was it lit or was Henry lighting it? Again, Murray tried to dirty up Henry and Bernard by bringing up "hypothetical" imaginary "facts," like the gun that Henry might have had on him at the DeGaulle parking lot.

"In ten minutes, going to two different apartments," Murray asked, "you wouldn't have had an opportunity to have gotten rid of the gun?"

"I guess so, but wasn't no gun."

"I'm just asking you, hypothetically?"

"Yeah, but I didn't have no gun."

Murray walked up to the evidentiary line by asking Bernard

about the blood patterns he'd seen as Henry bled out, questions designed to suggest that his best friend had been shot in the chest. Africk called us to the bench to issue the defense a warning. "I just want to be careful about where we're going...because if we're getting into where he says the wound was or where did the bullet exit, and that creates a whole can of worms."

Again, I pushed the judge to let Dr. Sperry testify about the nature of rifle shots. Again, the judge deferred ruling. Murray was sufficiently chastened that he stopped asking about blood patterns.

When Patrice Glover testified next, she wasn't as nervous as she'd been before, but she was similarly emotional. This time, I asked questions more slowly and gave her the time she needed to talk about her brother in a way that demonstrated how much he was loved.

I asked what Henry's future had looked like before Katrina. "He was going to school to be an electrician," she said. "He likes to fix all the stuff and work on stuff. Anything that I asked him to do for me, you know, he'll come do it for me." Tears streamed down Patrice's cheek. "My brother, I miss him so much."

As the trial progressed, it became clear how hard it would be for our witnesses to avoid talking about things they'd lived through but were excluded from the trial. At one point, after a poorly worded question by Murray, Patrice mentioned the beating at Habans. In response to Murray's objection, I explained, "This is a case that deeply affected all of the witnesses... What happened that day is a part of their experience. We've instructed them not to talk about it, but for people like Ms. Glover, the ability to separate and to make that academic decision to not talk about something that did happen is asking a lot..."

The judge instructed the jury to disregard the comment on the beating. It is hard for juries to "unhear" anything, so I'm sure this instruction raised the jury's suspicion that they were not getting the full story.

I had heard Officer Linda Howard give her account of the shooting many times. I had seen her emotionally overwhelmed, and I had seen her passive and defeated. It felt like I was a spectator on her journey through the stages of grief.

By the retrial, Howard had arrived at, of all things, a place of equanimity. She had recently retired from policing after twenty-eight years on the force and had taken a job with the New Orleans Recreation Department Commission, where she mentored children. For the first time since I'd known her, she seemed at ease. She remembered what she liked most about her NOPD experience: "I just enjoyed being a police officer just because I got a chance to help people."

This time when she told her story, the delivery sounded smoother, but still authentic. She articulated just how fearful she had been after watching Warren shoot Henry for no reason. "I was just fearful. I just wanted to leave that location… I didn't know what state of mind Officer Warren was in. He had just shot someone, and I was the only witness."

And she filled in the picture of Dugue's obstruction. "He told me that he really needed to get this statement done because they was trying to railroad Officer Warren, and he knew [Warren] didn't do anything wrong…and I said, 'Okay, then.'" When she returned to the scene with Dugue a few days later, and described the unjustified shooting in detail, she asked why he wasn't recording. "He said, 'Don't worry about it,' that he would take care of it."

It was the same refrain other officers used to brush off inconvenient inquiries—Scheuermann had said it to Joe Meisch as Tanner's car burned, and Italiano said it to John Schmidt when the ICE agent was briefing him about the connection between the shooting victim at Habans and the burned body at the levee. Not that this jury knew who any of those people were.

Tracey wrapped up by homing in on the main point.

"Do you have any doubt at all that Officer Warren shot the man as he was running away?" Tracey asked.

"No."

"Have you ever doubted that fact?"

"No."

★ ★ ★

Rick Simmons crossed Howard. Though far less combative than Murray, he nonetheless hammered her on some well-documented inconsistencies. Howard had spoken to the FBI many times, and had given slightly different locations of her position on the mall breezeway, including once when she had briefly misidentified where she'd been standing in a staged FBI photo at the crime scene.

"We're now eight years later [after the shooting], and your memory has improved?" Simmons mocked her.

Howard wouldn't budge: "The truth is the truth."

When Officer Keyalah Bell testified in the first trial, I had the feeling that, for her, it was a kind of redemption for her years of silence. By the retrial, my distinct impression was, she no longer wanted anything to do with the case.

In June 2010, when she first learned that Travis McCabe had been granted a new trial based on "newly discovered evidence," Bell evidently felt overwhelmed at the prospect of having, once again, to testify against the NOPD. She went out for a night of drinking and, while driving home, crashed into a parked car.

Bell was charged with driving while intoxicated and leaving the scene of an accident. After an internal investigation and lengthy appeal process, the NOPD fired her. She temporarily won reinstatement on a technicality, but at the time of trial, the department was still fighting the case as a part of its newfound desire to hold officers accountable.

Though Ashley had a new job as a supervisory special agent in Atlanta, she came back to New Orleans to join the team as we prepared witnesses for trial. Both she and Tracey spent a fair amount of time with Bell before she testified. "Bell would sit there with her arms folded," Ashley recalled. "She was guarded, very guarded." Tracey had a similar take: "She has already testified against former officers in the first trial and so she's distrusted by her colleagues, and she's got the civil service commission questioning her about whether she's going to be able to keep her job. Meanwhile, her plan to switch to a nursing career wasn't working out. It was a lot."

As little as she wanted to be there, Bell was vital to making the case, especially because we didn't call her former senior partner, Sergeant Nina Simmons, in our case-in-chief. Simmons's credibility had been shredded in the first trial, and the judge clearly despised her. Since the testimony she had provided against Italiano and McCabe would not be allowed at retrial, she was no longer a necessary witness. Bell could testify to practically everything Simmons would have been allowed to talk about regarding what had happened on the mall breezeway and in the nearby streets in the minutes after the shooting, and she was significantly more credible.

I made a last-ditch effort to call Dr. Sperry and introduce the new forensic evidence. Africk once again kicked the can down the road. It was incredibly frustrating having a key element of our case hanging on what the defense might or might not do. I wondered if this is what it felt like for Murray in the first trial, as he repeatedly lost his severance motion. At least his objections turned out to be useful on appeal. The prosecution cannot appeal a decision when it loses. And I wasn't sure if we could win without that forensic evidence.

After only two days of testimony, we rested our case. Given how long it took to present our evidence in the first trial, this was a remarkable turn of events. Henry's aunt, Rebecca Glover, was suspicious, worried that we had intentionally put on a weak case. I tried to explain about the judge's rulings, and assured her we were doing our best with the hand we'd been dealt, but she was having none of it. Aunt Rebecca was not doing much for my confidence.

The defense didn't have its witnesses ready, so the judge used the spare time to allow jurors to hold Warren's gun. "Let them see the weapon. You can pass it down. Each of you will have a chance to look at it. The scope, as well."

Each juror was given the opportunity to step out of the jury box and go to the back of the courtroom, where they could lift the gun and point it at the same unoccupied corner that I had used during my closing in the first trial.

"Do we have to touch it?" one juror asked the judge. That seemed to bode well for us.

As I watched some of the jurors uncomfortably handling the weapon, I flashed back to a trip that Julia Gegenheimer and I had taken to the FBI Academy at Quantico, Virginia, six weeks earlier. The FBI ballistics team loaned us the same model of the gun that Warren had used, a SIG Arms 550, and set up a target seventy-five feet away, slightly farther than the distance from which Warren had shot Henry.

Julia had never fired a gun in her life and was plainly nervous. With the benefit of some on-site instruction and the capabilities of the scope, she obliterated the target, grouping five rounds into an area the size of a quarter. Granted, shooting at the range is not the same as responding in real time under stress. Nevertheless, our little demo cemented in my mind the certainty that there was no way Warren thought he had missed.

I wished the jurors could have had that experience.

Warren's team called many more witnesses in the retrial, though I wasn't persuaded they added much. John Castelluccio was a retired NOPD officer who had ridden around with Warren in the days after Katrina. He hadn't testified during the first trial, so I didn't know what he might have to say.

Castelluccio testified about one time that he and Warren confronted "looters" a few days after the storm. "We came upon a Shell station that was in shambles, the doors had been kicked in. As we approached, [we] saw several subjects—adults, male, female, and some children and juveniles—coming from the Shell station carrying bags, convenience bags."

Castelluccio opted for a maximal response: "We drew our personal weapons that we were assigned from the department, told them to stop and drop the bags, so we could see their hands... They said they were getting foodstuffs from the Shell station... We patted them down for weapons. Asked them if they had permission to take the food things, and they said no... We told them to go on their way, and don't come back."

Rick Simmons asked, "During that time period...did [Warren]

have any discussions with you about looters or make any comments about looters?... Like, they are animals, or they should be shot?"

"No, sir."

Castelluccio was the defense's counterweight to Alec Brown who, as he had in the first trial, testified that Warren had described looters as animals who deserved to be shot. Castelluccio's testimony suggested that Warren wasn't always muttering darkly about looters. And, I guess, the fact that the two officers hadn't shot anyone on their patrols was evidence that Warren didn't want to shoot *all* "looters." But that seemed like a low bar for exculpatory evidence.

On cross, I returned to the ex-officer's interactions with civilians at the Shell gas station. To me, it demonstrated Warren's lack of empathy for citizens struggling to survive after Katrina.

I asked about the plastic bags being carried by the people at the Shell station, a group he said included two or three children.

"It was chips and things."

"So you took the food and the water away from them, and you sent them on their way?"

"Right."

I noted that the officers then took the food back to the police station for their own consumption.

Castelluccio was starting to get defensive. "Sir, this would have been considered, under normal times, *'evidence.'*"

"During Katrina, it was just considered *'food and water,'* correct?" I asked. He reluctantly agreed. I asked if there were any flat screen televisions in the plastic bags. He said no.

As is often true in police cases, the outcome would likely be determined by the defendant's testimony, something Warren's team was well aware of. Evidently, they had meticulously reviewed the transcripts from the first trial and noted where he had come across as uncaring and aloof.

The defendant on the stand was demonstrably new and improved. Rick Simmons asked Warren a series of questions on direct that allowed him to spell out for the jury how his notion of police service had changed after Katrina, especially after the shooting of his fellow Fourth District officer Kevin Thomas. "So that told me that, you know, even what could be a simple situation, you know, could turn into a very dangerous one very quickly."

His alertness was turned all the way up, he said, when Henry Glover "charged" the mall. He described the moment with, compared to the first trial, newfound clarity. "I'm looking back and forth between the two men, and they're coming at this gate... And the man in the lead, I see his right hand—you know, we're taught to watch hands, there's bars, there's obstructions and everything else, but I am trying to see what's in his hands, and in his right hand is an object."

The nonspecific "object" had previously been a problem for the defense. But Warren's vision had retrospectively gotten sharper: "I can tell you that I saw what I thought was the butt of a pistol and part of a barrel."

Warren added feelings that were absent from his weirdly detached performance the first time around. "And when I saw that, I thought I can't let him get through that gate. If he gets through that gate, I am going to die. If he gets through that gate, I am not going to be there for my son's third birthday. And as—at that point I came up and I fired."

This somewhat more emotional and socially conscious David Warren wanted the jury to understand he wasn't a racist, or someone who devalued Black lives after Katrina. "You know, I was repulsed by what [Alec Brown] had to say. I don't go around categorizing people in broad brushstrokes and saying that everybody is a particular way, you know... That's not how I speak."

Simmons asked him how he felt knowing that he took another person's life.

"It's a sad thing, it's not a good feeling. You know, it's a tragedy for the family, and I understand that. I mean, I'm a father, I have five children, I have a son, you know... [T]o [the Glovers] that loss is irreparable, and I understand that. As a father I do."

Simmons followed up: "Having said that, do you feel like you should have acted differently [on September 2]?"

Warren was unrepentant. "No, sir... I took the actions that I did because I thought I was going to die. I thought I wasn't going to be able to see my son turn three." (Interestingly, though Warren had four daughters, he only ever specifically referenced his son.)

"I took the actions that I took. I still feel to this day they were the correct actions."

I began my cross as bluntly as possible: "You killed Henry Glover on September 2, 2005?" To get the jurors to convict, I figured I had to convince them that Warren, from moment one, knew he'd hit the man he shot at.

"Yes, sir."

Unlike Magner's cross, which was designed to let Warren ramble on about guns, I structured my cross to show that he was well aware of the limitations on the police use of force. "Now, you know based on your training that you cannot shoot an unarmed man who poses no threat, correct?"

"Correct."

I asked him whether Katrina changed the rules of engagement. "Even during Katrina, you weren't authorized to just shoot looters at will, correct?"

"Correct."

"You can't think someone is an animal who is looting and just pick them off for no justification; you would agree with that, correct?"

"That is correct."

I asked Warren if he saw himself as an expert marksman. Some of his above-it-all superiority crept back into his testimony. "If shooting a perfect score on our course can classify you as an expert, then I guess I would have to say I'm an expert."

I asked Warren what he'd told Linda Howard after he'd taken his shot. "…[Y]ou didn't turn over to Linda Howard and say, 'I just saw a man with a firearm who was threatening our lives'? You didn't say that?"

"I don't remember what I said to Linda. I don't know if I said that—I mean, obviously I didn't say anything like that."

"You said 'I missed,' did you not?"

"I may have said I missed, yes."

I made a similar point, that he had never mentioned being

threatened by a gun, or an object that he perceived to be a gun, when Simmons and Bell responded after the shooting.

"Yes, I informed, explained that to Sergeant Simmons."

This was new. Warren now claimed for the first time that he had, in fact, told Simmons that he had seen an actual gun. For all of Nina Simmons's inconsistencies as a witness, she had always said that Warren never mentioned seeing a gun. He blamed her for not collecting evidence that would establish his innocence.

Warren, I sensed, was getting crafty. Since Simmons hadn't testified in this trial, Warren could place the blame on her without fear of contradiction. Once again, it seemed to me, Sergeant Simmons was being set up as the scapegoat.

Overall, I felt good about my cross-examination of Warren, but I worried that he seemed significantly more reputable and less heartless this time around. Would the jury buy his suggestion that Nina Simmons was responsible for not adequately documenting a police shooting?

I struggled with whether to call Nina Simmons in our rebuttal case. If there was anything in this trial that cried out to be rebutted, it was Warren's attempts to shift the blame to her. But I knew all too well that Simmons could be a confused and confusing witness. The defense could paint her, accurately, as a woman who had lied under oath to a grand jury, making Warren look trustworthy by comparison.

On the other hand, if the defense attacked her for her perjured grand jury testimony, they would open the door for us to discuss the NOPD cover-up of the shooting that Judge Africk had worked so hard to exclude. This was turning into a giant legal game of Chicken.

We decided to take the risk and got a few hours of sleep. Simmons, who had retired from the NOPD after the first trial, testified the next morning.

Limited to discrete testimony about the shooting scene, she held up well on the stand. She testified that Warren on the breezeway had made no mention of a gun in the man's hand.

"What did he tell you about his state of mind at the time of the shooting?"

"He didn't say anything about his state of mind. He was standing there and his demeanor to me was nonchalant...he was emotionless."

To close out her rebuttal testimony, I wanted Simmons to explain that the lack of investigation of the shooting scene had not been her choice, and that she had reported the shooting to her lieutenant. That was hardly the full story of the obstruction, but I hoped it gave the jury some sense that the NOPD's botched response to the shooting extended well beyond Sergeant Simmons.

Even that was too much for Julian Murray. He tried to have her testimony struck from the record. He complained, "She's basically started to talk about the Fourth District fraternity..." Africk waved him off, opining that Simmons had been an appropriate rebuttal witness.

Rick Simmons, for his part, barely laid a glove on the former sergeant on cross. That was pure self-preservation. The last thing he wanted to do was to open the door to the existence of an NOPD cover-up, right before closing arguments.

As a result, Nina Simmons came off as a forthright, credible witness, a significant contrast to the pummeling she took in the last trial. Again, I puzzle over the rules of evidence that often create a distorted version of reality.

As for Dr. Sperry's findings about the "snowstorm" effect that showed Henry having been shot in the back, the clock had finally run out. Judge Africk would not allow him to testify. It was another piece of the story that was missing. I worried that all those missing pieces could add up to reasonable doubt.

After closing arguments, essentially a replay of what both sides had produced two years earlier, we hunkered down for another brutal wait in our war room. For two days, we heard absolutely nothing, until we got a note from the jurors informing us that they were "hopelessly deadlocked." (Every jury in America that can't reach a decision seems to write that exact expression on their note to the judge.)

The judge brought the jurors back into the courtroom to give an *Allen* charge, instructing them to continue their deliberations. The *Allen* charge is sometimes known as the "dynamite charge," intended to push a jury into agreement, though the language of the standard jury instruction is rather subdued. "...[T]here is no reason to believe that the case could ever be submitted to twelve men and women more conscientious, more impartial, or more competent to decide it, or that more or clearer evidence could be produced." Africk told the jurors that they could take as long as they needed to come up with a unanimous decision.

Our team returned to our room and waited some more. I was convinced that the trial would end in a hung jury. It seemed highly unlikely that "guilty" and "not guilty" camps would unanimously agree on anything.

Forty-five minutes later, we got an unexpected phone call. The clerk informed us that the jury reached a verdict. The speed caught everyone off guard.

Typically, a verdict shortly after an *Allen* charge bodes well for the prosecution. I certainly believed the facts of the Warren shooting were damning on their face, but I didn't know how to read the jury's sudden change of heart.

Once again, the verdict occurred after regular court hours, and so the courthouse felt eerily near-empty, mostly just a few friends and family of the Glovers and Warrens, and members of the media.

As the jury entered the courtroom, one juror, a middle-aged White woman, appeared to be crying. I had never before seen a juror cry during the reading of a verdict and had no idea what that could mean.

The judge opened the proceedings with one of his stock musings on the criminal justice system. "There are no winners or losers here," he pronounced. "There is only justice." A nice sentiment, I thought, but far from my experience as a civil rights lawyer working with marginalized communities. The system I know produces no shortage of losers.

The room was quiet, and then the foreperson began reading the jury's verdict.

Not guilty. There was a collective gasp. Henry's sister Patrice screamed out, "He killed my brother!" Two family members lifted her by her arms and legs and carried her out of the courtroom, shrieking. It was as if she was learning about her brother's death for the first time.

I looked back at the jury box, and half of the twelve jurors were in tears. They must have had deep reservations about that verdict, not that it did anyone any good now. I just felt numb.

The jurors returned to the jury room adjacent to the courtroom, where the judge thanked them for their service. He told them that he appreciated that they had honored his order not to view outside news sources or use the internet during the trial. He told them that they could now read about the case.

The judge warned them, however, that they would learn something that he had kept from them during the trial: after David Warren had shot and killed Henry Glover, another police officer had burned his body. One juror threw up all over the jury room.

The next morning, Tracey and I called Linda Howard to check in with her. We were concerned that, after all we'd put her through as a witness to convict Warren, she'd be devastated by the "not guilty." Instead, she comforted us, acknowledging how hard this must be for *us*. Somehow, against all expectation, Howard had emerged from her ordeal stronger and more comfortable in her own skin, ready to empathize with what we were going through.

As I walked through the streets of New Orleans the day after the verdict, everywhere I looked, I saw the tabloid edition of *The Times-Picayune*. The front page was a full-sized picture of David Warren's smiling face with just two words—*Not Guilty*. It felt like he was taunting me.

I flew out of New Orleans that day for what I figured might be the last time. It wasn't how I'd hoped this chapter of my life would end.

CHAPTER 24

BREAKDOWN

December 2013 through April 2018

The convictions that DOJ had won in Glover in 2010 and Robair and Danziger in 2011 were the high-water mark for holding NOPD officers accountable for their crimes. By 2013, that tide was in full retreat.

The Danziger case began to fall apart after it was revealed that a senior prosecutor from the US Attorney's Office in New Orleans, who did not work on the case, posted numerous anonymous comments on Nola.com, the *Times-Picayune* website. He excoriated the NOPD as, among other things, a fish "rotten from the head down" and "a collection of self-centered, self-interested, self-promoting, insular, arrogant, overweening, prevaricating, libidinous fools." (We had considered this same prosecutor, Sal Perricone, for our original Glover legal team, but Mike Magner joined us instead.)

A subsequent investigation revealed two other prosecutors, also not on the prosecution team, made anonymous, if somewhat less incendiary, posts. The defense claimed this was a part of a "secret public relations campaign" to deprive the officers of a fair trial.

Judge Kurt Engelhardt railed against what he called "grotesque prosecutorial misconduct." Although the judge acknowledged that there was no evidence that any jurors had seen these posts, or that they had any bearing on the verdicts, he concluded that the "highly unusual, extensive and truly bizarre actions" nonetheless warranted vacating the convictions and granting new trials. However, what apparently drove the reversal was the trial judge's discomfort with the stiff sentences he'd been forced to mete out because of gun charges that carried mandatory minimums. One officer had received a sentence of sixty-five years.

At sentencing, Engelhardt, subsequently elevated to the Fifth Circuit Court of Appeals by Donald Trump, professed to be horrified by the prosecution giving several defendants reduced sentences to "flip" on the others, a standard prosecutorial tactic. I agreed with *The Washington Post*'s assessment that "Engelhardt's emotional 129-page ruling [for a new trial] is unconvincing in the extreme."

The Danziger case would float in limbo for another three and a half years. Finally, in the spring of 2016, the five officers accepted plea deals brokered by new lawyers from the US Attorney's Office and received vastly shorter sentences, between three and twelve years, with credit for time served.

As for Detective Sergeant Gerard Dugue, he was tried on multiple counts of obstruction of justice separately from the other defendants. Bobbi Bernstein prosecuted his stand-alone trial in January 2012, about a year after the original Glover trial.

Dugue testified in his own defense, and during his direct examination, said that he would never insert credibility determinations in his official reports. Of course, he had done just that in Robair, when he concluded that civilian witnesses were untrustworthy.

Bobbi tore him apart on cross, meticulously excavating his long-standing history of covering up police misconduct. But according to the judge's pre-trial ruling, the Robair case was off-limits, unless, of course, Dugue "opened the door." When Dugue claimed he was having difficulty remembering past cases, Bobbi asked the judge, "May I help him remember?"

Judge Engelhardt responded, "Go ahead."

Bobbi went back to her table and asked a paralegal to "Get me Robair," so she could impeach Dugue with examples from his report.

Dugue's attorney objected. The judge, who was generally hostile towards Bobbi, told her that Robair was still off-limits. Bobbi moved on to other examples; she had plenty of ammunition.

But later that day, Dugue's attorney moved for a mistrial, arguing that the mere mention of Robair's name had been unduly prejudicial. It felt like a half-hearted, last-ditch attempt by his attorney to save Dugue, who seemed well on his way to being found guilty. Shockingly, the judge declared a mistrial. He noted that it was impossible to know whether jurors had heard what she had said to the paralegal, but concluded, "That's a chance that I'm not willing to take." This was, without a doubt, the most bizarre grounds for a mistrial I've ever encountered.

Dugue's retrial had to wait until the rest of the Danziger legal mess could be sorted out. His fate would stay unresolved until late 2016 when he accepted a plea deal, brokered by the US Attorney's Office. He was convicted of one misdemeanor charge of "accessory after the fact" for his role in the Danziger Bridge shooting cover-up and sentenced to one year probation. He was the only Danziger defendant who never spent a day in prison. At least he would never investigate another case of police misconduct again.

The Glover case continued to have its own twists and turns. After Warren's acquittal, we were confronted with what to do about Travis McCabe. Warren—after having been found "not guilty" for the shooting—would be the key, and supposedly more credible, witness at McCabe's trial. DOJ opted not to retry McCabe.

Even Greg McRae, the lone remaining convicted defendant in the Glover case, got a reprieve from an unexpected corner, the US Supreme Court. The federal statute at the heart of McRae's obstruction of justice conviction prohibited destruction of "tangible objects" with intent to interfere with an investigation. It seemed to us that a human body and a car were about as tangible as you could get. In 2015, in *United States v. Yates*, the Supreme Court thought otherwise.

John L. Yates was a commercial fisherman busted for catching undersized red grouper, who covered up evidence of his crime by throwing the offending fish overboard. The issue before the Supreme Court was whether the undersized fish qualified as "tangible objects" under the statute. It was an absurd case to bring before the nation's highest court. (*Yates* failed what I called the "Kowalski test." My DOJ mentor Barry Kowalski once told me, "If someone asks you, 'Why are you making a federal case out of this?' you better have a damn good explanation.")

The captain's acts certainly seemed to meet the requirements of the statute. It was hard to argue that undersized fish were not "tangible objects."

And yet that is exactly what the court decided. The majority opinion determined that "tangible object" did not mean "all physical objects," but only the subset of objects "used to record or preserve information." Cars and bodies did not qualify.

The *Yates* decision required Africk to toss out the obstruction of justice charge, and once again resentence Greg McRae. At the hearing in February 2016, there was one conspicuous absence. Frank DeSalvo no longer represented McRae. McRae's new lawyer advanced an eleventh-hour "affirmative" defense, arguing that his client's sentence should be significantly reduced, because he suffered from post-traumatic stress disorder.

The attorney called a psychologist whose report asserted that there was "substantial evidence to support the fact that Officer McRae was suffering from post-traumatic stress disorder, which began shortly after the arrival of Hurricane Katrina and progressed quickly and intensely; further complicated by sleep deprivation, physical exhaustion, and a generalized sense of helplessness and hopelessness." He concluded: "In my opinion [McRae] did not understand the wrongfulness of his conduct and even more so, to exercise the power of rational thought about what he had undertaken."

I contended that even if McRae suffered from PTSD *now*, which he very well might, that had no bearing on whether he had the ability to appreciate that his actions were criminal at the time they were committed. Perhaps, I argued, the "trauma" that triggered his PTSD could have been the burning of Glover's body itself.

Africk rejected the new testimony, noting that "the court finds you [McRae] did not have a significantly impaired ability to understand the wrongfulness of the behavior, to exercise the power of reason, or to control a behavior you knew was wrongful."

But without the obstruction of justice charge, Africk reduced McRae's sentence from seventeen to twelve years.

The McRae resentencing hearing would not be my last time in a New Orleans courthouse. In February 2019, I found myself back in federal district court one last time to finish off the last of the Katrina-era cases.

Roland Bourgeois, a civilian, formed an all-White vigilante neighborhood watch group. Armed with a smattering of shotguns, rifles, and handguns, the group set up barricades of fallen trees to protect their mostly White neighborhood of Algiers Point. One vigilante said that the Fourth District police advised them to take matters into their own hands: "If they're breaking in your property, do what you gotta do and leave them [the bodies] on the side of the road."

The Algiers Point's ferry landing had been designated as an official evacuation site for the city and Bourgeois was worried about an influx of "outsiders." He made it clear to his neighbors just whom he meant, telling them, "Anything coming up this street darker than a brown paper bag is getting shot."

On the afternoon of September 1, three Black men made their way to the ferry landing to escape the city. Bourgeois fired his shotgun multiple times, hitting the three men and grievously wounding one man in the neck.

Once again, our office learned about the incident from an article written by A.C. Thompson. After a yearlong investigation by my Robair trial partner, Forrest Christian, a grand jury indicted Bourgeois in 2010 for hate crimes and obstruction of justice, almost five years after their commission.

After the indictment, Bourgeois's attorneys said he suffered from a medical condition that impaired his mental functioning and made it impossible for him to assist in his defense. They predicted Bourgeois did not have long to live. The court postponed the trial indefinitely.

Eight years later, Bourgeois was back from the near-dead, thanks to extraordinary advances in medicine. The Court declared him competent to stand trial. I was assigned the trial with another DOJ colleague. Not long before our scheduled trial date, Bourgeois pleaded guilty.

The judge sentenced Bourgeois to ten years. It turned out to be a life sentence. Only seven days after sentencing, he was found in his cell, dead, according to the corrections officials, from natural causes. It was hard to believe after waiting so long for "justice," this was how the last of the Katrina cases ended, another unsatisfying conclusion to another disgraceful episode.

CHAPTER 25

CHASING JUSTICE

2017 through 2021

For years, I kept a framed copy of the front page of the December 10, 2010, edition of *The Times-Picayune* in my DOJ office. The headline read: *3 Guilty in Glover Case*. After two of the convictions were overturned, I covered the *3* with a Post-it note on which I'd scribbled *1*, my personal asterisk on the legal resolution of the case.

Warren's acquittal was particularly hard to bear. The feeling had something in common with the loss I felt after Israeli prosecutors declined to charge anyone for the murder of my teenage friend Asel during my time in Jerusalem. Both killers walked free; neither society seemed to care enough about those deaths to hold anyone responsible. I hung the *Times-Pic* front page next to my framed photo of Asel to encourage me to fight even harder the next time.

In 2017, four years after a jury found Warren not guilty, I prosecuted a police abuse case in North Charleston, South Carolina, that promised to be that "next time."

Two years earlier, Walter Scott, a fifty-year-old Black man, was pulled over for a malfunctioning taillight. Less than two minutes later, Scott was gunned down by Officer Michael Slager. The North Charleston police department reflexively defended Slager's actions, claiming that Scott had attacked Slager with a Taser. But, miraculously, a local barber captured the shooting on a cell phone video as he walked to work. The footage was the clearest evidence I had ever seen of a bad shooting: the officer fired eight times at Scott as he was running away, five shots striking him in the back.

Scott's death was widely considered one of the catalysts of the national Black Lives Matter movement that had come into being after the 2014 police killings of Michael Brown in Ferguson, Missouri; Eric Garner in Staten Island, New York; and Tamir Rice in Cleveland, Ohio. (The Tamir Rice case was particularly close to my heart. I investigated the shooting for the DOJ but the department declined to move forward.)

Notwithstanding the video, Slager's state murder trial resulted in a hung jury. I led the DOJ team that prosecuted Slager for federal civil rights violations following the mistrial. Our successful pretrial strategy ultimately resulted in Slager pleading guilty.

The result was as good as any we could have hoped for, an all-too-rare case of a police officer convicted for unjustifiably taking a life. The Court called Walter Scott's death what it was—a murder—and sentenced Slager to twenty years in prison. Anthony Scott, Walter's brother, proclaimed, "Not only did we get justice today, but the truth was told." The headline that ran in the local paper the next day declared it a *Monumental Day for Civil Rights*. It was precisely the kind of case I had always dreamed of winning.

The truth was, my "triumph" felt empty. "Now what?" I thought. Was anything going to change? The fact that Michael Slager was going to spend at least the next seventeen years in prison wasn't likely to ameliorate any of the conditions that gave rise to the killing in the first place, such as the targeted law enforcement that disproportionately harms people of color.

If "winning" felt this bad, I needed a new job.

Don't get me wrong. Murder should be prosecuted, and law enforcement officers who kill without justification should be held accountable. Nothing sends a more powerful message to a community that it doesn't matter than when an agent of the state kills a member of that community and suffers no serious consequences. The failure to prosecute or convict is one thing that can reliably send a city up in flames: LA after Rodney King; Ferguson after Michael Brown; Baltimore after Freddie Gray.

However, prosecuting those who abuse their power, while certainly necessary, is an expensive, labor-intensive business. It's also a purely after-the-fact remedy—often many *years* after the fact—that doesn't do enough to prevent future harm. Roughly a thousand people lose their lives in police shootings every year, a rate that has stayed relatively constant for the past seven years, increased prosecutions notwithstanding.

Even though I spent fourteen years prosecuting cops who have done bad things, I have learned that, collectively, we overemphasize the power that individual cases have to fix past harms. We hold trials up as morality plays that pit "right" versus "wrong." When our side wins, we're quick to call it a victory for justice (even though that feeling doesn't last long.) When our side loses, we lament the unfairness of it all, even as we're proud of the righteousness of the cause.

In practice, trials are rarely the great arbiter of truth that we want them to be. I don't share Judge Africk's assessment that "the American jury system is the most powerful method yet devised for the ascertainment of truth." Given the adversarial nature of our system, juries are, at least potentially, a valuable protection against wrongful accusations. But jury trials never tell the whole story. Results often turn on technical matters, like legal rulings; which witnesses cooperate; and random chance, like which judge is assigned to the case or who happened to get called for jury duty that week.

And after the few wins we do have, we often send the wrong message. We label the offenders "bad apples"; we talk about how they failed to live up to our ideals. Then we return to business as usual, in effect letting the rest of the criminal legal system off the hook.

Following Warren's conviction in the first trial, Patrice Glover asked the judge to impose maximum prison sentences. She wanted those NOPD officers to pay for the death of her brother and the desecration of his body. I did too, and I asked the court for a significant prison time. Edna Glover struck a different, religious note: "I forgive these men, because if I don't forgive them, Jesus won't forgive me. And I would like justice to be served in Jesus's name."

Edna's message was that something worthy of being called "justice" should be about more than a long prison sentence. Prison is passive: a person is punished. No one needs to *do* anything to try to make things right. As an increasingly influential "restorative justice" movement has argued over the past several decades, real justice requires acknowledging responsibility for one's actions and the impact that it has had on others. It requires a genuine expression of remorse and the taking of concrete actions to repair the harm. In cases of state violence, it requires acknowledging the social and cultural context of the damage done—and working to ameliorate the conditions that made it possible. Prosecutions, as they exist today, virtually never accomplish these things.

For years I saw the Glover case as an unmitigated loss. But with time, I have come to realize that those two trials played a major role in a city-wide transformation that was far more powerful than any single win or loss in the courtroom.

The crimes unearthed during the federal investigations of the Glover, Robair, and Danziger cases were simply too awful for New Orleans to ignore. We had held a mirror up to the police department, and the community did not like what it saw. People demanded the city do better. Remarkably, it began trying.

In his last months in office in late 2016, Mayor Mitch Landrieu attempted to grapple with the emotional damage caused by police crimes after Katrina. He negotiated $13.3 million in financial settlements with the Glover and Robair families and with the families of the Danziger victims. On behalf of the city, he publicly apologized to them for the "terror" and "mayhem" that the police had visited upon them.

The apology was unprecedented. Mary Howell, who represented one of the Danziger families, put it this way: "You can't move forward, with any sense of justice or of healing, unless there is recognition of past harms."

Landrieu was attempting to leave behind, for a moment, the criminal justice framework of punishment and accountability, to reach for an almost religious conception of atonement. He arranged a memorial service, closed to the press and the public, that he hoped would reach both the sinners and the sinned against. One section of the chapel was reserved for the victims' families and their advisors, one section for the police command staff, and one for the clergy.

"Some of the police were friends with officers who had been convicted and were in prison," Howell said later. "By the end of the service, there were a lot of people crossing those aisles."

Genuine apologies create space for changing hearts and minds. They allow us to hit the "reset button," as Asel always wanted. Then we must begin the arduous process of fixing the problems that got us here.

After the federal prosecutions, New Orleans began remaking its police department in a way that no previous police scandals had ever managed to inspire and that, pre-Katrina, few people would have ever thought possible. For starters, the NOPD got serious about cleaning house. At least twenty-five officers were fired or resigned under investigation, including numerous high-ranking officers. These officers had used excessive force, lied, obstructed, or otherwise failed to live up to their obligations to protect and serve.

In 2013, in between the two Glover trials, New Orleans entered into an agreement with a different part of the Civil Rights Division, the Special Litigation Section, whose analysis of the persistent pattern of civil rights abuses within the NOPD served as the precursor to a 129-page "consent decree" between the city, the NOPD, and the federal judiciary to reform the police department.

It was the most extensive, and one of the most expensive, efforts ever undertaken to reimagine policing.

For the past decade, a team of federal court–appointed monitors has worked with the department to reassess every aspect of the job, from training and hiring protocols to "use of force" procedures, evaluating the department's progress along the way.

One of the most innovative reforms to spring from the consent decree is a program called EPIC (Ethical Policing Is Courageous). It aims to change a "passive bystander" culture in which officers fail to prevent misconduct and stay silent about their colleagues' abusive behavior. The federal prosecutions after Katrina provided all too many examples of officers who looked the other way.

While there have long been laws and rules requiring officers to stop such abuse, EPIC's approach recognizes what motivates or inhibits people from intervening, and provides officers with practical techniques to navigate and defuse those difficult situations. We all want fewer officers like Matthew Dean "Patches" Moore, the officer who watched Robair get beaten to death, or, for that matter, the three officers who stood by as Derek Chauvin murdered George Floyd. In the past decade, lawsuits for police misconduct have cost American cities around three billion dollars, money that would be far better spent addressing the true drivers of crime.

EPIC has sparked the creation of bystander intervention programs across the US. These days, NOPD sends EPIC "ambassadors" to work with police departments around the country, a mind-blowing turn of events for anyone who remembers the department of old.

After the Walter Scott case, I wanted to try to tackle some of the systemic problems that distort our criminal justice system. I'd grown tired of the simple-minded binary thinking that pits prosecutor against defendant, cops against the community. I was frustrated that our society keeps "criminalizing" problems that the system was not designed to solve, such as addiction, mental health, and poverty. Communities are awash in unaddressed trauma, which often manifests itself in new violence.

Every year, American police make about 10 million arrests, at a cost of hundreds of billions of dollars. Approximately 1.9 million people currently live behind bars, more people, and more people per capita, than anywhere else in the world. And yet 95 percent of these people return home, faced with severe barriers to gaining legal employment and reintegrating into their communities. Recent evidence suggests that this approach has a "criminogenic" effect, increasing the odds that incarcerated people will be released only to commit additional crimes.

These statistics don't factor in the generational trauma created by having more than five million children across the country who have had a parent incarcerated at some point in their lives. One study estimates these children are six times more likely to become incarcerated in the future than their peers who have not suffered this experience.

If this "tough on crime" approach really worked, America would be the safest country in the world. Hardly.

After the conclusion of the Walter Scott case, I kept in touch with Solicitor Scarlett Wilson, the chief local prosecutor in Charleston, an elected Republican, who had handled the state case. Like me, she had a growing understanding of how racial bias is built into the criminal legal system. For years, Solicitor Wilson had been collecting data on key prosecutorial decisions in Charleston and Berkeley Counties, such as charging, plea negotiations, and sentences. She wanted to analyze the data to see if her office was treating defendants fairly. If it wasn't, she wanted to do something about it.

In May 2020, as a global pandemic upended the world, I left the Justice Department to launch a non-profit initiative, Justice Innovation Lab. My hope was that we could analyze the solicitor's data to identify everyday practices in her office that lead to unfair outcomes. The power of digging into the data is that we can step back and see the collective impact of decisions—any of which can be justified in isolation—in a broad, system-wide context. The numbers allow us to ask different and better questions about whether we are really achieving what we want to achieve:

safe and fair communities. I began assembling a team with expertise in law, data science, behavioral psychology, policy, design-thinking, adult learning, and data visualization. Charleston would be our first real-life lab.

We started by looking at racial disparities in incarceration. Consistent with national trends, Black men collectively were incarcerated twice as long as White men, even though they only comprise 12 percent of the country's population.

I had assumed, given this huge difference in incarceration numbers, prosecutors must be treating Black and White people in the system unequally. But when we controlled for factors that impact sentences—such as severity and number of charges and past criminal record—we found that, overall, prosecutors were treating "similarly situated" defendants similarly, and yet with drastically unequal results. How could this possibly be so?

As we delved deeper, a story emerged. Much of it comes back to policing.

Black men were five times more likely to be arrested than White men in Charleston, a rate roughly similar to many other jurisdictions. The disparity was even greater for drug charges, where Black men were six times more likely to be arrested, even though local and national data suggest similar rates of drug use and drug sales across races. The disparities are greater still for the demographic that gets arrested most frequently: young Black men.

The police will typically explain racial disparities in incarceration by noting that violent crime is more prevalent in minority communities, and violent crimes come with long prison sentences. But that is only part of the story. What we discovered in Charleston was that differences in policing low-level offenses, such as drugs and low-value theft, accounted for much of the "incarceration gap."

Overpolicing of Black communities increases the likelihood that a Black person will be arrested for a low-level offense. They then return to their community with a criminal record and reduced opportunities for legal employment, which in turn increases the likelihood of being arrested again. With each new conviction, the penalties escalate dramatically and often include mandatory minimum sentences. The vicious circle continues. The effect at the community and family level is exponential and devastating.

Additionally, the wide net cast by these aggressive and targeted police practices often leads to cases that don't pass legal muster. Prosecutors increasingly correct for that. We discovered that Black defendants had their cases dismissed twice as often as White defendants for insufficient evidence, almost certainly because they were being arrested on weak charges far more frequently than White men.

These cases, however, often remained in the system for close to a year, profoundly impacting arrestees. Some were jailed or lost their jobs. Collectively, these cases cost those arrested millions of dollars in bond payments, all on charges later determined not to merit prosecution.

As a result, resources are diverted away from serving victims and solving serious crimes. The societal costs, including disruption to families, lost economic output, and lost opportunities, are immeasurable.

Our analysis unearthed a "system" problem that doesn't require "bad intent" on anybody's part. Even when prosecutors treat cases "equally," Black defendants receive massively unequal outcomes. Deeply rooted economic and social inequities, a fact of life for many communities of color, are only exacerbated by the criminal legal system, which, counter to its professed goal, produces more crime.

We worked with the solicitor's office to develop new screening procedures to identify and remove from the system cases with insufficient evidence. We have reduced the harm caused by unequal arrest patterns and flagged cases that might be better served by alternatives to prosecution. This will reduce the number of years people will be incarcerated.

Our work has reinforced what my former colleague once told me in Kosovo: that more than any other actor in the system, prosecutors have the greatest power to protect civil rights, if they choose to exercise it. They can hold police officers accountable, and not only by prosecuting them. Measures like better screening of cases can significantly reduce the harm suffered by entire communities.

Of course, our society needs to do more to address the root

causes of crime: untreated mental health issues, addiction, unaddressed trauma, and poverty. But Justice Innovation Lab represents a worthy first step: do less harm right now. Over the next three years, we intend to expand our work into eight new jurisdictions, which should positively impact hundreds of thousands of cases.

The Glover case was, in many ways, unique, the byproduct of extreme circumstances—Katrina—and a deeply troubled police department. Frankly, I chose to write about the case because it was so outrageous. I figured readers would be more likely to pay attention because the facts were so shocking.

But I also knew that the case was illustrative of just how broken the whole criminal legal system is. Factors that contributed to Glover's death and incineration, and the cover-up that followed—such as the dehumanization of marginalized citizens and a complicit "bystander culture"—exist, in varying degrees, in jurisdictions across the United States. The Glover case is a cautionary tale of what can happen when our institutional systems fail, and the worst impulses of humanity spin out of control.

All of which made this a hard book to write. I didn't want to write a depressing book. I didn't want people to throw up their hands and quit, lamenting the unfairness of life, or simply accepting bad outcomes as inevitable. Those cannot be our final takeaways.

For all the times that Martin Luther King, Jr., has been quoted—"The moral arc of the universe is long, but it bends towards justice"—the geopolitical developments of the past decade or so have persuaded a lot of people that maybe King got it wrong. I'm not one of them. As much as it may feel in the current moment that we're "bending" in the wrong direction, we should remind ourselves of how far we have come. Consider that our Constitution, about which I often waxed poetically in court, explicitly permitted the enslavement of human beings.

But we must also remember that the moral arc doesn't bend on its own. As King noted, "Human progress is neither automatic nor inevitable... Every step towards the goal of justice requires sacrifice, suffering and struggle; the tireless exertions and passionate concerns of dedicated individuals."

There are countless people in the trenches fighting every day to reimagine what justice looks like. They struggle to move that arc. I am grateful to work alongside them.

As a child in elementary school, the Biblical imperative that most resonated with me was *Tzedek, Tzedek Tirdof*, usually translated as "Justice, Justice you shall pursue." But the Hebrew verb *tirdof* also means "to chase." That is the image I have in my mind when I think about what we must do to repair the world.

We must chase justice. It is in an active pursuit. It can be slippery and hard to nail down. It can be exhausting. Chasing justice comes with the understanding that, far more often than we'd like, it will get away from us.

Our current criminal legal system is the result of choices made by many individuals over a long period of time. Some of these structures and practices were deliberately built to oppress others; sometimes, the harms are merely unintended consequences. People created these problems; people can fix them.

I am often asked how I stay positive; how have I not grown cynical? It's because I have no choice but to believe that we can build a better system of justice, and in so doing, make a better world. The alternative is simply unacceptable.

We get to choose how Henry Glover's story ends.

EPILOGUE

April through November 2022

Less than an hour after landing at Louis Armstrong International Airport, my co-author Joe Hooper and I wandered through Jackson Square in the heart of the French Quarter in the middle of the French Quarter Festival. I'd missed the scene: eating shrimp po' boys, drinking Abita beer and listening to an aural encyclopedia of American music—jazz, zydeco, and rock.

I hadn't been back to New Orleans in four years since the sentencing of the Katrina-era vigilante Roland Bourgeois. COVID had kept us away for most of the researching and writing of this book. But as the virus relaxed its grip on the country, I'd keenly looked forward to returning to the city where I came of age as a civil rights prosecutor.

The city I found in the spring of 2022 had changed quite a bit, in ways both engaging and disheartening.

The gentrified city of today is cleaner and more prosperous. COVID notwithstanding, the streets and bars were filled with tourists who'd come back in full force. The city's permanent population had swelled; 40,000 more people lived here than when I arrived to investigate the Glover case in 2009. (Even so, the city is only 80 percent of its pre-Katrina population.) The growth has been driven by an influx of mostly White transplants. There have been, among others, the hipsters, drawn in by the city's festive, music-saturated vibe; the so-called YURPs or "young urban rebuilding professionals"; and their more commercially-minded cousins who profitably fixed up and flipped houses in once storm-blighted neighborhoods. The Treme neighborhood where I once looked so out of place is a hell of a lot Whiter these days.

The end result is a city considerably less racially diverse than the one I remembered. After Katrina, approximately one third of the Black population didn't return, mostly due to a lack of affordable housing. The post-Katrina Road Home program allocated support funds based on estimated home value, not actual construction costs, leaving many lower-income homeowners without the capital to return and rebuild. The "Big Four" public housing complexes were razed to the ground, replaced with smaller mixed-income developments. Flooded-out, mostly Black neighborhoods like the Lower Ninth Ward and New Orleans East have yet to be built back to anything close to their former dimensions.

One thing that remained constant between 2009 and 2022 was that New Orleanians were still talking about the police. This time around, they were talking less about the NOPD committing crimes, and more about its inability to prevent or solve them. After the worst days of the pandemic passed and Americans resumed a semi-normal life, violent crime spiked in cities across the nation. Yet New Orleans still managed to stand out in a crowded field. In 2022, the city was on pace to lead the country in murders per capita.

Violent crime in New Orleans is nothing new. But almost everyone we talked to, regardless of where they fell on the economic and ideological spectrum, described a pervasive feeling of threat, especially walking the city at night. People were still talking about a bungled carjacking one month earlier in which four teenagers dragged the driver, a seventy-three-year-old woman, to her death. (These four teenagers, three of them young women, are set to be tried as adults, for second-degree murder.) The conversations recalled "the bad old days" of the early '90s, when the city suffered the distinction of being the nation's murder capital.

Certainly, the pandemic was behind much of the city's recent crime surge. It drove lockdowns and the ensuing joblessness, especially severe in a city dependent on tourism. Court closures hamstrung an already dysfunctional legal system. COVID damaged the city's overall mental health.

But a lot of New Orleanians seemed to be looking for a handier scapegoat. The federal consent decree has made a fat target. In remarks delivered at a press conference three months after our visit, the city's mayor, LaToya Cantrell, opined, "The consent decree handcuffs our officers by making their jobs harder, pestering them with punitive punishment and burying them with paperwork that is an overburden."

A theory advanced by the president of one police union is that the consent decree restrictions on police behavior have resulted in a mass exodus of police officers, which has driven up crime. Today's NOPD has, according to some estimates, barely half the number of officers it did before Katrina hit. Some of the departees have complained to the media about how the job has grown more dangerous and the respect from the public they serve has dwindled. If we want to stop crime, they argue, unshackle the police and let them police the way they want to.

I have seen one thing over and over again when people grow fearful of rising violence. It doesn't take long before they lean into their most punitive instincts and push for more aggressive policing and harsher punishments. That fervor, in response to the '90s crime wave, brought us mandatory minimum sentences, three strikes laws, and stop-and-frisk policing, with the result that the US became the incarceration capital of the world.

When we met up with civil rights attorney Mary Howell, she couldn't hide her contempt for the idea that justice reform has led to increased violence. "We have the police union saying the consent decree is the cause of crime in New Orleans," she told us. "Really? Really?"

Mary had been a leading voice for police reform representing victims in virtually every significant police misconduct case in New Orleans since the Algiers 7 case in 1980. She had been a formidable ally and mentor, and I'd missed her sharp tongue and bracing intellect.

"There is all kinds of corruption going on," she said. She blamed some of the poor police performance on officers not showing up to work. The department is in the middle of a major payroll fraud scandal that has implicated over fifty officers in double-dipping, working paid second jobs when they're supposed to be policing. "I always say, number one, see if the people who are in NOPD are actually on the job."

For all the reforms ushered in, clearly, a lot *hadn't* changed. But in Mary's view, the consent decree was a qualified success, "the floor, not the ceiling" of nonabusive policing in New Orleans.

In the years since the Glover case, complaints against the NOPD for excessive force have dropped dramatically, as have the number of police-involved shootings. There have been measurable strides in areas like community policing and body-worn cameras. "We'll never know about the people that weren't harmed and the violence that wasn't done because of it," she said.

But even Mary understands that the consent decree will be phased out and the critical issue will be whether there is the political will, and the resources, to sustain the hard-earned reforms. (It is likely the consent decree will be in a sunset period by the time this book is published.)

How the city and its police department will fare afterwards will be determined, she felt, less by the number of officers on the payroll than by their mindset: "If the police culture doesn't change, then the same bad things just keep happening over and over again."

On another day, in another conversation, Jim Letten, the former US Attorney during the Glover, Robair, and Danziger investigations, hit a similar note. His takeaway message to the NOPD officers and recruits he lectures to: "Don't let anyone ever tell you that policing constitutionally and legally is inconsistent with policing effectively, and even aggressively, if you have to. The two are not mutually exclusive, at all!"

I caught up with my former trial partners Tracey Knight and Mike Magner separately to get their thoughts on what had and hadn't changed since the Glover case. Tracey and Mike had both prospered since the trials, but on opposite sides of the courtroom.

Tracey had been promoted to criminal chief of the US Attorney's Office, overseeing all federal criminal prosecutions in the district. She maintains a docket of her own high-profile cases, including one against Joe Meisch, the former NOPD lieutenant who testified about seeing McRae and Scheuermann at the levee as Tanner's car went up in flames. After the first trial, Meisch was fired for "neglect of duty" for failing to report the burning. He became the business manager of St. Patrick's Catholic Church, and was later charged with embezzling close to $330,000 from the church.

Magner had retired from federal service and moved on to become a successful defense attorney, a not unusual transition. He was content with the move. "Representing clients, you're their last and best hope," he said. "That's rewarding."

Tracey and Mike agreed that the Katrina-era civil rights cases brought against NOPD had helped change the culture of the department for the better, the current crime wave notwithstanding. "It got rid of a lot of really bad cops," Tracey said. "We don't really see a lot of civil rights cases coming out of NOPD anymore."

Magner took a consoling long view: "Yes, the results in court were mixed. But it struck me as absolutely essential that law enforcement, and the federal government in particular, plant the flag, that there had to be some rule of law here, however imperfect."

★ ★ ★

I didn't have a current phone number for Linda Howard, but I remembered where she lived. I called a play from my old investigative playbook and dropped by unannounced. Linda was gardening and didn't recognize me at first, but before long, we were chatting on her patio. The Glover case wasn't too far from her mind—a month earlier, she'd attended a memorial service for Rebecca Glover, Henry's aunt, a well-known figure around New Orleans, and a fierce advocate for civil rights.

Linda and I talked about the philosophy she developed over twenty-eight years. "I never wanted to think I had the power," she told us. "I was just doing my job. Not trying to be above you or anything like that…" She arrested many people over the years, but she said she never cursed or talked down to them. "You leave them with their dignity. And they'll respect you for that."

As we began talking about the Glover case, the topic changed to fear and the strength required to overcome it. Building the Glover case required persuading a handful of officers to tell the truth about what they knew, regardless of the personal cost. Back when we first met, I recognized Linda Howard's courage in stepping forward to testify, but I don't think I adequately appreciated the risks she incurred.

Returning home after shifts was always frightening, she said. Her family had left the city two days after Katrina hit and she was alone. "I'd come home and I couldn't do anything or go anywhere," she said. "I couldn't even cut the grass. I was always scared that a car with dark windows would pass. I was like, 'Is this the one that's going to get me?'" After she testified in the trial, the Fourth District rank offered to transfer her, but she declined: "If someone was going to retaliate against me, at least I know the faces there."

To my knowledge, Linda was the only significant NOPD witness involved in the Glover case who left the department on her own terms, without a push or an outright dismissal. She almost made her full pension. "People said to me, 'You only have two more years to make your thirty,' but I say, 'Yeah, in those two years, I could be dead.'"

I knew Ashley would appreciate hearing Linda's voice, and vice versa, so I connected the two on speakerphone for their first conversation since the retrial. "Hey Ashley, it's Linda! How you doin'? I'm at home and that's good." Linda seemed content in retirement, tending to her garden and her home, and coaching nine- and ten-year-old girls in a local sports league.

Linda was pleased to hear that Ashley was thriving as well, having steadily moved up the ranks to lead International Operations at FBI headquarters, one of only three Black women currently in the Bureau in the "senior executive service," the highest level of government civil service.

Returning to our conversation, Linda told us that she didn't regret the way the Glover case upended her life for close to eight years. The fear, she said, lessened with time, a testament to her Christian faith and to her conviction that she had done the right thing.

"Do you think you were meant to be there, to watch what happened to Henry?" I asked.

She didn't hesitate. "Of course! For the truth to come out."

If Linda Howard looked back at the Glover drama without regret, that seemed to be all that Nina Simmons was left with.

Simmons retired from NOPD while under investigation for lying to the grand jury. Since then, she'd taught preschoolers ("I like introducing babies to new things: letters, numbers; their minds are so spongy") and helped her husband out with a security business. We met her in a downtown hotel lobby. I asked her what she had taken away from the Glover case.

"I regret having so much fear inside me," she told us. It was her anxiety about possible NOPD retribution, she said, that kept her from ensuring that senior leadership knew that Officer Howard had witnessed a bad shooting. "I was too fearful that they were going to get to her and kill her. I'll never live in fear like that again. It's not controlling me anymore."

The more we spoke about the case, the more obvious it was that her role in it had taken an emotional toll. She started the conversation by telling us that she was considering writing a book about her experiences. By the end, she had changed her mind. "I think the act of talking to you guys, I'm finished with this," she declared. "I think I just need to move on with my life from this." Her goal moving forward was to simply "help those who I can along the way."

For the past three years, I've wrestled with criminal justice from a "systems" perspective, identifying areas where process and policy lead to unnecessary and unfair harms, and figuring out how to fix them. Our trip to New Orleans had brought me back to individual *people*, and how they have the power to bend the system in the direction of justice or its opposite. Some, like Linda Howard, rose to the occasion; countless others lied or stayed silent. In my estimation, the five NOPD officers I prosecuted had been both heroic and villainous in the same week.

The passage of time helped me appreciate more deeply just what it took to speak out against injustice, especially for those with less power to make their voices heard.

William Tanner helped a stranger in desperate need, and he paid a price for that. He was beaten, stripped of his car and his dignity. But he didn't remain silent, and he wasn't deterred by the people who didn't believe him. Without his persistence, it is likely that no one would have ever found out what happened to Henry.

We met Tanner under the I-10 highway overpass, not far from where I canvassed for witnesses in the Robair case. We ducked into a nearby fried seafood restaurant, the same place where I'd last seen him in 2018 when I ran into him by accident. Not surprisingly, he hadn't remembered my name, but he knew who I was. "Hey, DOJ guy!" he yelled out.

Back then, he was as ebullient as I remembered from the Glover trials. This time around he was more subdued, and I had to wonder whether his peripatetic lifestyle might be catching up with him. "I move around from house to house," he said. "Never stay in one place for long." But his life philosophy remained upbeat:

"I died in 2000, so I must be doin' good," Tanner joked, an allusion to the surgery where he'd "flatlined" for about five minutes.

Tanner was more pessimistic when it came to the question of whether the Glover prosecution made any real difference in New Orleans. He didn't think the police force had improved much since then, and like everyone else we spoke with, he worried about rising crime.

But regardless of the case's longer-term impact, he was proud of the Good Samaritan role he had played. "[Every] September 2, people are talking about this case," he said. He told us that a photograph of his burned-out Chevy Malibu is on display at the Lower Ninth Ward Living Museum, a home turned museum that documents the impact of Katrina.

He was pleased that we were trying to keep that history alive. "As long as it's in a history, I'm good. Everybody loves a legend." Tanner flashed his lopsided grin. "I'm not a giant legend, but I am a legend."

To my mind, Merlene Kimble was another local hero.

After Officer Melvin "Flattop" Williams beat Raymond Robair to death, Merlene, then a woman in her sixties, made sure the world knew about it. Ultimately, she connected us with the witnesses that had allowed us to bring charges. "Some of those people was rockheads, drug addicts, dope dealers," she recalled for us. "But they came forward." Williams had a hard-won reputation for terrorizing the neighborhood. It took the community's collective bravery to stop him.

But the lasting impact of the Robair prosecution went beyond holding two police officers accountable for misconduct. Merlene told us that one time a young man approached her on the street and asked if he could hug her. Williams had arrested the man on false charges after he refused to sell drugs on his behalf. He had told her: "I almost lost my job, and my kids and my wife would have been homeless. When you got the [Williams] conviction, they let me out!"

Merlene gave him a smile. "Yeah, you could hug me."

★ ★ ★

Lastly, I reached out to Frank DeSalvo, hoping he might give me some insights on the part of the case that left me with so many unanswered questions: the burning of Henry Glover's body.

I haven't had many opportunities to compare notes with the defense attorneys I've battled at trial, particularly not one like De-Salvo whom I repeatedly tried to get removed from the case for what I considered ethically questionable tactics and conflicts of interest. Our in-court clashes notwithstanding, DeSalvo was always collegial, personable, and often funny. I learned a lot about how to be an effective advocate by seeing him in action. As many times as I'd watched him defend the indefensible, he was nonetheless a hard guy to hate.

He welcomed us into his office for a long conversation that felt more like visiting with an old professor than a former legal adversary. He said, at seventy-nine, he was still busy, still practicing law full-time, which he intended to do until he died. "I'm having fun. I like going to trial… And I don't know what [else] I would do." I suggested he might want to write a book about his career and the hundreds, if not thousands, of cases he'd tried. "I can't write about all the cases I won, how wonderful I was, 'cause these guys were guilty," he shot back. "You know, fuck that!"

Of course, it was the police cases he'd lost that were the occasion for some wound-licking. "Thirtysomething years I represented the police union [PANO] and up until the post-Katrina cases, I never lost a case. Never! And then I lose two." (Three, actually: Greg McRae in the Glover case, Melvin Williams in the Robair case, and one of the Danziger defendants.) He moved on from PANO about a decade ago and these days, he's even handled cases *against* the police department.

I brought the conversation around to the first Glover trial. De-Salvo was adamant that Scheuermann, who still worked for him as an investigator, was innocent of every charge we threw at him. McRae was guilty ("he admitted that he did it, couldn't get around that") but only, he said, of committing an irrational act under extreme stress, not participating in a cover-up of a police shooting.

DeSalvo insisted that none of the SOD officers knew on September 2 that Henry Glover had been shot by a fellow cop. "I'll go to my grave believin' that, nobody knew."

"And it's just a coincidence that McRae burns a body that happens to be the one guy who was shot by a police officer?" I asked.

"As a matter of fact, it was... I could tell you more, but I can't." We had to leave it at that.

I mentioned to DeSalvo that I was interested in talking with Scheuermann and with McRae, who had only recently been released from prison. He said he would pass on the invitation, and that I might even learn something new: "Been a lot of water under the bridge since then. Not everybody likes everybody now." DeSalvo mentioned that Scheuermann, who had known McRae only briefly before September 2, 2005, had been a loyal friend to McRae in prison. But McRae's longtime commanding officer, Captain Jeff Winn, had not.

I heard nothing from either man during our last few days in New Orleans, which wasn't surprising. Why would either of them want to talk to the person who tried his very best to send them to prison? I returned home and put the idea out of my head.

Two weeks later, I was startled by a text message on my phone: Mr. Fishman, this is Dwayne Scheuermann, would you be interested in talking tomorrow?

Of the five defendants from the Glover case, I always figured that Scheuermann would be the most likely to talk to me for this book. He wasn't shy about speaking his mind. He frequently commented on the *Times-Pic* website, Nola.com, and on Facebook about policing in general, and about past allegations of misconduct against him specifically. One such post: "...[N]o apologies for anything I ever did to a violent criminal."

In another post, directed at "the cop haters," Scheuermann commented that he was "not sufficiently impressed" with their hatred "towards cops and white people." He attached a photo to "say the rest" and demonstrate "what I have done and am prepared to do." In the photo, Scheuermann aims his rifle on the Claiborne Overpass a day before Henry was killed and burned. In the foreground, some Black civilians lay on the ground, presumably taking cover in fear. Kennon McCann, an unarmed Black man, was wounded in the incident. NOPD later cleared Scheuermann and SOD Captain Jeff Winn, his partner in the shooting, after a cursory investigation.

On our video call, Scheuermann was, as ever, respectful and affable, calling me "Mr. Fishman" and bantering about how he never thought he would be chatting with me again. He seemed almost giddy to talk to me. Why, I couldn't say.

DeSalvo had told us that Scheuermann "found God" after his acquittal. I hoped that might lead to some newfound honesty on his part, but the closest I came to an admission of wrongdoing was, "I'm not claiming I was an angel as a cop." But he continued to deny that he was a part of any cover-up of the Glover shooting. I asked him if he had regrets about sitting on the information that McRae had burned the body. He said he "could have did better," though he was short on specifics.

He continued to deny, as he had at trial, that he knew McRae would burn Henry's body in advance, that it was "100 percent Greg acting spontaneously." But he also said "everyone knew" about the burning, well before the federal investigation began, all the way up the chain of command to senior leadership. But they did nothing about it. "A lot of things were pushed to the side and forgotten about."

Our conversation ended abruptly as a massive thunderstorm interrupted my internet connection. Honestly, I didn't feel we had much more to say to each other.

The person I really wanted to speak with was Greg McRae. Maybe McRae would be able, and willing, to answer the questions about the case that had troubled me for years: "How did you learn that a police officer killed Henry?" "How high did the NOPD cover-up go?" Perhaps even, "What happened to Henry's skull?"

A week later, unexpectedly, McRae called me. While the list of questions I had only grew longer over the years, I hadn't figured out how I would approach the conversation. In fifteen years of prosecuting, I had never spoken to someone after I had convicted them. All I knew for sure was that I wanted our discussion to be unlike my cross-examination at trial, which I meticulously designed to send him to prison.

I began by acknowledging the collateral damage suffered by his family. It wasn't an apology per se; I had no regrets about my efforts to hold *him* accountable. But over the years, I regularly thought about McRae's family. His wife, Gail, died of cancer while he was in prison, and their daughter, adopted at twenty-two months old from China, was raised by Gail's sister and brother-in-law. For years, I worried about what had become of his daughter.

"I think what happened to Henry Glover is really a travesty that should never happen again in America," I said. "[But] I want to let you know that I'm fully cognizant of the impact it's had on your family, and I'm sorry for that."

This wasn't a conscious interview strategy, but it seemed to put McRae at ease. "You saying that means a lot," he said, his voice cracking with emotion. "We're not enemies, believe it or not." I was relieved to learn that his daughter was doing well, a top high school student who was getting ready to go off to college.

Between May and November 2022 Greg McRae and I spoke for about six hours over video. He often fumbled with the technology, and I thought about how disorienting it must be for him to reenter the world, in the midst of a global pandemic, having been cut off from a decade's worth of technological advancements. But he pressed on. He had a lot to get off his chest.

The first time we spoke in detail about the storm, it was mostly a free association. McRae rattled off a long list of the different dead bodies he encountered during Katrina, how each had impacted him. He spoke of watching rabid dogs feed on human remains. He remembered bodies by key details like clothing or location. In some cases, he removed keepsakes to return to family members. In the end, he never found any of them.

As he had on the witness stand, McRae sometimes broke down and cried. Back then, I wondered how much of the emotion was put on for the jury's benefit. This time, I did not. As he recounted the traumatic moments from after the storm, I thought about how hard, and often successfully, I'd fought to keep this material out of open court.

One incident, which I had never heard about before, seemed particularly significant for him. In the first days after Katrina, McRae grew concerned that the generators at the area hospitals would soon run out of fuel, jeopardizing the lives of anyone on life support. (Similar fears prompted Dr. Anna Pou, Rick Simmons's former client, to allegedly euthanize severely ill or incapacitated patients.) NOPD officers had sent word to Baton Rouge to send diesel fuel immediately.

The following day, McRae spotted a diesel truck as he walked down Canal Street. He ordered some other officers to gather empty jerricans so they could quickly distribute the fuel to the hospitals, but the truck's driver wouldn't let them offload it. McRae asked why.

The diesel was reserved for the city's aquarium. Whoever made those allocation decisions had chosen to prioritize fish over humans. McRae was furious, but the truck's driver and his partner were armed with a pistol and a rifle, and seemed primed for a shootout. "If there was anyone I should have killed," he told me, "it was the driver of that truck."

From that moment on, he said, something snapped inside him. He had used every skill he possessed to save lives, he said, and not only was it not enough, but the people at the top didn't seem to care one way or the other. "That's when I knew we were on our own."

After that, McRae said, he felt the need to dispose of the bodies he encountered. He said he placed corpses in trunks. A few days later, Henry's body arrived at the compound. He insisted he had no idea this man had been shot by a fellow officer.

Had he known David Warren was the shooter, he said, he would have never protected him and would have served him up to me "on a silver platter." The 2022 McRae had no love lost for Warren. McRae had never met him until they were indicted and hadn't spoken to him at any length until they'd briefly shared a jail cell a year after their trial. According to McRae, Warren was "a coward" and "clueless." Warren was afraid of Black people and obsessed with guns and hunting. "The Bible says we were meant to be hunters," Warren once told him. "David Warren should never have been a police officer," McRae told me. On that, we could agree.

If McRae hadn't known that a cop had shot Henry, why in the world did he burn the body? I asked him if he'd ever burned a body before. No. I asked him if he ever burned things with road flares before. No. I asked him what prompted him to think about using the flares. His answer couldn't have been more matter-of-fact: "I didn't go looking for them, but I remember seeing them and having them."

McRae readily acknowledged that years of policing had desensitized him. He had a long career working in what he described as some of the "most vile, dangerous" neighborhoods in New Orleans, and he'd even been shot at multiple times. "Unfortunately, from working in that environment, you become callous." He said it got to the point where he didn't always see the people he policed as fully human. The destruction caused by Katrina only made things worse.

At some point after Henry's body arrived at Habans, McRae explained, Captain Winn told him, "Get rid of it." (At trial, McRae testified that Winn had said, "We have to get it out of here," a more benign sounding command.) Glover wasn't the only body he had, in his words, "put places," and his supervisors knew it. So when Winn told him to "get rid" of Glover's body, he understood this to mean *get rid of it so no one ever sees it again.* Burning took care of that. McRae, once again, denied telling either Scheuermann or Winn about his disposal plan beforehand, though after the fact, he said, everyone in SOD knew what had happened.

I pushed back. During our investigation, our team interviewed over fifty SOD officers, and *none* of them admitted to knowing who burned the car or the body. How could we not assume that we'd stumbled onto a massive cover-up?

He shrugged. He said that in this case, "the blue wall" of silence had less to do with paramilitary solidarity than individual officers wanting to keep their own post-Katrina skeletons hidden in the closet. There is probably *some* truth to this. But it was also evident to me that many of the officers who lied to us were acting out of loyalty and a fierce desire to "protect their own."

"I'll accept, for this moment, that *you* didn't know the police shot Henry," I told him. "But I find it hard to believe that no one else knew."

"You know about the hat, right?" he asked me, out of the blue.

I had no idea what he was talking about. "You *know* the nickname he [Captain Winn] had for me?" McRae could sense my confusion. "I'm not sure how you missed that one," he said.

McRae lifted his laptop and walked me through his house into his walk-in closet. From the top shelf, he pulled down a black hat that Winn had given him for Christmas, either in 2005 or 2006, he wasn't sure which. On the front was a skull and crossbones. The back of the hat read, *The Wolf.*

McRae said the nickname came from the film *Pulp Fiction.* After the hapless hitmen John Travolta and Samuel L. Jackson accidentally kill someone, they call on Winston "The Wolf" Wolfe (Harvey Keitel) to clean up the bloody mess left in the back seat of the car. Without asking too many questions, The Wolf makes the incriminating physical evidence disappear.

The parallels were almost too neat. "Winn saw you as the cleaner," I blurted out.

McRae pulled back a bit. He wasn't suggesting Winn knew *in advance* that he would burn the car. McRae's point, he emphasized, was that, contrary to Winn's trial testimony, the captain certainly knew immediately afterwards.

I floated the possibility that Winn and/or Scheuermann knew Henry was shot by a police officer before they ordered McRae to "get rid" of the body, and that he had been manipulated by his ranking officers. He didn't embrace the idea, but he didn't write it off either. "I'm not gonna sit here and say you're wrong. But I'm gonna disagree with you." (McRae told me that he never wore the hat.)

(Not long after, I reached out to Winn, who was fired from NOPD after the Glover case, and now works for the St. Charles Parish Sheriff's Office, for comment. I texted him: I am working on a book about the [Glover] case and would be interested in speaking to you, if you are willing. His response was brief: WTF???? His lawyer later texted me a more lawyerly declination: Unfortunately, due to various circumstances...)

It has always been hard for me to look at McRae and *not* see a guy thrown under the bus by the entire police department. He was, to be sure, responsible for the damage he had done. But in taking the fall for the entire department, he ensured that few others received their share of the blame. To what degree the events of September 2 were coordinated, or simply *just happened*, I doubt that I (or even McRae) will ever know. In a way, it is more disturbing for me to contemplate the possibility that a crime of this magnitude—the police incinerating and "disappearing" an American citizen—could have been the product of cops on autopilot and not conscious design.

It would be easy for me to see McRae as a monster. Once, I did. In law enforcement, we want to know that we got the "bad guy," as if there is such a thing as "good guys" and "bad guys." Most of the time, I don't think that's true. There are humans and there is context. Most of the people I have met who have hurt others have themselves been damaged. Trauma produces more trauma. McRae is living proof.

McRae acknowledged the harm he caused the Glovers, while giving himself a kind of out. "I'm not making excuses for myself," he said, "[but] I think I helped more people in my twenty-seven-year career than I hurt."

I wondered at some moments if I was empathizing too much with McRae. I didn't buy everything he told me, but I did believe he was trying to be forthright. He even said he'd be willing to speak to other police departments to help improve the relationship between law enforcement and communities of color. He said that if the Glover family were willing, he'd like to apologize for his actions in person even as he recognized that wasn't likely to happen.

I called Patrice Glover, whom, because of scheduling problems, we hadn't been able to see in New Orleans. Seventeen years after her brother was murdered, her emotions were still raw. "I haven't healed yet. I still cry when I talk about it." She wasn't ready to talk to McRae; she had her own trauma to work through.

What made the loss of her brother so difficult, she said, was that it was the police, the arm of the government that had pledged to serve and protect *her*, who had taken Henry, and his body, away.

"In this world we call America," she said, "how could it possibly be like that? That's the ultimate hurt, in *America*, for us to be treated like that." She was still shocked that countless officers knew what had happened to her brother, but "no one would step up."

Patrice, like everyone else, was concerned about the rising level of violence in the city, and fewer cops on the street to combat it. We don't just need more cops, she said, but more *good* cops who care about protecting her community and who are willing to work with the residents to make it safer. "Let's do it now," she said. "Too many hurt families, hurting communities, hurting loved ones."

As for her own recovery, Patrice felt she needed to talk to others who had lost loved ones to police violence. There is something uniquely horrible when it's your own government that rips out your heart, she said, and only people who had lived through it could really understand. I connected her with such a group, Families United 4 Justice, a nonprofit organization that provides support and services to families impacted by police violence.

"I think that's the cure for me."

Seventeen years after Henry's death, ten years after his killer walked free, the outlook for our society, in all too many respects, is discouraging. Our violently polarized political culture has eroded confidence in institutions that, for all of their flaws, protect us from the most severe threats to our society and our planet, be it catastrophic weather events or viral pandemics. One thing I learned from working in war zones early in my career: institutions are easy enough to destroy, but extremely difficult to repair.

Much of the problem comes back to the age-old story of Us and Them. It is, sadly, almost instinctual when we encounter people who don't think or look like us to see them as less than fully human. That's what makes it possible, under the right circumstances, for us to do the terrible things we are capable of doing to each other. It doesn't have to be this way. We all have the capacity to listen better, exercise more empathy, and define "Us" more broadly.

Coming back to New Orleans and talking with people like Linda Howard and William Tanner and Merlene Kimble gives me some grounds for hope. Three people with seemingly relatively limited influence set in motion events that transformed the city's police department, however imperfectly. I was left with the thought that if the rest of us can do what is within our power to improve the worlds we inhabit, even just a little, then collectively we can move closer to that elusive ideal of justice.

★ ★ ★ ★ ★

ACKNOWLEDGMENTS

It is impossible to achieve anything of real significance alone. I am so grateful for the many people who have helped make this book a reality.

First, to my writing-partner, Joseph Hooper. I have known from the earliest months of the investigation that I needed to tell this story. And yet I struggled for many years to put it down on paper. Thank you for dedicating so much of your life to this project, and for helping me find my voice, and for making this book a reality. I could not have done this without you.

To my agents. To Sam Stoloff, for believing in this book and persisting in getting it published, notwithstanding forty rejections. To Jody Hotchkiss, for helping ensure this story can also be told cinematically.

To our editor, Peter Joseph, thank you for recognizing the importance of this story, for bringing it to a wider audience, and for all of your advice that helped shape this book into what it is today.

To the team at Hanover Square. To Eden Railsback and Grace Towery for all your work. To Shirley Komosa for legal guidance, Emer Flounders and Kathleen Carter for publicity, and Jennifer Stimson for copyediting.

To my sisters in crime fighting, Ashley Johnson, who truly puts the "special" in Special Agent, and Tracey Knight. And to Laura Orth, who always had my back. I am grateful to have shared this experience with you. Thank you for reliving these events with me, and for all of your feedback along the way.

To Bobbi Bernstein, Forrest Christian, Frank DeSalvo, Julia Gegenheimer, Mary Hahn, Linda Howard, Mary Howell, Merlene Kimble, Jim Letten, Mike Magner, Brendan McCarthy, Greg McRae, Dwayne Scheuermann, Anthony Scott, Nina Simmons, William Tanner, A.C. Thompson, and those of you who asked to remain anonymous, for generously offering your perspectives on the events described in this book.

To my friends and colleagues at the FBI, Civil Rights Division, and the United States Attorney's Office who were a part of the teams that investigated and prosecuted these cases, and many more like these. You know who you are. These cases would not have been possible without you.

To the OWMB, for helping me process Asel's death, and for remembering his life with me. A special thank-you to Alex Berg, Ned Lazarus, Leslie Lewin, Larry Malm, Jen Marlowe, Ben Rempell, and Adam Shapiro for your feedback and support.

To the many people who offered me constructive comments at various stages of the writing process. This book is undoubtedly better because of your insights: Don Braman, Lindsay Eberts, Nick Edwards, Peter Fishman, Mary Howell, Jarvis Idowu, Ashley Kolaya, Laurie Liss, Fiona Macaulay, Ann Macaulay, AMF, Dayna Bowen Matthew, Dominique Morisseau, Rory Pulvino, David Reese, Kelli Ross, Jess Sorensen, Wendy Stiver, Matt Watkins, Joanie Weaver, and Berry Welsh.

To the many people who helped shape me into the lawyer I

am. Until recently, I wouldn't have thought to call you mentors. I simply saw you as friends who were more senior and taught me stuff. Only with time did I truly appreciate the profound impact you had on my career: Bobbi Bernstein, Mark Blumberg, Markus Funk, Gerry Hogan, Sami al-Jundi, Barry Kowalski, Jenny Lyman, Karima Maloney, Robert Moosey, Anne Olesen, Kristy Parker, John Richmond, and Brian Steel.

To my team at Justice Innovation Lab, thanks for joining me on the journey to build a more fair and effective justice system. I am grateful to work alongside you every day to bend the arc of the universe towards justice.

To my parents. Thank you for ensuring that I never doubted that I was loved. Mom, I am so sorry that you are not here to read this book. I hope you know, wherever you are, that I am working every day to make the world a better place. Dad, thank you for your support as I found my way, for opening up a world of possibilities to me, and for your willingness to grow alongside me.

To A and J, thanks for supporting me and showering me with love. My life is richer with you in it. Thank you for reminding me every day why I continue to do this work.

And finally, to Fiona. Thank you for being my partner in life for the last twenty years. You have helped me broaden my perspective, imagine new possibilities, and become a better version of myself. Thank you for being by my side during the most intense moments of my career, and for holding down the fort while I was away on the road, even as you juggled your own impressive career. Thank you for helping me tell our story. And thank you for being my partner in raising two of the most wonderful human beings I know. I love you.

Jared Fishman

Deepest thanks to my friend Jared Fishman for inviting me to share this venture with him. On the page, we complemented each other almost uncannily well. Off the page, we did pretty well too.

Also, thanks to our editor, Peter Joseph, at Hanover Square

who had the imagination to see what *Fire on the Levee* could be and to the Hanover Square/Harlequin team that helped bring it into being, especially Eden Railsback for her tireless eleventh-hour editorial support. And thanks to my agent, Linda Loewenthal, who has helped guide my (somewhat sporadic) book career for more years than I care to count, and to Sam Stoloff, *Fire on the Levee*'s dedicated lead agent. And, finally, thanks to John Colapinto, Ben Dickinson, Bill Doyle, Michael Doyle, Kate Doyle Hooper, Peggy O'Neal, and John Thackary who, in different ways, made this book possible for me.

Joseph Hooper

ENDNOTES

Unless otherwise noted, the direct quotes in chapters 2–5, 7, 8, and 10 are taken verbatim from the court transcripts of the two Henry Glover trials: United States District Court, Eastern District of Louisiana, November 8–December 9, 2010 and December 4–10, 2013. According to the author's best recollection, these quotes are very similar to what was said in earlier investigation interviews, although no records exist to document their precise wording.

Unless otherwise noted, the direct quotes in chapters 13–21 are taken verbatim from the court transcript of the first Glover trial.

Unless otherwise noted, the direct quotes in chapter 22 are taken verbatim from the court transcript of the Raymond Robair trial, United States District Court, Eastern District of Louisiana, April 4–13, 2011.

Unless otherwise noted, the direct quotes in chapter 23 are taken verbatim from the court transcript of the second Glover trial.

PROLOGUE

1 "...I want you to know..." AP video footage of the September 2, 2005 helicopter trip taken by President Bush, Governor Blanco, and Mayor Nagin, and Bush's remarks at the New Orleans airport afterwards, found at: https://www.youtube.com/watch?v=it3Kx7TJLq0 An evocative journalistic account of Bush's tour that day provided by then *Newsweek* White House Correspondent Holly Bailey in a *Yahoo! News* article, "What I saw visiting post-Katrina New Orleans with President Bush," August 26, 2015.

2 "...that had warehoused..." Various estimates of the size of the population taking refuge inside the New Orleans Superdome have been advanced; in the immediate aftermath of the disaster, 20,000 was the number frequently cited, see: *New York Times*, "Superdome: Haven Quickly Becomes an Ordeal" by Joseph B. Treaster, September 1, 2005. But more recent accounts have put the figure at 30,000. See PBS *Frontline*, "Law & Disorder" interview with former governor Kathleen Blanco, June 10, 2010: https://www.pbs.org/wgbh/pages/frontline/law-disorder/interviews/blanco.html Also: *USA TODAY*, "Refuge of last resort: Five days inside the Superdome for Hurricane Katrina" by Nate Scott, August 24, 2015.

3 "...walking around like zombies..." New Orleans Police Department recorded interview with officer Linda Howard, April 18, 2009.

4 "...know how to shoot and kill..." PBS *Frontline*, "Law & Disorder," August 25, 2010, includes video footage of Governor Blanco making this statement to the press.

CHAPTER 1

1 "...a recently published article from *The Nation*..." *The Nation*, "Body of Evidence" by A.C. Thompson, December 17, 2008.

2 "(The old-fashioned-sounding term first shows up..." *Michigan Law Review*, "The Meaning of 'Under Color of' Law," Vol. 91, Issue 3, 1992.

3 "But as the pathologist told Thompson..." Video interview with Dr. Kevin Whaley, PBS *Frontline*, "Law & Disorder," August 25, 2010.

4 "Why don't you come on down?" Author's best recollection of the phone conversation.

CHAPTER 2

1 "You can call me Jared…" Author's best recollection of the conversation.

2 "If you live in a predominantly White area…" *Los Angeles Times*, "Sheriff Rescinds Order to Stop Blacks in White Areas," by J. Michael Kennedy, December 4, 1986.

3 "…they started beating on me…" The two NOPD officers prosecuted for physically abusing the detainees at the Habans School, Dwayne Scheuermann and Greg McRae, were found not guilty of those charges in the Glover trial.

4 "In lieu of recordings…" The FBI's reliance on written 302 memos, instead of recorded interviews, is discussed on this website, Grand Jury Target: Tracking Key Issues in White Collar Prosecutions, "What is an FBI 302? The Problematic Nature of FBI Agents' Interview Memos" by Sara Kropf, May 18, 2017: https://grandjurytarget.com/2017/05/18/what-is-an-fbi-302-the-problematic-nature-of-fbi-agents-interview-memos/

5 "(Black New Orleanians have marched in the streets on Mardi Gras…" There are many good histories of the Mardi Gras Indians, including the following: https://mardigrasneworleans.com, "Mardi Gras Indians History and Tradition"; Curbed New Orleans, "Super Sunday 2019: The history behind Mardi Gras Indian tradition and culture" by Eric Craig, March 16, 2017: https://nola.curbed.com/2017/3/16/14937428/super-sunday-mardi-gras-indian-tradition-history-culture

   New Orleans civil rights attorney Mary Howell also provided context and detail.

6 "I never heard back." Edna Glover's quotes are the author's best recollection of what was said.

7 "I was excited I had a job…" Patrice Glover quotes about her family memories from December 18, 2020 interview. According to the author's best

recollection, they are similar to what she told him and Ashley Johnson during their first meeting in February 2009.

8 "...I couldn't get any answers..." Patrice Glover interview December 18, 2020.

9 "'Momma, what's going on?'" Patrice Glover's memories of the "Algiers 7" police assault on the Fischer Projects, December 18, 2020 interview.

10 "The so-called Algiers 7 case was grotesque..." Sources include a comprehensive article by Brendan McCarthy, NOLA.com, "Infamous Algiers 7 police brutality case of 1980 has parallels to today," November 7, 2010: https://www.nola.com/news/crime_police/article_e292c330-498e-556c-a05a-743766901be0.html

   Also see: *The New York Times Magazine*, "The Thinnest Blue Line," by Paul Keegan, March 31, 1996; US Department of Justice, Office of Justice Programs, "Shielded from Justice: Accountability in the United States," 1998; PBS *Frontline*, "Law & Disorder," transcript of November 23, 2009 interview with Mary Howell: https://www.pbs.org/wgbh/pages/frontline/law-disorder/interviews/howell.html

   Also, authors' interviews with Mary Howell, July 15, 2019 and April 26, 2022.

   For a detailed historical overview of policing in New Orleans, from Spanish colonial times through 1983, see: https://nolacrimereport.files.wordpress.com/2017/08/history-of-the-new-orleans-police-department-1984.pdf

11 "A federal appeals court..." The summary by the Fifth Circuit Court of Appeals is quoted in an obituary of Otis Buckner III, an NOPD whistleblower who helped call attention to the police abuses, published in AP News, "Ex-New Orleans officer dies, whistleblower against brutality," June 6, 2022: https://apnews.com/article/houston-new-orleans-algiers-africa-police-brutality-ac5090420ae69b4bc0f5e722fb742bfa; *United States of America v. John E. Mckenzie, Dale Bonura and Stephen Farrar*, 768 F.2d 602 (5th Cir. 1985).

12 "...the city was roiled by the killing of Adolph Archie..." Sources include: *The New York Times*, "In America; Disgracing the Badge," by Bob Herbert, September 18, 1995; US Department of Justice, Office of Justice Programs, "Shielded from Justice: Accountability in the United

States," 1998; PBS *Frontline*, "Law & Disorder," August 25, 2010, transcript of November 23, 2009, interview with Mary Howell online; and the author's more recent conversations with Howell.

13 "It seemed unfathomable to me that a person could be jailed for owing the government money." For a full discussion of punitive court-related fines and fees, see: Brennan Center for Justice, "Fines & Fee" online. Also: United States Department of Justice, Civil Rights Division, "Investigation of the Ferguson [Missouri] Police Department," March 4, 2015. Source for Gretna, Louisiana's use of fines and fees: NOLA.com, "Gretna is the 'arrest capital' of the U.S. website says," July 19, 2019. The article reports the findings of a study by the website Fusion which, using FBI statistics, found that Gretna makes slightly more than one arrest per citizen.

14 "Last time I saw my brother..." The Edward King quotes in this chapter concerning the events of September 2, 2005 and their impact are from a PBS *Frontline*, "Law & Disorder," August 25, 2010 video interview by A.C. Thompson. The author's best recollection is that King used similar language when he and Ashley Johnson interviewed him in jail in February 2005.

15 "He beat me good..." Edward King did not testify in the Glover trial but the jury found Lieutenant Dwayne Scheuermann not guilty on charges of physically abusing the two Habans School detainees who did testify: William Tanner and Bernard Calloway.

16 "I can't believe you're here." Author's best recollection of King's response.

17 "...a light bulb kind of went on..." Interview with Ashley Johnson, June 9, 2019.

18 "When it's the police who do this to you..." Author's best recollection of the exchange.

CHAPTER 3

1 "You have to understand what it was like..." The conversation with the anonymous SOD officer is according to the author's best recollection.

2 "[W]e didn't know what day it was..." Quote is from the testimony of NOPD Sergeant Purnella Simmons at trial, November 19, 2010. According to the author's best recollection, she shared similar Katrina memories during their initial interviews in 2009.

3 "...like a parent would give a child..." Ashley Johnson interview, July 26, 2020.

4 "He didn't tell me anything about them." This exchange between the author and Ashley Johnson is according to the author's best recollection.

CHAPTER 4

1 "We asked about the report..." Robert Italiano testified in the Glover trial, December 1–2, 2010 that he meant to convey to FBI agent Ashley Johnson that in the months that followed Katrina the department was only writing up reports for serious crimes and the discharge of an officer's weapon did not rise to that level. He also testified that he remembered that he had signed off on a report concerning David Warren's firearm discharge only after his meeting with the FBI. He maintained at trial that he never saw the Henry Glover missing persons report. The jury found Italiano not guilty on charges of obstruction of justice and lying to the FBI.

2 "...these were not 'normal times.'" Robert Italiano's quote fragment and the assertions he makes about the events of September 2, 2005 during the meeting at the FBI are found in his testimony in the Glover trial, December 1–2, 2010.

3 "The Division was created as a part of..." A good overview is provided by the United States Department of Justice website, justice.gov, "About the Division." For a historical perspective, see justice.gov, "The Department of Justice's Civil Rights Division: A Historical Perspective as The Division Nears 50," March 22, 2006.

4 "...'You ain't got to do him like that.'" Bernard Calloway's account of the beating at Habans School is disputed by SOD officers Dwayne Scheuermann and Greg McRae whom a jury found not guilty of these abuse charges.

5 "I knew his mind wasn't going to be right..." Author interview with Patrice Glover, February 11, 2021.

6 "Everybody looked like a shadow..." From NOPD Detective Sergeant Gerard Dugue's recorded interview with Officer Linda Howard, April 18, 2009. She expressed herself similarly to the author and Ashley Johnson during their April 2009 interview, according to the author's best recollection.

7 "She kept her eyes on the two men running." At trial, David Warren disputed his partner Linda Howard's account. He testified that she was not in a position to see the shooting or the man, Henry Glover, who was shot at. He testified that he shot Glover as he was rushing towards them, not in the back, as Howard asserted. Howard's recorded interview with NOPD Detective Sergeant Gerard Dugue is ambiguous on these points.

8 "...blocked by a locked gate that separated the mall from the lot." David Warren testified, contrary to Linda Howard's assertion, that the gate was not locked.

9 "'He asked me if it was a good shooting.'" Robert Italiano testified at trial that he had little or no recollection of speaking with Officer Howard the evening of September 2, but that he would never have asked her, or any officer, to draw a conclusion about justifiability of an officer firing his weapon.

CHAPTER 5

1 "I went through the breezeway..." Gerard Dugue recorded interview with Linda Howard, April 18, 2009

2 "...or smelling a scent can trigger recall..." Sources: "Memory for Emotional Events" by Jonathan W. Schooler & Eric Eich, Psychological and Brain Sciences, UC Santa Barbara; "The Return of the Repressed: The Persistent and Problematic Claims of Long-Forgotten Trauma," Elizabeth Loftus et al., *Perspectives on Psychological Science*, October 4, 2019.

3 "The report was classified as a Signal 21..." NOPD Report, December 2, 2005, for Police Discharge of Firearm on September 2, 2005.

4 Typically, grand jury testimony remains secret. However, when Sergeant Simmons testified at trial, she was impeached by the defense with the portions of her grand jury testimony that are discussed in this chapter. The content of her grand jury testimony was discussed at length in multiple court proceedings.

5 "...a .45 bullet struck Thomas's head..." Sources: *The Times-Picayune*, "Hurricane Katrina aftermath shooting of police officer described," Gwen Filosa, January 15, 2010 and "Orleans jury convicts one man, frees other in cop shooting," Gwen Filosa, January 16, 2010; NOLA.com, "Man convicted of shooting NOPD officer is sentenced to 35 years," Paul Purpura, March 11, 2011. For a skeptical take on the jury verdict in the Thomas case, see the website: jamiljoyner.net/trial-summary.

6 "I got it from Italiano." The direct quotes attributed to Travis McCabe interview are Ashley Johnson's best recollection of the late 2009 interview, backed up by her near-contemporaneous notes. The quotes are taken verbatim from Johnson's testimony at the Glover trial, November 23, 2010.

CHAPTER 6

1 "...I'm probably one of two Black people there..." Ashley Johnson interview September 4, 2020.

2 "She is very proper..." Ashley Johnson's recollections about childhood, family and the importance of the Church in her life, from March 10, 2021 interview.

3 "...to make split-second judgments..." From 1989 Supreme Court case, *Graham v. Connor*, 490 U.S. 386 supreme.justia.com/cases/federal/us/490/386/

4 "...when you absolutely, positively need to kill someone..." *The Boston Phoenix*, "The New Hampshire seminar to take when you absolutely, positively need to kill someone tomorrow," Chris Wright, November–December 2, 1999.

5 "...249 officers walked off the job..." Wave website, "Police Chief: 249 New Orleans Officers Left Posts Without Permission During Katrina,"

September 27, 2005: https://www.wave3.com/story/3904630/police-chief-249-new-orleans-officers-left-posts-without-permission-during-katrina/

6 "By any chance were you White in 2005?" Author's best recollection of Ashley Johnson's comment.

7 "...guilty of something, even if we didn't catch them this time." Author's best recollection of Alec Brown's paraphrase of his NOPD colleague's policing philosophy.

8 "Police need to stick together..." Travis McCabe testified at trial that he never said this to Alec Brown nor that Brown should ignore the burned body by the levee. The jury found McCabe guilty of obstruction of justice, lying to the FBI and perjury. However, Judge Africk subsequently vacated his sentence and McCabe was never retried.

9 "...looters 'were all animals...'" David Warren testified at trial that, contrary to Alec Brown's testimony, he never told him that looters were animals who deserved to be shot.

10 "...ushering in a period known as the Second (or *Al-Aqsa*) Intifada." For two very different perspectives on the Israel-Palestine conflict, see jewishvirtuallibrary.org/background-and-overview-of-al-aqsa-intifada and palestineonline.org/al-aqsa-intifada/, also palquest.org/en/overallchronology?sideid=6526

   Also of note: The Second Intifada, 20 Years On: Thousands Died in a Struggle That Failed by Gideon Levy, Haaretz, September 26, 2020. Available at The Second Intifada, 20 Years On: Thousands Died in a Struggle That Failed - Israel News - Haaretz.com: https://www.haaretz.com/israel-news/2020-09-26/ty-article-magazine/.premium/the-second-intifada-20-years-on-thousands-died-in-a-struggle-that-failed/0000017f-dc6f-d856-a37f-fdef7f110000

11 "Sami was a Palestinian..." Sami al Jundi wrote a highly recommended memoir describing his evolution from political prisoner to non-violent political activist, *The Hour of Sunlight: One Palestinian's Journey from Prisoner to Peacemaker* by Sami al Jundi and Jen Marlowe, Bold Type Books, 2011.

12 "Amnesty International estimated that at least 80 percent…" Amnesty International, "Israel and the Occupied Territories: Broken lives—a year of intifada," November 13, 2001.

13 "He was like an observer, or a journalist…" Seeds of Peace, "Ned Lazarus Diary No. 5" *Slate*, November 9, 2001: https://www.seedsofpeace.org/page/126/?history

14 "The Or Commission concluded, 'The police reaction…'" Haaretz.com, "The official summation of the Or Commission report," February 9, 2003.

15 "I don't think they shot him for no reason." Author's best recollection of what the Seeds of Peace teenager said.

CHAPTER 7

1 "…best-guess reconstruction of the letters…" At trial, Dwayne Scheuermann testified that, contrary to Bernard Calloway's testimony, he was not wearing any clothing with stitched letters on it the morning of September 2, 2005.

2 "But that productivity came with a price…" Sources include: *The Times-Picayune*, "Indicted New Orleans police lieutenant with history of abuse allegations was never flagged for intervention" by Brendan McCarthy and A.C. Thompson, October 24, 2010: https://www.nola.com/news/crime_police/article_058b785f-88ae-58ca-88eb-871d1ba91ffa.html. And for more detail: *ProPublica*, "Some of the Complaints Levied Against Lt. Dwayne Scheuermann" by McCarthy and Thompson, October 24, 2010: https://www.propublica.org/article/some-the-complaints-levied-against-lt-dwayne-scheuermann Background information and context provided by Mary Howell, July 15, 2019, interview.

3 "…whereas most cops never fire their guns in their entire careers." Pew Research Center, "A closer look at police officers who fired their weapon on duty," Rich Morin and Andrew Mercer, February 8, 2017.

4 "In a PBS *Frontline* report that aired…" *Frontline* "Law & Disorder," by Brendan McCarthy and A.C. Thompson, August 25, 2010.

5   "A New Orleans blog that covered…" "NOPD versus Hurricane Katrina," a blog post written by retired law enforcement officer Charles "Chuck" Hustmyre, now a screenwriter and prolific true-crime author; see: chuck-hustymre.com The blog post no longer seems to be available online.

6   "DeSalvo commented in print…" NOLA.com, "New Orleans police lawyers think FBI should butt out of some cases" by Jarvis DeBerry, April 20, 2010: https://www.nola.com/opinions/article_ac78ed3e-f7f1-5483-bcb4-44bf4f9656f0.html

7   "…clear all of the NOPD officers…" NOLA.com, "FBI looks at cases involving New Orleans Police Department officers" by Laura Maggi, June 2, 2009: https://www.nola.com/news/article_29a83f52-d181-5285-a873-162f79d02ae5.html

8   "SOD, like similar SWAT units…" A comprehensive account is *Rise of the Warrior Cop: The Militarization of America's Police Force* by Radley Balko, Public Affairs, 2014. Balko, a veteran journalist, now posts on Substack: radleybalkosubstack.com

9   "We met him in a fast-food restaurant…" The exchanges with this anonymous NOPD officer, here and elsewhere in this chapter, are the author's best recollection of the conversations.

10 "…a reason to trust you…" Ashley Johnson's observations about her interviewing style and her experiences as a social worker in a psychiatric unit from March 10, 2021 interview.

11 "…as a 'legend,' noting 'a gnawing sense of anxiety…'" NOLA.com, "Federal probe digs deeper into NOPD's actions after Hurricane Katrina" by Brendan McCarthy, September 7, 2009: https://www.nola.com/news/crime_police/article_22d7870a-ac0b-5a10-8be5-a901daacbc6a.html

12 "…we could be the 2009 Charlie's Angels." From an Ashley Johnson email to the author.

13 "But by the '90s, the department had added…" A scrupulous account of the hiring practices of the NOPD and the police abuse scandals of the '90s is provided in *Black Rage in New Orleans: Police Brutality and African American Activism from World War II to Hurricane Katrina* by Leonard

N. Moore, Louisiana State Press, 2010. For a more popular account, see: *Murder Behind the Badge: True Stories of Cops Who Kill* by Stacy Dittrich, Prometheus Books 2010, Chapter 9: Evil in Blue—Antoinette Frank and Chapter 14: She Filed a Complaint, So He Killed Her—Len Davis. See also: *Killer With a Badge* by Chuck Hustmyre iUniverse 2004, a full recounting of the Antoinette Frank story. Journalistic accounts include: *The New York Times Magazine*, "The Thinnest Blue Line," by Paul Keegan, March 31, 1996.

14 The "want less crime" quote is from Dittrich, *Murder Behind the Badge*.

15 "We had police officers doing bank robberies…" Mary Howell video interview, PBS *Frontline*, "Law & Disorder," August 25, 2010. Howell is, in the author's opinion, a highly reliable resource for NOPD history. She provided invaluable details and context over the course of researching this book, in several interviews, shorter conversations, and email exchanges.

16 "The personification of the NOPD officer…" The Len Davis story is recounted in the sources already listed covering NOPD scandals in the '90s.

17 "…the story of Antoinette Franks, a young Black female officer…" The Connie Vu quote is included in both the Chuck Hustmyre and the Stacy Dittrich books.

18 "That could be you down the road." Ashley Johnson interview, March 10, 2021.

19 "Between you and the dead guy…" The author's best recollection of Ashley Johnson's remark.

20 "I think we've been called worse things…" Author's best recollection of his exchange with the anonymous SOD officer.

21 "What's our strategy?" Author's best recollection of the exchange between him and Ashley Johnson.

CHAPTER 8

1 "Abbott climbed to his attic to escape…" This account of Abbott's harrowing escape from his flooded house is included in the estimable *The*

Great Deluge: Hurricane Katrina, New Orleans, and the Mississippi Gulf Coast by Douglas Brinkley, HarperCollins, 2006, pp. 138–141.

2 "...but within a day he was back on the job..." "NOPD versus Hurricane Katrina" blog post, Charles "Chuck" Hustmyre.

3 "In 1998, he was patrolling..." Sources for all three incidents when Abbott was shot, including the trial of Brandy Jefferson: NOLA.com, "New Orleans policeman shot in the leg while working detail Uptown; officer had been shot previously" by Ramon Antonio-Vargas, July 24, 2017. Also "NOPD officer struck by 6 bullets in 3 shootings finds new calling" by Mike Perlstein, February 14, 2019: www.wwltv.com/article/news/investigations/mike-perlstein/nopd-office-struck-by-6-bullets-in-3-shootings-finds-new-calling/289-a1cc0f13-e754-41ee-8336-7d8016d29c12 For more detail on the Jefferson case, see the case law document: https://case-law.vlex.com/vid/state-v-jefferson-no-889885258

4 "...working as an officer peer support counselor." 4WWL-TV.com, "NOPD officer struck by 6 bullets in 3 shootings finds new calling" by Mike Perlstein, February 14, 2019: www.wwltv.com/article/news/investigations/mike-perlstein/nopd-office-struck-by-6-bullets-in-3-shootings-finds-new-calling/289-a1cc0f13-e754-41ee-8336-7d8016d29c12

5 "...the officer was found not guilty of malfeasance..." NOLA.com, "Prosecutors compare case of NOPD dog that died to Danziger Bridge, Glover cases" by Claire Garofaro, February 2, 2013.

6 "...in the vicinity of the Maurepas Swamp Wildlife Management Area..." The Conservation Fund: https://conservationfund.org/projects/maurepas-swamp-wildlife-management-area and Cajun Pride Swamp Tours: cajun-prideswamptours.com

7 "...score of seedy, barely veiled sex parlors..." NOLA.com, "Erotic massage parlors retain strong foothold in New Orleans, as police focus dwindling resources elsewhere" by Jim Mustian, December 1, 2015: https://www.nola.com/news/erotic-massage-parlors-retain-strong-foothold-in-new-orleans-as-police-focus-dwindling-resources-elsewhere/article_42f15b3c-f0ac-5d2b-a7d6-460746e43c95.html

8 "... Burns and five other men...entered the spa." Best source is the

case "plea document," under the section called "the factual basis," Case 2:06-CR-203-EEF-DEK. This requires a specialized "Pacer" account to bring up online.

9 "...grabbed one of the men by the shirt..." Sergeant Sandoz disputed Joshua Burns's testimony. Sandoz testified that he never struck any of the detainees at Habans.

10 "Burns saw Italiano and Scheuermann walk away..." At trial, both Italiano and Scheuermann testified that they had no specific recollection of having a private conversation with each other but that it could have happened.

CHAPTER 9

1 "...but rather a video taken by a retired corrections officer..." *ProPublica*, "New Evidence Surfaces in Post-Katrina Crimes" by A.C. Thompson, July 10, 2009.

2 "We found this completely burned-out vehicle." About a minute of Istvan Balogh's video footage, including his quoted narration, was shown on PBS *Frontline*, "Law & Disorder," August 25, 2010.

3 "The magnitude of the way..." Video interview, Istvan Balogh, PBS *Frontline*, "Law and Disorder," August 25, 2010.

4 A good starting point to explore the theme of photography and death is *On Photography* by Susan Sontag, Picador/Farrar, Straus and Giroux, 1973, her classic meditation on the morality of photography. Her second book on photography is notable for its focus on suffering, *Regarding the Pain of Others*, Picador/FSG 2003. It includes the memorable line: "Ever since cameras were invented in 1839, photography has kept company with death." Another good source: *Photography and Death: Framing Death throughout History* by Racheal Harris, Emerald Publishing 2020.

5 "Photography played a prominent role in the extrajudicial executions..." *Photography and Death: Framing Death throughout History* provides a useful history and analysis in Chapter 4: "Violence: The Lynching Photograph."

6 "...most famously the photograph that ran in *Jet*..." See *Time*, "When One Mother Defied America: The Photo That Changed the Civil Rights Movement," July 10, 2016. Also, UMBC's Online Exhibition, "The Power of a Photograph: The Lynching of Emmett Till": https://fatwts. umbc.edu/the-power-of-a-photograph-the-lynching-of-emmett-till/

7 For a trenchant discussion of the legacy of lynching, its outsize place in Black memory and as an object of White amnesia, see *On the Courthouse Lawn: Confronting the Legacy of Lynching in the 21st Century* by Sherrilyn A. Ifill, Beacon Press, 2007.

8 "One of the greatest predictors of 'adverse events'..." CCJ Task Force on Policing, "Officer Wellness Policy Assessment," May 2021: https://counciloncj.foleon.com/policing/assessing-the-evidence/xiv-officer-wellness/

9 "Fuck it, he is dead..." This representation of the temporary FBI agent's disturbing encounter with the NOPD SOD officer is the author's best recollection of the events.

10 "..Haitian emigres first brought the seeds of vodoun..." Interview with Grete Viddal, PhD, New Orleans anthropologist and vodoun scholar, December 3, 2022

11 "Did you hear they found a car..." The conversations with the anonymous Fourth District officer are the author's best recollection of what was said.

12 "...(the images of dead soldiers..." For a discussion of staged photographs of battlefield dead, most famously by Mathew Brady's team during the Civil War, see *Regarding the Pain of Others* by Susan Sontag and *Photography and Death: Framing Death throughout History* by Racheal Harris.

13 "Was he shot, was he hit on the head..." Video interview, Dr. Frank Minyard, PBS *Frontline*, "Law and Disorder," August 25, 2010.

14 "...she personally performed about 155 autopsies..." Testimony of Dr. Dana Troxclair, Glover trial, November 18, 2010.

15 "...double what the National Association of Medical Examiners...": https://www.thename.org/

16 "When I heard he was found..." Video interview, Dr. Kevin Whaley,
PBS *Frontline*, "Law and Disorder," August 25, 2010.

CHAPTER 10

1 "Ruiz, like Josh Burns before him, confirmed..." Again, Italiano and
Scheuermann each testified that they had no specific recollection of having a private conversation with each other but that it could have happened.

2 "...like driving off a cliff..." According to the author's best recollection,
Meisch used this expression during investigation interviews.

3 "'It's all right. I'm handling it.'..." Dwayne Scheuermann's testimony at
trial is somewhat different than Meisch's account. Scheuermann testified
that he told Meisch that "we" will handle it later. He denied taking sole
responsibility for the burning car.

4 "Did you know, we are under martial law?" David Warren testified at
trial, contrary to Linda Howard's testimony, that he never mentioned
martial law to her. Alec Brown makes the same assertion at trial, which
Warren also denies.

5 "...as a member of that first generation of Black women..." Sources on the
racial politics of the NOPD include: *The New York Times Magazine*, "The
Thinnest Blue Line," by Paul Keegan, March 31, 1996; US Department of
Justice, Office of Justice Programs, "Shielded from Justice: Accountability
in the United States," 1998; PBS *Frontline*, "Law & Disorder," August 25,
2010, transcripts of interviews with Mary Howell and with David Benelli,
retired NOPD lieutenant and former president of the police union PANO,
available online; *Murder Behind the Badge: True Stories of Cops Who Kill* by
Stacy Dittrich, Prometheus Books 2010; *Killer With a Badge* by Chuck Hustmyre, iUniverse 2004.

6 Ashley Johnson and Tracey Knight's observations about Linda Howard
and NOPD racial politics from interview with Johnson and Knight, August 19, 2020.

7 "I lived in Algiers..." From interview with Tracey Knight, April 27, 2021.

8 "...an estimated 1.5 million gallons of crude oil..." The National Oceanic

and Atmospheric Administration's executive summary puts the amount of oil spilled at 134 million gallons over a period of 87 days, which comes to approximately 1.5 million gallons per day. https://www.gulfspillrestoration. noaa.gov/wp-content/uploads/Chapter-2_Incident-Overview_508.pdf

CHAPTER 11

1 "Moreover, there is ample research…" US Department of Justice, Office of Justice Programs, National Institute of Justice, "Five Things About Deterrence," https://www.ojp.gov/pdffiles1/nij/247350.pdf; University of Michigan Law School Scholarship Repository, "Racial Disparity in Federal Criminal Sentencing" by M. Marit Rehavi and Sonja B. Starr, 2014, https://repository.law.umich.edu/cgi/viewcontent.cgi?article=24 13&context=articles; FAMM, Families for Justice Reform, "The Case against Mandatory Minimum Sentences," https://famm.org/wp-content/ uploads/The-Case-against-Mandatory-Minimum-Sentences.pdf

2 "…NOPD officers responded to a call…" The author drew on a handful of conversations with Mary Howell, who represented the Madison family, victimized in the Danziger Bridge shootings, and with Forrest Christian and Bobbi Bernstein, Department of Justice prosecutors, who worked on the federal prosecution of the case. The entire story of the Danziger episode, including the legal battles that ensued, is told with admirable clarity and style in *Shots on the Bridge: Police Violence and Cover-Up in the Wake of Katrina* by journalist Ronnie Greene, Beacon Press, 2015.

3 "Detective Jeffrey Lehrmann, one of the first officers to cooperate…" Lehrmann accepted a plea deal in return for a reduced sentence.

4 "Detective Dugue was accused of playing a key role in this cover-up." Dugue ultimately accepted a plea deal, in 2016, for his role in the Danziger cover-up and received a sentence of one year probation.

5 "…you're covering it up for them." From interview with Ashley Johnson, April 6, 2021.

6 "…approximately 10 million arrestees…" An excellent single source for arrest and incarceration statistics and analysis is: Prison Policy Initiative, "Mass Incarceration: The Whole Pie 2022" by Wendy Sawyer and Peter Wagner, March 14, 2022: prisonpolicy.org/reports/pie2022.html

7   "Every one of them faces detention hearings." Recognizing that bail often results in low-income people being jailed even though they may pose no risk, many states have eliminated cash bail in recent years. However, each defendant has a hearing to determine whether they will be released pending trial or detained as a "risk of flight" or "danger to the community."

8   "...obscure right-wing Christian radio show..." NOLA.com, "Attorney for the ex-N.O. cop: Others killed Glover" by Brendan McCarthy, June 28, 2010.

9   "...God is always politically correct." The direct quotes from "Politically Correct" are from a transcript of the June 24, 2010 episode, no longer available online.

10 "...not the best decisions that were made..." Frank DeSalvo's quotes are verbatim from the court's Conflict of Interest hearing, April 21, 2010.

CHAPTER 12

1   "...'a quantity of Officer Thomas's brain cells...'" From prosecution court filing, Government's Response Regarding the Admissibility of (1) The Conditions in Orleans Parish Following Hurricane Katrina and (2) Specific Incidents Affecting Defendants' State of Mind, footnote 4.

2   "I may have said..." PBS *Frontline*, "Law & Disorder," August 25, 2010 and *ProPublica*, "After Katrina, New Orleans Cops Were Told They Could Shoot Looters" by Sabrina Shankman, Tom Jennings, Brendan McCarthy, Laura Maggi, and A.C. Thompson, July 24, 2012.

3   "In a radio interview..." PBS *Frontline*, "Law & Disorder" includes a recording of Nagin making that assertion in a radio interview.

4   "These troops know how to shoot and kill..." PBS *Frontline*, "Law & Disorder," August 25, 2010.

5   "...exceeded 40,000.)" PBS *Frontline*, "Law & Disorder," interview with former governor Kathleen Blanco, June 10, 2010. Douglas Brinkley, in *The Great Deluge*, asserts that the 40,000 troops that Blanco asked for "proved an accurate assessment of the troop strength needed," p. 413.

6 "Rwanda was home to perhaps..." The best book, in the author's opinion, on the Rwandan genocide, is *We Wish to Inform You That Tomorrow
You Will Be Killed with Our Families: Stories from Rwanda* by Philip Goure-
vitch, Farrar, Straus and Giroux, 1999. Two good sources on the Rwandan "gacaca" judicial process are: BBC News, "Rwanda 'gacaca' genocide
courts finish work," June 18, 2012, and Africa Research Institute, "How
Rwanda judged its genocide," Phil Clark, May 2, 2012: https://www.
africaresearchinstitute.org/newsite/publications/how-rwanda-judged-
its-genocide-new/

7 "Get back before I shoot your Black ass." Quoted in the prosecution's
motion to introduce evidence of Officer Greg McRae's alleged prior
bad acts, "Notice of Intention to Offer 404(b) Evidence," filed with the
Court on September 1, 2010.

8 "You don't think so?" This is the author's best recollection of his conversation with Tracey Knight.

9 "...saw firsthand the high volume..." A good source for on-point statistics is: D.C.gov, District of Columbia Sentencing Commission, 2021 An-
nual Report—SCDC: https://scdc.dc.gov/node/1593206. According to
the report, in DC, 94 percent of people sentenced for felonies are Black,
and more than half are Black men aged eighteen to thirty.

10 "Recent research suggests the opposite..." A telling analysis of misdemeanor prosecutions in Suffolk County, Massachusetts, is: SSRN,
"Misdemeanor Prosecution" by Amanda Agan, Jennifer L. Doleac, and
Anna Harvey, August 26, 2022: https://papers.ssrn.com/sol3/papers.
cfm?abstract_id=3814854

11 "I don't think I could have..." ACLU District of Columbia, "Racial Disparities in Stops by the Metropolitan Police Department: 2020
Data Update": https://www.acludc.org/en/racial-disparities-stops-
metropolitan-police-department-2020-data-update According to this
analysis, in DC, Black people experience more than 90 percent of the
searches that lead to no warning, ticket or arrest.

12 "...are seven times more likely..." National Registry of Exonerations,
"Race and Wrongful Convictions in the United States 2022," September 2022.

13 "...are 2.5 times more likely..." *PNAS*, "Risk of being killed by po-
    lice use-of-force in the U.S. by age, race/ethnicity, and sex" by Frank
    Edwards, Hedwig Lee, and Michael Esposito, August 2, 2019: https://
    www.prisonpolicy.org/scans/police_mort_open.pdf

14 "...comment to Officer Brown that looters 'deserve to be shot.'" David
    Warren testified that he did not make such a comment to Brown.

15 "...federal hate crimes require proof..." *United States v. Mullet, et al.*,
    822 F.3d 842 (6th Cir. 2016): https://cases.justia.com/federal/appellate-
    courts/ca6/15-3212/15-3212-2016-05-04.pdf?ts=1462379451

16 "...more complicated, and subtle, forms of racial bias." *The Color of Law:
    A Forgotten History of How Our Government Segregated America*, by Rich-
    ard Rothstein, Liveright, 2017.

17 "Algiers Point, where the Glover family decamped..." New Orleans
    Historical, "African Presence in Algiers" by Ann Cobb, February 7,
    2020: https://neworleanshistorical.org/items/show/1589

18 "The earliest policing structures..." *The New Yorker*, "The Invention of
    the Police" by Jill Lepore, July 13, 2020.

19 "...conduct such as walking 'without purpose'..." Vera, a national ad-
    vocacy and research group working to end mass incarceration, by Kica
    Matos and Jamila Hodge, June 17, 2021, "The Chains of Slavery Still
    Exist in Mass Incarceration": https://www.vera.org/news/the-chains-
    of-slavery-still-exist-in-mass-incarceration

20 "In Alabama, by 1898..." AAREG, African American Registry, "The
    American Convict Leasing Program: A Story": https://aaregistry.org/
    story/the-american-convict-leasing-program-a-story/

21 "It has been perpetuated..." A foundational analysis connecting slavery
    and Jim Crow and today's race-biased culture of mass incarceration is
    The New Jim Crow: Mass Incarceration in the Age of Colorblindness by Mi-
    chelle Alexander, The New Press, 2010.

22 "People with felonies..." Prison Policy Initiative, "Nowhere to Go: Home-

lessness among formerly incarcerated people" by Lucius Couloute, August 2018: https://www.prisonpolicy.org/reports/housing.html

23   "It was frustrating not to be able to talk about race..." Tracey Knight interview, April 27, 2021.

CHAPTER 13

1   "...only 2 percent of federal criminal cases go..." Vanderbilt Law Review, Vol. 75:5:1461, Andrew Guthrie Ferguson, footnote 5.

2   "...the 1986 Supreme Court decision in *Batson v. Kentucky*..." In *Batson v. Kentucky*, 476 U.S. 79 (1986), the U.S. Supreme Court attempted to eliminate racial discrimination in jury selection by prohibiting the use of peremptory challenges to intentionally strike prospective jurors based on their race.

3   "...after a review of a conviction on appeal." The Curtis Flowers case was one such example. In 2019, the Supreme Court overturned the murder conviction of Curtis Flowers after a prosecutor in Mississippi had struck forty-one out of forty-two Black juror candidates. Flowers had been on death row *for 23 years* before the decision. New evidence uncovered in the investigative podcast *In the Dark* helped free Flowers. See: https://www. clarionledger.com/story/news/2020/09/10/how-investigative-podcast-in-dark-helped-free-curtis-flowers/5747054002/

4   "...a video surfaced from a district attorney's..." *The New York Times*, "Former Philadelphia Prosecution Accused on Racial Bias," April 3, 1997.

CHAPTER 15

1   "...and *Get Christie Love!*, starring Teresa Graves." Teresa Graves, playing a New York City police detective, was only the second female African American lead in a network TV drama, following Diahann Carroll in *Julia*.

2   "You lie, you die." NOLA.com, "Implementation of NOPD 'If you lie, you die' policy is not so clear-cut" by Brendan McCarthy, February 21, 2011: https://www.nola.com/news/crime_police/article_ 69269d9a-f115-5b73-a93a-914128c4831d.html

CHAPTER 16

1 "...Simmons was on the team..." *Five Days at Memorial: Life and Death in a Storm-Ravaged Hospital* by Sheri Fink, Crown, 2013.

2 "Modern cognitive science..." A thoughtful and influential analysis on why people hold the beliefs they do can be found in *The Righteous Mind: Why Good People Are Divided by Politics and Religion* by Jonathan Haidt, Random House, 2012.

3 "...in wrongful convictions.)" Innocence Project, "Cross-racial identification and jury instruction," May 20, 2008: https://innocenceproject. org/cross-racial-identification-and-jury-instruction/See also: Cornell Law Review, "Cross-Racial Identification Errors in Criminal Cases" by Sheri Lynn Johnson, Volume 69, Issue 5, June 1984. https://scholarship.law.cornell.edu/cgi/viewcontent.cgi?referer=&httpsredir=1&article=4357&context=clr

4 "...after the Supreme Court case..." *Garrity v. New Jersey*, 385 U.S. 493 (1967) established protections for government employees compelled to participate in criminal investigations.

CHAPTER 18

1 "...in the prosecution of Blackwater personnel..." *Jurist*, "Blackwater, Garrity and Immunity: What Does It All Mean?" by Jeremiah Lee, November 12, 2007: https://www.jurist.org/commentary/2007/11/blackwater-garrity-and-immunity-what/

2 "The head of SOD, Captain Jeff Winn..." Winn was fired by NOPD in May 2011 for his failure in 2009 to inform the department's internal investigation that Greg McRae had burned Henry Glover's body. See: https://www.nola.com/news/crime_police/article_01f75596-f65d-58bb-9015-05e013ec2e35.html

As of this writing, Winn still works in law enforcement in the Sheriff's Office in St. Charles Parish, west of Orleans Parish (New Orleans proper).

3 "...no one stood stronger..." Ed Bradley, *60 Minutes*, "Order Out of Chaos," September 10, 2005: www.cbsnews.com/news/order-out-of-chaos/

4 "...walking reasonable doubt." Mike Magner, from interview, April 28, 2022.

5 *ProPublica*, "Did New Orleans SWAT Cops Shoot an Unarmed Man" by A.C. Thompson, Brendan McCarthy, and Laura Maggi, December 15, 2009: https://www.propublica.org/article/did-new-orleans-swat-cops-shoot-an-unarmed-man-1215

CHAPTER 20

1 "...might appeal to different kinds..." Jonathan Haidt's *The Righteous Mind: Why Good People Are Divided by Politics and Religion* is instructive here.

CHAPTER 21

1 "'He's a police officer..." *The Times-Picayune*, "2 cops walk in beating, burning, cover-up" by Laura Maggi, December 10, 2010.

2 "...only 121 officers were charged..." *The New York Times*, "Few Police Officers Who Cause Deaths Are Charged or Convicted" by Shaila Dewan, September 24, 2020.

3 "When I first met you..." The author's best recollection of what he said to Edna and Patrice Glover at that time.

4 "...into the back of an African American teenager..." Source on sentencing and prison time served: *The New York Times*, "Ex-Chicago Officer Who Killed Laquan McDonald Won't Face Federal Charges" by Alyssa Lukpat, April 18, 2022.

5 "...their families become collateral damage." For a comprehensive look at the impact of incarceration on families and communities, see *Doing Time on the Outside: Incarceration and Family Life in America* by Donald Braman, University of Michigan Press, 2007.

CHAPTER 22

1 "...By the time we came to Katrina..." PBS *Frontline*, "Law & Disorder," transcript of November 23, 2009, interview with Mary Howell, available online.

2 "...four NOPD officers were charged with murder." *Black Rage in New Orleans* by Leonard N. Moore, Louisiana State University Press, 2010.

3 "At one point in 2010..." *ProPublica*, "Post-Katrina Shootings by Police Get Federal Attention" by A.C. Thompson, Laura Maggi, and Brendan McCarthy, February 19, 2010: See also: NOLA.com, "Federal investigations of NOPD run up against statute of limitations" by Laura Maggi, September 7, 2010. https://www.nola.com/news/crime_police/article_50ba75cf-4695-59d9-b461-40051aad35c2.html

   The final resolution of the cases: One officer was convicted of perjury and obstruction of justice in the Danny Brumfield fatal shooting, see: "NOPD Officer Sentenced in Post-Katrina Shooting" by Sarah Moughty, Frontline Documentaries, April 11, 2012: https://www.pbs.org/wgbh/frontline/article/nopd-officer-sentenced-in-post-katrina-shooting/

   No charges were ever filed in the Matthew McDonald shooting death. See: NOLA.com, "A decade after Danziger Bridge Shootings, killings still cast a shadow" by Andy Grimm, September 5, 2015: https://www.nola.com/news/crime_police/article_00bb8d39-aa35-5959-b613-873905a4e734.html

4 "...describe as a 'legend'..." NOLA.com, "Death of Raymond Robair in 2005 being investigated by FBI" by Brendan McCarthy, July 26, 2010: https://www.nola.com/news/crime_police/article_66545c3d-391c-527e-8754-8072889da36f.html

5 "...we tracked down some of the people who had watched the beating..." The author's conversations with the Treme residents during the Robair investigation are according to his best recollection.

6 "The elected coroner, Frank Minyard..." Minyard's obituary on the 4WWL TV website: https://www.wwltv.com/article/obits/dr-frank-minyard-longtime-orleans-parish-coroner-dies-at-91/289-9aaa1430-efdc-427a-8578-9435d9bbe988

7 "What's your email address?" The author's brief exchange with Dwayne Scheuermann is according to his best recollection.

8 "The appellate decision came down..." The Fifth Circuit Court of Appeals decision can be found at: *United States v. McRae*, 702 F.3d 806 (5th Cir. 2012).

9 "...the most conservative appeals court..." *The Guardian*, "How Trump reshaped the Fifth Circuit to become 'the most extreme' US Court" by David Smith, November 15, 2021: www.theguardian.com/law/2021/nov/15/fifth-circuit-court-appeals-most-extreme-us

See also: MBLB News, "In a Recent Civil Rights Case, Fifth Circuit Reinforces Qualified Immunity/Serves to Protect Police Officers," April 21, 2021: https://mblb.com/municipal-law/fifth-circuit-reinforces-qualified-immunity-serves-to-protect-police-officers-in-civil-rights-case/

CHAPTER 23

1 "...his proudest moment as an attorney..." Louisiana Bar Foundation video, 2004 Distinguished Attorney, Julian R. Murray, Jr., March 22, 2017: https://www.raisingthebar.org/new-orleans/item/69-julian-r-murray-jr-new-orleans

2 "...with driving while intoxicated..." NOLA.com, "New Orleans police officer who testified in Henry Glover case arrested on hit-and-run, DWI charges" by Laura Maggi, May 7, 2011.

3 *Daubert v. Merrell Dow Pharmaceuticals, Inc.*, 509 U.S. 579 (1993), is a United States Supreme Court case determining the standard for admitting expert testimony in federal courts.

CHAPTER 24

1 "...that tide was in full retreat." *The New York Times*, "Post-Katrina Police Prosecutions in New Orleans Face Setbacks" by Campbell Robertson, December 12, 2013.

2 "'...a collection of self-centered...'" Blog post quotes from *Shots on the Bridge: Police Violence and Cover-Up in the Wake of Katrina* by Ronnie Greene, Beacon Press, 2015.

3 "Engelhardt's emotional 129-page ruling..." *Washington Post*, "No Justice in New Orleans Danziger Bridge Case," September 21, 2013.

4 "That's a chance..." Quoted in *The New York Times*, "Re-trial in a Case Tied to Post-Katrina Deaths" by The Associated Press, January 28, 2012.

5 "...accepted a plea deal..." NOLA.com, "'Finally over': Last Danziger defendant pleads guilty, sentenced to probation" by Emily Lane, November 4, 2016: https://www.nola.com/news/crime_police/article_f383ff60-a451-5f87-9a78-257c7efef892.html

6 "...the Supreme Court thought otherwise." Supreme Court of the United States, Syllabus, *Yates v. United States*, 574 U.S. 528 (2015): https://www.supremecourt.gov/opinions/14pdf/13-7451_m64o.pdf

7 "But without the obstruction of justice charge..." Four years earlier, the Fifth Circuit Court of Appeals had overturned Greg McCabe's conviction on the novel charge that his burning of Henry Glover's body deprived the Glover family of "access to the courts" for financial redress, arguing that the prosecution had not established that any member of the family was planning on filing a lawsuit. However, eliminating that one conviction did not result in any reduction of McRae's sentence.

8 "...darker than a brown paper bag..." *The New York Times*, "White Man Sentenced to 10 Years for Shooting Black Men after Hurricane Katrina" by Julia Jacobs, February 14, 2019.

9 "If they're breaking in your property..." Quoted in *ProPublica*, "Post-Katrina, White Vigilantes Shot African-Americans With Impunity" by A.C. Thompson, December 19, 2008: https://www.propublica.org/article/post-katrina-white-vigilantes-shot-african-americans-with-impunity

CHAPTER 25

1 "...catalysts of the national Black Lives Matter..." Howard University School of Law, Law Library, Black Civil Rights, Black Lives Matter Movement: www.library.law.howard.edu/civilrightshistory/BLM

2 "The Tamir Rice case..." *New York Times*, "Justice Dept. Is Said to Quietly Quash Inquiry into Tamir Rice Killing" by Charlie Savage and Katie Benner, October 29, 2020.

3 "Anthony Scott, Walter's brother, proclaimed..." https://www.thestate.com/news/local/crime/article188525374.html

4   "The headline that ran..." *The Post and Courier*, "Ex-police officer Michael
     Slager pleads guilty to civil rights charge in Walter Scott shooting; state
     murder case dropped" by Andrew Knapp and Brenda Rindge, May 2,
     2017: https://www.postandcourier.com/news/ex-police-officer-michael-
     slager-pleads-guilty-to-civil-rights-charge-in-walter-scott-shooting/ar-
     ticle_c6836d4c-2f2f-11e7-a651-7f3c5a7bbf12.html
         Also see, *New York Times*, "Michael Slager, Officer in Walter Scott
     Shooting, Gets 20-Year Sentence" by Alan Blinder, December 7, 2017,
     for coverage of how the federal judge regarded the shooting as murder
     in arriving at a sentence.

5   "...a rate that has stayed relatively constant..." *The Washington Post*,
     "Four years in a row, police nationwide fatally shoot nearly 1,000 peo-
     ple" by John Sullivan, Liz Weber, Julie Tate, and Jennifer Jenkins, Feb-
     ruary 12, 2015. Also see: *The Washington Post*'s police shooting database
     2015-2022: https://www.washingtonpost.com/graphics/investigations/
     police-shootings-database/

6   "...increasingly influential 'restorative justice' movement..." The author
     is particularly appreciative of the work of Danielle Sered, executive di-
     rector of the New York City-based nonprofit, Common Justice, and the
     author of *Until We Reckon: Violence, Mass Incarceration, and a Road to Re-
     pair*, The New Press, 2019.

7   "...he publicly apologized..." NOLA.com, "Mayor Mitch Landrieu apol-
     ogizes for NOPD's Hurricane Katrina-era crimes" by Jarvis DeBerry,
     December 20, 2016: https://www.nola.com/opinions/article_edcd62b4-
     bd8a-59c6-a1e2-80010f1d1ea5.html

8   "You can't move forward..." Quotes from Mary Howell interview, July
     15, 2019.

9   "...a program called EPIC..." The EPIC program is described in the New
     Orleans city government website, http://epic.nola.gov/home/ As the site
     explains, EPIC is currently working with Georgetown University Law
     Center's ABLE (Active Bystandership for Law Enforcement) Project,
     a national police peer intervention program, to expand the reach of its
     training and insights. See: https://www.law.georgetown.edu/cics/able/

10   "...the three officers who stood by..." the *Washington Post*, "George

Floyd's death could have been prevented if we had a police culture of intervention" by Christy E. Lopez, May 29, 2020.

11 "…10 million arrests, at a cost of billions…" Prison Policy Initiative, "Mass Incarceration: The Whole Pie 2022" by Wendy Sawyer and Peter Wagner, March 14, 2022: https://prisonpolicy.org/reports/pie2022.html
    Another good source is The Marshall Project, "The United States of Incarceration," Issue 6: https://www.themarshallproject.org/2020/11/11/the-united-states-of-incarceration
    For the cost of incarceration, see: https://arrestrecords.com/cost-of-incarceration-in-the-us/

12 "And yet 95% of these people…" Mid-America Prison Ministries, "95% of All Prisoners Eventually Released": midamericaprisonministries.org/eventually-released/

13 "…more than five million children…" The Anne E. Casey Foundation, "Parental Incarceration": https://aecf.org/topics/parental-incarceration

14 "…Justice Innovation Lab." See: justiceinnovationlab.org

15 "…our first real-life lab." For some examples of JIL's work in Charleston, SC, see: https://why-screen-charleston-sc.justiceinnovationlab.org/ and https://charleston-disparity-in-prosecution.org/

16 "…'similarly situated' defendants…" The idea of a "similarly situated" defendant is a statistical concept. It is very rare to find truly similar individuals to compare, but this is the best way JIL knows to evaluate bias in the system.

17 University of Chicago researcher Hannah Shaffer is doing particularly interesting research in this area. Her book, *Prosecutors, Race, and the Criminal Pipeline*, is scheduled to be published in 2023.

EPILOGUE

1 "The city's permanent population…" For an overview of New Orleans demographic changes, especially its racial composition, since Hurricane Katrina, see: *The Nation*, "White New Orleans Has Recovered from Hur-

ricane Katrina; Black New Orleans Has Not" by Gary Rivlin, August 29, 2016: https://www.thenation.com/article/archive/white-new-orleans-has-recovered-from-hurricane-katrina-black-new-orleans-has-not/

A fuller account of the city's bungled, and racially biased post-Katrina rebuilding efforts, is found in Rivlin's invaluable *Katrina after the Flood*, Simon & Schuster, 2016.

See also: *FiveThirtyEight*, "Katrina Washed Away New Orleans's Black Middle Class" by Ben Casselman, August 24, 2015: https://fivethirtyeight.com/features/katrina-washed-away-new-orleanss-black-middle-class/

2 "In 2022, the city was on pace..." The Marshall Project, "New Orleans Battled Mass Incarceration. Then Came the Backlash over Violent Crime" by Jamiles Lartey, July 6, 2022: https://www.themarshallproject.org/2022/07/06/new-orleans-battled-mass-incarceration-then-came-the-rise-in-violent-crime

3 "...dragged the driver..." NOLA.com, "Grand jury returns indictments in carjacking death of Linda Frickey; teens to be tried as adults" by Jillian Kramer, April 28, 2022: https://www.nola.com/news/courts/article_ee680b6c-c721-11ec-8ed1-5f8a7fc82317.html

4 "...made a fat target." For a good round-up of the consent decree's more recent political travails, see: NOLA.com, "New Orleans Police Department seeks end to consent decree despite open issues" by Matt Sledge, December 17, 2020: https://www.nola.com/news/courts/article_196e0746-3ffe-11eb-8a7f-a3923b682aae.html

5 "...burying them with paperwork..." NBC News, "New Orleans mayor says police consent decree must end, citing retention issues" by David K. Liu, August 4, 2022. The website contains a video clip of Mayor LaToya Cantrell's comments on the consent decree and a discussion of the recent drop in NOPD force levels: https://www.nbcnews.com/news/us-news/new-orleans-mayor-says-police-consent-decree-must-end-citing-retention-rcna41620

Another good analysis of the decline in officer numbers and morale is: NOLA.com, "New Orleans officers, leaving in droves, air grievances in exit interviews" by John Simmerman, July 24, 2022: https://www.nola.com/news/article_5ffa853c-0a04-11ed-9285-6be02e4e976d.html

In a similar vein, also by Simmerman: "As officers flee New Orleans Police Department in droves, few apply to replace them," June 26, 2022:

https://www.nola.com/news/crime_police/article_75ccd4ba-f3f1-11ec-9b2c-1be4e201c386.html

6 "Really? Really?" Quotes from interview with Mary Howell, April 26, 2022.

7 "...have dropped dramatically..." You can find reports on the NOPD consent decree at nola.gov/nopd/nopd-consent-decree. See also: *The Christian Science Monitor*, "How New Orleans police went from 'most corrupt' to model force" by Patrik Jonsonn, February 26, 2019: https://www.csmonitor.com/USA/Justice/2019/0226/How-New-Orleans-police-went-from-most-corrupt-to-model-force

8 "Don't let anyone ever tell you..." Author's interview/conversation with former US Attorney Jim Letten, April 29, 2022.

9 "...embezzling close to $330,000..." NOLA.com: "New Orleans police ex-lieutenant charged with embezzling almost $330,000 from Catholic Church" by Ramon Antonio Vargas, September 25, 2020: https://www.nola.com/news/crime_police/article_56ce8800-ff75-11ea-a610-6b7ad275a392.html

10 "...their last and best hope..." Mike Magner interview, April 28, 2022.

11 "...a lot of really bad cops..." Tracey Knight interview, May 25, 2022.

12 "...a fierce advocate for civil rights." Rebecca Glover obituary: https://obits.nola.com/us/obituaries/nola/name/rebecca-glover-brown-obituary?id=6597988

13 "Linda and I talked about the philosophy..." Linda Howard interview, April 27, 2022.

14 "I like introducing babies to new things..." Purnella Simmons interview, April 29, 2022.

15 "...he was more subdued..." William Tanner interview, April 28, 2022.

16 "...his burned-out Chevy Malibu..." Lower Ninth Ward Living Museum: https://www.neworleans.com/listing/lower-ninth-ward-living-museum/32476/

17 "...was another local hero." Merlene Kimble interview, April 26, 2022.

18 "...felt more like visiting with an old professor..." Frank DeSalvo interview, April 25, 2022.

19 "One such post..." Dwayne Scheuermann's posts seem to be no longer available online.

20 "On our video call..." Author's video call with Dwayne Scheuermann, May 16, 2022.

21 "...reserved for the city's aquarium." An additional source on the aquarium situation during Katrina: *Los Angeles Times*, "Aquarium Becomes Watery Grave for Sea Life" by Karen Kaplan and Alan Zarembo, September 10, 2005. See also the account in Douglas Brinkley's *The Great Deluge*. He notes that the aquarium served as a temporary communications center for NOPD during the flooding.

22 "...Captain Winn told him, 'Get rid of it.'" At trial, Captain Jeff Winn used more anodyne language: "I made the decision to move the body from the compound to the other side of the levee."

23 "I called Patrice Glover..." Patrice Glover interview, August 27, 2022.

24 "I think that's the cure for me." For more information on Families United 4 Justice, see the fu4jgroup website.

25 "...age-old story of Us and Them." An illuminating analysis of how our adversarial two-party political system has devolved into an all-out Us vs. Them conflict is found in *Why We're Polarized* by Ezra Klein, Avid Reader Press/Simon & Schuster, 2020.